Unleashing the Art of Digital Forensics

Unleashing the Art of Digital Forensics is intended to describe and explain the steps taken during a forensic examination, with the intent of making the reader aware of the constraints and considerations that apply during a forensic examination in law enforcement and in the private sector.

Key Features:

- Discusses the recent advancements in Digital Forensics and Cybersecurity
- Reviews detailed applications of Digital Forensics for real-life problems
- Addresses the challenges related to implementation of Digital Forensics and Anti-Forensic approaches
- Includes case studies that will be helpful for researchers
- Offers both quantitative and qualitative research articles, conceptual papers, review papers, etc.
- Identifies the future scope of research in the field of Digital Forensics and Cybersecurity

This book is aimed primarily at and will be beneficial to graduates, postgraduates, and researchers in Digital Forensics and Cybersecurity.

Unleashing the Art of Digital Forensics

Edited by
Keshav Kaushik, Rohit Tanwar,
Susheela Dahiya, Komal Kumar Bhatia, and
Yulei Wu

CRC Press
Taylor & Francis Group
Boca Raton London New York

CRC Press is an imprint of the
Taylor & Francis Group, an **informa** business
A CHAPMAN & HALL BOOK

First edition published 2023
by CRC Press
6000 Broken Sound Parkway NW, Suite 300, Boca Raton, FL 33487-2742

and by CRC Press
4 Park Square, Milton Park, Abingdon, Oxon, OX14 4RN

CRC Press is an imprint of Taylor & Francis Group, LLC

ISBN: 978-1-032-06975-3 (hbk)
ISBN: 978-1-032-06989-0 (pbk)
ISBN: 978-1-003-20486-2 (ebk)

DOI: 10.1201/9781003204862

Typeset in Palatino
by MPS Limited, Dehradun

Contents

Preface

The 21st century has witnessed a number of cyberattacks in various forms that target individuals, property, and even the entire nation. Examples of cyberattacks include hacking, defamation, DDoS, and ransomware. The entire universe is on the radar of cybercriminals and programmers. The financial advancement of any country is affected by these gatecrashers in some way or another. These computerized crimes remain close to psychological warfare as the biggest obstacle in the economic improvement of the general public. Indeed, even the terrorists are utilizing digital means and a few nations are occupied with digital reconnaissance to disturb the basic foundations with an expectation to drop down financial status of these nations. The advanced legal sciences information is high time prerequisite in this basic circumstance. The Internet instability exposed genuine dangers and weaknesses. Additionally, the internet witnesses successive cybercrime episodes all throughout the planet.

Digital forensics includes examination and investigation of digital proof, keeping up with integrity and chain of custody for prosecution purposes. Disk imaging is the initial phase in safeguarding digital forensic evidence in anticipation of postmortem examination and examination. The majority of the cybercrime examinations have various jurisdictional intricacies. The 3A's of digital forensics techniques are Acquiring proof without change, Authenticating held onto information, and Analyzing information without modification. This work acquaints the reader with the universe of digital forensics in a functional and open way. The text is written to fulfill the requirement for a book that presents scientific technique and sound forensic thinking along with hands-on examples for normal assignments in a computer forensic examination.

Unleashing the Art of Digital Forensics is intended to describe and explain the steps taken during a forensic examination, with the intent of making the reader aware of the constraints and considerations applied in law enforcement and in the private sector. On reading this book, the reader will have a proper overview of the field of digital forensics, embarking on the journey of becoming a computer forensics expert.

This book is an accomplished assortment of best-in-class approaches used in the fields of Cybersecurity, Digital Forensics, and Cyber Law, respectively. It will be valuable for the new scientists and specialists working in the field to rapidly know the best performing strategies. It will help them in realizing their ideas, analyzing various approaches, and delivering the best one to society. This book will be helpful as a textbook/reference book for undergraduate and postgraduate students as a number of reputed universities have Digital Forensics as a part of their curriculum these days.

Editors

Mr. Keshav Kaushik is an Assistant Professor in the Department of Systemics, School of Computer Science at the University of Petroleum and Energy Studies, Dehradun, India. He is pursuing a Ph.D. in Cybersecurity and Forensics. He is an experienced educator with over six years of teaching and research experience in Cybersecurity, Digital Forensics, the Internet of Things, and Blockchain Technology. Mr. Kaushik received his B. Tech degree in Computer Science and Engineering from the University Institute of Engineering and Technology, Maharshi Dayanand University, Rohtak. In addition, M. Tech degree in Information Technology from YMCA University of Science and Technology, Faridabad, Haryana. He has qualified GATE (2012 & 2016). He has published several research papers in International Journals and has presented at reputed International Conferences. He is a Certified Ethical Hacker (CEH) v11, CQI and IRCA Certified ISO/IEC 27001:2013 Lead Auditor, and Quick Heal Academy certified Cyber Security Professional (QCSP). He has delivered professional talks and keynote speeches at national and international platforms.

Dr. Rohit Tanwar received his bachelor's degree (B. Tech) in CSE from Kurukshetra University, Kurukshetra, India, and master's degree (M. Tech) in CSE from YMCA University of Science and Technology, Faridabad, India. Dr. Tanwar was awarded his Ph.D. degree in 2019 from Kurukshetra University. He has more than 10 years of experience in teaching. Currently, he is working as an Assistant Professor Senior Scale in School of Computer Science, UPES Dehradun. His areas of interest include Network Security, Optimization Techniques, Human computing, Soft computing, Cloud computing, Data Mining, etc. He has more than twenty publications to his credit in different reputed journals and conferences. He has been associated with many conferences throughout India as TPC member and session chair, etc. Dr. Tanwar is an editor of two books that are under processing with CRC Press and Scrivener Publishing (Wiley). He is a special issue editor in the journal EAI Endorsed on Transactions on Pervasive Health and Technology (Scopus Indexed). He is associated with the International Journal of Communication Systems (SCIE) (WILEY), and International Journal of Information Security and Privacy (IJISP) (Scopus, ESCI), IGI Global as an active reviewer. He is supervising two Ph.D. research scholars in the fields of security and optimization.

Dr. Susheela Dahiya, Ph.D. (IIT Roorkee) is working as Assistant Professor at the University of Petroleum and Energy Studies (UPES), Dehradun. She received her M. Tech. (Computer Science & Engineering) and Ph.D. degree from IIT Roorkee. She had also qualified NET and GATE. She has more than eight years of academic/research experience. Her research work is focused on satellite image processing, video processing, cyber security, and cloud computing and deep learning. She is also supervising her Ph.D. students in these areas. She has published several research papers in SCI and Scopus indexed journals and conferences.

Dr. Komal Kumar Bhatia is working as a Professor at Department of Computer Engineering at J. C. Bose University of Science and Technology has a work experience of 19 years. He received his B.E., M.Tech. and Ph.D. degrees in Computer Engineering in 2001, 2004, and 2009, respectively. He has guided seven Ph.D. scholars and is currently guiding five Ph.D. scholars. He has also guided more than sixty M.Tech. Dissertations. He has published more than a hundred research papers in reputed journals and conferences and his areas of interest are Information Retrieval Systems, Hidden Web, and Web Mining. Currently, he is also working as Dean, Faculty of Informatics & Computing and Chairman of the Department of Computer Engineering. He is also a member of several professional bodies at national/international level.

Dr. Yulei Wu is a Senior Lecturer with the Department of Computer Science, College of Engineering, Mathematics and Physical Sciences, University of Exeter, United Kingdom. He received the B.Sc. degree (First Class Honors) in Computer Science and the Ph.D. degree in Computing and Mathematics from the University of Bradford, United Kingdom, in 2006 and 2010, respectively. His expertise is on intelligent networking, and his main research interests include computer networks, networked systems, software-defined networks and systems, network management, and network security and privacy. He has authored one book (Springer) and edited/co-edited three books (two with CRC Press and one with The IET). His research has been supported by the Engineering and Physical Sciences Research Council, National Natural Science Foundation of China, University's Innovation Platform and industry. He is an Editor of IEEE Transactions on Network and Service Management, IEEE Transactions on Network Science and Engineering, Computer Networks (Elsevier), and IEEE Access. He is a Senior Member of the IEEE, and a Fellow of the HEA (Higher Education Academy).

Contributors

Sujata Bali
University of Petroleum & Energy Studies (UPES)
Dehradun, Uttarakhand, India

V.Y. Bharadwaj
CMR Institute of Technology
Kundalahalli Bangalore, India

Susheela Dahiya
University of Petroleum & Energy Studies (UPES)
Dehradun, Uttarakhand, India

Manik Garg
VMware Software India Private Limited
Kalyani Vista, Bengaluru, Karnataka, India

Bhavana Kaushik
University of Petroleum & Energy Studies (UPES)
Dehradun, Uttarakhand, India

Keshav Kaushik
University of Petroleum & Energy Studies (UPES)
Dehradun, Uttarakhand, India

Bharti Nair Khan
University of Petroleum & Energy Studies (UPES)
Dehradun, Uttarakhand, India

Tripti Misra
University of Petroleum & Energy Studies (UPES)
Dehradun, Uttarakhand, India

Shreyas S. Muthye
Independent Digital Forensic Consultant
Nagpur, Maharashtra, India

Smita M. Pachare
Universal Business School
Karjat, Maharashtra, India

Urmila Pilania
Manav Rachna University
Faridabad, Haryana, India

S. Pooja
GLA University
Mathura, Uttar Pradesh, India

Vikas Sagar
Deputy HOD (AI branch), NIET
Greater Noida, Uttar Pradesh, India

K.N.D. Saile
CMR Institute of Technology
Kundalahalli, Bangalore, India

Ravi Sheth
Rashtriya Raksha University
Gandhinagar, Gujarat, India

Ashish Shukla
Rashtriya Raksha University
Gandhinagar, Gujarat, India

Raahat Devender Singh
Panjab University
Chandigarh, Punjab, India

Vanshika Singh
University of Petroleum & Energy Studies (UPES)
Dehradun, Uttarakhand, India

Tanisha Singla
University of Petroleum & Energy Studies (UPES)
Dehradun, Uttarakhand, India

Rohit Tanwar
University of Petroleum & Energy Studies (UPES)
Dehradun, Uttarakhand, India

Suhasini Verma
Manipal University
Jaipur, Rajasthan, India

Vidhisha Vyas
IILM University
Gurugram, Haryana, India

G.Y. Vybhavi
Geetanjali College of Engineering and Technology
Telangana, India

1

Data Hiding—Steganography and Steganalysis

K.N.D. Saile[1], V.Y. Bharadwaj[1], and G.Y. Vybhavi[2]
[1]*CMR Institute of Technology, Hyderabad, Telangana, India*
[2]*Geetanjali College of Engineering and Technology, Hyderabad, Telangana, India*

CONTENTS

DOI: 10.1201/9781003204862-1

1.1 Introduction

The wide usage of internet and advancement in related technology relates to the vital role of communication. Digitalization and data transfer over the internet have increased drastically thus maintaining confidentiality is a major concern. Confidentiality is an important component of the CIA—confidentiality, integrity, and availability—triad in information security. Figure 1.1 shows the CIA triad.

Confidentiality of data can be attained by masking and hiding information using different techniques. Two of such data-hiding techniques, namely, cryptography and steganography, are shown in Figure 1.2.

In this chapter, we will discuss steganography, its various techniques, and the methods to perform steganalysis.

1.2 Steganography: Background and Literature Survey

1.2.1 Background

Steganography is a communication method used between two parties, where a third party is not aware of the hidden information. Steganography is the technique of concealing the data. The word *steganography* is derived from the Greek word *steganos-graphein* (Wikipedia, 2021) which technically means covered writing. The Greek interpretation is στεγανός (covered) and γραφία (writing).

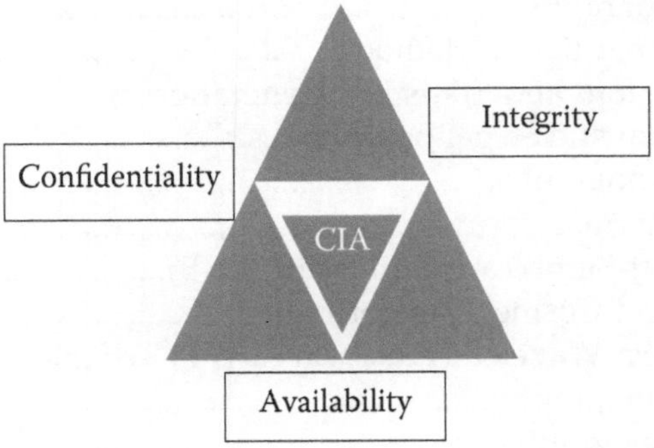

FIGURE 1.1
CIA Triad.

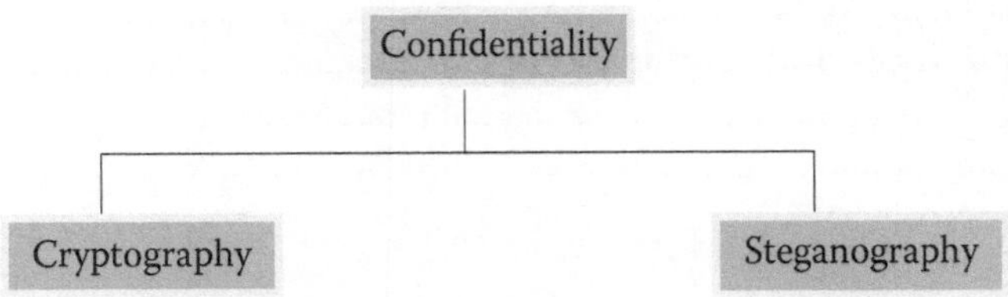

FIGURE 1.2
Types of Data-Hiding Techniques Used in Maintaining Confidentiality.

Steganography was used in physical forms before the invention of computers. During the historical times, steganography was used by the emperors to hide messages from other emperors, using wax. One of the practices was writing on the wood and covering the wood with wax. The person at another end was able to read the message by scrapping off or by melting the wax on the wood. These pieces of wood, called wax tablets, were most commonly used in ancient history.

During World War II, messages were sent between two ends using microdots. These are typically smaller in size than the full stop (.). These dots were covered using an adhesive and the person at another end would be able to read the code placing the paper against the light rays (Parah et al., 2019). Another technique was using the Morse code. Only the person who understands the Morse code would be able to decode the information. These were few techniques followed before the invention of computers. Later, with the advent of computers and the internet, digitalization gave scope for the development of new steganographic techniques, which we shall see in Section 1.5.

Figure 1.3 shows a transcript, dated 1591, of Steganographia by Johannes Trithemius (1462–1516), where each text is changed to another form using steganography.

1.2.2 Literature Survey

Steganography has undergone many enhancements with the growing technology since its begining. Research is underway to propel a better level of confidentiality for the information. According to Ashwin et al. (2012), the data can be concealed in various methods by using masking, filtering, and techniques of least significant bit. Humanth Kumar et al. (2013) enhanced the earlier technique by adding Advanced Encryption Algorithm also known as AES to an image. A. Joseph Raphaelet et al. (2010) proposed a technique where both cryptography and steganography were combined to form a hybrid architecture and

FIGURE 1.3
Steganographia. (Source: https://en.wikipedia.org/wiki/Steganography (last edited on May 6, 2022))

provide better security. Armin Bahramshahry et al. (2007) proposed a technique where the users at both ends are provided with a unique ID, name, and password. After the data transmission is completed, a unique key was generated by an automatic id generator for getting the hidden information.

According to Wajgade and Kumar (2013), using a hash key for the encryption and concealing the data proved better security. Seth et al. (2010) provide a technique wherein the image is transformed by spatial domain, and Wai Wai Zin (2011) enhances the technique by using the wavelet transformation on the images. N.V Rao et al. (2011) proposed a method using Rivest, Shamir, Adleman (RSA) encryption techniques and latter techniques performed practically well in the paper demonstrated by Channalli and Jadhav (2009).

More works have been conducted in the field of images by changing the form of images such as the bitmap format or .png format. Rig Das et al. (2012) have worked in this area and found good results in the format of the image (Singh & Malik, 2013). Many researchers have worked on using encryption algorithms such as Blowfish, RC4, AES, DES, Triple-DES encryption of algorithms for encryption the secret key and combined them with a steg image to develop better privacy of the data. According to Karthik et al. (2013) the Huffman coding over the color image also helps in having better confidentiality.

Initially the research was conducted only for text steganography, later on with the computational power, the steganography techniques moved on to images, video and thus developing the hybrid architectures in steganography.

1.3 Importance of Steganography

Confidentiality, Integrity, and authentication are the components of information security. Confidentiality of the information can be achieved only by maintaining the secrecy of data from intruders. This can be achieved by cryptography and steganography.

Cryptography is the art of computer science where the data are encrypted using a public key by user A and decrypted using a private key at another end B. Here, if the pattern of the key is deciphered, the intruder can intervene and get access to the data. However, steganography is the technique where the data are masked or hidden with different techniques making the creepy eyes unaware of the message in it. Hence to maintain the confidentiality of data and avoid stealing the data, steganography is needed. Figure 1.4 shows the data communication between two parties and how an eavesdropper can intervene in the communication channel.

1.4 Cryptography vs. Steganography

It is a well-known fact that cryptography and steganography are the two major methods to provide confidentiality of the data. Steganography is used to communicate the message by using different data-masking techniques, whereas Cryptography communicates using encryption techniques. As shown in Figure 1.5, cryptography secret keys exchanged between two parties are called the public key and private key. Person A encrypts the data using Public

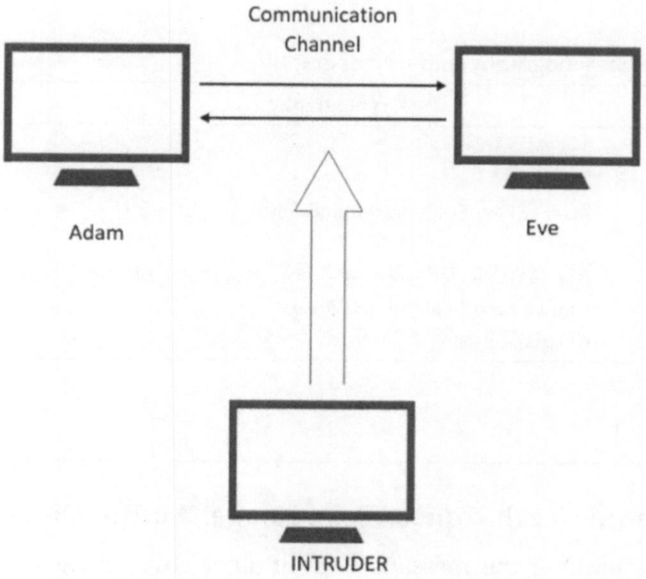

FIGURE 1.4
Data Communication.

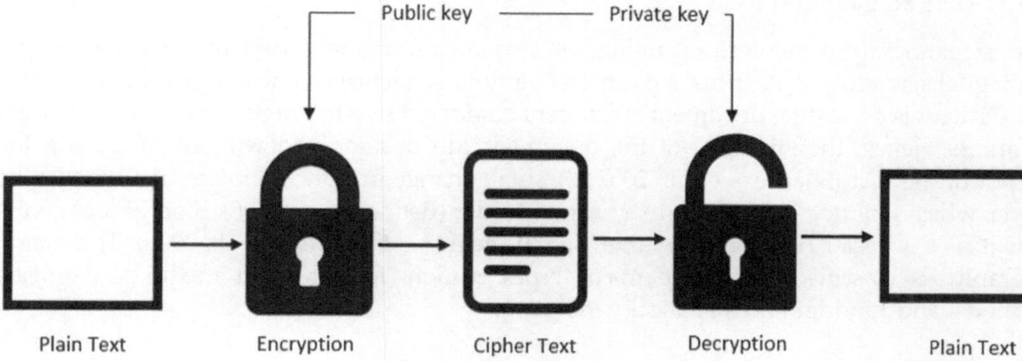

FIGURE 1.5
Cryptography: Encryption and Decryption.

Key and Person B decrypts the data using his private key. If the eavesdropper can decipher the private key he can intrude the communication process and steal the data, whereas steganography is a method of concealing the secret message with a cover message using different forms such as image, text, video, etc. (Ahmed Laskar, 2012). In steganography, the secret message and the cover image are bounded together to form a stego-object by an embedding process (Petitcolas et al., 1999). After the message is received at the receiver end, the hidden message is revealed by the extraction process. A secret key is shared between the two parties. (i.e., the sender and the receiver) before the extraction process. (Uliyan et al., 2018). These are the major differences between steganography and cryptography, while others (Ekatpure et al., 2015) are shown in Table 1.1.

TABLE 1.1
Differences between Steganography and Cryptography

Criteria	Cryptography	Steganography
Principle carrier	Text	Text, audio, video
Secret data	Text	Pay load
Keys	Private key, Public key mandatory	Optional
CIA triad	Yes	Yes
Algorithms	RSA, AES, substitution, and transposition algorithms	Steg images, LSB
Visibility	Can be seen in an altered format	Not visible
Attacks	Cryptanalysis	Steganalysis

1.5 Steganographic Techniques: Text, Image, Audio, Video, and Network

Steganography is masking the message with another cover image. There are different techniques used in steganography. The secret message can be hidden with different methodologies such as text, image, audio, video, and network (Figure 1.6). Now, let's have a detailed discussion of the different techniques used.

1.5.1 Text Steganography

Text steganography involves changing the textual information from the existing text by adding tabs, spaces, context-free grammars, random sequence characters, etc. (Benett, 2004). The structure of a textual document is different compared to other digital mediums of images or audio. Hence, the structure of the document can be modified without disturbing the output of the text (Shahreza et al., 2007). A small change in punctuation marks can also be made, which will not be readable to a normal reader (Bender et al., 1996). Storage and access of text files is easier compared to other digital mediums (Shahreza et al., 2006). Text steganography is classified into three major types namely format-based methods, linguistic methods, and random and statistical generation.

1.5.1.1 Format-Based Methods

As the name suggests the format of the word or punctuation marks is used to hide the data. Full stops and commas can be named with the secret messages (Agarwal, 2013).

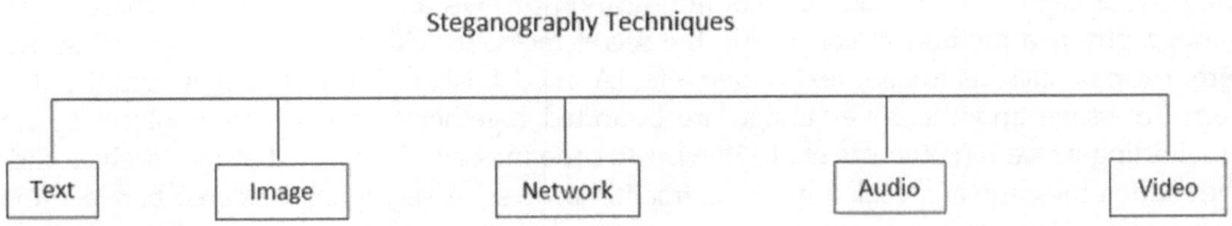

FIGURE 1.6
Steganography Techniques.

TABLE 1.2

Punctuation and Their Corresponding User-defined Codes

Punctuation	Code
!	00
.	01
?	11
"	10
:	110
;	101

Each of the punctuations can be given a code as shown in Table 1.2, and hence the data can be hidden.

For example, another technique is using codes based on the spelling of a word. There doesn't exist any difference in the meaning of the word but the spelling varies for the US and UK format. Let's say for example the word "colour" and "color." Colour is for UK style and color is the US style of writing the spelling. Hence, here the coding for a country-style could be 0(zero) and for another country, it is 1(one) (Shirali-Shahreza, 2008). Other techniques is coloring the white spaces with another color to indicate some kind of hidden information present in the text. When a certain format is included in the embedding process of the secret message with a cover image, then it is called a format-based method.

1.5.1.2 Random and Statistical Generation

This is another technique for text steganography where a randomized method is used in the generation of the cover messages. Markov Chain methods can be used to generate the cover message (Hernon Moraldo, 2012). Here, there is usage of context-free grammar for the cover text using the mimic functions that are based on probabilities (Wayner, 1992). According to authors, this is also one of the steganographic techniques. Few words that are out of context are also added to divert the meaning of the sentence and add as a cover text to the secret message. For example,

- **Secret Message:** "The message code is the ASCII value of every second word of the first sentence in the paragraph."
- **Stego File:** Every student is important for a teacher and for every message the message code is the ASCII value of every second word of the first sentence in the paragraph shared to the students makes an impact in their journey. They remember the values taught by their teacher and make themselves to be a nobleman.

  If you observe the stego-file, few words are unrelated to the context which shows the original message is concealed with other words.

1.5.1.3 Linguistic Steganography

It is one of the most commonly used techniques where the semantics of the words is compromised. The existing text is replaced, by using a similar kind of thesaurus synonyms by both the sender and receiver. A cat can have synonyms such as tomcat, kitten, pussy cat, tom, etc. A tiger can have synonyms such as cheetah, leopard, lion, jaguar, etc. "My pet tom is taken to the park today." It means the pet cat has been taken to the park today. So here the linguistic changes of a cat being shown as a tom are made.

These are the major techniques of text-based steganography that are added to attain confidentiality of information.

1.5.2 Image Steganography

Image steganography uses a cover image to hide secret messages. Before getting into the details of image steganography, we need to understand images and their work. Image steganography can be attained in four different ways: watermarking, LSB—least significant bit hiding, direct cosine transformation, and wavelet transformation (Morkel et al., 2005). We will discuss these techniques in detail further.

1.5.2.1 Watermarking

Watermarking is a part of steganography used to protect messages from unauthorized usage (Bhatt et al., 2015) Watermarks are used to provide security to the ownership of the data. The watermarks are imbibed in the image in such a way that they can't be modified by cropping, compression, filtering, etc. Images have few areas called patches that are invariant to attacks. These areas can be identified by Scale Invariant Feature Transform also known as SIFT. These kinds of patches can be identified and the watermarking can be imbibed into it.

1.5.2.2 Least-Significant Bit Hiding (LSB)

A pixel is the smallest unit of an image and a group of these pixels makes an image. Each pixel consists of three colors RGB—Red, Green, Blue—for colored images, whereas a grayscale image consists of white and black. If you want to represent Red color then the code is 100, which means 1 part of red, 0 part of blue and green. An 8-bit system comprises 8-bit binary code that can be accommodated ranging from 0 to 255. 0 being the least 00000000 and 255 being the largest 11111111. These RGB colors and shades can be accommodated within these values of 0 to 255. Let's consider Table 1.3 for a better understanding of the colors.

In the LSB technique, the least significant bit is converted with the binary values of the secret message. Say, for example, your secret message is number 50. This number is converted into a binary format which is 110010. This obtained binary value is replaced

TABLE 1.3

Proportion of RGB colors

Colors	Proportion of Red	Proportion of Green	Proportion of Blue
Red	11111111	00000000	00000000
Blue	00000000	00000000	11111111
Green	00000000	11111111	00000000
Purple	10000000	00000000	11111111

TABLE 1.4

RGB values of sample pixels

Colors	Proportion of Red	Proportion of Green	Proportion of Blue
Pixel 1	00101101	00011100	11011100
Pixel 2	10100110	11010010	10101101
Pixel 3	00001100	00101101	00001100

TABLE 1.5

RGB values of an image with a secret message in pixels

Colors	Proportion of Red	Proportion of Green	Proportion of Blue
Pixel 1	00101101	000111011	11011100
Pixel 2	10100110	11010011	10101100
Pixel 3	00001100	00101101	00001100

with the least significant bit, mostly the last digit of the pixel value, and transmitted to the receiver. Table 1.4 provides the values of the original image.

These pixel values are now replaced with a binary value of the secret message which is as follows. The last bit of each binary value has the embedded secret message value, as shown in Table 1.5.

The values in bold are the secret message values and in the image it shows a slight variation in the color, which the receiver understand during the steganalysis.

1.5.2.3 Direct Cosine Transformation

DCT is the acronym for Direct Cosine Transformation in image processing. DCT is the technique mainly used in image compression, which alters the image from a spatial to frequency domain. DCT is used in steganography in the following way.

i. The image is segmented into an 8 × 8 block of pixels from all the sides of the image.
ii. DCT is applied on all the segmented blocks of the image, which compresses the image
iii. The DCT coefficients are scaled using quantization, and compression is applied on each block.
iv. The secret message is concealed in the DCT coefficients and transmitted.

1.5.2.4 Direct Wavelet Transform (DWT) Technique

DWT transforms the image using Haar-DWT, which comprises two major operations. The first operation is the vertical transformation and the second operation is the horizontal transformation. In the first step, the scanning of the image is done left to right horizontally and in the second step from top to bottom vertically. Each pixel is added to the corresponding pixel and similarly, the subtraction is performed. Every output of addition and subtraction is stored. This is repeated until the entire image is scanned. The summation of pixels represents the low frequency and the difference of the pixels represents the high frequency. Similarly, this process is repeated for the vertical operations also. The sub bands formed give a set of low-frequency and high-frequency images that are similar to the original image (Narasimmalou et al., 2012; Raftari et al., 2012).

1.5.3 Audio Steganography

Audio steganography is a technique where the secret message is hidden in an audio file. The bits of the audio file are altered which compromises the quality of the audio file. The change in the quality of the file cannot be identified by the human auditory system. Few techniques to achieve audio steganography are LSB, spread spectrum, DWT's, phase encoding, parity encoding, etc. (Divya et al., 2012). LSB is the simplest way of concealing the information in an audio file. The least significant bits of the audio files samples are replaced with the secret message bits, hiding the message from the third party. While using LSB the secret key encrypted using either AES, Blowfish, or DES algorithms. Spread spectrum techniques convert the time-based domain into the frequency domain using the Fourier transforms. This frequency-based conversion can be used for secret message transfer. DWT's covert the spatial domain into the frequency domain. This conversion changes the digital file into low- and high-frequency data that can be associated with the original message. The changes in the parity of the audio files is used in parity encoding of audio steganography. Due the change in parity, the secret message can be concealed. The data are hidden in the form of AU, WAV, and MP3 formats.

1.5.4 Video Steganography

A video consists of 3 parts: the audio, video, and data. All these three together are called video container. Each of them can be used as data-hiding technique. Each frame of the video can be used in the concealing process. Choosing the right frame plays a major role as data loss might occur. The frames identified will be encoded similar to images using DCT coefficients. LSB is another technique that can be used for data hiding in video frames and formats. In simple terms, video steganography can be considered as the combination of audio and image steganography. This can be achieved either by embedding the secret message to the raw uncompressed data and later compressing it or by directly concealing the message in the compressed data.

1.5.5 Network Steganography

Network steganography is also known as protocol steganography. As the name suggests the secret message is concealed into any of the protocols of the OSI model and transferred over the network (Lubacz et al., 2012). For example, A secret message can be hidden in the header of a TCP/IP packet. Voice samples modification on VIP, hiding data in TCP segments, information embedding in padding, intentionally corrupted frames, etc. If the secret message can be passed over on the available layers of TCP/IP and OSI model, this is called network steganography.

TABLE 1.6
Attacks on Steganography

Attack	Location
Steg Only	Only stego object is used for analysis
Known cover attack	The cover and the stego both are known
Chosen stego attack	Steganographic algorithms and stego-object are known
Known stego attack	Cover object and steganographic tools are used.

1.6 Steganalysis: Introduction, Approaches and Tools

1.6.1 Steganalysis and Approaches

Steganalysis is the process of identifying the hidden secret message in steganography (Wikipedia, 2021). In steganalysis, few attacks, as shown in Table 1.6, check for the hidden message, while a few try to manipulate the data and a few change the location of the data present. All these attacks are targeted on the steg-object. The followings are few attacks on steganography.

The steganalysis can be achieved in three different ways: Visual approach, Structural approach, and Statistical approach.

1. In *Visual approaches*, the images are identified by observing the images and tracing out the altered bits by seeing the image directly.
2. In *Structural approaches*, the structures of the cover image are changed. The original image and the image with a secret message have variations of few pixels in the color that was altered. This approach identifies the file formats and structures to perform the steganalysis.
3. *Statistical approaches* use some mathematical and statistical ways to identify the hidden message.

1.6.2 Steganalysis Tools

These tools are used for detecting the presence of steganography. Stegdetect is an open-source tool that detects images generated by JSteg, JPHide, Invisible Secrets, Camouflage, and many more. StegSpy is a freeware that identifies steganography generated by the Hiderman, JPHideandSeek, Masker, JPegX, and Invisible Secrets tools. Stegbreak detects JSteg-Shell, JPHide, and OutGuess 0.13b generated messages.

1.7 Steganography Tools and Applications

There are many open-source and licensed software available to perform steganography few of which are as follows:

- *Stegosuite* is a tool written in Java that can hide information in images.
- *Steghide* is used for image and audio files. This is open-source software.

- *Xiao Steganography* is used to hide BMP and Wav formats.
- *SSuite Picsel* hides text in an image file.
- *Open puff* used for audio, video, flash, and image formats.

The main uses of steganography include the following:

- Confidential data communication
- Access control for digital media
- Protection against data alteration
- Maintain CAI triad
- Secret storage of data

Steganography is mainly used for secret communication purposes in the defense systems along with few others which are as follows:

- On military services
- Online transactions
- Medical services
- Intellectual property rights
- Financial and banking sectors
- Media piracy

1.8 Conclusion

Steganography is the technique to hide secret information from intruders with the help of a variety of media. Text, image, audio, video, and network steganographies are the different media used for concealing a secret message. Steganography provides a greater range of security compared to cryptography, because in steganography the existence of a secret message is not known to the naked eye. Each of the media has different techniques to achieve steganography as discussed in Section 1.5. Though there are few difficulties in the techniques, they provide good confidentiality of the data. The steganography also has a wide scope for research in the recent times with the machine learning approaches.

References

Agarwal, M. (2013). Text Steganographic Approaches: A Comparison. *International Journal of Network Security & Its Applications*, *5*(1), 91–106. doi: 10.5121/ijnsa.2013.5107

Ahmed Laskar, S. (2012). Secure Data Transmission Using Steganography and Encryption Technique. *International Journal on Cryptography and Information Security*, 2(3), 161–172.

Ashwin, S., Ramesh, J., & Gunavathi, K. (Dec 2012). Novel and Secure Encoding and Hiding Techniques Using Image Steganography: A Survey. *IEEE Xplore International Conference on Emerging Trends in Electrical Engineering and Energy Management*, pp. 171–177.

Bahramshahry, A., Ghasemi, H., Mitra, A., & Morada, V. (2007). Design of a Data Hiding Application Using Steganography. *Databases*, 1–6.

Bender, W., Gruhl, D., Morimoto, N., & Lu, A. (1996). Techniques for Data Hiding. *IBM Systems Journal*, *35*, 313–336.

Benett, K. (2004). Linguistic Steganography—Survey, Analysis and Robustness Concerns for Hiding Information in Text. Purdue University, CERIAS Tech. Report 2004–2013.

Bhatt, S., Ray, A., Ghosh, A., & Ray, A. (2015). Image Steganography and Visible Watermarking Using LSB Extraction Technique. *2015 IEEE 9th International Conference on Intelligent Systems and Control (ISCO)*, pp. 1–6.

Channalli, S., & Jadhav, A. (2009). Steganography an Art of Hiding Data. *International Journal on Computer Science and Engineering*, *1*(3), 137–141.

Das, R., & Tuithung, T. (2012). A Novel Steganography Method for Image Based on Huffman Encoding. *IEEE 3rd National Conference on Emerging Trends and Applications in Computer Science*, pp. 14–18. doi: 10.1109/NCETACS.2012.6203290

Divya, S. S., & Reddy, M. R. M. (2012). Hiding Text in Audio Using Multiple LSB Steganography and Provide Security Using Cryptography. *International Journal of Scientific & Technology Research*, *1*(6), 68–70.

Ekatpure, P. R., & Benkar, R. N. (2015). A Comparative Study of Steganography & Cryptography. *International Journal of Science and Research*, *4*(7), 670–672.

Hernon Moraldo, H. (2012). An Approach for Text Steganography Based on Markov Chains. *4th WSEAS Workshop on Computer Security*, pp. 21–35.

Joseph Raphael, A., & Sundaram, D. V. (2010). Cryptography and Steganography—A Survey. *International Journal of Computer and Technology Applications*, *2*(3), 626–630.

Karthik, J. V., & Venkateshwar Reddy, B. (Sept 2013). Authentication of Secret Information in Image Steganography. *International Journal of Latest Trends in Engineering & Technology*, *3*(1), 97–104.

Kumar, H., Shareef, M., & Kumar, R. P. (March 2013). Securing Information Using Steganography. *IEEE Xplore International Conference on Circuits, Power and Computing Technologies*, pp. 1197–1200.

Lubacz, J., Mazurczyk, W., & Szczypiorski, K. (2012). Principles and Overview of Network Steganography.*IEEE Communications Magazine*, *52*. doi: 10.1109/MCOM.2014.6815916

Morkel, T., Eloff, J. H., & Olivier, M. S. (2005). An Overview of Image Steganography. ISSA.

Narasimmalou, T., & Allen, J. R. (2012). Optimized Discrete Wavelet Transform Based Steganography. *2012 IEEE International Conference on Advanced Communication Control and Computing Technologies (ICACCCT)*, pp. 88–91. doi: 10.1109/ICACCCT.2012.6320747

Parah, S., Bashir, A., Manzoor, M., Gulzar, A., Firdous, M., Loan, N., & Sheikh, J. (2019). Secure and Reversible Data Hiding Scheme for Healthcare System Using Magic Rectangle and a New Interpolation Technique. *Healthcare Data Analytics and Management*, 267–309. doi: 10.1016/B978-0-12-815368-0.00011-7

Petitcolas, F., Anderson, R., & Kuhn, M. (1999). Information Hiding—A Survey. *Proceedings of The IEEE*, *87*(7), 1062–1078. doi: 10.1109/5.771065

Raftari, N., & Moghadam, A. M. E. (2012). Digital Image Steganography Based on Assignment Algorithm and Combination of DCT-IWT. *2012 Fourth International Conference on Computational Intelligence, Communication Systems and Networks*, pp. 295–300. doi: 10.1109/CICSyN.2012.62

Rao, N. V., & Philjon, J. T. L. (June 2011). Metamorphic Crypto—A Paradox between Cryptography and Steganography using Dynamic Encryption. *IEEE Xplore International Conference on Recent Trends in Information Technology*, pp. 217–222.

Seth, D., Ramanathan, L., & Pandey, A. (2010). Security Enhancement: Combining Cryptography and Steganography. *International Journal of Computers Applications*, *9*(11), 3–6.

Shahreza, M. H. S., & Shahreza, M. S. (2006) "A New Approach to Persian/Arabic Text Steganography. *Proceedings of 5th IEEE/ACIS Int. Conf. on Computer and Information Science and 1st IEEE/ACIS Int. Workshop on Component-Based Software Engineering, Software Architecture, and Reuse*, pp. 310–315.

Shahreza, M. S., & Shahreza, M. H. S. (2007). Text Steganography in SMS. *2007 International Conference on Convergence Information Technology*, pp. 2260–2265.

Shirali-Shahreza, M. H. (2008). Text Steganography by Changing Words Spelling. *2008 10th International Conference on Advanced Communication Technology*, 3, 1912–1913.

Singh, A., & Malik, S. (May 2013). Securing Data by Using Cryptography with Steganography. *International Journal of Advanced Research in Computer Science and Software Engineering*, 3(5), 404–409.

Uliyan, D., Al-Husainy, & Mohammed. (2018). Image Steganography Technique Based on Extracted Chains from the Secret Key. *Journal of Engineering and Applied Sciences, 13*, 4235–4244.

Wajgade, V. M., & Kumar, D. S. (2013). Stegocrypto—A Review of Steganography Techniques using Cryptography. *International Journal of Computer Science & Engineering Technology, 4*, 423–426.

Wayner, P. (1992). MIMIC Functions. *Cryptologia, 16*(3), 193–214. doi: 10.1080/0161-119291866883

Wikipedia.org. (2021). Steganography—Wikipedia. [online] Available at: https://en.wikipedia.org/wiki/Steganography. Last edited May 6, 2022.

Zin, W. W. (March 2011). Implementation and Analysis of Three Steganographic Approaches. *IEEE Xplore International Conference on Computer Research and Development*, pp. 456–460.

2

International Cyberspace Laws: A Review

Manik Garg[1], Susheela Dahiya[2], and Keshav Kaushik[2]
[1]*VMware Software India Pvt. Ltd., Bengaluru, Karnataka, India*
[2]*School of Computer Science, University of Petroleum & Energy Studies (UPES), Dehradun, Uttarakhand, India*

CONTENTS

2.1 Introduction

Cyber security is like another mini world in this digital space and, like other sectors, it needs to have its own laws. The more connected we are via the global internet network, more prone to cyber attacks we become. Both good and bad guys are using the same resources; while you could be fetching out just some information, someone can be after

DOI: 10.1201/9781003204862-2

yours. This is where laws come in. They help in keeping you safe even in a virtual digital world. Contrary to the title, there is no single "International Cyberspace" Law as such but the law that applies to you depends on which country you are currently residing and from where you are accessing the data (in terms of VPN) and in some cases to whom does the data belong. Keeping these factors in mind, different laws have different rules and regulations to follow while working both online and offline and handling information. Cyber Security is not just about the internet, it is about the information and rights of a particular individual both in terms of physical as well as known physical breaches.

2.2 Compliance Obligations—Standards, Laws, and Regulations

While there is no central law to enforce across the world, there are different internationally recognized standards that can be willingly implemented to help set up the controls needed for effective and efficient security. Many of them aim at different domains of security and privacy and vary by the type of infrastructure they can impact. Together the standards, laws, and regulations make the applicable "compliance obligations." Compliance obligations are a set of laws, regulations, and standards/requirements that apply to a particular individual or organization based on the nature, location, and audience of the activities.

2.3 Information Security Standards

A standard is a document containing a set of guidelines or requirements laid down by a particular organization known as the standardization body in a particular domain. It takes years to create a standard after a set of people continuously review the requirements based on feedback from industry stakeholders. Any standard may or may not be internationally recognized based on the aim and intent of creation. Usually, standards are independent and applicable across organizations and borders. It is not mandatory to implement a standard as per law, but some specific states or customers can make it a requirement to abide by a particular standard to get the business or for operations. Many international organizations work toward creating the standards in the information security field such as International Organization for Standardization (ISO), National Institute for Standards and Technology (NIST), International Electrotechnical Commission (IEC), British Standards Institute (BSI), etc. Some of the most widely used standards in Information Security are presented next.

2.3.1 ISO 27001

This is the most widely used standard across the globe for setting up an Information Security Management System (ISMS). It is referred to as *ISO/IEC 27001:2013* that specifies the requirements for establishing, implementing, maintaining ISMS. This standard is created by a joint effort of ISO and IEC and is the second version after the ISO/IEC 27001:2005.

FIGURE 2.1
ISMS Clauses Based on ISO 27001:2013.

This standard lays down the basic requirements for implementing cybersecurity in an organization. It contains 10 clauses, as shown in Figure 2.1.

These clauses together help set up the ISMS—Information Security Management System. It also contains the list of 114 controls from ISO 27002 standard as Annexure A. Together these clauses and controls cover various domains of cybersecurity across an organization. The controls are divided into the below-mentioned 14 domains from A5 to A18:

- **Information Security Policies:** This domain addresses the need for information security policies under various domains and their regular reviews.
- **Organization of Information Security:** This domain discusses the controls related to internal organization, roles, communication, and security of mobile devices.
- **Human Resource Security:** This domain talks about various controls in HR domain like screening, terms and conditions, disciplinary process, infosec awareness, etc.
- **Asset Management:** This domain addresses the requirements like asset inventory, ownership, acceptable use, classification, labelling, disposal, and management of removal media.
- **Access Control:** This is an important domain talking about user access provisioning and deprovisioning, access reviews, privileged access management and password management systems.
- **Cryptography:** This domain discusses requirements related to a cryptographic policy and management of keys.
- **Physical Security:** This domain addresses the controls related to physical security perimeter, entry restrictions, cabling, user assets and clear desk clear screen policies.
- **Operations Security:** This domain talks about important aspects like change management, capacity management, malware protection, backup, logging and monitoring, clock synchronization, vulnerability management and software installation restrictions.

- **Communications Security:** This domain discusses the network security controls, information transfers, and non disclosure agreements.
- **System Acquisition Development and Maintenance:** This domain addresses the software development lifecycle security, testing principles, and security of test data.
- **Supplier Relationships:** This domain addresses various aspects of vendor management along with onboarding checks.
- **Information Security Incident Management:** This domain discusses reporting security events, incident lifecycle, and evidence collection.
- **Information Security Aspects of Business Continuity Management:** This domain talks about business continuity plans, disaster recovery, and ongoing tests.
- **Compliance:** This domain discusses legal and contractual requirements and independence of security reviews.

This standard is the first choice for any organization looking forward for implementing Information Security. Also, this is a certifiable standard i.e., an organization can obtain a certification from an accreditation body stating its compliance with the requirements of ISO/IEC 27001 and can showcase it as proof of being secure.

Let's discuss the compliance certification cycle in more detail. The compliance certification cycle for ISO 27001 contains various phases that can change for each organization based on their scope and product implementation. This is first decided with the help of a document known as the "Statement of Applicability or the SOA." This document lays down all the ISO 27001 Clauses and controls along with a status showing whether they are applicable or not for the organization. To scope out a control, an organization needs to have a proper Business justification or a technical exception. The ISO 27001 Certification Process can be divided into different phases as shown in Figure 2.2.

Some of these phases will repeat after each other to support continuous improvement as suggested by the standard. ISO 27001 is a documentation-heavy standard i.e., it relies a lot on documented evidence. Thus, while aiming for ISO 27001 Compliance, an organization needs to create a lot of documentation around its processes and classify them as either Policy, Procedures, or Guidelines.

Another major focus of ISO 27001 is on Risk Management. It is covered as part of Clause 6 Planning and then again as part of Clause 8 Operation. To drive Risk Assessment and Risk treatment practices, 27001 focusses on another piece of document known as the "Risk Treatment Plan," or the RTP. This document describes the actions taken to address a particular risk in the environment.

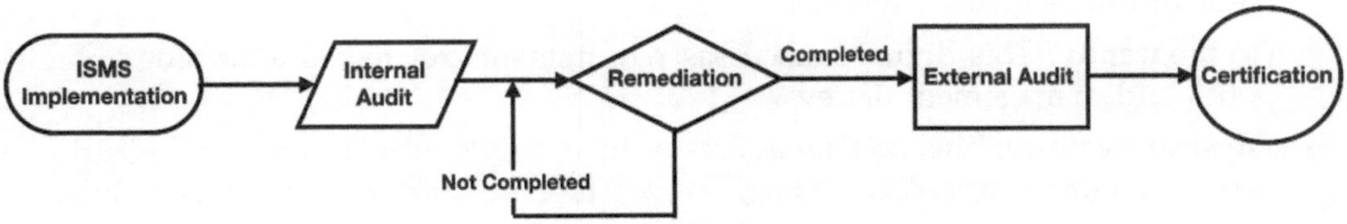

FIGURE 2.2
ISO Certification Cycle.

ISO 27001 categorizes any finding from the assessment into the following three categories:

1. **Opportunity for Improvement:** This describes any additional guidance or implementation that can help in increasing the effectiveness of the control.
2. **Minor Non-Conformity:** This refers to a Minor gap in the control implementation and a slight deviation from ISO 27001 control requirement but not majorly affecting the ISMS.
3. **Major Non-conformity:** This refers to a major gap in a control implementation or an absence of a control thus, majorly affecting the ISMS.

OFI and Minor NCs doesn't affect the ISO 27001 Certification but a Major NC can stop an organization from obtaining the certification. The copy of ISO 27001 Certification can be procured from the official ISO website [1,2].

2.3.2 ISO 27017

This standard is referred to as *"ISO/IEC 27017:2015 Information technology — Security techniques — Code of practice for information security controls based on ISO/IEC 27002 for cloud services."* This standard focuses on implementing the ISO/IEC 27001 controls and some additional guidance on cloud services. It is an extension standard to ISO/IEC 27001:2013 covering aspects of Cloud Security by adding specific requirements in ISO/IEC 27001 Annexure A controls and introducing an additional Annexure of its own.

ISO 27017 is not used as an independent certifiable standard but is often used in addition with ISO 27001 as a joint certification. This is majorly used by Cloud Providers and Cloud Customers to establish a secure control landscape in the cloud environment. It discusses the controls in alignment with the Shared Responsibility Model. It discusses domains like Asset Management, Access Control, Network Security, Operations Security, etc. [3].

2.3.3 NIST SP 800-53

This standard is created by the "National Institute of Standards & Technology." The standard addresses the "Security and Privacy Controls for Information Systems and Organizations." It is majorly used for U.S. federal Systems but can be implemented by other organizations as well. It addresses areas like Risk Management and helps in implementing the baseline security controls.

It addresses 18 domains in Information Security listed as follows:

1. **AC:** Access Control
2. **PM:** Program Management
3. **SI:** System and Information Integrity
4. **AU:** Audit and Accountability
5. **CA:** Security Assessment and Authorization
6. **PL:** Planning
7. **IA:** Identification and Authentication
8. **CM:** Configuration Management
9. **IR:** Incident Response

10. **AT:** Awareness and Training
11. **MA:** Maintenance
12. **CP:** Contingency Planning
13. **MP:** Media Protection
14. **SA:** System and Services Acquisition
15. **PE:** Physical and Environmental Protection
16. **PS:** Personnel Security
17. **RA:** Risk Assessment
18. **SC:** System and Communications Protection

The current version for this standard is the 5th Revision, which was released on September 23, 2020. All NIST standards are publicly available free of cost for anyone to access and implement at [4].

2.3.4 PCI DSS

PCI DSS stands for "Payment Card Industry Data Security Standard." This is a worldwide accepted standard in the digital payments industry created by the "Payment Card Industry Security Standards Council" comprising of Visa, MasterCard, American Express, JCB International and Discover Financial Services. Though it is not a regulation as per the government but is mandated by a lot of credit card companies like Visa and Mastercard. Any application processing payments in any form is usually required to adhere to PCI DSS compliance. This standard is also publicly available at [5]. The latest version of this standard is PCI DSS v3.2.1. The standard states that any organization/application that accepts, processes, stores, or transmits any payment-related information needs to abide by the PCI DSS rules.

It focuses on the six control objectives listed as follows:

1. The first objective is to build and maintain a Secure Network and Systems for addressing network security related requirements.
2. The second objective is to Implement Strong Access Control Measures for preventing unauthorized access and concurrent authentication.
3. The third objective is to Protect Cardholder Data by encrypting and preventing unauthorized disclosure.
4. The fourth objective is to Regularly Monitor and Test Networks by implementing logging and monitoring controls.
5. The fifth objective is to Maintain a Vulnerability Management Program for providing protection against any zero-day vulnerabilities.
6. The sixth objective is to Maintain an Information Security Policy for efficient and regular management of the whole information security process.

The above-stated control objectives are further classified into 12 requirements:

1. To protect cardholder data, install and maintain a firewall config and use proper configuration of network devices like routers, to segregate and protect the network appropriately.

2. Never use vendor-supplied default passwords for system and other security parameters as default passwords are available on vendor websites or as part of documentation.
3. Protect the stored cardholder data even in case of a physical breach.
4. Across open, public networks use encrypted transmission of cardholder data to avoid attacks like Man in the Middle and sniffing.
5. Use an anti-virus software program and update it regularly to be aware of all new virus definitions.
6. For development and maintenance of secure systems and applications follow strong security design principles.
7. Restricted access to cardholder data by business need to know.
8. To implement accountability of actions, assign a unique ID to everyone having access to a particular computer.
9. Restricted physical access to cardholder data so that no one can destroy or alter the data at an infrastructure level.
10. Test security systems and processes regularly.
11. Track and monitor all access to detect any unauthorized actions to network resources and cardholder data.
12. Maintain a policy that addresses information security for all personnel.

PCI DSS is laid out in a very detailed manner with specific terms for each role and requirement.

The key terms discussed throughout PCI DSS are as follows:

1. **SAQ** (Self-Assessment Questionnaire)
2. **ROC** (Report on Compliance)
3. **AOC** (Attestation on Compliance)
4. **ISA** (Internal Security Assessor)
5. **QSA** (Qualified Security Assessor)
6. **ASV** (Approved Scanning Vendor)
7. **POI** (Point of Interaction)
8. **PA DSS** (Payment Application Data Security Standard)
9. **CDE** (Card Holder Data Environment)
10. **EPP** (Encrypting PIN Pads)
11. **SRED** (Secure Read & Exchange Modules)
12. **UPT** (Unattended Payment Terminals)
13. **TPP** (Third Party Processor)
14. **PSP** (Payment Service Provider)
15. **DSE** (Data Storage Entity)
16. **VNP** (VisaNet Processor)
17. **DSOP** (Data Security Operating Policy)
18. **DISC** (Discover Information Security Compliance)

19. **SDP** (Site Data Protection)
20. **QIR** (Qualifies Integrators & Resellers)

2.3.5 Service Organization Controls

Service organization control (SOC) reports are a very important part of compliance reporting for any service organization. They represent the validation of AICPA SOC controls. These controls consist of Common Control Criteria, COSO Principles, and some detailed points of focus. These reports are required to validate the five Trust Service Principles: Security, Availability, Process integrity, Privacy, and Confidentiality.

There are three types of SOC reports containing different control domains and testing strategies as discussed below:

1. **SOC 1:** This is a financial attestation report that validates the management business objectives.
2. **SOC 2:** This report describes the security control environment in a service organization for customers to understand the level of controls implemented.
3. **SOC 3:** This describes an organization's internal control in the field of confidentiality, availability, and integrity.

SOC 2 reports are the most important ones in the cybersecurity industry. These reports can be further divided into the following two types:

1. **SOC 2 Type I:** These reports consist of a basic overview of the security controls landscape. They are usually a result of the "Test of Design" on the organization's environment. They are meant to be shared with customers or the general public so that they can understand what security controls are in place.
2. **SOC 2 Type II:** These reports are result of a detailed "Test of Effectiveness." They are an extended version of Type I reports that explain how the security controls are implemented and validates their functioning by means of testing of various samples across the control domain. These are to be shared with customers that are important and need to understand the whole control domain. Type II reports contain a lot of confidential information so sharing of such reports is highly restricted.

To obtain any of these reports, an organization needs to go through a rigorous external audit with an independent authorized auditor. Customers usually rely on these reports to save redundant testing efforts on vendor's environment.

Note: It is not a mandate for a service organization to have an SOC assessment but depending on the need an organization can choose to go for 1 or more of these assessments. [6]

2.4 Laws and Regulations

Usually, in the field of legal studies laws and regulations are defined as separate entities. However, in cybersecurity, no such segregation has been seen. For now, any set of rules and regulations that are mandated by a particular government to be established and followed within their jurisdiction bounds is a law in that particular area. In this section, we will discuss various Cyber Security laws and their applicable areas.

2.4.1 EU-GDPR

EU-GDPR stands for "European Union's General Data Protection Regulation." This law is the most widely recognized privacy law in the world and one of its kind. This law aims at protecting the rights of individuals residing in the European Union and the European Economic Area irrespective of location or country of residence. It addresses the privacy related rights and is applicable to anyone processing or storing the data of these individuals. This law was made in April 2016 but implemented in May 2018.

The law relies on the following six principles:

1. **Lawfulness, fairness, and transparency:** Everything should abide by law, and nothing should be hidden from the individual who owns the data.
2. **Purpose Limitation:** Restricted use of data according to the purpose defined and communicated.
3. **Data Minimization:** Avoid collecting data that is not needed as part of business requirement.
4. **Accuracy:** The data should be always updated and accurate.
5. **Storage Limitation:** Any personal data should be only stored until it is needed.
6. **Integrity and Confidentiality:** Any processing on data should not compromise its integrity and confidentiality.

It states that the data of an individual cannot be processed without consent unless there is at least one legal reason to do so.

According to GDPR, a Data Subject (an individual whose data is being referred to) has the following rights:

1. **Right to Information:** To request the processor/ controller to disclose information about what personal data is stored or processed about him/her and can ask a reason for that.
2. **Right to Access:** To access their personal data to view what is processed and to request a copy of the same.
3. **Right to Withdraw Consent:** To revoke any consent that was provided previously and thus stopping the processing of their personal data.
4. **Right to Object:** To object the processing of his/her data for a specific purpose.
5. **Right to Rectification:** To request any modification to their personal data if they believe it is not correct or updated.
6. **Right to Object to Automated Processing:** To request manual processing instead of automated processing of their personal data.
7. **Right for Data Portability:** To request transfer of data to another controller or processor in a machine-readable format.
8. **Right to be Forgotten:** To request deletion of their data permanently. This is also known as Right to Erasure.

The above-mentioned rights are provided to Data Subjects in the Articles 15–22 of the GDPR. However, Personal or household activities, Law Enforcement and National Security are exempted from any applicability of GDPR. [7]

2.4.1.1 Processor vs. Controller

These two terms are discussed and used throughout the GDPR. Processor refers to the entity performing operation on the data while controller if the person controlling what needs to be processed and is the main entity in an agreement with Data Subject. In some scenarios, processor and controller can be the same entity whereas sometimes processor can also additionally bring in other entities known as sub processors to process some or all aspects of the data.

2.4.1.2 PII—Personally Identifiable Information

The personal data mentioned throughout the GDPR is known as PII. PII is any data related to the Data Subject that can help in the identification of data subject like SSN, contact number, address, email address, etc.

EU-GDPR also discusses the fines and penalties to be levied in case of any violation to the GDPR compromising the rights of EU citizens.

2.4.2 CCPA

CCPA stands for "California Consumer Privacy Act." This act aims at protecting the rights of the citizens of California state in the U.S. and was implemented in June 2018. It addresses the following rights:

1. **Right to Know:** This provides the citizens right to know about what information is stored and processed regarding them by any business.
2. **Right to Delete:** This provides the citizens right to request deletion of any data a business holds about them.
3. **Right to Opt-out:** This provides the citizens right to prevent the sale of their personal information.
4. **Right to Non-discrimination:** This provides the citizens right to exercise their CCPA rights no matter what.

The California voters also passed the California Privacy Rights Act in November 2020 which is an extension to the CCPA and expands the rights of the citizens. [8]

2.4.3 SOX

SOX stands for "Sarbanes Oxley Act." This US federal law was enacted in July 2002. Though this law focuses on accuracy of financial information still there are a lot of aspects in this law that mandates security of any applications processing financial information of users or the company. This law is applicable to any publicly listed company in the United States. The act mandates testing of IT General Controls (ITGCs), IT Application Controls (ITACs) and some key financial reports. It addresses domains like

Provisioning & Deprovisioning of User Access, Review of User Access, Shared Account Access, Privileged Access, etc.

2.4.4 FISMA

FISMA stands for "Federal Information Security Management Act." This act was enacted in 2002 and requires all federal agencies to implement controls for protecting sensitive data. FISMA has the following Data Security Requirements apart from physical security control space:

1. **Information System Inventory:** There should be a proper asset inventory of all information processing systems.
2. **Risk Categorization:** Appropriate risk categorization should be there as per severity, likelihood, and impact.
3. **System Security Plan:** All systems should be secure and tested regularly.
4. **Security Controls:** Security controls should be implemented to address data security requirements.
5. **Risk Assessments:** Risk Assessments should be conducted to identify and mitigate risks in the environment.
6. **Certification and Accreditation:** Identify and obtain appropriate compliance accreditations.
7. **Continuous Monitoring:** Continuously log and monitor all controls to ensure appropriate working.

The FISMA compliance can be obtained by following the data security practices and implementing certain NIST standards such as the SP 800-53. [9]

2.4.5 PIPEDA

PIPEDA stands for "Personal Information Protection and Electronic Documents Act." This act is a Canadian law regarding Data Privacy. This was first enacted in April 2000, and it applies to the private sector organizations [10]. The 10 principles on which PIPEDA is based are shown in Figure 2.3.

Apart from these principles the PIPEDA addresses the following rights for the Data Subjects:

1. **Right to Access:** This provides the user right to request access his/her personal data as stored by the business.
2. **Right to Rectification:** This provides the user right to request modification in his/her personal data if found inaccurate.
3. **Right to Erasure:** This provides the user right to request deletion of data subject to purpose.

2.4.6 HIPAA

HIPAA stands for "Health Insurance Protection and Applicability Act." This federal law is applicable in the United States and deals with the security of Protected Health

FIGURE 2.3
PIPEDA Principles.

Information (PHI). It governs the use and disclosure of patient health information by entities known as "covered entities." The covered entities address by HIPAA are Health Plans, Healthcare Providers, Healthcare Clearinghouses, and Business Associates.

HIPAA Privacy rule allows the permitted uses of the health information regarding the following:

- Disclosure to individual's information
- Payment for treatment of healthcare operations
- Opportunity to decide about the disclosure of Protected Health Information
- Incident to an otherwise permitted use or disclosure and
- Limited dataset for research, public health, or healthcare operation.

HIPAA also allows the permitted uses of the health information for any other public interest and benefit activities like identification concerning deceased persons, essential government functions, when required by law for Judicial and administrative proceedings, workers' compensation, donation of cadaveric organ, eye, or tissue, victims of abuse or neglect or domestic violence, to prevent or lessen a serious threat to health or safety etc.

With respect to security, HIPAA ensures the availability, confidentiality, and integrity of all electronic protected health information. It also detects and safeguards the health information against anticipated threats to the security of the information and unauthorized uses or disclosures.

An organization functioning outside the US, but processing PHI of US Citizens can also be obligated to obtain HIPAA Compliance. [11]

2.4.7 Information Technology Act—India

Commonly known as the IT Act, this Indian law was enacted in 2000 with an amendment in 2008 known as the "IT Amendment Act." This law describes cybercrimes and penalties associated with them if committed in the Indian Jurisdiction bounds. The original act contained 94 sections which were then amended in 2008 to include any crimes introduced due to modern technological advancements.

The act addresses the offences from sections 65 to 78. The offences include:

1. Computer system hacking
2. Receiving any stolen communication device or computer
3. Using password of another person
4. Attempting to secure access to a protected system
5. Failure/refusal to decrypt data or to maintain records
6. Publishing images containing sexual acts, child porn or private images of others
7. Tampering with computer source documents
8. Cheating using computer resource
9. Failure/refusal to comply with orders
10. Publication for fraudulent purpose
11. Acts of cyberterrorism
12. Misrepresentation
13. Confidentiality and privacy breach
14. Disclosure of information in breach of lawful contract
15. False electronic signature certificate publishing in certain particulars
16. Any information which is obscene in electronic form

As per this law, foreign nationals can also be penalized if any cybercrime involves a computer or network located in India. [12]

2.5 Conclusion

Always remember though security and privacy seems pretty much the same, they are very different concepts. Security refers to protecting the assets and information related to any organization or user and thus implementing relevant controls to achieve this. Whereas privacy is a concept of rights of users related to their PII—Personally Identifiable Information. Thus, different laws and standards cover these aspects differently and we should take this into consideration.

We discussed various laws, regulations, and standards throughout this chapter. All of these apply differently in different scenarios and have different target audience. People involved in the governance practices of the organizations need to identify the applicable and relevant compliance obligations for their organizations. As an individual, everyone should be aware of their nation's IT law and the implications of breaking them. We have discussed most of the cyberspace laws in brief. More detailed information can be obtained by visiting their official sources and documentations. There is no international cyberspace law currently, but, of course, we need one and it can be a whole separate set of guidelines or a combination of the currently available ones.

References

1. ISO/IEC 27001:2013 Information technology—Security techniques—Information security management systems—Requirements
2. ISO/IEC 27002:2013 Information technology—Security techniques—Code of practice for information security controls
3. ISO/IEC 27017:2015 Information technology—Security techniques—Code of practice for information security controls based on ISO/IEC 27002 for cloud services
4. https://www.nist.gov—Accessed on July 8, 2021
5. https://www.pcisecuritystandards.org—Accessed on June 27, 2021
6. https://www.aicpa.org/interestareas/frc/assuranceadvisoryservices/socforserviceorganizations.html—Accessed on June 28, 2021
7. https://gdpr-info.eu/—Accessed on June 28, 2021
8. https://oag.ca.gov/privacy/ccpa—Accessed on August 3, 2021
9. https://www.cisa.gov/federal-information-security-modernization-act—Accessed on June 15, 2021
10. https://www.priv.gc.ca/en/privacy-topics/privacy-laws-in-canada/the-personal-information-protection-and-electronic-documents-act-pipeda/—Accessed on June 25, 2021
11. https://www.cdc.gov/phlp/publications/topic/hipaa.html#:~:text=The%20Health%20Insurance%20Portability%20and,the%20patient's%20consent%20or%20knowledge—Accessed on June 21, 2021
12. https://www.indiacode.nic.in/bitstream/123456789/13116/1/it_act_2000_updated.pdf—Accessed on July 18, 2021

3

Unraveling the Dark Web

Susheela Dahiya[1], Manik Garg[2], and Keshav Kaushik[1]
[1]*School of Computer Science, University of Petroleum & Energy Studies (UPES), Dehradun, Uttarakhand, India*
[2]*VMware Software India Pvt. Ltd., Bengaluru, Karnataka, India*

CONTENTS

3.1 Deep Web: The Unknown

Most of the people, especially, young generation spend majority of their time on the internet on a daily basis. Smartphones, Smart Homes, and all other gadgets have made it nearly impossible to stay without the internet. We can find a site for nearly anything and everything on the public internet. You just have to go to a web browser, go to a search engine, enter your need, and hit ENTER. It is as simple as that. But do you see everything? Do you know everything that is on the internet? No, you don't. Because it is not visible or in technical terms, it is not addressable. As shown in Figure 3.1., the World Wide Web (www) consists of three parts: Visible Web, Deep Web, and Dark Web.

The area of the internet that is visible to common people is known as Visible Web and the area which is not visible to common people is known as the Deep Web. The Dark Web

DOI: 10.1201/9781003204862-3

FIGURE 3.1
A Metaphorical View of Internet.

is a part of Deep Web. These are websites that exist but are not indexed on search engines. This doesn't mean that these sites are illegal, it just means they are hidden or not for public use e.g., a bank's internal website. Only 10 percent of the global internet is for public use; the remaining 90 percent is Deep Web.

3.1.1 How to Access the Deep Web?

Generally, we access websites using the name provided as a part of Domain Name System (DNS). Every website on the internet is represented by an IP Address of its hosting server. The only difference between a public website and a Deep Web page is that latter doesn't have a Domain Name associated with it. To access a Deep Web website, you need to know its IP address. Usually, these websites require an authentication mechanism to log in. So, in a nutshell, you should be an authenticated and authorized user with knowledge of the whereabouts of the website through your organization.

3.2 Dark Web—Illegal Dark Web

We just discussed the Deep Web in the previous sections. Another aspect of the hidden web is the infamous Dark Web. The Dark Web is not the same as the Deep Web, rather it is a part of the Deep Web, and this part is illegal. It works in the same way as the Deep Web but contains pages of black markets, weapon houses, drug dealings, and a lot more. People usually get confused between the Dark and Deep Web, but they are different. The Dark Web is more of an unmanaged internet but not necessarily unmonitored. The Dark Web got its boost through various top marketplaces such as the Silk Road. So, the difference lies in the usage and the content. The Deep Web serves a legitimate content that has a restricted audience, thus is not indexed on the public web; whereas the Dark Web serves illegal content to anyone who wishes to access it through a special mechanism.

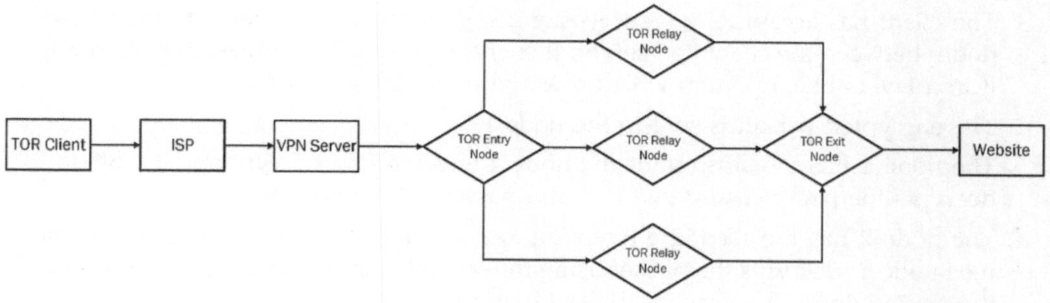

FIGURE 3.2
Working of the TOR Browser Using TOR Relays.

3.2.1 How to Access the Dark Web?

Dark Web webpages have a unique domain name. They all end with onion like the public web ends with .com, .org, etc. But you can't access any .onion domain using normal browsers. You have to use a concept known as Onion routing and a browser known as TOR (The Onion Router) to access these URLs. However, it is legally not allowed to browse the Dark Web due to the activities carried out there.

Figure 3.2 showcases the end-to-end flow of how TOR works and helps in accessing Dark Web sites. The detailed process regarding the nodes relay will be covered in the next subsection.

3.2.2 Onion Routing

This concept works like the structure of an onion. The data to be sent are not sent as it is in packets, rather the packet is encapsulated by layers of encryption and different routes to provide anonymity. These encapsulated packets travel through different nodes jumping from one location to another providing anonymity. Each node removes one layer of encryption to know the destination of the next node. The final layer contains the destination. This technique makes it difficult for anyone to track the user activity since there is not IP address allotted to the browser.

Let's understand the process of data flow in onion routing with the help of Figure 3.3 (Kaur and Randhawa, 2020).

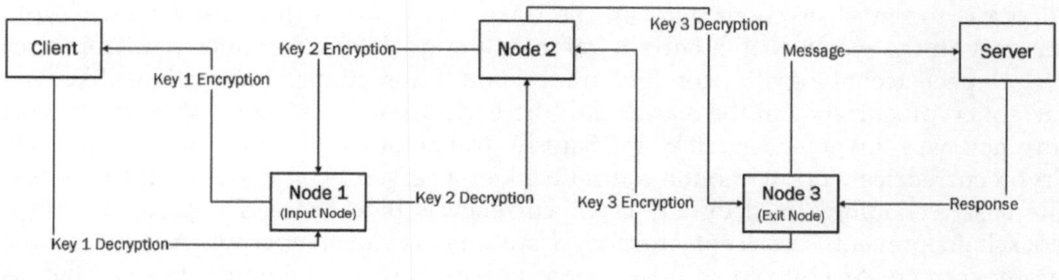

FIGURE 3.3
Data Flow on the Working of Onion Routing.

1. The client has access to "*n*" encryption keys where *n* represents the number of nodes between the client and server. It encrypts the packet *n* times thus wrapping it in *n* layers like an onion which must be removed one by one.
2. The encrypted packet is sent to the node 1.
3. The node 1 has the address of the node 2 and the first encryption key. Node 1 decrypts the packet using that key and passes it to the node 2.
4. The node 2 has the second encryption key and the address of the first and the next node. It decrypts the packet using the second encryption key and passes it to the next node until it reaches the last exit node.
5. The third node (*n*th node) which is an exit node decrypts the packet and finds a GET request and passes to the destination server.
6. The destination server fulfils the request of the client as a response.
7. The response is sent to the client in the reverse direction with a layer of encryption added by every node using their encryption key.
8. Finally, the encrypted response reaches the client, and the client will decrypt it with the help of the decryption keys.

3.2.3 Vulnerability in Onion Routing

We just discussed the end-to-end functionality of the onion routing. This concept acts as a base in TOR Browser for providing anonymity over the Dark Web. But is it 100% secure and effective? The answer is no, there is one security vulnerability in onion routing that can compromise anonymity. Though it is very difficult to exploit this flaw, still it is not an impossible scenario. The vulnerability can be exploited as follows: *If an attacker is listening in on a server at the same time. He can match the request at the destination to a request made by the client on the other side of a network. He can do so by analyzing the length and the frequency of the characters found in the intercepted request/response at the destination server and then tracking them down and knowing their online activity.*

3.3 Dark Web Currencies

Bitcoin is the most used currency on the Dark Web. This is the most famous crypto currency in the world with a current value of around $48000 per bitcoin. Bitcoin uses peer-to-peer technology to conduct trades and transactions. It functions like any current cryptocurrency in the market and there are around 4000 cryptocurrencies. This currency was invented in 2008 by Satoshi Nakamoto and came in use in 2009. Cryptocurrencies work without a central bank or a server using nodes on the network. The base technology used by any cryptocurrency is Blockchain. The core concept of blockchain prevents the cryptocurrency from any sort of tampering. Anyone on the internet can create a bitcoin address which is necessarily a unique private key. There is no public mapping of real-world owners to bitcoin addresses thus maintaining the

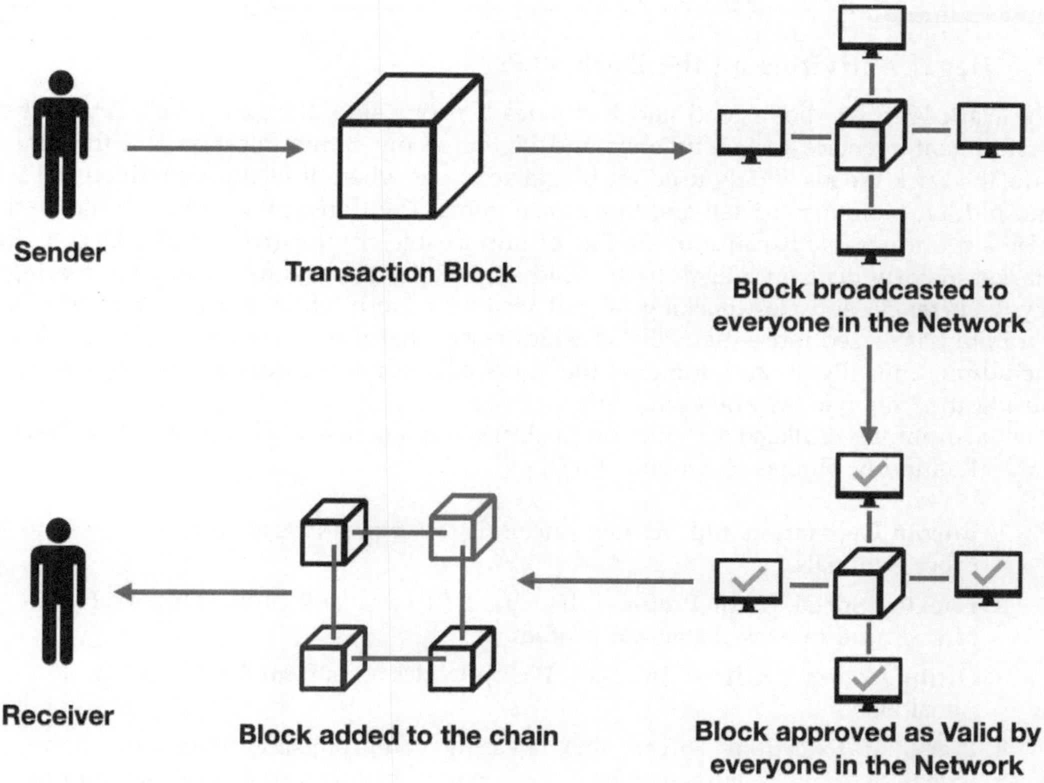

FIGURE 3.4
Process for Crypto Currency Transaction.

anonymity of transactions. Since there is no central authority or bank managing the transactions and everything is recorded on a public hyper ledger with bitcoin addresses, it is practically impossible to trace a transaction. Bitcoin has been used for several illegitimate activities such as drug trades, payments over the Dark Web, ransom payments for malware attacks, and so on (*Bitcoin Part 1: Here's How the Cryptocurrency Works,* n.d.). The process of a crypto currency transaction is shown in Figure 3.4.

Contrary to the use of bitcoin in the Dark Web, it is also used as a real-world trading currency and investment option through legitimate Bitcoin exchanges. These exchanges collect the personal information of the owners and map them to a bitcoin address thus maintaining traceability for each transaction. These are governed and overseen by the law. Since bitcoin works on the concept of mining and peer approval, its real-world value is very volatile. Many countries have made it illegal to trade in cryptocurrencies while some organizations are highly promoting the use and acceptance of cryptos. Some other famous cryptocurrencies used both over the Dark Web and the public internet are Ethereum, Dogecoin, XRP, etc.

3.4 Illegal Activities on the Dark Web

The Dark Web has both good and bad sides. On one side, the Dark Web is used by government agencies for anonymous and highly secure communication. On the other side, the Dark Web is widely used for illegal activities where it facilitates hidden sellers and hidden customers to sell and buy stolen items. The transactions done on the Dark Web are untraceable because of the use of untraceable cryptocurrency. The Dark Web market majorly deals in illegal drugs, ready-to-sell human organs, money laundering, cryptocurrency, software hacking, stolen weapons, porn, child pornography, etc. In 2015 FBI has seized more than 200000 IP addresses that use to share the black markets including "Silk Road" and some of the users and administrators are being arrested during the time (Godawatte et al., 2019).

Some examples of illegal activities on the Dark Web are listed below (*Dark Web Crimes*, n.d.), (Rafiuddin, Minhas, & Dhubb, 2017).

1. **Bitcoin Generation and Selling:** Bitcoin is the logical crypto currency used by cyber criminals.
2. **Hacking Social Media Profiles:** There are URLs available on the Dark Web that can be used to hack Instagram profiles.
3. **Hiring Contract Killers:** The Dark Web provides a platform for hiring a professional killer.
4. **Blackmail/Extortion:** Threats like releasing compromising photos of affairs (either such photo exists or not) in exchange of payment of a stated amount of bitcoin.
5. **Fake Documents:** Fake documents like VISA, Passports, Educational and Birth Certificates, Citizenship, etc. can be purchased from the Dark Web.
6. **Illegal Drugs Sales:** Silk Road was the most highly publicized online marketplace on the Dark Web for illegal sales of drugs, which was shut down by FBI in 2013. After that Agora was the one, which was shut down in 2019.
7. **Illegal Arms Sales:** According to estimates, approximately. "Tens of thousands of dollars" worth of guns are illegally sold each month on the Dark Web. Europe, Denmark, and Germany are the three largest sources of arms on the Dark Web.
8. **Child Pornography:** It includes exploiting the children for sexual stimulation, abuse of child during sexual acts, and use of sexual images of child pornography. It is very difficult for an average user to find these sites. PLAYPEN (taken down by the FBI in 2015) was the biggest child pornography site of that time on the entire Dark Web with approximately 200000 members. In 2018, approximately 144000 persons were using the Dark Web to access child pornography in Britain.
9. **Human/Sex Trafficking:** Human and sex trafficking are the crimes that take place on the Dark Web into secrecy. In 2015, an experimental internet search tool was used by the New York County D.A.'s Office to catch and prosecute the leader of a sex trafficking ring.
10. **Terrorism:** The Dark Web has been used both for recruitment and planning attacks by terrorist groups.

11. **Online Hackers:** Online hackers use to leak someone's personal and sensitive information over the Dark Web like personal records, credit card information, etc.
12. **Illegal Wildlife Trade:** There are many wildlife products like rhino horn, elephant tusk, ivory statue, and ivory case that are being traded illegally over the Dark Web.
13. **Counterfeit Credit Cards:** It is the most common Dark Web crime. It includes fabrication of counterfeit credit cards, stealing and selling of user's credentials of credit card and using for financial transaction.
14. **Cyber Attacks:** There are many cyber attacks that can be performed over the Dark Web like DD4BC (DDoS "4" Bitcoin), a group of cyber criminals which threatened victims via email with a DDoS attack till ransom is not paid in the form of bitcoins. This group has attacked more than 140 companies since its emergence in 2014.

3.5 Cyber Attacks via the Dark Web

There are several cyber attacks that can be launched via the Dark Web. As the attacker's identity is anonymous, it easy to attack the target. Cyber attacks can be categorized into following categories.

3.5.1 Active Attacks

In active attacks, there is an alteration/modification in the information available on the system which makes a direct impact on the system, and system resources. The victim can easily notice these types of attacks. Congestion/clogging attacks, traffic and timing correlation attacks, SQL injection (SQLI), cross-site scripting (XSS) attacks, man-in-the-middle attacks, authentication attacks, and phishing are the examples of active attacks that can be launched via the Dark Web.

3.5.2 Passive Attacks

In passive attacks, there is no impact on the system and system resources as the information remains unchanged. It is very difficult for the victim to notice these types of attacks. Correlation attacks, traffic fingerprinting attacks, Distributed Denial of Service (DDoS) attacks are the examples of passive attacks that can be launched via the Dark Web. Government organizations like FBI has taken down many illegal activities such as drug trafficking and child pornography running on the Dark Web by getting information about them through passive attacks on the Dark Web.

3.6 Social Media and the Dark Web

The Dark Web is a minor subset of the Deep Web that consists of sites purposely hidden from the public eye, such as those that use secret computer networks such as the TOR

Browser to connect to the Internet. When you use TOR, your traffic is routed via numerous computers all over the world before arriving at a website, masking your IP address and geolocation. The multiplicity of unlawful businesses and markets strewn over the Dark Web demonstrate that anonymity has a wide range of applications. That is also, why users should use TOR with caution since hackers can steal your data if your machine is not adequately protected.

Reddit (*Dark Web Social Networks and Identity*, n.d.), a well-known Surface Web social media network that blurs the lines of what conventional social media is characterized as, is a suitable location to start investigating these concerns. In terms of user engagement, Reddit is perhaps the most well-known social media network that adheres to the ideals of security and confidentiality. The overall layout of the platform places a greater emphasis on debate and external information than on personal identification. People seldom publish about themselves to keep others up to date; alternatively, personal information is frequently shared as a means of obtaining advice or learning. Several people do not really have their names associated to their accounts in relationship advice, for instance, thus the information is not adding to a real-life identity. Reddit is an example of a successful site where users may operate anonymously while still realizing the rewards.

Generally, when it pertains to providing a decent experience in the same areas, generic Dark Web social media sites fall short of Facebook, Instagram, Twitter, and others. Discovering an anonymized and private Reddit substitute appears to be more doable than finding one for Instagram. And although maintaining a constant connection with individual people on these more anonymous networks may be difficult, if not impossible, unchaining your identification may be invigorating, even if it means sacrificing some utility.

Because social media is assisting in the broad distribution of Dark Web products and services, assaults can come from anybody, anyplace, and at any moment. This can't go on like this. Cybercriminals utilizing social media networks require a far more aggressive response from social media firms. Humans can work together just to discourage cybercriminals from using social media to flog their products and make it difficult for them to draw the audience to their Dark Web shopping operations, if we recognize that social media is not simply a conduit for delivering dangers but also a market for selling them.

Accounts are being used by cybercriminals to sell these items openly or as a marketing tool to direct consumers to more specifications on the Dark Web. On social networking sites, fraudsters have gotten increasingly aggressive. One Facebook account stands out in my recollection because it was aggressively promoting on Twitter to attract customers and was giving the possibility to exchange or discover about exploits. Cybercriminals have turned to social media to broaden their reach and reach a larger audience. The distinctions between genuine clear web platforms and fraudulent Dark Web markets have blurred because of social media.

The Digital Shadows (*The Number of Stolen Logins Circulating On Dark Web Increased By 300 Percent since the Year 2018/Digital Information World*, n.d.) team's most recent analysis uncovers the full scope of stolen account login information spreading among cybercriminals on the Dark Web. Approximately 15 billion hijacked identities from 100,000 breaches are now accessible to cybercriminals, according to the researchers, who probably spent 18 months analyzing criminal forums and markets throughout the Dark Web. Since 2018, the figure has risen by 300 percent (Digital shadows). Figure 3.5. shows the graphical representation of percentages for the stolen login accounts on the Dark Web.

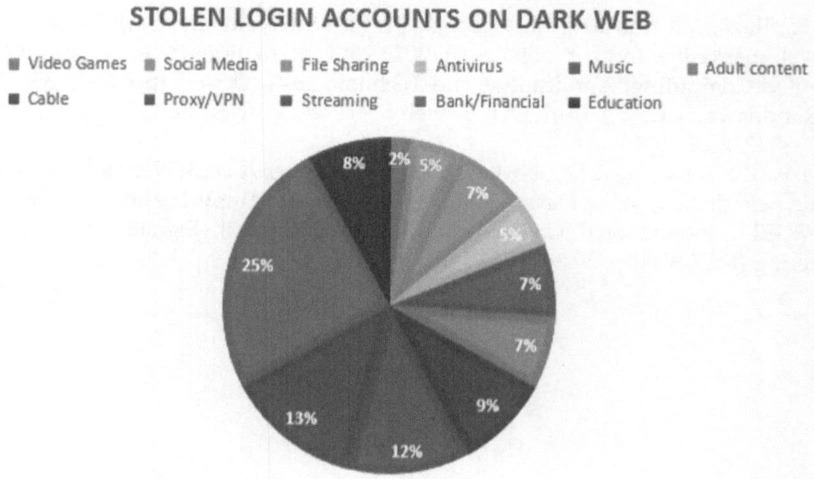

FIGURE 3.5
Percentages of Stolen Login Accounts on the Dark Web.

3.7 Conclusion

The Dark Web is a large marketplace that generates a huge amount of revenue per day. Generally, the person who wants to perform an activity (legal/illegal) uses the Dark Web to hide his/her identity. Most of the activities performed on the Dark Web are criminal such as hacking, proxying, selling of drugs and weapons and child pornography. The government agencies need to frame strong laws to regulate the use of the Dark Web. Along with numerous drawbacks, the Dark Web is also being used as a tool by government officials for online surveillance, planning and executing sting operations over TOR. With the help of the anonymity feature of TOR, FBI shut down many websites performing illegal activities on the Dark Web.

References

Bitcoin part 1: Here's how the cryptocurrency works (no date). Available at: https://www.moneycontrol.com/news/business/personal-finance/bitcoin-part-1-heres-how-the-cryptocurrency-works-6400621.html (Accessed: 12 May 2022).

Dark Web Crimes (no date). Available at: https://www.findlaw.com/criminal/criminal-charges/dark-web-crimes.html (Accessed: 7 November 2021).

Dark Web Social Networks and Identity (no date). Available at: https://www.logoffmovement.org/post/dark-web-social-networks-and-identity (Accessed: 17 November 2021).

Digital Information World (no date). The Number of Stolen Logins Circulating On Dark Web Increased By 300 Percent since the Year 2018. Available at: https://www.digitalinformationworld.com/2020/07/the-number-of-stolen-logins-circulating-on-dark-web-increased-by-300-percent-since-the-year-2018.html (Accessed: 12 May 2022).

Godawatte, K., Raza, M., Murtaza, M., & Saeed, A. (2019, December). Dark Web along with the Dark Web marketing and surveillance. In 2019 20th International Conference on Parallel and Distributed Computing, Applications and Technologies (PDCAT) (pp. 483–485). IEEE.

Kaur, S., & Randhawa, S. (2020). Dark web: A web of crimes. *Wireless Pers Commun* 112, 2131–2158. 10.1007/s11277-020-07143-2

Rafiuddin, M. F. B., Minhas, H., & Dhubb, P. S. (2017, September). A Dark Web story in-depth research and study conducted on the Dark Web based on forensic computing and security in Malaysia. In 2017 IEEE International Conference on Power, Control, Signals and Instrumentation Engineering (ICPCSI) (pp. 3049–3055). IEEE.

4

Memory Acquisition Process for the Linux and Macintosh Based Operating System Using Open-Source Tool

Ravi Sheth and Ashish Shukla
Rashtriya Raksha University, Gandhinagar, Gujarat, India

CONTENTS

4.1 Introduction and Literature Survey

In the era of digitization, cyber offenders are constantly enhancing their knowledge and skills for performing various ethical activities. Due to the growth and enhancement in the technologies the advanced forensic features are being introduced in present computer systems that gives the protection to rightful users those who have set protection but at the same time it will also aided to cyber offenders and this cause make the investigation process more difficult and challenging. Currently, the usage of Linux and Macintosh based operating systems are being increased. Every year these operating systems comes with the new privacy features for the users which enhance the security

DOI: 10.1201/9781003204862-4

features. Users are able to convert whole operating system data in to the encrypted form which makes difficult for forensic experts to retrieve the original data in a shorter amount of time without having the credentials of the user's account. Sometimes this encrypted data may have the different credentials compare to the account credentials. In such case it is always challenging task for the cyber experts to get the data from the memory and find the artifacts [1–4]. Generally, the cyber forensic experts followed a traditional method for acquiring digital forensic artefacts. Experts would simply use plug and play tools to acquire and analyze the data. For many years, such a process only means to retrieve the digital evidences. The method that captures every bite of artefacts, is continuous and repeatable, and does not change any content of the digital evidence. The benefit of this method, also known as a dead acquisition, which allowed during the court of trial as important evidence [5]. Advanced forensic characteristics of current operating systems encourage many computer experts to explore various methods of collecting digital artefacts. The most important difference between the new and traditional method is to collect the data from the volatile memory functioning in live system. Memory forensics, a relatively emerging and developing field for cyber experts that allows for the recovery of encrypted credentials, process list, packet information, packet exchange process and undisclosed process from physical memory [6]. Creating a memory dump or acquisition process always include the usage of open source or commercial tools to get the data or artifacts from the memory. There are many such tools are available for Windows operating systems like FTK imager, MAGNET RAM Capture, Belkasoft RAM Capturer and many more, but there are two very less effective open source and commercial tools available for Linux and Macintosh operating systems despite their growing market share. To create a memory dump or memory acquisition of memory from Linux and Macintosh operating system is more complicated and complex. It also includes the high amount of risk having the loss of artifacts. Considering all these facts many cyber forensic experts blindly trust on the tools without having the understanding and without testing and evaluating their results and performance measure and certainly this leads you towards the failure. The objective of this chapter is to give detail idea about the available volatile memory acquisition tools that mainly and specially developed for Linux and Macintosh computer systems. Examiners has to understand the authenticity of tools and risk of using them like our proposed method gives the positive rates of the tools based on to create the memory dump without system failure.

4.2 Linux Memory Acquisition Process

To analyze volatile memory data in Linux, first we need to run Linux based Operating System Ex. Kali Linux, on virtual box our host Device. Tool for memory forensics in Linux is LiME TOOL. LIME—LINUX MEMORY EXTRACTOR [7].

4.2.1 Software Acquisition Tools: Linux

LIME is a working as a Linux memory extraction tool. It has a feature of LKM i.e., Loadable Kernel Module using that memory dumping process is being done from the device having Linux based operating system. It will reduce the communication overhead between kernel space and user while the dumping process is being performed. Due to this it permits to generate and create a memory dump which can be forensically correct compare to other similar tools available for the Linux acquisition process.

4.2.2 Features of Lime

LiME is a very essential tool for acquiring the data from the Linux operating system it has a capability to perform on network interface, to process on footprint and to create a hash value of the memory dump.

4.2.3 System Information and Specification of Linux-Based Operating System

The table given below shows the system overview of the linux operating system.

System Information	System Specification
Host System Model Name:	DESKTOP-6TMVT1K
Operating System:	Windows 10 Pro
Processor Name:	Intel(R) Core(TM) i7-8700 CPU
Memory:	8GB
Device ID:	281B1CA9-7544-4D4F-891B-14942CAA237F
Product ID:	00330-80201-64589-AA683
Serial Number (system):	C1MT3Q6EH3QD
Processor Speed:	3.20GHz
Virtual Platform Name	Virtual Box
Guest (Virtual-Linux System):	Kali-Linux-2021.2 (Debian-64)
Number of Processor:	2
RAM Memory Size:	2GB
ROM Memory Size:	80 GB
Processor Speed:	3.20GHz

4.2.4 Methodology for Creating Memory Dump

The LiME Tool needs to be download on the suspicious machine. To run the LiME Tool, we need to login as a root in our kali linux terminal to login as root.

1. To run the LiME Tool, we need to login as a root in our kali linux terminal to login as root Sudo -I (sudo hyphen i).
2. LiME compilation. Once this process gets done the Lime Loadable Kernel Object (LKO) shall be created.
3. Enter the following commands:
    a. cd LiME (compilation of LiME Tool)
    b. ls (To view the presence of LKO)
    c. cd src
    d. ls

e. make (make command will help to create kernel object which we can use to insert module from kali machine)
f. sudo insmod./lime-4.19.0-kali4-amd64.ko "path=LinuxMemory.mem format=raw" (Here, examiner needs to define the address and the type of the format for creating memory dump)
g. ls (Then we can check whether our Memory has created or not.)
h. md5sum LinuxMemory.mem (Hash of Dumped Memory)

Step 1: Download the tool from the Github repository.

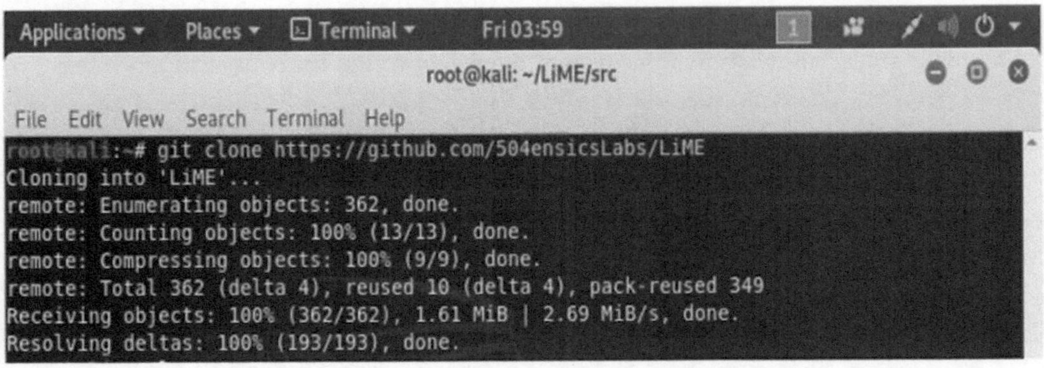

Step 2: Compilation of LiME Tool.

Step 3: To create kernel object which we can use to insert module from kali machine.

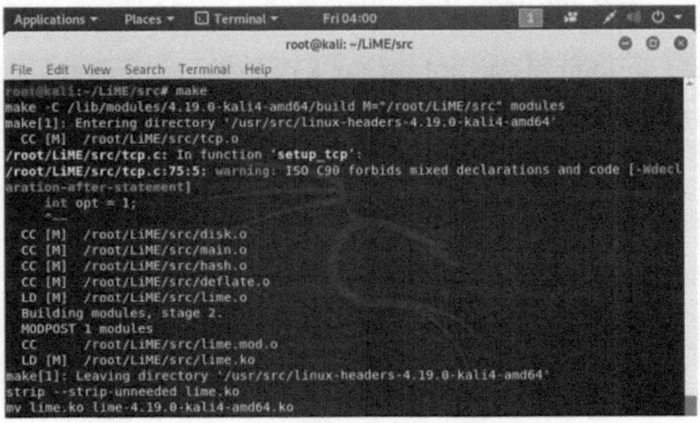

Step 4: To define the address and the type of the format for creating memory dump.

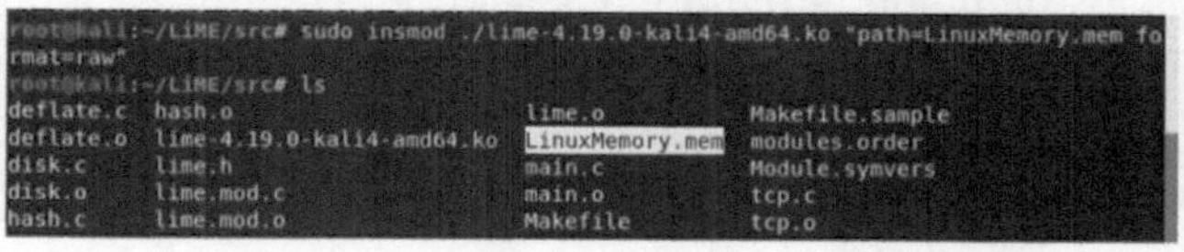

Step 5: Generating Hash of Dumped Memory.

4.3 Artefacts Available in Macintosh Memory

Like windows operating system volatile memory of Macintosh operating system also having the list of credentials, number of processes, network communication packets and other files [5]. It is always difficult to find all the artifacts present in the memory if memory has been unplugged by the forensic experts. Memory analysis is always useful in certain cases like malware and network traffic analysis. Cyber experts can easily trace out such activities based on the behavior of the process being executed in the memory.

The understand the presence and impact of malware and network data the memory forensics is considered as an ideal process. Using this the network traffic as well as malicious process can be easily traced out. According to Roberts [8], the advanced threat landscape contains memory-resident malware or viruses [8], almost every threat does not available in the hard disk, rather such processes made to execute in memory only. Without checking the content of the volatile memory such threats cannot be traced out or identified. Network communication packets are also there in the process list of the memory while sending and receiving. It will remain present until data gets overwrite. A memory acquiring process required certain amount of time to collect the artifacts related to network traffic depending on the capacity and usage of memory. Add on to this, in many cases previously executed network packets can also be retrieved [6].

4.3.1 Macintosh Memory Acquisition Process

Creating a memory dump or Memory acquisition process is a very first steps to performs the activities of memory forensics. As mentioned above very few tools are available for this process and required admin or root privileges for Macintosh systems. Once this process gets over, the data or artefacts can be found in memory dump that must be analyzed with tools mainly designed for operating system working on the kernel version.

4.3.2 Software Acquisition Tools: Macintosh

Internet sources and research & study of various experts it has been noticed that BlackBag- A Cellebrite Company, MacQuisition and OSXPMem are the most acceptable tools that having the capacity to work for different version of Macintosh operating system. For this research we have used OSXPMem tool for capturing the memory dum from the Macintosh operating system OSXPmem is an open-source and easy to use memory acquisition tool. This tool is available on GitHub website [10].

4.3.3 System Information and Specification of Macintosh-Based Operating System

The table given below shows the system overview of the macintosh operating system.

System Information	System Specification
System Model Name:	MacBook Air
Operating System:	Mojave 10.14.6 (18G8022)
Model Identifier:	MacBookAir7,2
Processor Name:	Intel Core i5
Memory:	8GB
L3 Cache:	3 MB
Hyper-Threading Technology:	Enabled
Hardware UUID:	0502838A-9764-566F-AED8-06A92DB5B8D4
L2 Cache (per Core):	256 KB
SMC Version (system):	2.27f2
Serial Number (system):	C1MT3Q6EH3QD
Processor Speed:	1.6 GHz
Boot ROM Version	426.0.0.0.0

4.3.4 Methodology for Creating Memory Dump

The OSXPmem is the only an open-source tool that provides very ease of process for creating the memory dump of volatile memory functioning in Macintosh. The OSXPmem having two major components user mode and kernel extension [10]. The user mode component is responsible to convert the readable section of volatile memory and store it into its compatible format. A kernel extension called "pmem.kext" provides the access of volatile memory in read only mode. While executing it in to the kernel level it provides the device file ("/dev/pmem/") and through which examiner can read the memory file that gives the read only access to volatile memory.

1. To get it installed this tool in the system we should have an access of root for that first open a terminal ("sudo su").
2. Extract the archive that shall create the directory name "OSXPMem" containing the binary "osxpmem," as well as the kernel extension "pmem.kext."
3. Enter the following commands:
    a. cd OSXPMem
    b. sudo chown -R root:wheel osxpmem.app/ (To start the tool)
    c. sudo osxpmem.app/osxpmem -o mem.aff4 (By default it creates memory dump in aff4 format (Advanced forensics format))
    d. sudo osxpmem.app/osxpmem -e /dev/pmem -o mem.raw mem.aff4 (Here, examiner needs to define the address and the type of the format for creating memory dump.)

Step 1: Download the tool from the Github repository.

```
user — -bash — 80×24
Last login: Wed Dec  5 01:24:58 on ttys001
Users-Mac:~ user$ sudo wget https://github.com/google/rekall/releases/download/v
1.5.1/osxpmem-2.1.post4.zip
Password:
--2018-12-05 01:59:46--  https://github.com/google/rekall/releases/download/v1.5
.1/osxpmem-2.1.post4.zip
Resolving github.com (github.com)... 192.30.253.112, 192.30.253.113
Connecting to github.com (github.com)|192.30.253.112|:443... connected.
HTTP request sent, awaiting response... 302 Found
Location: https://github-production-release-asset-2e65be.s3.amazonaws.com/198647
41/062e9aa2-210d-11e6-9e5d-64ac29aeaa1a?X-Amz-Algorithm=AWS4-HMAC-SHA256&X-Amz-C
redential=AKIAIWNJYAX4CSVEH53A%2F20181205%2Fus-east-1%2Fs3%2Faws4_request&X-Amz-
Date=20181205T095948Z&X-Amz-Expires=300&X-Amz-Signature=a8cac0ef4845f98721893db9
56179f2fc5de700fc88db719d4fe565e5b240107&X-Amz-SignedHeaders=host&actor_id=0&res
ponse-content-disposition=attachment%3B%20filename%3Dosxpmem-2.1.post4.zip&respo
nse-content-type=application%2Foctet-stream [following]
--2018-12-05 01:59:48--  https://github-production-release-asset-2e65be.s3.amazo
naws.com/19864741/062e9aa2-210d-11e6-9e5d-64ac29aeaa1a?X-Amz-Algorithm=AWS4-HMAC
-SHA256&X-Amz-Credential=AKIAIWNJYAX4CSVEH53A%2F20181205%2Fus-east-1%2Fs3%2Faws4
_request&X-Amz-Date=20181205T095948Z&X-Amz-Expires=300&X-Amz-Signature=a8cac0ef4
845f98721893db956179f2fc5de700fc88db719d4fe565e5b240107&X-Amz-SignedHeaders=host
&actor_id=0&response-content-disposition=attachment%3B%20filename%3Dosxpmem-2.1.
post4.zip&response-content-type=application%2Foctet-stream
Resolving github-production-release-asset-2e65be.s3.amazonaws.com (github-produc
```

Step 2: Unzip osxpmem-2.1.post4.zip.

```
user — -bash — 80×24
Users-Mac:~ user$ unzip osxpmem-2.1.post4.zip
Archive:  osxpmem-2.1.post4.zip
   creating: osxpmem.app/
   creating: osxpmem.app/libs/
  inflating: osxpmem.app/libs/libaff4.0.dylib
  inflating: osxpmem.app/libs/libcrypto.1.0.0.dylib
  inflating: osxpmem.app/libs/libcurl.4.dylib
  inflating: osxpmem.app/libs/libglog.0.dylib
  inflating: osxpmem.app/libs/libiconv.2.dylib
  inflating: osxpmem.app/libs/liblzma.5.dylib
  inflating: osxpmem.app/libs/libpcre++.0.dylib
  inflating: osxpmem.app/libs/libpcre.1.dylib
  inflating: osxpmem.app/libs/libraptor2.0.dylib
  inflating: osxpmem.app/libs/libsnappy.1.dylib
  inflating: osxpmem.app/libs/libssl.1.0.0.dylib
  inflating: osxpmem.app/libs/liburiparser.1.dylib
  inflating: osxpmem.app/libs/libuuid.16.dylib
  inflating: osxpmem.app/libs/libxml2.2.dylib
  inflating: osxpmem.app/libs/libxslt.1.dylib
  inflating: osxpmem.app/libs/libz.1.2.8.dylib
   creating: osxpmem.app/MacPmem.kext/
   creating: osxpmem.app/MacPmem.kext/Contents/
   creating: osxpmem.app/MacPmem.kext/Contents/_CodeSignature/
  inflating: osxpmem.app/MacPmem.kext/Contents/_CodeSignature/CodeResou
```

Step 3: Start the OSXpmem tool.

```
user — -bash — 80×24
Users-Mac:~ user$ sudo chown -R root:wheel osxpmem.app/
Password:
Users-Mac:~ user$ 
```

This comes in the case when system integrity protection is on and which prevents it. In such case this option needs to be disabled. To do this we have to start system into recovery mode.

Step 4: (In case error message gets displayed: Unable to load driver).

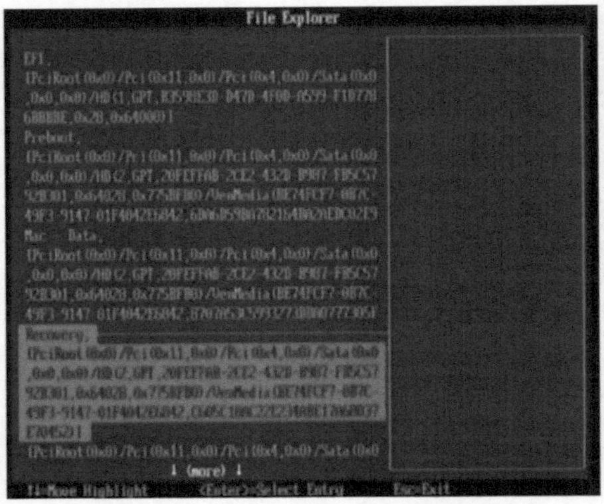

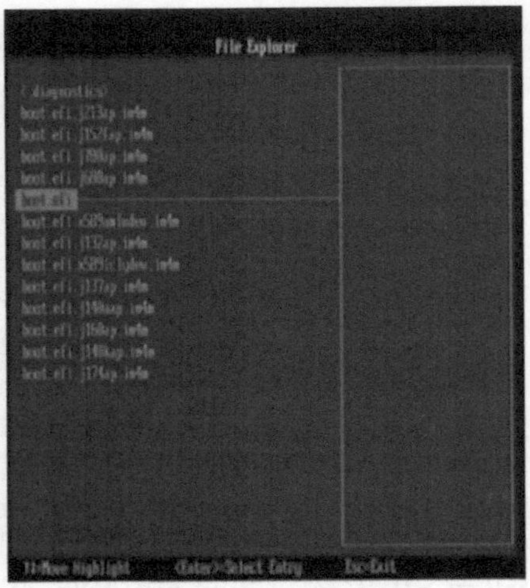

Step 4: (In case error message gets displayed: Unable to load driver).

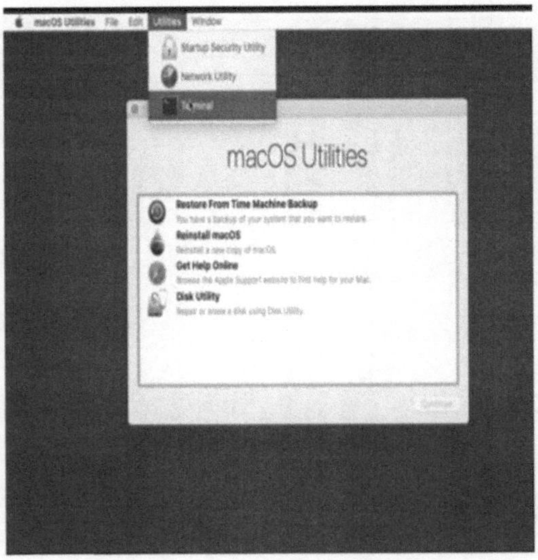

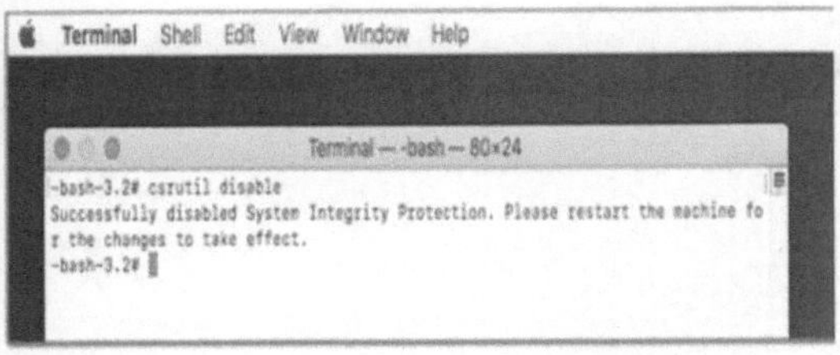

Step 5: To create a memory dump in aff4 format.

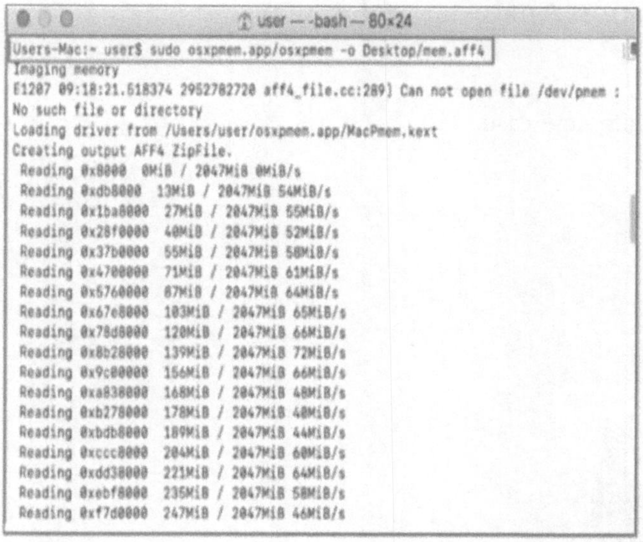

Step 6: To analyze the memory dump in Autopsy or Bulk extractor tool, need to convert the .aff4 format to .raw format.

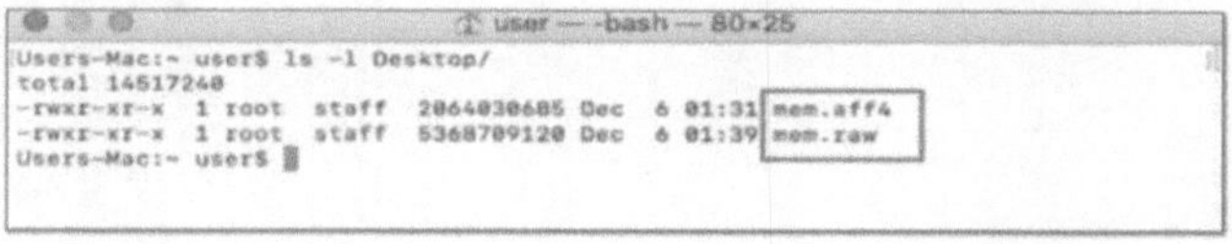

4.4 Autospy Digital Investigation Analysis Tool

Step 1: Open Autospy Tool and create new case.

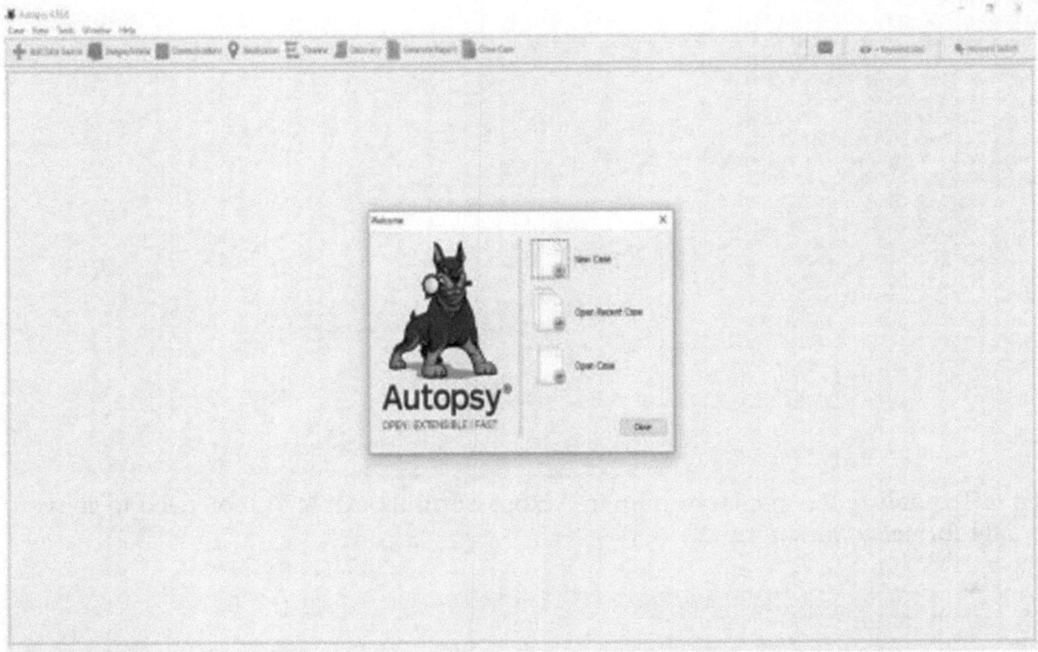

Step 2: Enter case information.

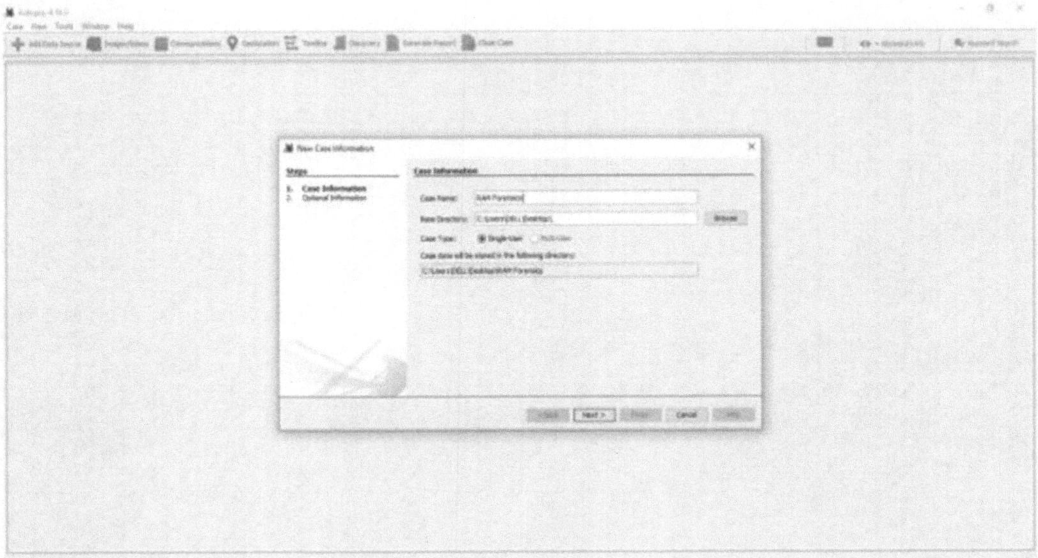

Step 3: Enter optional information.

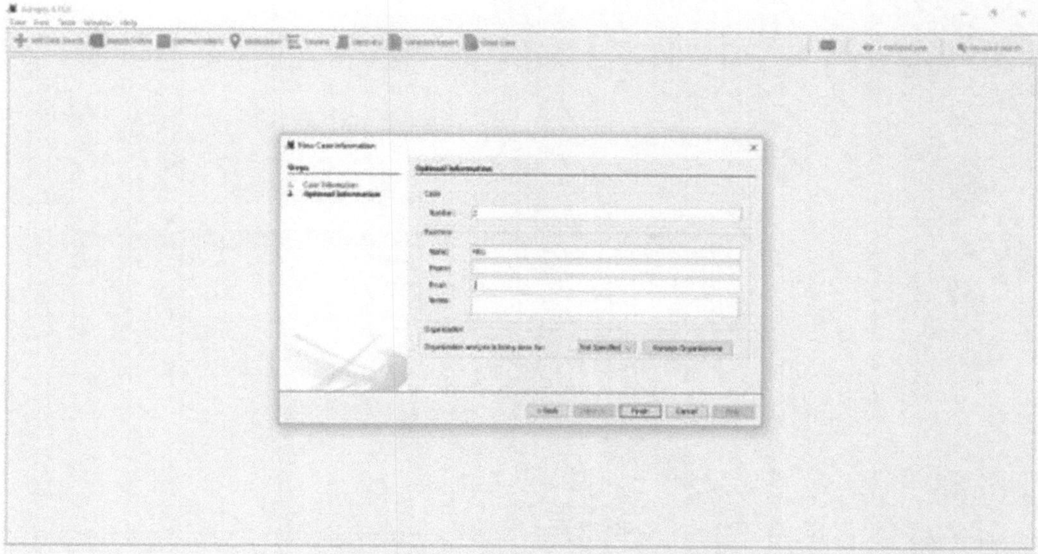

Step 4: To open RAM Imaging file (.mem), we have to choose "unallocated space image file" in "select Type of Data Source to Add".

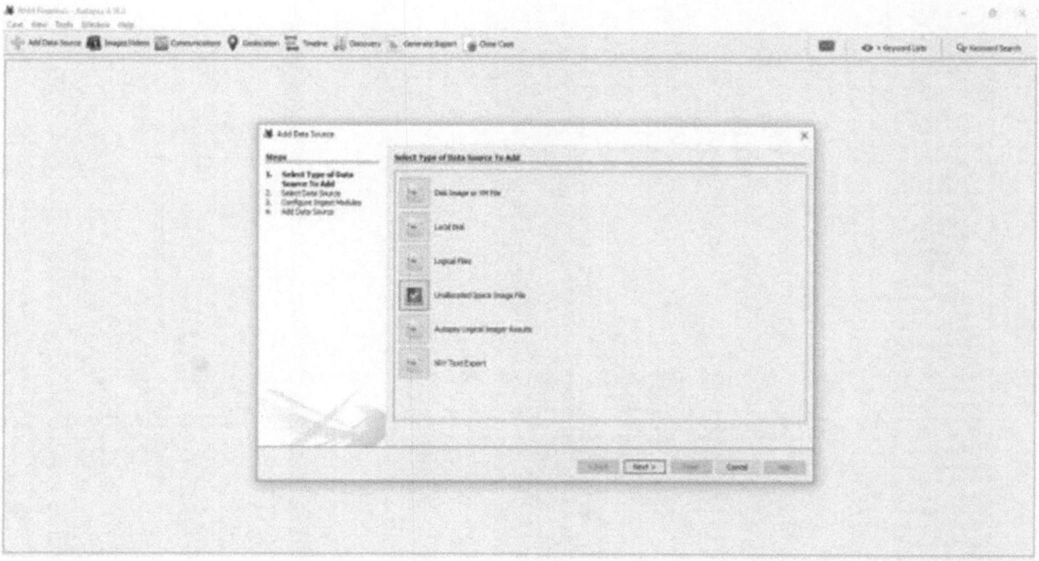

Linux memory artifacts.

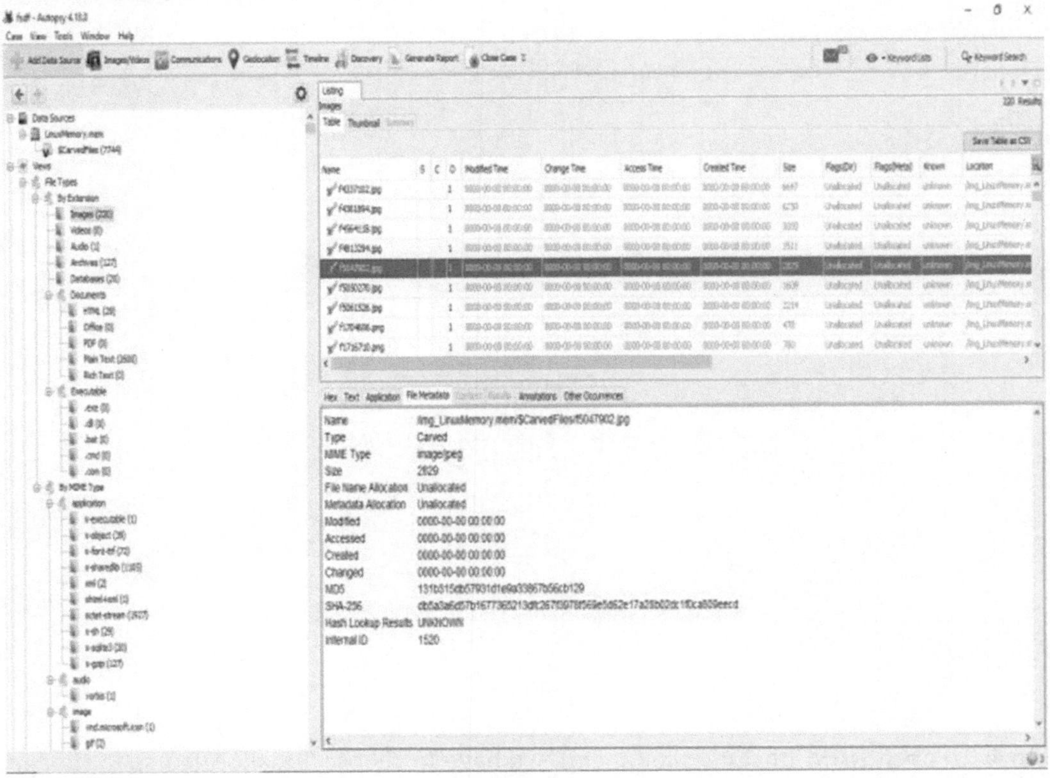

Linux memory artifacts LiME terminal output of memory captured email located in memory.

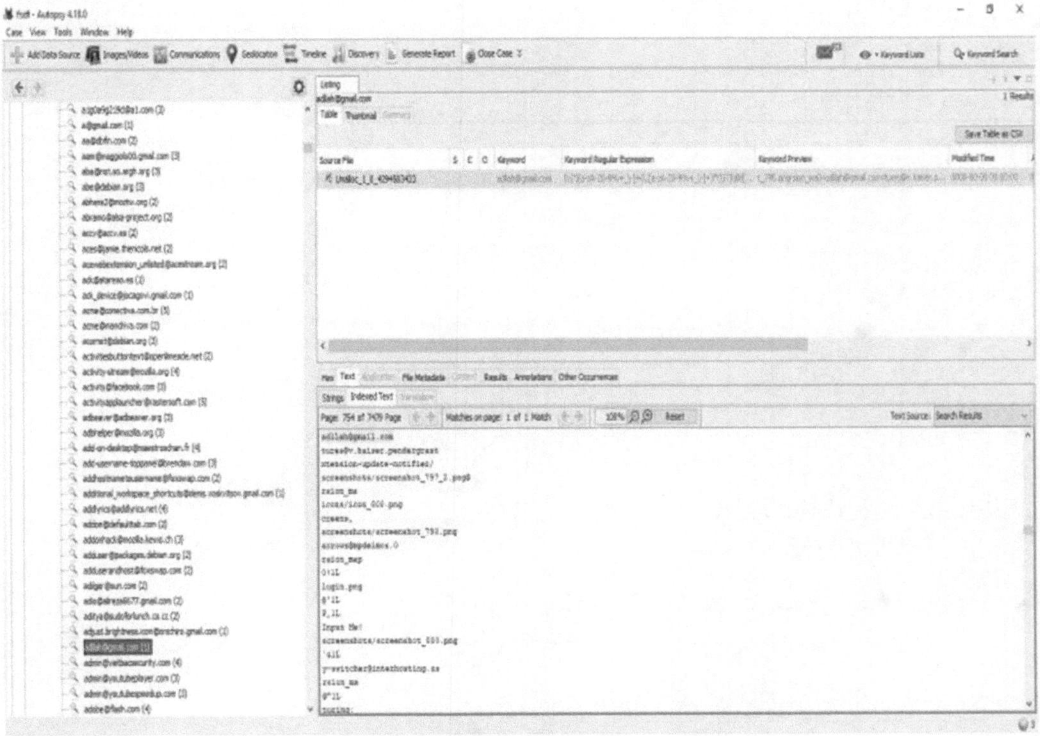

Macintosh memory artifacts (Linux memory artifacts OSXPMem terminal output of memory captured from VM user's login password located in memory).

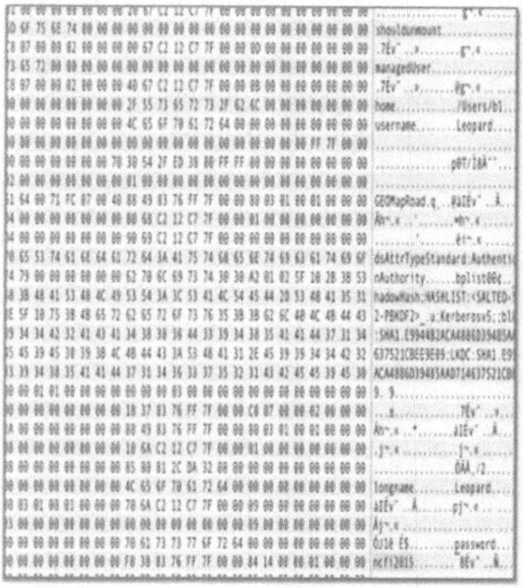

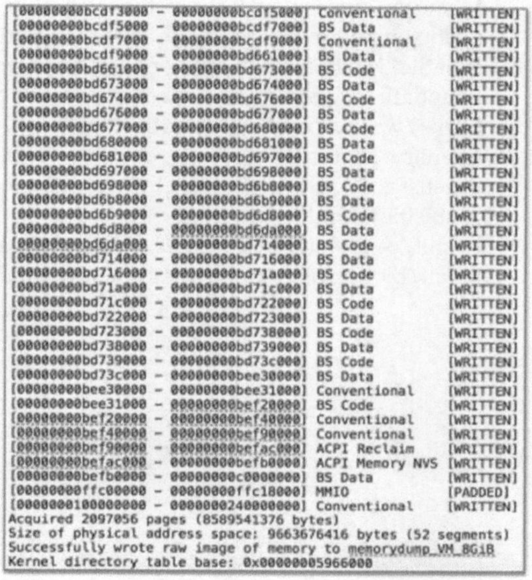

4.5 Conclusion

The results of acquisition process of memory show that LiME and OSXPMem tools working very effectively for Linux and Macintosh operating system respectively. The memory dump has been created without any loss of data and system damage. Later on, the created memory dump has been imported in the open-source tool like Autopsy for collecting the artifacts. Main advantage of said tool is it performing without any dependency related to the various.

References

1. M. Ligh et al. (2014.), *Art of memory forensics. Indianapolis*, published by Wiley
2. Carving process retrieved from R. Beverly et al. (2011). Forensic carving of network packets and associated data structures, Sciencedirect.com, 2011. [Online]. Available: http://www.sciencedirect.com/science/article/pii/S174228761100034X, Accessed: July. 10, 2021.
3. A. Aljaedi et al. *Comparative analysis of volatile memory forensics: Live response vs. memory imaging*, in 2011 IEEE Third Int'l Conf. on Privacy, Security, Risk and Trust, Boston, MA, 2011, pp. 1253–1258.
4. Waits, C. (2008, August). *Computer Forensics: Results of Live Response Inquiry vs. Memory Image Analysis. Computing Sciences.* https://www.csc.villanova.edu/~nadi/csc8710/papers/Forensic.pd
5. Ovie L. Carroll (2008), Computer Forensics: *Digital Forensic Analysis Methodology, United States Department of Justice Executive Office for United States Attorneys Washington,* DC, Volume 56 Number 1, Available: http://www.justice.gov/sites/default/files/usao/legacy/2008/02/04/usab5601.pdf

6. Reddy N. (2019), Mac OS Forensics. In: *Practical Cyber Forensics. Apress, Berkeley, CA.* Available: 10.1007/978-1-4842-4460-9_4
7. LiME resources retrieved from 504ensicsLabs/LiME: LiME (formerly DMD). GitHub. Memory Acquisition Process for the Linux and Macintosh Based Operating System Using open-source tool https://github.com/504ensicsLabs/LiME
8. Volatile Memory resources retrieved from Volatility Foundation. (n.d.). The Volatility Foundation–Open-source memory forensics. Volatility Foundation. [Online]. Available: http://www.volatilityfoundation.org/#!about/cmf3., Accessed: July. 11, 2021.
9. Memory acquisition process retrieved from OSX 10.9 memory acquisition. (n.d.). Rekall Forensics blog. Available: https://blog.rekall/forensic.com/2014/03/osx-109-memory-acquisition.html
10. Rekall/osxpmem.cc at master · Google/rekall. (n.d.). GitHub. https://github.com/google/rekall/blob/master/tools/pmem/osxpmem.cc

5

Deepfakes—A Looming Threat to Our Society

Raahat Devender Singh
Panjab University, Chandigarh, Punjab, India

CONTENTS

5.1 Introduction

When BuzzFeed and Jordan Peele created the fake Obama public service announcement in April 2018 (BuzzFeedVideo, 2018), it engendered a wave of wonder and excitement, which was soon replaced by a wave of trepidation and creeping vexation when the disturbing reality of the situation began to sink in. This video quickly became one of the most recognizable examples of deepfakes, aside from all the videos people created by replacing various actors' faces in movie clips with those of other celebrities (Collins, 2018a, 2018b; *The New York Times*, 2019).

Deepfake, which is a portmanteau of "deep learning" and "fake," refers to the artificial intelligence–based image synthesis technique that is used to merge and overlay existing images and videos of human faces onto other images or videos. Before learning more about deepfakes, let's take a look at a few snapshots from some famous deepfake videos (Figures 5.1 and 5.2).

DOI: 10.1201/9781003204862-5

FIGURE 5.1
Fake Obama Public Service Announcement. Snapshots from the fake PSA video created by BuzzFeed and Jordan Peele. Source: Jordan Peele. https://www.buzzfeed.com/in/tag/jordan-peele (accessed May 12, 2022).

FIGURE 5.2
Snapshots from some deepfakes. (a) Kate McKinnon as Hilary (Courtesy: Life2Coding). (b) Clinton Nicolas Cage as Lois Lane and Loki, respectively. (c) Nicolas Cage as Jean-Luc Picard in *Star Trek* (Courtesy (b and c): Nic Cage DeepFakes, YouTube, NBC, Paramount Pictures, Warner Bros. Pictures, Walt Disney Studio).

5.2 Typical Fake Video Creation Operations

Creation of a typical fake video requires the assistance of certain operations. Let's take a look at them before delving any further into the realm of deepfakes.

a. *Face swapping*, or *face replacement*, is the process of replacing a person's entire face or parts of a face in a target video with that or those of another person from a source video or several source images. This is basically a video–apposite version of the analogous image–based face–swap operation, whereby in digital images, the face of one person is replaced by that of another.
b. *Deepfake*, as mentioned previously, is a combination of "deep learning" and "fake," which is an AI–based technique that is used to merge and overlay images and videos of human faces onto other images or videos. What differentiates a deepfake video from any other kind of fake video is the use of deep learning.
c. When producing a fake video where the target person is supposed to engage in a monologue or a dialogue, the mouth region of the person also needs to be manipulated accordingly. This can be done with the help of *facial animation*. Facial animation can also be used to synthesize an entirely new face, which can then be superimposed onto the face of a target person (who can either be the same as the source person or someone different).

   Furthermore, in order to create a more realistic fake video, facial animation may need to be performed in conjunction with *expression animation*, whereby the facial expressions of the target person are also manipulated in correspondence with their mouth.
d. Another operation that falls under the category of facial animation is *facial re–enactment*, which is the process where the facial expressions of a target person in the given video are replaced with those of a source person.
e. Sometimes, facial and expression animation are performed in conjunction with another operation called *speech animation*, aka *lip–sync synthesis*, which involves one of two things: Either the audio in the target video is replaced with another audio clip of the same person speaking in another video or in the same video at some other moment in time, or the audio in the target video is completely fabricated. Please note that the possibility of accomplishing the latter is subject to availability of a good vocal impressionist who can mimic the voice of the target person, or access to voice modification technology such as Adobe VoCo ("About Adobe VoCo") or WaveNet ("About WaveNet").

When creating a fake video, various combinations of the aforementioned operations can be used. In the fake videos thus produced, either the face and/or expressions of a target person are manipulated, or the involvement of a target person in a particular activity is altered or fabricated. It is also possible to alter the context of the words spoken by the target person, or to create a video with an entirely fake speech.

5.3 Deep Learning-Based Fake Content Creation

Over the past few years, deep learning has found increased utility in the digital content manipulation domain (Upchurch et al., 2016; Antipov et al., 2017; Huang et al., 2017; Lu et al., 2017; Lample et al., 2017; Karras et al., 2018; Bansal et al., 2018; Cao et al., 2019; Zhang et al., 2019; Naruniec et al., 2020; Siarohin et al., 2020). The technology behind deepfakes is *Generative Adversarial Networks* or *GANs*. Generative Adversarial Networks is a relatively new neural network first introduced in 2014 by Ian Goodfellow and others (Goodfellow et al., 2014). The objective of GANs is to produce fake images that are as realistic as possible.

There are two components involved in GAN:

1. **The Generator:** generates the images
2. **The Discriminator:** classifies whether the image generated is a fake image or a real one

Figure 5.3 shows some images from an effective GAN model called StyleGAN.

FIGURE 5.3
These people are not real—all of these faces were synthesized by StyleGAN. (Courtesy: https://github.com/NVlabs/stylegan.)

Simply stated, a GAN[1] trains a generator and a discriminator in an adversarial relationship.

While the generator creates new images from the latent representation of the source material, the discriminator attempts to determine whether or not the image is generated correctly. (The latent representations are generated by an encoder that reduces the image to a lower dimensional space by only retaining the key facial features.) Any defects or abnormalities in the images thus created are immediately caught by the discriminator, thus allowing the generator to create images that mimic reality extremely well. Both algorithms improve constantly in a zero-sum game.

There is nothing new about the act of replacing one face in an image by another, but recent deepfake methods exploit powerful GAN models that have been exclusively designed to focus on facial manipulation, and the most common manipulation being performed these days is *face swapping*, where the face of the person in a video is swapped with the face of another. Very simply, the process of face swapping consists of two phases: *Training* and *Video Generation*.

a. **Training:** In the training phase, two sets of sample images are required. The first contains only samples of the original face that is to be replaced. These samples can be extracted from the target video (i.e., the one that will be manipulated). This first set of images can be expanded by incorporating additional images from another source or multiple sources to obtain more realistic results. The second set of images consists of only the desired (source) face that will be injected into the video at hand. In order to simplify the training process, it is desirable to have both the source and the target faces under similar viewing and illumination conditions.

   These two image sets are then used to train an autoencoder. The autoencoder consist of an encoder, which reduces the images to a lower-dimensional latent space (i.e., a latent representation), and a decoder, which reconstructs the images from this latent representation.

b. **Video Generation:** After the completion of the training process, the latent representation of a face generated from the source (original) person present in the video can be passed to the decoder network that has been trained on faces of the target person that needs to be inserted into the video. As shown in Figure 5.4, the decoder then tries to reconstruct a face of the new (target) person, using the information corresponding to the face already present in the video. This decoding process is repeated for every frame in which a face needs to be swapped.

Another common manipulation strategy is *facial expression manipulation*, where the source video of a person is used to drive an image of another person to re-enact the facial expressions in the source (driving) video. (Please refer to this video (DisneyResearchHub, 2020) for a quick and informative demonstration).

The fake Obama PSA created by Jordan Peele and BuzzFeed (BuzzFeedVideo, 2018), the fake Trump video created by Russian–linked trolls (Harding, 2018), the fake Kim Jong-Un video (RepresentUs, 2020), deepfake Queen of England (Channel 4, 2020), deepfake Adele (*The New York Times*, 2019), and this compilation (WatchMojo.com, 2019) remain some of the best available exemplifications of deep learning–assisted fake videos; no technical papers documenting the creation of these videos have been made available.

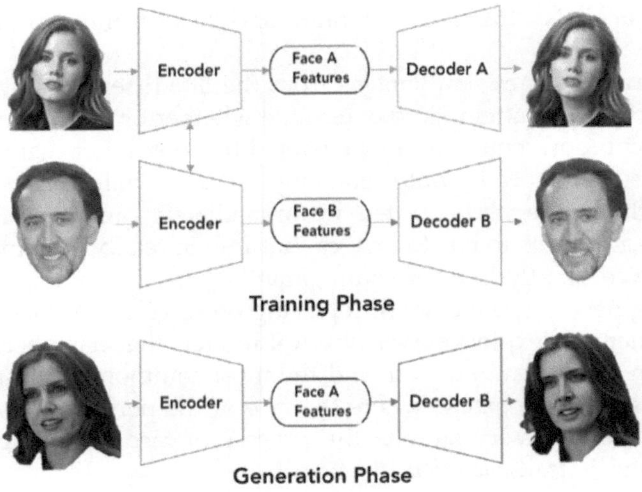

FIGURE 5.4
To make it possible to create a deepfake, both source and target latent faces need to be forcefully encoded on the same features. This can be accomplished by using two networks that share the same encoder but have different decoders. This is the training phase. When a face-swap needs to be performed (generation phase), we can simply encode the input face using the encoder and decode it using the target face decoder. That is, features of face A are decoded using Decoder B (which basically converts face A [original face] into face B [target or new face]). (Courtesy: Güera & Delp, 2018.)

5.4 Dangers of Deepfakes

In a world where seeing is believing, photographic and video data is a truly indispensable source of information, and is regularly employed for post–event analysis and decision–making purposes in journalism, politics, civil and criminal investigations and litigations, surveillance and intelligence operations, and military undertakings. Even in our day to day lives, we treat photographs and videos as a "taken–for–granted" kind of evidence; we see them and we intrinsically believe them. But this power of persuasion is not without its dangers, because while it is often perceived as a representational, or perhaps even an ontological equivalent of what it depicts, the fact remains that in a world where deepfake technology exists, visual data is neither self–proving nor necessarily true.

The amount of deepfake content online is growing rapidly. According to a report from a start-up called Deeptrace, at the beginning of 2019, there were 7,964 deepfake videos on the Internet; towards the end of 2020, this count had reached 14,678. Since then, the amount of deepfake content on the Internet has continued to increase (Toews, 2020).

At the very least, deepfakes can cause massive damage to reputation (for instance, a deepfake of a public figure saying or doing something questionable). At the very worst, they can cause large scale mayhem. It is not difficult to imagine the consequences if the masses can be shown some fake video that they believe to be real. Imagine being shown deepfake footage of a prominent elected official taking bribes or engaging in some another illicit activity right before an election; or of our law enforcement personnel causing offences against civilians; or a world leader declaring war against another nation. In a situation where there is even a modicum of uncertainty regarding the authenticity of video data, the consequences could be far-reaching and catastrophic. And given the fact that deepfakes can be created using simple apps these days, such footage can be easily created by anyone: political groups, state-sponsored actors, and even malicious individuals (Chesney & Citron, 2018, 2019; Tucker, 2019; Fish, 2019; Marr, 2019; The Guardian, 2019).

The Brookings Institution, in a recent report, summed up the range of social and political dangers that deepfakes pose: "distorting democratic discourse; manipulating elections; eroding trust in institutions; weakening journalism; exacerbating social divisions; undermining public safety; and inflicting hard-to-repair damage on the reputation of prominent individuals, including elected officials and candidates for office" (Galston, 2020).

What's even more distressing is that people have already started using the mere existence of deepfakes to discredit true and genuine video evidence. Even if there is video of someone doing or saying something, they can simply state that it was a deepfake. And what's disconcerting about this situation is that it would be almost impossible to prove it wasn't!

In two separate incidents, politicians in Brazil (Thomas, 2020) and Malaysia (Ker, 2019) have tried to dodge the repercussions of compromising video evidence by asserting that the evidence was fabricated and that the videos were deepfakes. In both incidents, the public opinion has remained divided because no one has been able to incontrovertibly establish that the videos were, in fact, not deepfakes.

5.4.1 Some Grim Examples

In April 2020, a political group in Belgium produced and published a deepfake video of the prime minister of Belgium wherein the minister is giving a speech linking the COVID-19 pandemic to environmental damage caused by humans, subsequently calling for drastic actions against climate change (XR Belgium, 2020). Many people believed the video to be real.

In an even more cunning maneuvre, the mere possibility of a video being a deepfake can be exploited to stir confusion in the minds of citizens and deceive them regardless of whether or not deepfake technology was even actually used. An incident that happened in Gabon, Africa, presents an excellent example of this.

Toward the end of 2018, the president of Gabon, Ali Bongo, had not been present in the public eye for several months. This absence engendered rumors that Bongo's health had deteriorated significantly and he was no longer healthy enough for office; some even insinuated that he had passed away. Bongo's administration, in an effort to assuage such rumors, declared that the president was going to address the nation in a televised event on New Year's Day. This decision did not turn out to be a good one. In the video address (Gabon 24, 2019), Bongo seemed rigid and constrained, and exhibited strange facial expressions, and abnormal physical characteristics and speech patterns. The peculiarity of the entire video caused many to suspect that the administration was trying to hide something from the public. Bongo's political opponents pounced on the opportunity and immediately claimed that the footage was a deepfake created by Bongo's administration and that he was either debilitated or even dead.

Within hours, social media blew up with the deepfake conspiracy, in the wake of which, the political situation in Gabon destabilized quickly. Within a single week, the military had launched a coup (which was the first in the country since 1964). The reasoning for the coup was that the New Year's video was evidence that something was not quite right with the president. Even till this day, no one can definitively establish whether or not Bongo's video was authentic, although most people believe that it was. (The military coup proved to be unsuccessful; President Bongo has since reappeared and remains in office).

But whether or not the New Year's video was real is not even the point. The more substantial realization here is that the widespread availability and use of deepfake technology is making it more and more difficult for people to separate the real from the fake, and this confusion is something that malicious individuals with agendas will undeniably capitalize on—with calamitous consequences.

The aforementioned are merely the tip of the iceberg as far as the threat of deepfake videos are concerned. As this technology advances, the ramifications will be much more severe and damaging.

5.5 Deepfake Detection

Deepfakes are quickly becoming the scourge of our time, and with each new technological advancement, our capability to separate the truth from the fabricated realities diminishes a little. The task of forgery detection in digital images and videos has been engaging researchers for decades now, but almost all of that innovation has been limited to the detection of manipulations such as copy–paste forgeries (Singh & Aggarwal, 2017a, 2017b, 2021).

Considering the relatively recent nature of the developments in the domain of deepfake creation, advancements in the domain of deepfake detection are still considered to be in their early stage. In the upcoming sections, we will discuss some of the most notable research in this field.

5.5.1 Deepfake Detection: Current State of Affairs

Earliest attempts at deepfake detection were based on painstakingly curated features obtained from abnormalities that inevitably arise during the production of a typical fake video. Contrarily, more recent methods use deep learning techniques to automatically detect and utilize discriminatory artifacts and features to separate authentic videos from deepfakes.

One of the earliest works in deepfake detection used Photo Response Non–Uniformity (PRNU) analysis (Koopman et al., 2018). [PRNU is the unique uncorrelated patter of noise that every digital recording device introduces in every image or video that it records. This noise is caused due to the inhomogeneity of the imaging sensors that are used in the recording device, which arise because of the differences in the sensitivities of the silicon wafers used in the imaging sensors.] the authors in (Koopman et al., 2018) demonstrated that mean normalized cross correlation scores of PRNU between authentic videos and deepfakes varied significantly. They did this by first obtaining average PRNU patterns for the test videos (both authentic and deepfakes), followed by calculating normalized cross correlation scores for these patterns, followed by calculating variations in correlation scores and the average correlation score for each video, and finally applying the Welch's t-test to the results to assess the statistical significance of the obtained variations. The results of this method are shown in Figure 5.5.

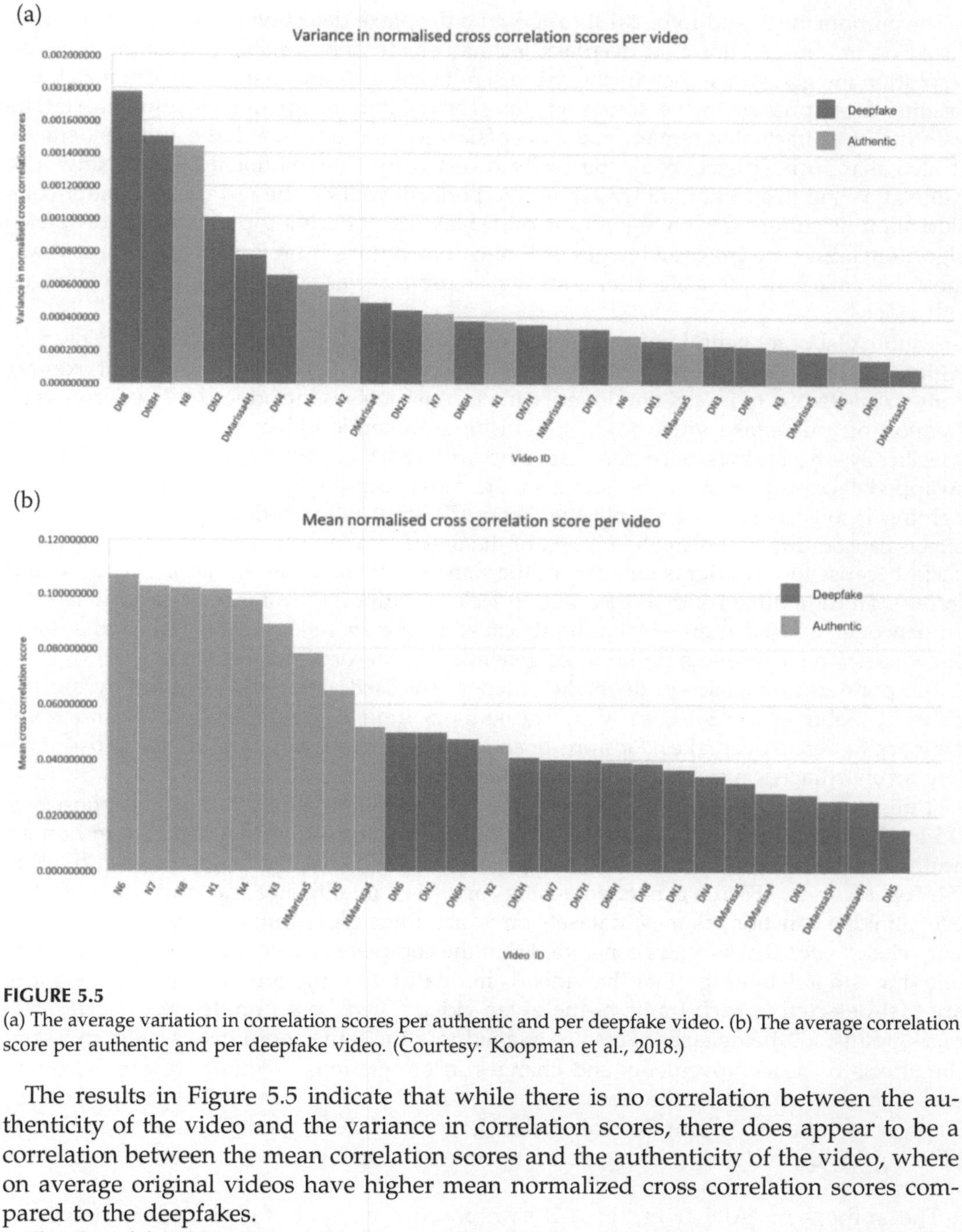

FIGURE 5.5
(a) The average variation in correlation scores per authentic and per deepfake video. (b) The average correlation score per authentic and per deepfake video. (Courtesy: Koopman et al., 2018.)

The results in Figure 5.5 indicate that while there is no correlation between the authenticity of the video and the variance in correlation scores, there does appear to be a correlation between the mean correlation scores and the authenticity of the video, where on average original videos have higher mean normalized cross correlation scores compared to the deepfakes.

The deepfake detection method proposed in (Yang et al., 2019) was based on the observations that deepfakes are created by injecting fabricated face regions into the source image, and this process introduces errors that can be revealed when 3D head poses are estimated from the face images. They further trained Support Vector Machines (SVM) classifiers based on the differences between head poses estimated using the full set of facial landmarks and those in the central face regions to differentiate deepfakes from real images or videos.

The authors in (Li and Lyu, 2018) proposed a deepfake detection technique, which was based on the observation that deepfake techniques are only capable of creating limited-resolution images, which then further need significant warping so that they can match the original faces present in the source videos. These kinds of operations result in certain identifiable artifacts that remain in the deepfake videos thus created; the authors demonstrated that such artifacts could be easily detected by Convolutional Neural Networks (CNNs). While this technique was shown to perform well on the test dataset under consideration, it suffers from a significant drawback: its underlying premise that deepfake algorithms can only generate images of limited resolutions is no longer true. These days, most deepfake generation algorithms are able to produce very high–resolution fake images and videos.

A more elaborate neural network based deepfake detection approach was proposed in (Güera & Delp, 2018). The authors thereof used both CNNs and Recurrent Neural Networks (RNNs) to model and identify the inconsistencies introduced by the process of creation of a deepfake video for distinguishing authentic video from fake ones. More specifically, the authors used three specific artifacts: First, the inconsistencies between swapped faces and rest of the scene in the video caused by multiple camera views, lighting inconsistencies, or simply the use of different video codecs. Second, boundary effects caused due to the amalgamation of the new face with the rest of the frame (which occur because the encoder is unaware of the skin or other scene information present in the frame). Third, anomalies that arise due to lack of temporal awareness caused when the autoencoder is used frame–by–frame (because of the frame–by–frame usage, the autoencoder has no awareness of the faces generated in the previous frames).

Temporal discrepancies in deepfake videos were used as forensic artifacts by the authors in (Sabir et al., 2019) as well. The authors trained a combined CNN and RNN network to detect deepfakes, facial re–enactment, and face–swapping in videos based on low level artifacts caused by manipulations on faces.

A deepfake identification technique based on eye–blinking detection was proposed in (Li et al., 2018). The authors thereof state that the mean resting blinking rate in human adults is 17 blinks/min or 0.283 blinks per second, and that the length of each blink is 0.1–0.4 seconds. Faces generated using artificial intelligence do not possess the eye–blinking function, as most datasets on which these algorithms are trained lack faces with closed eyes. The authors concluded that the complete absence or reduced rate of eye blinking is a tell–tale sign that the video is not natural. In the proposed technique, faces are first detected in each frame of the given video. Then, based on detected facial landmark points, all the detected faces are aligned into the same coordinate system to lessen the effects of head movements and changes in orientations. Regions corresponding to each eye are then extracted to form a stable sequence. After these initial pre–processing steps, Long–term Recurrent Convolutional Networks (LRCN) model is used to detect eye blinking by quantifying the degree of openness of an eye in each frame. Figure 5.6 illustrates one of their results.

The authors in (Afchar et al., 2018) proposed a compact facial forgery detection network called MesoNet that was based on two existing neural networks called Meso–4 and MesoInception–4. This network was specifically designed to detect deepfake videos generated using *Fakeapp* and *Face2Face*. The primary observation made by the authors after performing several successful tests that effectively distinguished deepfakes from authentic videos was that while faces in authentic videos exhibit high details in the eyes, nose, and mouth areas, deepfake faces lack details in those areas. Figure 5.7 shows maximum activation for several neurons of the last

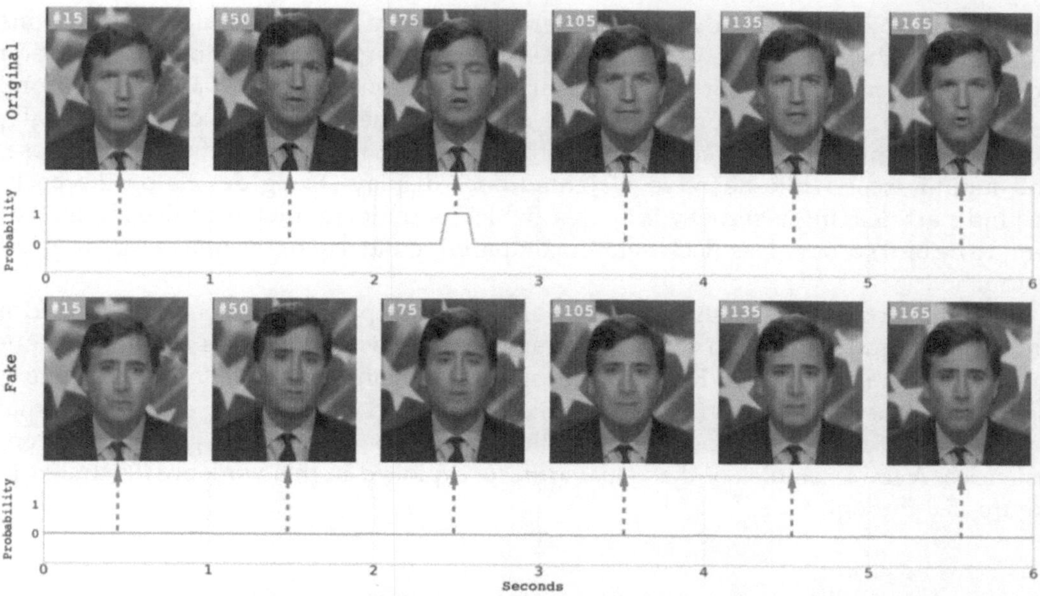

FIGURE 5.6
Example of eye blinking detection in an original video (top row) and a deepfake (bottom row). While in the original video, an eye blink can be detected within 6 seconds, in the deepfake, no blinks are detected, which is physiologically abnormal. (Courtesy: Li et al., 2018.)

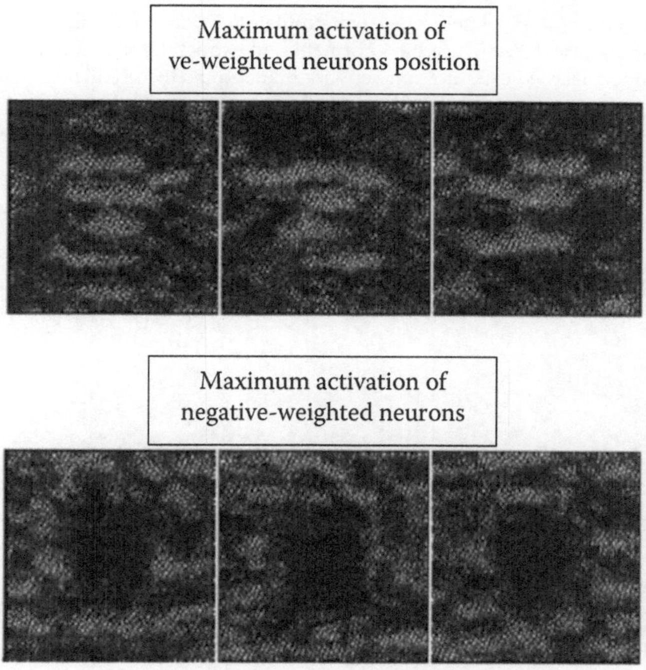

FIGURE 5.7
Maximum activation of some neurons of the hidden layer of Meso4. While positive-weighted neurons activation display images with highly detailed eyes, nose, and mouth areas, negative-weighted ones display strong details on the background part, leaving a smooth face area. (Courtesy: Afchar et al., 2018.)

hidden layer of Meso–4. The authors observed that they could separate those neurons according to the sign of the weight applied to their output for the final classification decision, thus accounting for whether their activation pushes toward a negative score, which corresponds to the forged class, or a positive one for the real class. Strikingly, positive–weighted neurons activation display images with highly detailed eyes, nose, and mouth areas while negative–weighted ones display strong details on the background part, leaving a smooth face area, which is understandable as deepfake faces tend to be blurry, or at least lack details, compared to the rest of the image that was left untouched.

In the method proposed in (Rössler et al., 2019), deepfake detection was deemed a binary classification problem and every frame of the given video was classified as authentic or fake using CNNs. Figure 5.8 illustrates the manipulation detection pipeline.

The technique proposed in (Matern et al., 2019) exposed deepfakes by exploiting visual artifacts, such as global inconsistencies, illumination variations, and geometric inconsistencies. A few examples of the visual artifacts exploited in this work are illustrated in Figures 5.9 through 5.12.

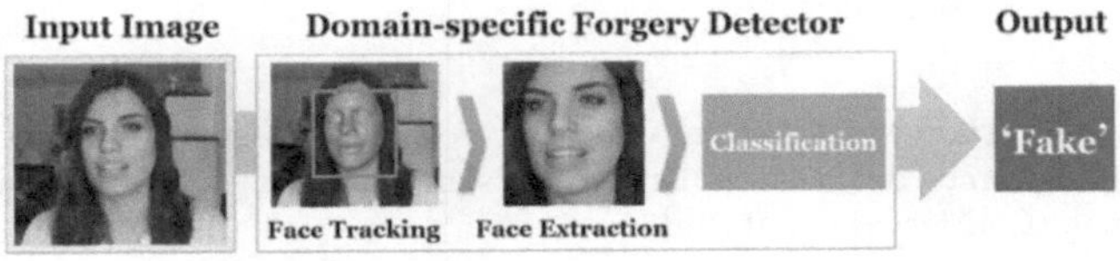

FIGURE 5.8
Domain-specific forgery detection pipeline for facial manipulation detection: the input image is processed by a robust face tracking method; the authors use the information to extract the region of the image covered by the face; this region is fed into a learned classification network that outputs the prediction. (Courtesy: Rössler et al., 2019.)

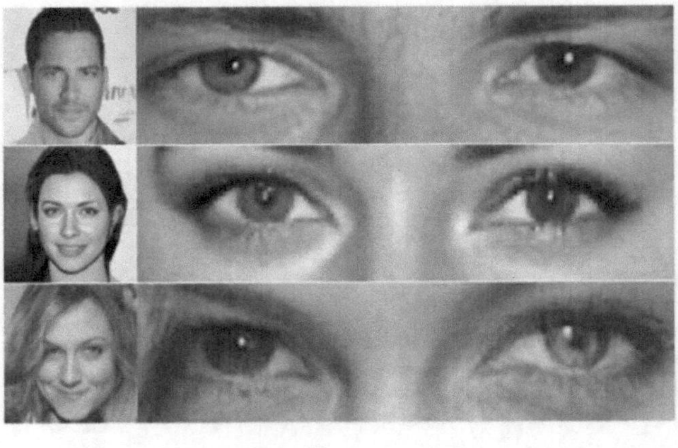

FIGURE 5.9
Global inconsistencies in GAN-generated faces. Significant differences between the colors of the two irises. Heterochromia, which is a biological phenomenon of having different colored irises, is actually quite rare. (Courtesy: Matern et al., 2019.)

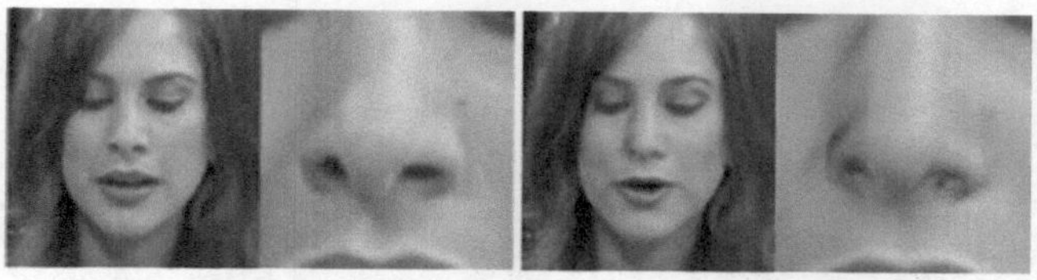

Real Face Deepfake Face

FIGURE 5.10
Shading artifacts in deepfakes. Significant shading artifacts arising from illumination estimation errors and imprecise geometry of the nose. (Courtesy: Matern et al., 2019.)

Real Faces Deepfake Faces

FIGURE 5.11
Unrealistic specular reflections in deepfakes. A lot of deepfake videos exhibit unrealistic specular reflections. There are either no specular reflections in the eyes, or the reflections appear as a white blob. Lack of specular reflections makes the eyes in the deepfake videos appear dull. (Courtesy: Matern et al., 2019.)

Real Faces Deepfake Faces

FIGURE 5.12
Missing geometry in deepfakes. In deepfake videos, not unlike the specular reflections in the eyes, teeth are not rendered with precision and are thus generated as white blobs. (Courtesy: Matern et al., 2019.)

Real Face GAN-Generated Face

FIGURE 5.13
A side-by-side comparison of real and GAN-generated faces in image and frequency domain. The left side shows an example and the mean DCT spectrum of the FFHQ data set (this dataset consists of real faces). The right side shows an example and the mean DCT spectrum of a data set sampled from StyleGAN trained on FFHQ (this dataset consists of fake faces). In the image domain, both images look real. However, in the frequency domain, one can easily spot multiple clearly visible artifacts for the GAN-generated images. (Courtesy: Frank et al., 2020.)

The authors in (Frank et al., 2020) suggested leveraging frequency analysis for deepfake image recognition. When examined in the frequency domain, GAN–generated facial images exhibit observable artifacts (as demonstrated in Figure 5.13).

Frequency analysis was exploited in (Wang et al., 2020) and (Durall et al., 2020) as well. Figure 5.14 shows the frequency spectra for real images and fake images from several datasets.

5.5.2 Deepfake Detection: A Novel Idea

Deepfake detection is usually deemed a classification problem, and deep learning models are further used to classify video as authentic or deepfakes. One significant disadvantage of these kinds of methods is that they require sizable databases of authentic and deepfake videos for proper training of the classification models. And although the number of deepfake videos is continually growing, it is not nearly enough for setting a benchmark against which various deepfake detection methods can be tested. Another disadvantage is the problem of overfitting, where the trained models perform extremely well on the test data under consideration but are rendered significantly less effective when applied to new data. Moreover, deep learning based deepfake detection methods rely on quite an assemblage of content–specific thresholds and parameters that need to be fine–tuned in order to get the model to work effectively. This process is not only prone to errors and highly time consuming, but is also responsible for poor performance of the deepfake detectors in realistic scenarios.

All in all, it can be stated that while the existing deepfake detection methods have shown some success in laboratory setting, further research is required into developing relatively simpler and less complex solutions to the challenge of deepfake detection.

With that in mind, a simplistic deepfake detection scheme based on *optical flow analysis* is presented here. Optical flow refers to the pattern of apparent motion of objects in the

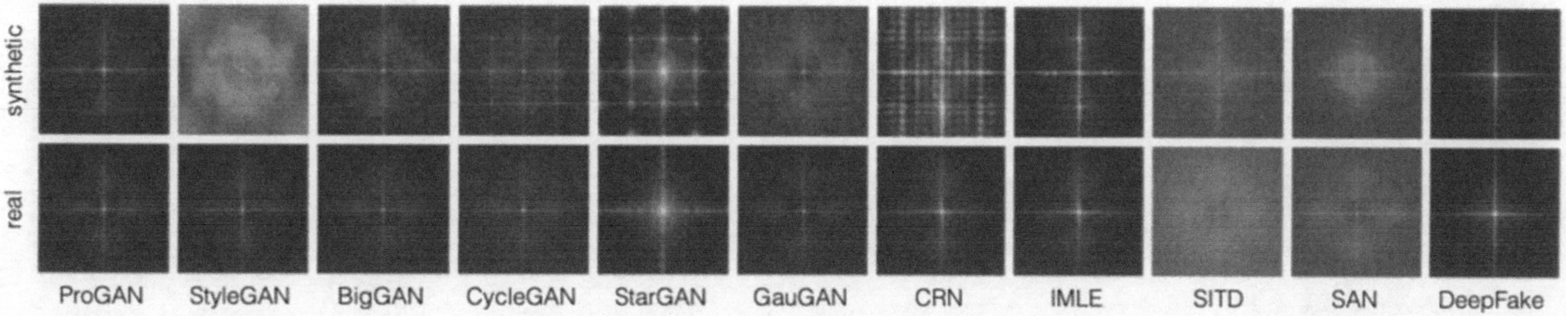

FIGURE 5.14
Frequency analysis on datasets consisting of real images and fake images. Average spectra of each high-pass filtered image are shown, for both the real and fake images. Periodic patterns (dots or lines) can be observed in most of the synthetic images, while BigGAN and ProGAN contains relatively few of such artifacts. (Courtesy: Wang et al., 2020.)

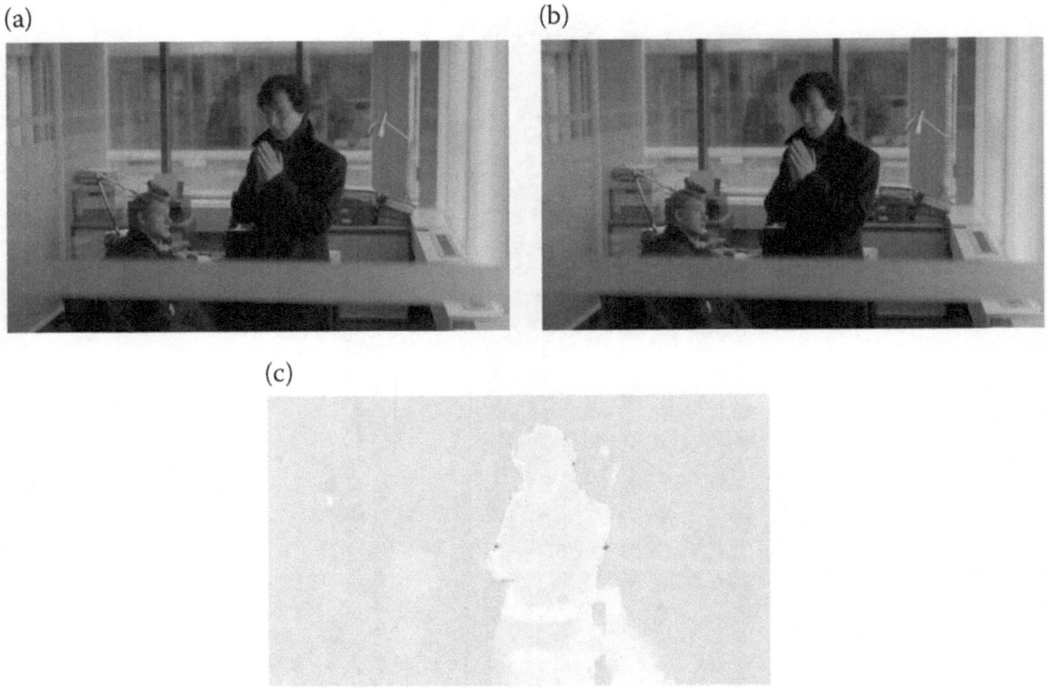

FIGURE 5.15
(a) and (b) represent successive frames from a video sequence, while (c) represents the estimated flow field between these frames. Based on the variations in the optical flow fields, as illustrated in (c), one can distinguish the scene elements that are at motion and those scene elements that remain stationary (and become a part of the background). (Courtesy Video: BBC One.)

frames of a video sequence, and is sensitive to even the slightest variation in object positions between two successive frames (see Figures 5.15 and 5.16).

In a natural video, variations in optical flow from one frame to the next remain more or less uniform, but in case of modified videos (such as those exhibiting a deepfake face) optical flow behaves in an abnormal manner, and these abnormalities serve as the fingerprint of the forgery.

Figure 5.17 presents some results of optical flow analysis performed on the fake Obama PSA introduced in the beginning of this chapter. Optical flow patterns are computed for the entire deepfake PSA, and for the sake of comparison, the same is done for another random original PSA. Sample frames from the two videos are also shown.

Optical flow is supposed to be an indicative of movement of pixels from one frame to the next; all the white regions in these results correspond to those pixels that change from one frame to the next. When a person speaks, their entire face and upper body undergo subtle variations and movements, even if these movements are as slight as possible. As we observed in Figures 5.15 and 5.16, optical flow is powerful enough to identify and capture these movements. The optical flow patterns exhibited by the real PSA show movements in the entire face and upper body of the speaker (as is naturally expected). However, optical flow patterns in the fake PSA tend to be concentrated only near the mouth region, with zero to little optical flow activity in the rest of the face or the upper

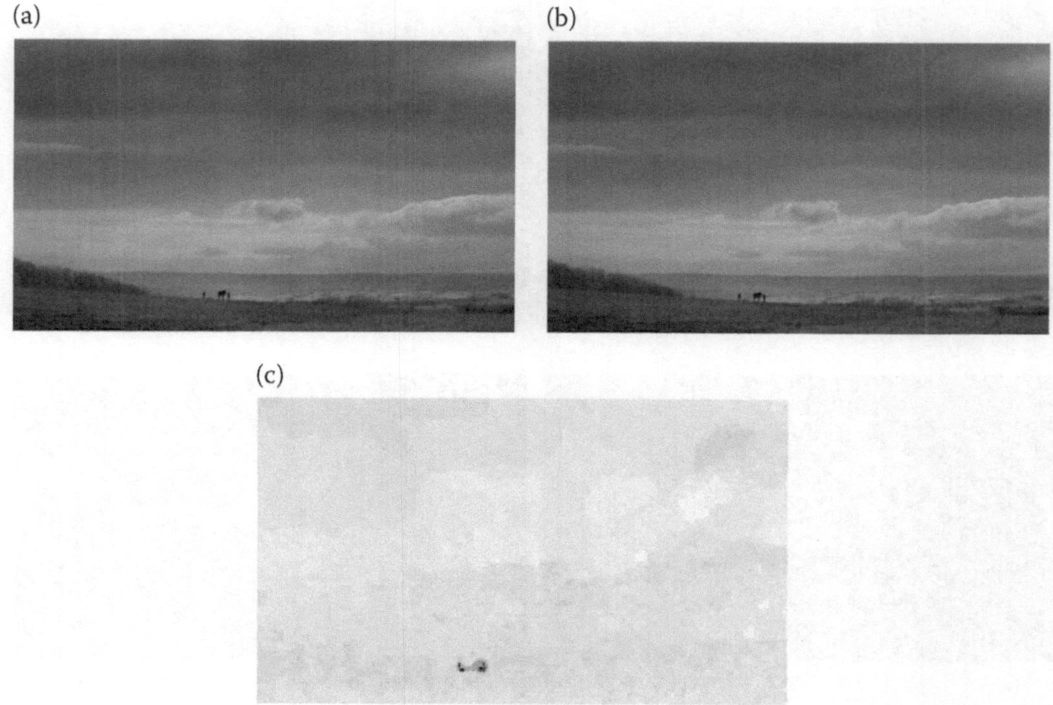

FIGURE 5.16
(a) and (b) represent successive frames from a video sequence, while (c) represents the estimated flow field between these frames. Even the slightest displacement of objects between the two frames affects the optical flow between these frames, as is apparent from the image in (c). (Courtesy Video: BBC/HBO/VRT.)

body. This is because of the way in which this video was faked: The deepfake PSA was created by manipulating the mouth region of Obama (while the rest of the facial area remained untouched). This discrepancy, though not readily observable in the actual fake video, can be noticed due to the abnormalities that appear in the optical flow patterns of the video.

The optical flow–based method just described is a simple solution to the problem of detecting deepfakes, and we are in dire need of more of such simple solutions if we are to consider ourselves ready to tackle the challenges that deepfake technology is posing (and will continue to pose) in our society.

5.6 Conclusion

Ubiquity of aphorisms like "seeing is believing" and "a picture is worth a thousand words," not only lend credence to the epistemologically unique status of visual evidence, but also accord great value to such evidence. Photographs and videos carry within themselves enough information to help us form an opinion as to the reality of the situation being depicted in the scene at that exact moment in time. They seem almost to

Sample frames from an original Obama PSA

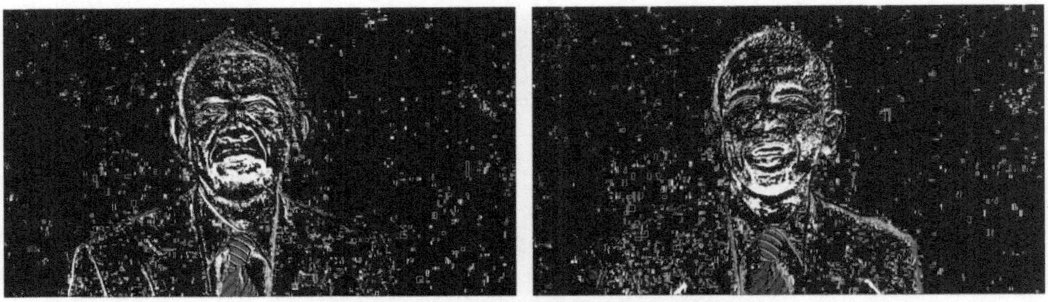

Optical flow patterns for the original PSA

Sample frames from the fake Obama PSA

Optical flow patterns for the fake PSA

FIGURE 5.17
Optical flow analysis for deepfake detection. Sample frames from the fake Obama PSA and an original Obama PSA, along with their respective optical flow patterns. (Sample Images Sources: Row 1 whitehouse.gov.; Row 3 Jordan Peele/BuzzFeed.)

compel belief, and this power of persuasion stems both from their capacity to convey verisimilitude and the mechanical quality of their assertion to objectivity. This is why we recognize this data as not only self–sufficient but also self–evident.

However, with recent advances in the artificial intelligence domain, deepfake technology has come to light, and in a very short span of time, it has managed to strike a major blow to the trustworthiness of digital images and videos. Though there have been some advances in the domain of deepfake detection, the best tools we have our disposal are still our own common sense and keen–eyedness. We must learn to be skeptical of the content we have become so accustomed to consuming in our everyday lives, and be vigilant of the world around us and how it is portrayed to us in the form of digital audio–visual data. Only then can we be truly safe from this very real and growing threat.

Note

1. For more details about the working of GANs, please refer to these videos (CodeEmporium, 2019; Serrano, 2020). This webpage on deepfakes ("About Deep fake") will also serve as a useful read. More advanced readers can refer to this video (Arxiv Insights, 2019) for more information.

References

About Adobe VoCo. Retrieved from https://en.wikipedia.org/wiki/Adobe_Voco on July 3, 2021. Last edited May 3, 2022.

About Deepfake. Retrieved from https://en.wikipedia.org/wiki/Deepfake on February 6, 2021. Last edited May 11, 2022.

About WaveNet. Retrieved from https://en.wikipedia.org/wiki/WaveNet on July 3, 2021. Last edited January 28, 2022.

Afchar, D., Nozick, V., Yamagishi, J., and Echizen, I. (2018, December 11–13). *MesoNet: a compact facial video forgery detection network* [Paper presentation]. IEEE International Workshop on Information Forensics and Security (WIFS), Hong Kong, China. DOI: 10.1109/WIFS.2018.8630761

Antipov, G., Baccouche, M., and Dugelay, J. (2017, September 17–20). *Face aging with conditional generative adversarial networks* [Paper presentation]. IEEE International Conference on Image Processing (ICIP), Beijing China. DOI: 10.1109/ICIP.2017.8296650

Arxiv Insights (2019, September 13). *Face editing with Generative Adversarial Networks*. Retrieved from https://www.youtube.com/watch?v=dCKbRCUyop8

Bansal, A., Ma, S., Ramanan, D., and Sheikh. Y. (2018, September 8–14). *Recycle-GAN: Unsupervised Video Retargeting* [Paper presentation]. 15th European Conference on Computer Vision (ECCV), Munich, Germany.

BuzzFeedVideo (2018, April 17). *You Won't Believe What Obama Says In This Video!* Retrieved from https://www.youtube.com/watch?v=cQ54GDm1eL0

Cao, J., Hu, Y., Yu, B., et al. (2019). 3D aided duet GANs for multi-view face image synthesis. *IEEE Transactions on Information Forensics and Security*, 14(8), 2028–2042.

Chesney, R. and Citron, D.K. (2018). *Deep fakes: a looming challenge for privacy, democracy, and national security*. 107 California Law Review, 1753, U of Texas Law, Public Law Research Paper No. 692, U of Maryland Legal Studies Research Paper No. 2018-21, SSRN: https://ssrn.com/abstract=3213954. DOI: 10.2139/ssrn.3213954

Chesney, R. and Citron, D.K. (2019, January). *Deepfakes and the new disinformation war: The coming age of post-truth geopolitics*. Retrieved from https://www.foreignaffairs.com/articles/world/2018-12-11/deepfakes-and-new-disinformation-war

Collins, J. (2018, January 30). *Nic Cage deepfakes mini compilation*. Retrieved from https://www.youtube.com/watch?v=2jp4M1cIJ5A

Collins, J. (2018a, February 2). *Nic Cage Deepfake Compilation 4 (+ trump house of cards)*. Retrieved from https://www.youtube.com/watch?v=-zrkFWRiL2M

Collins, J. (2018b, January 30). *Nic Cage deepfakes mini compilation*. Retrieved from https://www.youtube.com/watch?v=2jp4M1cIJ5A

CodeEmporium (2019, January 20). *Evolution of Face Generation | Evolution of GANs*. Retrieved from https://www.youtube.com/watch?v=C1YUYWP-6rE&t=330s

Channel 4 (2020, December 25). *Deepfake Queen: 2020 Alternative Christmas Message*. Retrieved from https://www.youtube.com/watch?v=IvY-Abd2FfM&t=132s

Durall, R. Keuper, M., and Keuper, J. (2020, June 13–19). *Watch your upconvolution: CNN based generative deep neural networks are failing to reproduce spectral distributions* [Paper presentation]. IEEE/CVF Conference on Computer Vision and Pattern Recognition (CVPR), Seattle, WA. DOI: 10.1109/CVPR42600.2020.00791

DisneyResearchHub (2020, June 29). *High Resolution Neural Face Swapping for Visual Effects*. Retrieved from https://www.youtube.com/watch?v=yji0t6KS7Qo

Fish, T. (2019, April 4). *Deep fakes: AI-manipulated media will be weaponised to trick military*. Retrieved from https://www.express.co.uk/news/science/1109783/deep-fakes-ai-artificial-intelligence-photos-video-weaponised-china

Frank, J., Eisenhofer, T., Schönherr, L., et al. (2020). *Leveraging Frequency Analysis for Deep Fake Image Recognition*. Cornell University Archive, arXiv:2003.08685v3 [cs.CV].

Gabon 24. (2019, January 1). *Discours À La Nation Du Président Ali Bongo Ondimba*. Retrieved from https://www.facebook.com/tvgabon24/videos/324528215059254/

Galston, W.A. (2020, January 8). *Is seeing still believing? The deepfake challenge to truth in politics*. Retrieved from https://www.brookings.edu/research/is-seeing-still-believing-the-deepfake-challenge-to-truth-in-politics/#cancel

Goodfellow, I.J., Pouget-Abadie, J., Mirza, M., et al. (2014, December 8–13). *Generative Adversarial Networks* [Paper presentation]. 28th International Conference on Neural Information Processing Systems (NIPS), Montreal, Canada.

The Guardian. (2019, September 2). *Chinese deepfake app Zao sparks privacy row after going viral*. Retrieved from https://www.theguardian.com/technology/2019/sep/02/chinese-face-swap-app-zao-triggers-privacy-fears-viral

Güera, D. and Delp, E.J. (2018, November 27–30). *Deepfake Video Detection Using Recurrent Neural Networks* [Paper presentation]. 15th IEEE International Conference on Advanced Video and Signal Based Surveillance (AVSS), Auckland, New Zealand. DOI: 10.1109/AVSS.2018.8639163

Harding, N. (2018, May 26). *'Deepfake' videos produced by Russian-linked trolls are the latest weapon in fake news war, official monitors warn*. Retrieved from https://www.telegraph.co.uk/news/2018/05/26/deepfake-videos-produced-russian-linked-trolls-latest-weapon/

Huang, R., Zhang, S., Li, T., et al. (2017, October 22–29). *Beyond face rotation: Global and local perception GAN for photorealistic and identity preserving frontal view synthesis* [Paper presentation]. IEEE International Conference on Computer Vision (ICCV), Venice, Italy. DOI: 10.1109/ICCV.2017.267

Karras, T., Aila, T., Laine, S., et al. (2018, April 30–May 3). *Progressive Growing of GANs for Improved Quality, Stability, and Variation* [Paper presentation]. 6th International Conference on Learning Representations (ICLP), Vancouver, BC.

Ker, N. (2019, June 12). *Is the political aide viral sex video confession real or a Deepfake?* Retrieved from https://www.malaymail.com/news/malaysia/2019/06/12/is-the-political-aide-viral-sex-video-confession-real-or-a-deepfake/1761422

Koopman, M., Rodriguez, A.M. and Geradts, Z. (2018, August 29–31). *Detection of Deepfake Video Manipulation* [Paper presentation]. 20th Irish Machine Vision and Image Processing Conference (IMVIP), Belfast, Northern Ireland. ISBN 978-0-9934207-3-3

Lample, G., Zeghidour, N., Usunier, N., et al. (2017, December 4). *Fader networks: Manipulating images by sliding attributes* [Paper presentation]. 31st International Conference on Neural Information Processing Systems (NIPS), Long Beach, California. ISBN: 978-1-5108-6096-4

Li, Y. and Lyu, S. (2018). *Exposing DeepFake Videos By Detecting Face Warping Artifacts.* Cornell University Archive, arXiv:1811.00656v3 [cs.CV].

Li, Y., Chang, M.C., and Lyu, S. (2018, December 11–13). *In ictu oculi: Exposing AI created fake videos by detecting eye blinking* [Paper presentation]. IEEE International Workshop on Information Forensics and Security (WIFS), Hong Kong, China. DOI: 10.1109/WIFS.2018.8630787

Lu, Y., Tai, Y., and Tang. C. (2017). *Conditional cycleGAN for attribute guided face image generation.* Cornell University Archive, arXiv:1705.09966 [cs.CV].

Marr, B. (2019, July 22). *The best (and scariest) examples of AI-enabled deepfakes.* Retrieved from https://www.forbes.com/sites/bernardmarr/2019/07/22/the-best-and-scariest-examples-of-ai-enabled-deepfakes/?sh=1b053ccc2eaf

Matern, F., Riess, C., and Stamminger, M. (2019, January 7–11). *Exploiting visual artifacts to expose deepfakes and face manipulations* [Paper presentation]. IEEE Winter Applications of Computer Vision Workshops (WACVW), Waikoloa, HI. DOI: 10.1109/WACVW.2019.00020

Naruniec, J., Helminger, L., Schroers, C., and Weber, R.M. (2020). High-Resolution Neural Face Swapping for Visual Effects. *Computer Graphics Forum*, 39(4), 173–184.

The New York Times (2019, August 14). *Deepfakes: Is This Video Even Real? | NYT Opinion.* Retrieved from https://www.youtube.com/watch?v=1OqFY_2JE1c

Rössler, A., Cozzolino, D., Verdoliva, L., et al. (2019, October 27–Nov 2). *FaceForensics++: Learning to Detect Manipulated Facial Images* [Paper presentation]. IEEE/CVF International Conference on Computer Vision (ICCV), Seoul, South Korea. DOI: 10.1109/ICCV.2019.00009

RepresentUs (2020, September 29). *Dictators - Kim Jong-Un.* Retrieved from https://www.youtube.com/watch?v=ERQlaJ_czHU

Sabir, E., Cheng, J., Jaiswal, A., et al. (2019, June 16–20). *Recurrent convolutional strategies for face manipulation detection in videos* [Paper presentation]. IEEE Conference on Computer Vision and Pattern Recognition (CVPR), Long Beach, California.

Serrano, L. (2020, May 5). *A Friendly Introduction to Generative Adversarial Networks (GANs).* Retrieved from https://www.youtube.com/watch?v=8L11aMN5KY8

Siarohin, A., Lathuilière, S., Tulyakov, S., et al. (2020). *First Order Motion Model for Image Animation.* Cornell University Archive, arXiv:2003.00196v3 [cs.CV].

Singh, R.D. and Aggarwal, N. (2017). Video Content Authentication Techniques: A Comprehensive Survey, *Multimedia Systems*, 1–30.

Singh, R.D. and Aggarwal, N. (2017). Detection and Localization of Copy–Paste Forgeries in Digital Videos, *Forensic Science International*, 281, 75–91.

Singh, R.D. and Aggarwal, N. (2021). Optical Flow and Pattern Noise–Based Copy–Paste Detection in Digital Videos, *Multimedia Systems*, 27, 449–469.

Thomas, D. (2020, January 23). *Deepfakes: A threat to democracy or just a bit of fun?* Retrieved from https://www.bbc.com/news/business-51204954

Toews, R. (2020, May 25). *Deepfakes Are Going To Wreak Havoc On Society. We Are Not Prepared.* Retrieved from https://www.forbes.com/sites/robtoews/2020/05/25/deepfakes-are-going-to-wreak-havoc-on-society-we-are-not-prepared/?sh=4be255487494

Tucker, P. (2019, March 31). *The newest AI-enabled weapon: Deep-Faking photos of the earth.* Retrieved from https://www.defenseone.com/technology/2019/03/next-phase-ai-deep-faking-whole-world-and-china-ahead/155944/

Upchurch, P., Gardner, J.R., Bala, K., et al. (2016). *Deep feature interpolation for image content changes*. Cornell University Archive, arXiv:1611.05507 [cs.CV].

WatchMojo.com (2019, June 22). *Top 10 Deepfake Videos*. Retrieved from https://www.youtube.com/watch?v=-QvIX3cY4lc

Wang, S.Y., Wang, O., Zhang, R., et al. (2020, June 13–19). *CNN-generated images are surprisingly easy to spot…for now* [Paper presentation]. IEEE/CVF Conference on Computer Vision and Pattern Recognition (CVPR), Seattle, WA. DOI: 10.1109/CVPR42600.2020.00872

XR Belgium. (2020, April 13). *The truth about covid-19 and the ecological crisis—a speech for Sophie Wilmes*. Retrieved from https://tube.rebellion.global/videos/watch/2ad12b6bbb53-473c-ad74-14eef02874b5?title=0&warningTitle=0

Yang, X., Li, Y., and Lyu, S. (2019, May 12–17). *Exposing deep fakes using inconsistent head poses* [Paper presentation]. IEEE International Conference on Acoustics, Speech and Signal Processing (ICASSP), Brighton, UK. DOI: 10.1109/ICASSP.2019.8683164

Zhang, H., Xu, T., Li, H., et al. (2019). StackGAN++: Realistic image synthesis with stacked generative adversarial networks. *IEEE Transactions on Pattern Analysis and Machine Intelligence*, 41(8), 1947–1962.

6

Challenges in Digital Forensics and Future Aspects

Shreyas S. Muthye
Independent Researcher, Nagpur, Maharashtra, India

CONTENTS

6.1 Introduction

Computers have evolved over the years so have the complexities associated with them. Experts come across certain hindrances or restrictions in their investigations which add complexities during analysis. With every new gadget that enters the market, a new forensic practice needs to be prepared in case it turns up as digital evidence someday. People don't realize the research and time that goes into creating digital forensic infrastructure with proper tools and personnel. In this chapter, we'll look into what roadblocks do digital forensic professionals run into and what is being done to improve the investigation practices. We'll discuss briefly how the job of a digital forensic expert is more arduous in the presence of these challenges.

DOI: 10.1201/9781003204862-6

6.2 Challenges

This section discusses the various challenges in digital forensics. Main challenges in digital forensics are shown in Figure 6.1.

6.2.1 Human Factor

The rise in cyber attacks over the past years is quite alarming, an organization needs a strong blue and red team that keeps the organization safe digitally. As per reports, there is a serious shortage of trained digital and cyber forensic experts and the need is high. This is applicable to both private businesses and law enforcement agencies. Both, private and law enforcement agencies have been hesitant about building digital forensic centers. This situation has created two main problems—first, lack of employed experts and second, overworked experts at current labs.

Digital evidence is present in almost all investigations in some form or another such as smartphones, flash memory cards, storage disks, HDDs, etc. On multiple occasions, this evidence is handled by untrained personnel and they end up damaging it. Digital forensic evidence is very sensitive in nature and needs to be processed with caution and care. Untrained personnel often employ improper techniques which leads to unsuccessful examination. On the other side, overworked personnel might take longer to complete the examination which slows down the investigation process (Zuhri, 2017).

Another aspect that is not talked about is the ethics factor of the personnel. Apart from training experts with the technical knowledge required in the field, it is also important to teach them the code of conduct and ethics of work. These experts will work on sensitive cases and the investigation solely lies on the work of the expert; therefore, it is very important for them to hold to their values and perform their duty with utmost sincerity and integrity.

A lot of time and money is required to build a digital forensic setup—from selection of devices, acquiring special software, hiring skilled personnel, and training. This gets heavy on the pocket, and as corporates try to save money and law enforcement agencies face budget cuts frequently, often digital forensic infrastructure gets neglected.

FIGURE 6.1
A Diagram Showing the Different Challenges in Digital Forensics in a Branched Manner.

6.2.2 Encryption

It's the age of "privacy" or so they say, however, encryption is a term that is more talked about now than before. Encryption is a process through which data are mathematically altered with the help of algorithms to secure them. Simply said, encryption allows a user to safeguard their data by changing it to an illegible format. We find encryption in our Whatsapp chats, Mobile devices backup, secure folders, etc. As a mobile or computer user, the choice of encryption is available for all levels—from start-up to folders and files. Although it gives users a sense of security and safety, it makes the job of a digital forensic expert much more involuted (Balogun, 2013).

The OEMs (Original Equipment Manufacturers) have increased the security of many of their devices with a "device lock" option—where if multiple times wrong passcode is entered the device gets locked and the data won't be accessible. In many cases, digital forensic experts obtain encrypted devices which require a "key" (passcode) to access the data. An encrypted device/drive is not of much use until it gets decrypted. In such a scenario, the digital forensic examiner will have to resort to other advanced measures such as JTAG and Chip-off that involve disassembly of the device. These techniques are irreversible which means that once dissembled the device cannot be brought back to its original state.

PC tools such as TrueCrypt, VeraCryprt, Bitlocker, etc. allow users to create encrypted folders and files on a system. As users are becoming more concerned about their privacy, they are using more such tools to store their important files and hence we circle back to our point—encrypted data are a roadblock (Casey & Stellatos, 2008; Dezfouli, 2014).

In recent years, we have seen a rise in ransomware and malware attacks, while some attacks deleted the data some locked access to it. Again, the locked data were basically encrypted by malware with the hacker having its decryption key. Software companies did research on such malware and created "decryptors" which helped users to unlock their data and access it without paying hackers the ransom. Decryption tools are difficult to make and don't have a 100% success rate but are still useful. Encryption standards are also getting more advanced and complex with time. Decryption is a time-consuming and resource-heavy process, which requires a powerful forensic workstation (Casey & Stellatos, 2008; Singh et al., 2019).

6.2.3 High Storage Capacity

Currently, common specifications for a computer include four or more GBs of RAM, some powerful graphics card, and GBs or TBs of storage. Gone are the days when a 500 GB hard drive was considered to be huge, storage is now measured in terabytes now. Since storage media has become more affordable and durable, users opt for systems with a larger storage capacity.

While at first, this might seem like a great and giant "pro" for the user, it sure is a bigger "con" for the digital forensic expert. High-capacity storage media that hold lots of data require more time for their "forensic imaging." Even though forensic systems have become more capable and faster, a bit-stream backup of such drives is a time-consuming process. We know that digital forensic examination is done on forensic copies of digital evidence and until "forensic imaging" is not completed, the digital forensic examiner can't start the analysis of the evidence. Hence, the takeaway is "Bigger storage media will require more time and the examination process will be slower."

Another "con" associated with high-capacity storage media is the "cost of examining," we know the thumb rule for imaging that "forensic imaging of a storage device needs to be done on a higher capacity storage media," therefore the forensic examiner will require storage media of higher capacity than the evidence storage media for forensic imaging. This will require the digital forensic laboratory to store high-capacity storage drives ready for imaging at all times. Such purchases increase the maintenance and running expenses of a laboratory which is an important aspect of digital forensics.

6.2.4 Anti-forensics

Research and stats show that hackers are some of the smartest people around and it can be seen in their work. Just like other criminals, cyber criminals have also developed tools and techniques to cover their tracks. The "digital footprint"—a log of the digital activity of a user—is what the forensic experts aim to recover and cyber criminals try to alter or destroy. Such practices that are used by cyber criminals to counter the digital forensic process are collectively known as "anti-forensics" (Conlan, 2016).

Anti-forensics comprise tools and techniques, which attack the digital forensic process at different stages. The sole purpose of employing anti-forensics is to render the digital evidence useless.

Anti-forensic practices include the following:

- **Data Alteration:** This generally includes tampering and modification of file header, metadata, timestamps, etc. Portions of data or complete datasets are deleted or modified to create junk evidence which is done to disrupt the investigation.
- **Obfuscation:** This refers to altering the trail by creating fake web history, changing IP addresses, MAC addresses, etc. Along with this, culprits use log cleaners and other techniques to clean their fingerprints, all this is done to throw the investigation off course and trouble the digital forensic investigators.
- **Malware Encoding:** Files are laced with malicious code to attack the forensic examiner's system. Hacker/attacker will encode files with malware or will hide malware encoded files in the drive which when triggered will cause obstruction to the forensic system and tools to derange the investigation.
- **Destruction:** Destroying the storage media beyond repair is a very common method used by cyber criminals to dispose of the evidence. Another method is *Degaussing* where the storage media is wiped clean with the use of strong electromagnets. The electromagnetic pulse disturbs and damages the integrity of storage media and completely destroys the data. The chances of data recovery from degaussed storage media are negligible. *Data Wiping* is an advanced data deletion practice where the drive's data are deleted and then overwritten by useless data multiple times. This also makes data recovery very difficult and, in most cases, only fragments of data are recovered.
- **Data Hiding:** Data hiding primarily involves two practices: *Encryption* and *Steganography*. We know what challenge encryption is in digital forensics, steganography is a bit different. Here, the actual data are hidden behind a different set of data such as pictures, audio, video, etc. Unlike Encryption where encrypted data are visible but inaccessible, in steganography, the files appear to be normal and are easily accessible too. This makes the detection of steganography a difficult task.

6.2.5 Internet of Things and Smart Wearables

The rise of Internet of Things (IoT) devices and smart wearables have added another category of digital evidence. IoT devices are used in homes and offices such as smart TVs, air conditioners, speakers, doorbells, vacuum cleaners and these contain important information about the user's Wi-Fi, account information, passwords, IP location, etc. (Lillis et al., 2016; Singh et al., 2019) (Figure 6.2).

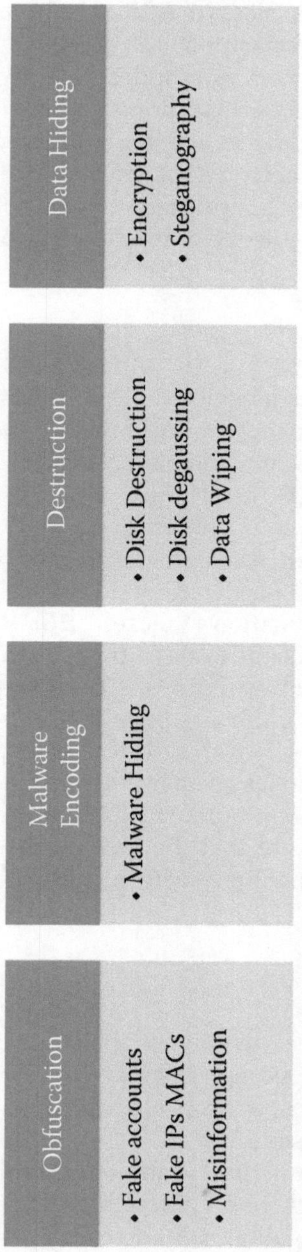

FIGURE 6.2
Anti Forensic Techniques—Different Techniques Displayed in a Tabular Manner.

Smart wearables include smartwatches, smart bands, fitness trackers, smart rings, etc. These are mostly connected to a smartphone via Bluetooth and also store some information in them. Some fitness trackers work independently and have built-in GPS, such devices store information regarding GPS location and activity of a user.

Both smart wearables and IoT devices are built differently from smartphones and therefore it is not convenient to connect to a system and access their data. Data collection from these devices can be tricky, they have different ports, software, firmware, etc. Digital forensic experts will need good knowledge of hardware also to work with IoT and smart wearables.

6.2.6 Software Plurality

We have looked at the new gadgets available in the market, it is obvious that these devices must be running on some software too. And this is where the next challenge comes in. A plethora of software choices is available as per the function of the device. For computers, there are Windows, iOS, and Linux which itself has hundreds of flavors (Linux distributions).

The job of a digital forensic expert has increased significantly, as he/she will need to study the device, then identify the hardware and software present on the device and based on that select tools for examination (Vincze, 2016). With such a diversity of software, the digital forensic examiner needs to stay updated with trends regarding them and keep tools ready at their disposal. Preparedness is key to any investigation, maintaining such an elaborate tool inventory is quite a tedious task.

Not all tools are cross-platform, selection of tools for a specific operating system and hardware takes time. Take smartphones as an example—Android OS has many versions, if the digital forensic examiner has an outdated tool and the smartphone has the latest android version installed, chances are that the tool would not support the device. The reverse of this situation is also possible where old mobiles and smartphones are not supported by newer software.

6.2.7 Cloud Storage

We have discussed storage media before now we shall look into the other storage. Almost all smartphone users have a cloud storage account which is synced with many services such as GPS info, documents, photos, backup, etc. This makes Cloud Storage a gold mine of digital evidence with many possibilities.

Cloud Storage Investigation is quite tricky due to multiple factors which include data availability, server location, time sync, etc. Digital forensic examiners run into obstacles at every step involved in the investigation. Cloud storage of a particular account can be accessed via multiple devices at the same time and changes can be made damaging the integrity of data. Even data isolation is not practically carried out yet and is only proposed in theory. Hence, we can infer that cloud storage architecture is not very well suited for forensic examination (Jain, 2019).

In an event of a cloud forensic investigation, the digital forensic examiner depends a lot on the cloud service providers (CSP) for the support in form of permissions required to carry out the investigation. The legal aspects are a hassle, jurisprudence issues and privacy laws; these altogether slow down the pace of investigation. Combine all this with lack of dedicated tools and we'll finally understand much efforts are put when investigating cloud-related cases.

6.2.8 Cryptocurrency

Cryptocurrency has taken the world by storm; even though it is not yet legalized in many countries but has gained quite a momentum and has a growing userbase. Currently, there are over thousands of cryptocurrency projects online and that number keeps on increasing with new projects getting added every day that promise its users brilliant return on their investments.

A major reason for the boom of cryptocurrency is the rise of ransomware attacks (Borreguero Beltrán, 2019). Cyber criminals ask for ransom in form of some cryptocurrency such as Bitcoin, Ethereum, Ripple, etc. Cryptocurrency works differently than the traditional banking system, it functions on the blockchain which is a decentralized ledger of all transactions. However, this mechanism is "pseudo-anonymous" as it only keeps a track of the "wallet id" and no other credentials such as name, address, country, etc. This results in investigations involving cryptocurrency painstaking. Tracing these transactions is laborious due to limited availability of tools and the use of IP hiding/spoofing tactics used by hackers.

To add to the woes, there are only a few tools that help the digital forensic expert in cryptocurrency investigations. This situation will surely improve in the future when more commercial tools will be made available for the experts. Every day new cryptocurrencies emerge on the web, this might fascinate the everyday user but for the digital forensic investigator it is taxing as they may encounter it in an investigation and will need to find tools for its analysis.

6.3 Future Aspects

We have looked at the different challenges that digital forensic experts endure, but all is not lost and how the situation may improve soon. Efforts are being taken by governments, private institutions, and individuals to look for solutions. Digital forensics is well past its infant stage and is now recognized as an important field of work. Law enforcement agencies are working 24/7 to improve their processing of digital evidence. They are working together with digital-forensic-based companies to find innovative solutions are work efficiently. From new software, hardware, and improved practices, a lot is stored for the future of digital forensics.

6.3.1 Artificial Intelligence and Machine Learning

Artificial Intelligence (AI) and Machine Learning (ML) are the buzzwords in the industry at the moment. Even the field of digital forensics can employ this technology to speed up work. AI and ML can be used in E-Discovery, experts can train models and deploy them for cases with huge amounts of data to look for specific strings, patterns, etc. With digitalization of the data of law enforcement agencies, huge datasets are available for analysis, these can be vital for research and investigation. There are many use cases of this technology such as growing smart city projects all over the world, where governments are using digital surveillance as a step to curb and prevent crime (Ngejane et al., 2021). Data from video cameras, toll booths, etc. can be collected and later used in analysis in case of ant criminal activity (Alqahtany et al., 2015; Rigano, 2019). This will upgrade the infrastructure and create a healthy environment for preventive forensics. Apart from speeding up work, it will also get more digital forensic projects in the market which will generate employment and create a new field of work.

6.3.2 DFaaS

We know digital forensic infrastructure costs a fortune due to which it is not easily adopted by all, a solution for this can be Digital Forensics as a Service (DFaaS). DFaaS is a model where an entity can provide digital forensic laboratory services to law enforcement agencies, corporates, and individuals. It would be quite useful when cyber forensic labs are not available or are not fully equipped to perform analysis of digital evidence. This model will provide a better chance for law enforcement agencies and private entities to team up and work together to provide this essential service. Here, the central lab can house all services/technologies under one roof which would save a great amount of time in investigations (Lillis et al., 2016; Singh et al., 2019). The DFaaS can also be deployed via cloud for convenience. This model can be a good chance of law enforcement agencies and private corporations/individual contractors to work together.

6.3.3 Open-Source Software

As previously discussed, cost is a big issue for companies or law enforcement agencies when they need to invest in digital forensic infrastructure and we know that commercial forensic software is expensive. Hence, a viable option is an Open-Source Software. Open-source software is mostly free to use and has the source code accessible for public to view and modify as per requirement.

Open-source software does not counter commercial software but it allows the user to explore the features of the software and even check its capabilities. It also allows the user to create a customized version of the tool for a specified purpose. Cyber Forensic experts already use open-source tools such as Autopsy, Wireshark, Volatility, etc. for examination and analysis so we know that these tools are capable (Carrier, 2003).

Platforms such as Raspberry Pi can be used to create lightweight cyber forensic systems, these systems can be used at small forensic labs which have a shortage of funds. Combining Raspberry Pi integrated forensic systems and open source tools can be used to create training systems as well as simple digital forensic examination systems. Many experts sing praises for Open Source software and believe that it is an underused and underrated asset that needs to be exploited more.

6.4 Conclusion

Cyberspace has an ever-changing horizon with new threats and technologies appearing every day. The challenges that we discussed will only get more elaborate in the future, therefore experts in this industry must collaborate on R&D projects to be better prepared for the challenges (Vincze, 2016).

The previous generation of law enforcement officers were not the most "tech-savvy" people but with time this has changed for good. This makes the process of digital forensics faster as now even the nonfield experts realize the importance of digital evidence.

Moreover, it is now realized by all that digital evidence cannot be ignored. Although slow, a positive approach toward the upgradation of the digital forensics infrastructure is now seen in governments across the world.

It is great to see the enthusiasm of cyber forensic experts when it comes to taking on challenges and only with this positive attitude, we'll be able to move ahead.

6.5 Literature Review

In this chapter, we have covered the different technicalities and situations which pose as challenges to the digital forensic process and the field in general. Right from the starting stage of the forensic process till the end stage, we have discussed that how much pre-requisite work needs to be done by experts in the field of digital forensics.

The discussion of the challenges is comprehensive yet it is kept brief. The complexities of each aspect are explained, such as Cloud Storage, Anti-Forensics, Human Factor, etc.

After covering all present and future challenges, this chapter concludes with a discussion on the steps taken toward improving the situation such as how technologies such as AI and ML are being amalgamated in the field or how Open Source is an underused asset.

References

Alqahtany, S., Reich, C., Clarke, N., & Furnell, S. (2015). *(PDF) Cloud Forensics: A Review of Challenges, Solutions and Open Problems* Research gate. Retrieved October 15, 2021, from https://www.researchgate.net/publication/276277307_Cloud_Forensics_A_Review_of_Challenges_Solutions_and_Open_Problems

Balogun, A. M., & Zhu, S. Y. (2013, December 11). *Privacy Impacts of Data Encryption on the Efficiency of Digital Forensics Technology*. arXiv.org. Retrieved October 15, 2021, from https://arxiv.org/abs/1312.3183

Borreguero Beltrán, A. (2019, September 30). *A Forensics Approach to Blockchain. Pàgina inicial de UPCommons*. Retrieved October 15, 2021, from https://upcommons.upc.edu/handle/2117/168894

Casey, E., & Stellatos, G. J. (2008, April 1). *The Impact of Full Disk Encryption on Digital Forensics. ACM SIGOPS Operating Systems Review*. Retrieved October 15, 2021, from https://dl.acm.org/doi/10.1145/1368506.1368519

Conlan, K., Baggili, I., & Breitinger, F. (2016). Anti-forensics: Furthering digital forensic science through a new extended, granular taxonomy. Digital Investigation, 18, S66–S7510.1016/j.diin.2016.04.006

Carrier, B.D. (2003). Open Source Digital Forensics Tools The Legal Argument, 1.

Dezfouli, F., & Dehghantanha, A. (2014). *Digital Forensics Trends and Future – University of Salford*. University of Salford Institutional Repository. Retrieved October 15, 2021, from https://usir.salford.ac.uk/id/eprint/34014/1/digital%20forensics.pdf

Jain, P., & Mahalkari, A. (2019). *Review of Cloud Forensics: Challenges, Solutions and Comparative Analysis. IJCA*. Retrieved October 15, 2021, from https://www.ijcaonline.org/archives/volume178/number34/30761-30761-2019919220?format=pdf

Lillis, D., Becker, B. A., O'Sullivan, T., & Scanlon, M. (2016). *Current Challenges and Future Research Areas – Mark Scanlon*. MarkScanlon.co. Retrieved October 15, 2021, from https://www.markscanlon.co/papers/CurrentChallengesAndFutureResearchAreas.pdf

Ngejane, C. H., et al. (2021) "Digital Forensics Supported by Machine Learning for the Detection of Online Sexual Predatory Chats." *Forensic Science International: Digital Investigation.* Elsevier. Retrieved February 18, 2021, from https://www.sciencedirect.com/science/article/abs/pii/S2666281721000032

Rigano, C. (2019). *Using Artificial Intelligence to Address Criminal Justice Needs* Office of Justice Programs. Retrieved October 15, 2021, from https://www.ojp.gov/pdffiles1/nij/252038.pdf

Singh, A., Adeyemi, I., & Venter, H. (2019). *(PDF) Digital Forensic Readiness Framework for Ransomware Investigation* Research Gate. Retrieved October 15, 2021, from https://www.researchgate.net/publication/329998174_Digital_Forensic_Readiness_Framework_for_Ransomware_Investigation_10th_International_EAI_Conference_ICDF2C_2018_New_Orleans_LA_USA_September_10-12_2018_Proceedings

Vincze, E. A. (2016). *Challenges in Digital Forensics.* Taylor & Francis. Retrieved October 15, 2021, from https://www.tandfonline.com/doi/full/10.1080/15614263.2015.1128163

Zuhri, F.A. (2017). *"Cyber Forensic Challenges Semantic Scholar."* https://www.semanticscholar.org/paper/CYBER-FORENSIC-CHALLENGES-Zuhri/2acd9931ad1b8341fc065ce9fedf0b3e0b350f11 (accessed May 12, 2022).

7

Cybercrimes against Women in India: How Can the Law and the Technology Help the Victims?

Sujata Bali
University of Petroleum and Energy Studies, Dehradun, Uttrakhand, India

CONTENTS

7.1 Introduction to Women in Cyber World

> The growing digitization and mobility would open up more ways for women to participate in economic activity and help in gender diversity
>
> **Ms. Chanda Kochhar**
> *Former CEO, ICICI Bank (Vijayakumar, 2015)*

This statement in 2015 by one of the then-leading woman achievers in India reassured that there is greater hope in the Internet age for the Indian womenfolk.

Information and Communication Technologies (ICTs) have definitely helped in ensuring the fast-paced progress of human activities, whether it is business, travel, or simple interaction between people of the world. Nevertheless, what ICTs have also done is that they have provided a new playfield for troublemakers and lawbreakers. Technological advancement has increased the pace of expansion of the Internet. The access to the Internet moved at an unbelievable pace from Internet cafes to personal computers to mobile phones.

A mobile phone in hand gave women a greater confidence to step into and cross the henceforth dark alleys, isolated roads which led them to a relatively safer place of work or

DOI: 10.1201/9781003204862-7

other desirable destinations (Women & Mobile: A Global Opportunity: A study on the mobile phone gender gap in low and middle-income countries, 2021). However, the friendly mobile phone soon became a foe with unwarranted calls, and with the advent of the Internet era, far-reaching perpetrators of crimes against women.

7.2 Research Gaps

1. The cybercrimes against women are recognized and underreported in India.
2. There are limited studies and discussions regarding cybercrimes against women in the field of sociolegal-technical research.
3. Cybercrimes against women can be prohibited only through recognition of its existence and its severity.

7.3 Research Methodology

The issue of cybercrimes against women is discussed through the related Indian legislations and literature. The research publications from the last 20 years obtained from distinguished academic and research databases such as Jstor, SCConline, National Crime Records Bureau Report of 2019, other newspaper reports are considered while analyzing the technological, social, legal, and psychological aspects of cybercrimes against women.

7.4 Cybercrimes or Cyber Targeting against Women

> Your online reputation is your reputation.
>
> *(Fertik & Thompson, 2010)*

By use of text, images, videos, and sounds over the Internet, women have been becoming victims of cybercrimes and the number of these crimes against women is constantly increasing (Kaushik, 2014). Cyberstalking, harassments, bullying, blackmailing, cyberdefamation, pornography, obscenity, morphing, and e-mail spoofing are some of the online crimes committed against women.

Cyberstalking "[It] involves invading the privacy by following a person's movements across the Internet by posting messages on the bulletin boards, entering the chat rooms frequented by the victim, constantly bombarding the victim with messages and emails with obscene language" (Kaushik, 2014). It has been observed that women are targeted excessively, particularly between the ages of 16 years to 35 years, for cyberstalking by men (Kaushik, 2014). Cyber harassments, Cyberbullying, blackmailing, cyberdefamation, pornography, obscenity online are virtual versions of real-world crimes that women have been facing. In morphing, the image is distorted by anyone without authorization and spoofing involves faking an email as the original.

These are the prevalent types of cybercrimes against women but the list keeps increasing with new technological advancements (Brody, 2018).

7.5 Legislative Approach against Cybercrimes in India

Right on, at the onset of the 21st century, the Parliament of India legislated the Information Technology Act, 2000. Though the Act was initially mostly aimed at providing a law-enabled environment for e-commerce, at a later point, it was amended to cover various cybercrimes against women as well (The Information Technology (Amendment) Act, 2008).

Chapter XI of the Information Technology Act, 2000 initially dealt with various offenses such as tampering with computer source documents (The Information Technology Act, 2000, Section 65), hacking with a computer system (The Information Technology Act, 2000, Section 66), publishing of information, which is obscene in electronic form (The Information Technology Act, 2000, Section 67), access to the protected system (The Information Technology Act, 2000, Section 70), breach of confidentiality and privacy (The Information Technology Act, 2000, Section 72), publication for the fraudulent purpose (The Information Technology Act, 2000, Section 74), etc. Later wrongs like identity theft (The Information Technology Act, 2000, Section 66 C), cheating by impersonation (The Information Technology Act, 2000, Section 66D), posting sexually explicit material (The Information Technology Act, 2000, Section 67 A, 67B) were included as offenses.

However, the scheme of the Act from its inception has been facilitative of business rather than curbing wrongs in the cyber world. Women in particular have not been seen as an identifiable section of society in the formation of laws on the Internet. This has resulted in most of the cases of cybercrime against women, still within the scope of traditional laws, e.g., under the Indian Penal Code, 1860 (see Sections 506, 503, and 384) and The Indecent Representation of Women (Prohibition) Act, 1986 which attracts punishment between two and five years for indecent representation of women through advertising, publishing, writings, paintings, figures, or otherwise.

To an extent, the erstwhile Section 66A of the Information Technology Act, 2000 which was capable of controlling "bad talk" in the web world was mostly utilized to curb freedom of speech instead. Due to its conflict with fundamental rights, the Supreme Court of India declared Section 66 A of the Information Technology Act, 2000 unconstitutional (Shreya Singhal v. Union of India, 2015).

7.6 Cyber Victimization in General and From Female Victims' Perspective

Though various governments and lawmakers of the world have shown a proactive approach to fighting cybercrimes, most of the laws and approaches are criminal-centric rather than victim-centric. The law, the news as well as academic research has ignored the victims of cybercrimes as a stakeholder in the fight against cybercrimes.

The identified adverse impacts of cybercrimes include loss of reputation, emotional pain, loss of jobs, and even subsequent physical attack. Researchers have noted that life-threatening cases of online abuse have also caused death through suicide or through targeted attacks (Lipton, 2010).

It is obvious that cyber victimization can cause all victims irrespective of gender or age to withdraw from even healthy, online interactions. However, the impact on women is long-lasting and regressive. For those, who seek support for this prophecy of mine, let me cite the noted data of Indian girls who drop out of school due to never-complained sexual harassment and the common observation that Indian women tend to find it safer to go out only in groups. These examples can be used as a basis to draw a conclusion that how one "bad experience" can lead to the withdrawal of women from unsafe "public spaces" whether in the real or cyber world. The rest of the society of course usually either ignores or compels such withdrawal.

7.7 Issues with Reporting of Cybercrimes against Women in India

India's National Crimes Record Bureau (NCRB) maintains the record of total cybercrimes against women in the following broad seven categories of cybercrimes against women:

1. Cyber Blackmailing/Threatening (Sections 506, 503, and 384 of the Indian Penal Code read with Information Technology Act)
2. Cyber Pornography/Hosting/Publishing Obscene Sexual Materials (Sections 67A/67B (Girl Child) of Information Technology Act read with Indian Penal Code)
3. Cyber Stalking/Cyber Bullying of Women (Section 354D Indian Penal Code read with Information Technology Act)
4. Defamation/Morphing (Section 469 Indian Penal Code read with Indecent Representation of Women (Prohibition) Act & Information Technology Act)
5. Fake Profile (Information Technology Act read with Indian Penal Code)
6. Other Crimes against Women

Figure 7.1 gives a graphical representation of the distribution of cybercrimes against women in these categories.

As per the latest available data, NCRB reported 8,379 total cases all over India. First, less than 10,000 cases reported of cybercrimes in a country, which has a female population of around 58 crores as per the 2011 census (CensusinfoIndia, 2011), seems a great example of massive underreporting of these crimes. Second, looking at the categorization of these cybercrimes, effectively around 71% (5,967 cases out of the reported 8,379) are categorized as "other crimes against women." It is safe to conclude that cybercrimes against women have not been recognized as a distinct category, not even at the reporting level.

The National Commission for Women and Children also facilitates direct reporting of cybercrimes against women on its portal through its complaints and investigation cells. In

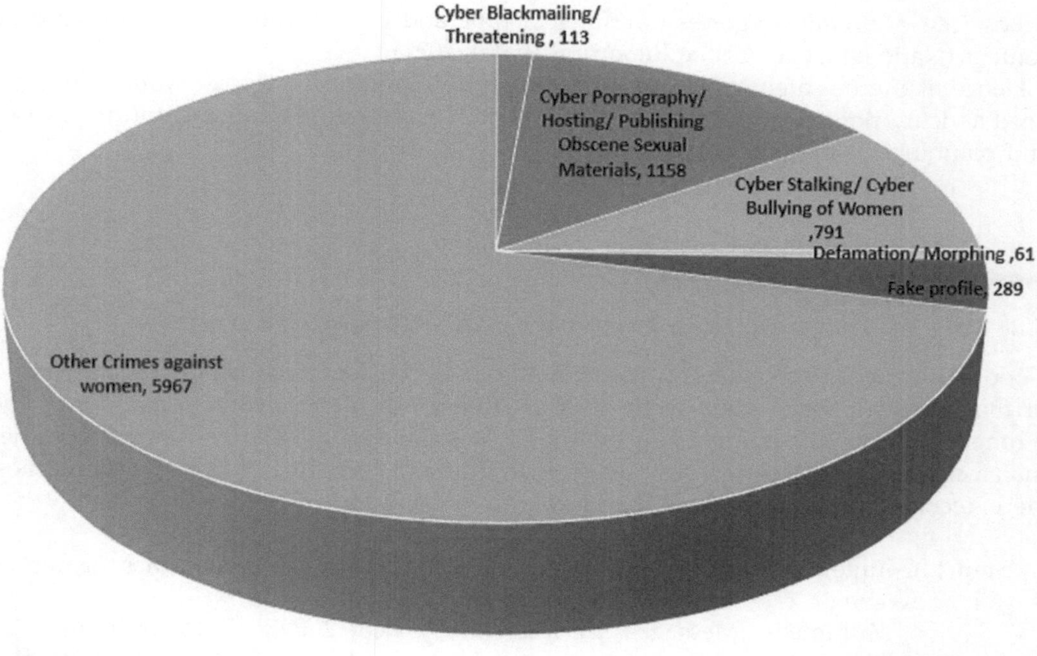

FIGURE 7.1
Reported Cybercrimes against Women (National Crime Records Bureau (NCRB), 2019).

addition, through it, the police investigations are monitored (National Commission for Women, 2021).

As per news reports, cybercrimes are on the rise and the Ministry of Home Affairs (MHA) explicitly interacts with the States and UTs and advises them to expedite the disposal of cybercrime relating to women and children (3.17 Lakh Cyber-crimes in India in Just 18 Months, Says Government, *The Times of India*, 2021).

In 2019, India's MHA launched CCPWC (Cybercrime Prevention against Women and Children) Scheme, which focused on the following five directions:

1. Online Cybercrime reporting through a central citizen portal.
2. Forensic through the national cyber forensic laboratory.
3. Capacity Building of police, prosecutors, judiciary, and all other concerned stakeholders for detection, investigations, forensics, etc.
4. Research & Development in association with research and academic institutions of national importance.
5. Awareness Creation as a pre-emptive approach.

On the first three of the above-stated units of CCPWC, action has been initiated, however, as of July 2021, as per details available on the MHA website action on Research and Development and Awareness Creation is still not a priority (Details about CCPWC [Cybercrime Prevention Against Women and Children] Scheme, 2021).

Even in 2021, looking closely at working of the National CyberCrime Reporting Portal, an offender forces an anonymous victim/informer of a cybercrime related to women to choose out of broad categories of crimes of rape and transmission of sexually obscene content (National Cyber Crime Reporting Portal, 2021).

Hence, it can be safely concluded that reporting cybercrimes against women in India need a victim-perspective approach. It will help in ascertaining the rising nature of cases and planning the best course of action to deal with the same.

7.8 Role of Technology in Preventing and Curing Cybercrimes

Good Law's job is to create terror in the mind of a wrongdoer and confidence in the mind of the wronged, while good technology facilitates the life of everyone and stops the wrongdoer from disturbing the growth of humankind. A preventive approach rather than a curative approach will help the women from not becoming victims of cybercrimes. Here, technology can help more than law.

Step 1: Counter technology helping in the commission of cybercrimes against women

Multimedia Messages Services (MMS), Peer 2 Peer (P2P), webcam, e-mails, chat rooms, are the common known technological tools easily used by perpetrators of cybercrimes against women. Creating technology that can easily counter these abused technologies, will be taking away the power of technology from wrongdoers.

Step 2: Technological tools to help women to have a safe cyberspace

Easily accessible tools such as Web filters and blocking software can be first line of defense against cybercrimes in the hands of women.

Step 3: Create technology supporting cyber forensic investigators

Supporting cyber forensic investigators with the help of trustworthy technological tools can help in ensuring justice for the victims of cybercrimes.

Making most of Lack of Visual Evidence (LOVE), the criminals have highlighted the inefficiency of traditional laws to deal with new-age crimes (Fatima, 2011).

7.9 Concluding Remarks and Suggestions

Dealing with such cybercrimes can leave invisible scars on the mind of the victims. The increasing rate of offenses committed over the Internet and the unpreparedness of the legal system to take on the offenders and support victims is evident.

This chapter tried to look at the role of the legal system in dealing with the issue of cybercrimes against women and in giving an essential support system to the victims of these crimes and found a vacuum in most places.

Based on this research, the author concludes with the following remarks and suggestions:

1. While advising women to be safe in the online world, most of the time, there has been apathy and at times insensitivity while dealing with women victims of cybercrimes on the part of enforcement and judicial authorities. The victims have been turning to nongovernmental organizations (NGOs) and private counselors for seeking help in such cases. However, such help is discretionary and not available to all victims. The State should sensitize and prepare the NGOs through seminars and workshops to recognize this issue and help the victims.
2. Continuous multidisciplinary research into the reasons, platforms, kinds, and effects of cybercrimes generally and particularly against women is required. Sociology, law, and technology experts need to come together to combat this menace.
3. There is a need for cyber education to facilitate the victims about their rights and the cybercriminals about their wrongs. Sometimes, the reasons for these wrongs may not be intentional harm but guileless unthinking on the part of the wrongdoer. Going forward, the MHA-launched CCPWC can utilize common and popular means of communication for awareness such as television, radio, social media networking sites, etc.
4. Amongst all rights of cyber-victim, "right to be forgotten" with the support of Internet Service Providers will be most crucial to facilitate the healthy participation of female victims in the cyberworld.
5. Principally, the online networking sites must provide users with greater options for regulating their privacy. For example, earlier the social networking site *Facebook*'s settings did not enable you to keep your profile picture restricted for download by others. Now, it does. A user-friendly setting and proactive display of information on restricting one's privacy can go a long way in ensuring a decrease in cybercrimes. Right now, India is on the verge of passing its standalone data protection laws, yet having practices better than the minimum mandate of law, always helps.
6. The State needs to promote greater online responsibility. From laws that are more stringent covering cybercrimes against women to ensuring psychological help for women-victim; beginning to end measures are essential to have an effective redressal of cybercrimes against women. Only then, the cherished ideals of freedom and dignity can become a virtual reality for women in India and every other artificial public space.
7. Peculiar crimes such as dowry deaths, honor killings haunt women in the real world, and the law has recognized these, it's time to recognize the vulnerability of women in the virtual world too, and identify and name the cybercrimes distinctly, not just in a few broad categories.
8. The thin line, which perpetrators of cybercrimes need to cross and physically harm the targets of their crimes, makes it necessary to have provision for restraining the wrongdoer from approaching the victim. Western countries frequently use the tool of "restraint order" to ensure this. This is the time that the Indian Courts use it liberally to ensure the peace of mind of the victim.
9. MHA-supported CCPWC scheme rightly focuses on capacity building of prosecutors, judiciary, forensics, however, the financial support needs to be enhanced and must include financial incentives for developing tools to counter cybercrimes against women.

10. MHA-supported CCPWC scheme highlighted the relevance of the Research and Development Unit with academic institutions, it is about time to realize it, help the cause of women victims of cybercrimes by ensuring the best of the minds working on its prevention.

Only when both law and technology collaborate, we can nip in the bud the evil of cybercrimes against women, and the cyber world becomes the human-made utopia envisioned and achieved.

References

"3.17 Lakh Cyber-crimes in India in Just 18 Months, Says Government." *The Times of India*, March 9, 2021. Retrieved from www.timesofindia.indiatimes.com: https://timesofindia.indiatimes.com/business/india-business/3-17-lakh-cyber-crimes-in-india-in-just-18-months-says-government/articleshow/81414259.cms (accessed May 12, 2022).

Brody, L. "How Cryptocurrency May Be Harmful to Women on the Dark Web and Beyond." May 7, 2018. Retrieved from www.glamour.com: https://www.glamour.com/story/how-cryptocurrency-may-be-harmful-to-women-on-the-dark-web-and-beyond

CensusinfoIndia. 2011. Retrieved from http://www.dataforall.org/dashboard/censusinfoindia_pca/

Details about CCPWC (Cybercrime Prevention against Women and Children) Scheme. July 30, 2021. Retrieved from www.mha.gov.in: https://www.mha.gov.in/division_of_mha/cyber-and-information-security-cis-division/Details-about-CCPWC-CybercrimePrevention-against-Women-and-Children-Scheme (accessed May 12, 2022).

Fatima, T. *Cybercrimes*. Lucknow: Eastern Book Company, 2011.

Fertik, Michael and David Thompson. *Wild West 2.0: How to Protect and Restore Your Online Reputation on the Untamed Social Frontier*. New York: AMACOM, 2010. Available at Wild West 2.0: How to Protect and Restore Your Reputation on the Untamed Social Frontier (zlibcdn.com).

The Indian Penal Code. 1860. Sections 506, 503, and 384. Retrieved from https://www.indiacode.nic.in/bitstream/123456789/2263/1/A1860-45.pdf

The Information Technology Act. 2000. Section 65. Retrieved from https://www.indiacode.nic.in/bitstream/123456789/6827/1/itact2000.pdf

The Information Technology Act. 2000. Section 66. Retrieved from https://www.indiacode.nic.in/bitstream/123456789/6827/1/itact2000.pdf

The Information Technology Act. 2000. Section 66C. Retrieved from https://www.indiacode.nic.in/bitstream/123456789/6827/1/itact2000.pdf

The Information Technology Act. 2000. Section 66D. Retrieved from https://www.indiacode.nic.in/bitstream/123456789/6827/1/itact2000.pdf

The Information Technology Act. 2000. Section 67. Retrieved from https://www.indiacode.nic.in/bitstream/123456789/6827/1/itact2000.pdf

The Information Technology Act. 2000. Section 67A, 67B. Retrieved from https://www.indiacode.nic.in/bitstream/123456789/6827/1/itact2000.pdf

The Information Technology Act. 2000. Section 70. Retrieved from https://www.indiacode.nic.in/bitstream/123456789/6827/1/itact2000.pdf

The Information Technology Act. 2000. Section 72. Retrieved from https://www.indiacode.nic.in/bitstream/123456789/6827/1/itact2000.pdf

The Information Technology Act. 2000. Section 74. Retrieved from https://www.indiacode.nic.in/bitstream/123456789/6827/1/itact2000.pdf

The Information Technology (Amendment) Act. 2008. India. Retrieved from https://www.indiacode.nic.in/bitstream/123456789/15414/1/21_new_it_amendment_act2008.pdf#search=The%20Information%20Technology%20(Amendment)%20Act.%20(2008)
Kaushik, N. A. "Cyber Crimes against Women," *GJRIM* 4, no. 1 (June 2014): 38–39.
Lipton, J. D. "Combating Cyber-Victimization" *Expresso.* 2010. Retrieved from http://works.bepress.com/jacqueline_lipton/11
National Commission for Women. 2021. Retrieved from www.ncw.nic.in: http://ncw.nic.in/ncw-cells/complaint-investigation-cell
National Crime Records Bureau (NCRB) Cyber-Crimes against Women in India. 2019. Retrieved from https://ncrb.gov.in/sites/default/files/crime_in_india_table_additional_table_chapter_reports/Table%209A.10_1.pdf
National Cyber Crime Reporting Portal. July 30, 2021. Retrieved from https://cybercrime.gov.in/Webform/Crime_ReportAnonymously.aspx
Shreya Singhal v. Union of India, 1523 (SC 2015). Retrieved from https://main.sci.gov.in/jonew/judis/42510.pdf
Vijayakumar, S. "Digitisation to Open Up More Opportunities for Women." *The Hindu*, November 2, 2015. Retrieved from http://www.thehindu.com/business/Industry/icici-bank-ceo-chanda-kochhar-on-digitisation-opportunities-for-women/article7834210.ece
"Women & Mobile: A Global Opportunity: A Study on the Mobile Phone Gender Gap in Low and Middle-Income Countries." July 26, 2021. Retrieved from https://www.gsma.com/mobilefordevelopment/wp-content/uploads/2013/01/GSMA_Women_and_Mobile-A_Global_Opportunity.pdf

8

Role of Technology and Prevention of Money Laundering

Smita M. Pachare[1], Suhasini Verma[2], and Vidhisha Vyas[3]
[1]*Associate Professor, Department of Finance, Universal Business School, Karjat, Maharashtra, India*
[2]*Associate Professor, Department of Business Administration, Manipal University, Jaipur, Rajasthan, India*
[3]*Professor, IILM University, Gurugram, Haryana, India*

CONTENTS

DOI: 10.1201/9781003204862-8

8.1 Introduction

8.1.1 Money Laundering: Meaning and Background

Money laundering is "any act or attempted act to conceal or disguise the identity of illegally obtained proceeds so that they appear to have originated from legitimate sources" (Hamin et al., 2014). It is the process of converting black money earned from unlawful activities to white money and making it appear as if it is earned by legal means. The intention behind money laundering is to hide money and other resources from the government authorities in order to avoid taxation, judgment enforcement, or deliberate seizure. There is no accounting of the illegal income, leaving no scope for tax charging, and thus having an adverse effect on the growth and development of the economy.

Article 1 of EC Directive 1991 defines money laundering as "the conversion of property, knowing that such property is derived from serious crime, for the purpose of concealing or disguising the illicit origin of the property or of assisting any person who is involved in committing such an offense(s) to evade the legal consequences of his action, and the concealment or disguise of the true nature, source, location, disposition, movement, rights with respect to, or ownership of property, knowing that such property is derived from serious crime."

The most common sources of black money are where the money comes from drug trafficking, corruption, terrorist activities, embezzlement, etc. These criminals are always on lookout the ways of easy laundering systems and newer ways to convert this illegally earned money, which is mostly in cash, to white money. To fund activities such as terrorism, illicit arms deals, financial forgeries, smuggling, or drug trafficking, a large corpus of money is created and criminal establishments search for ways to use these resources without arousing suspicions and doubts about their illicit origin.

The reports of IMF suggest that global money laundering is estimated to be around 2%–5% of World GDP. As per the Basel AML Index, India was ranked 79th in 2015, 78th in 2016, and 52nd in 2019. These data clearly show India's exposure to money laundering risk which is increasing at a very fast rate.

8.1.2 The Money Laundering Process

The money laundering process most commonly occurs in three key stages as explained in Exhibit 8.1. The stages are placement, layering, and integration (Kumar, 2015).

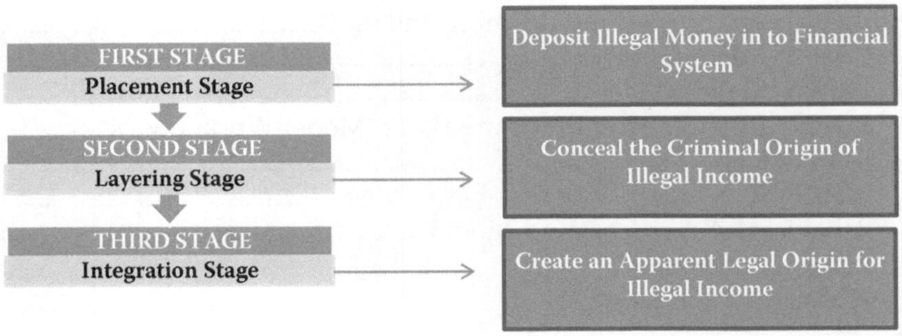

EXHIBIT 8.1
Money Laundering Process.

8.1.2.1 Placement Stage

Money laundering starts with placing dirty money into the financial system. The proceeding of the criminal activities—drug trafficking, corruption, etc.—comes in the form of cash, in order to wash this dirty money, it is inserted into the legitimate system through many ways like directly depositing the money in the bank in smaller amounts, casinos, buying costly items in cash, and then re-sale them for checks or account transfers, etc.

8.1.2.2 Layering Stage

The next stage is layering, also known as the structuring stage. It is considered the most complex component of the whole money laundering process. Layering consists of concealing the source of dirty money by putting layers of transactions in such a way that it becomes very difficult even for authorities to detect the sources of money. Depositing and transferring the money in different banks, withdrawing and depositing many times, changing the currency, buying costly items, intentionally involving many financial institutions, opening shell companies, etc. (Kaur, 2019) are a few of the ways, which puts layers on the transactions to conceal the source of illicit money.

8.1.2.3 Integration Stage

This stage is the final stage in the process of money laundering. In this phase, cash is reintroduced into the economy and appears to proceed with the legitimate transaction. After so much layering and whitewashing, this money is enjoyed, spent, invested in businesses and shares, etc. as clean money. Generally, criminals spend this money without being caught (see Exhibit 8.2).

8.1.3 Money Laundering: Common Tactics

The oldest method of money laundering is based on paper or cash. As the system grows newer ways and instruments are developed to cater various growing needs of institutions and individuals, the methods of money laundering have also expanded.

Technology has changed almost everything in our lives and financial transactions are no exception. In the past few decades, new payment methods—debit cards, credit cards, mobile payment services or digital wallets, internet payment services like online banking, digital currencies, etc.—are widely accepted payment methods. In this interconnected world, money can be transacted anywhere in the world, mostly without the intervention of third party, at an unprecedented speed. Moreover, technological development has

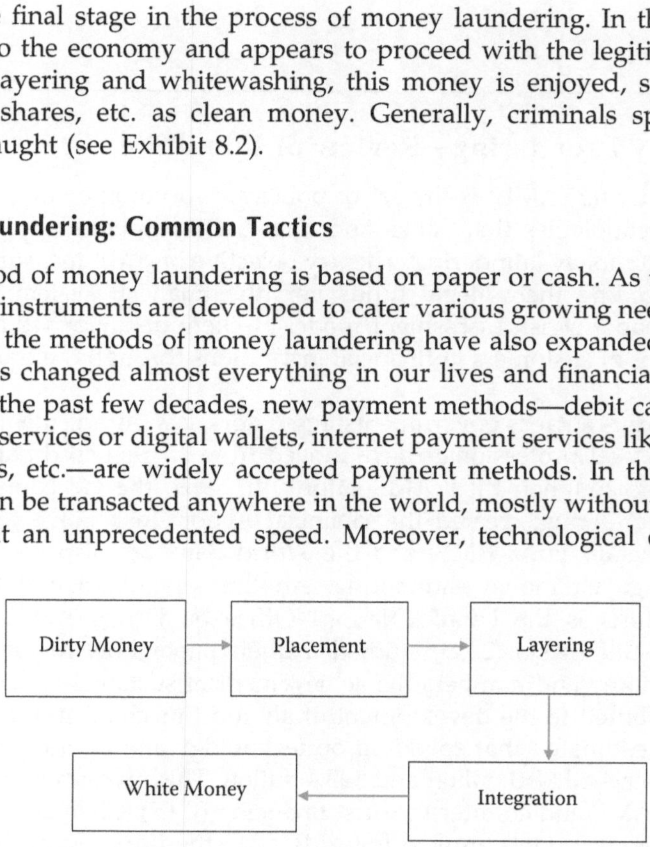

EXHIBIT 8.2
Money Laundering.

provided the business and individuals the ease of transactions, as well as the money launderer the newer doors. Minimal Know Your Customer (KYC) requirement in the digital world, globalized payment methods, absence of regulation, or less stringent regulation on Fin-Tech services provides a perfect platform to perform fraudulent financial activities. Due to its speed, global reach, simplicity, and low cost, online platforms are an obvious choice to launder money. They may "sell" merchandise, book rides, hotels, etc. through stolen credit cards, and declare the proceeds as money earned through legal sources.

8.1.4 Money Laundering: Why It Is a Serious Problem

Organized crime—drug trafficking, terrorist activities, etc.—cannot survive in absence of money. Fraudsters and criminals require a huge amount of money to perform these activities and a large amount of cash is difficult to circulate in the economy. Hence, they use financial institutions and perform many fraudulent activities to fulfill their objectives. Not only do these organized crimes pose a serious problem before mankind and mar economic development but also pose a challenge to the system to face regulatory compliances, financial security, dent of reputation, liquidity crunch, operational failure, and so on (Alford, 1993). Detection and prevention of money laundering are becoming a mammoth task for organizations as the size, nature, and complexity of the same are increasing at a fast pace (Palshikar & Apte, 2014).

8.2 Anti-Money Laundering—Review of Literature

Anti-money laundering (AML) is the set of policies, procedures, laws, other regulatory principles, and technologies that banks and financial institutions apply and enforce to detect and prevent money laundering. The key objective of AML measures is to dissuade criminals from feeding their illegal funds into the financial system. Marques (2015) proposed in his paper a risk assessment model of client behavior which aimed at analyzing the behavior of customers in financial institutions through the transactions carried out there.

All the stakeholders such as governments, regulators, law enforcement agencies, public authorities, banks, and professionals have moved from a rule-based paradigm to a risk-based approach, to toughen their AML efforts. In 1989, the G7 countries, seeking to combat money laundering, created the Financial Action Task Force (FATF, 2010). The International Monetary Fund (IMF) and the World Bank are also key institutions that advance efforts against money laundering. Another organization that is working to support AML efforts is the United Nations Office on Drugs and Crime (UNODC). Dobrowolski and Sulkowski (2019) studied in their paper how money laundering destabilizes the economy and hampers the achievement of sustainable development goals. Their work contributed to the development of an audit mechanism for AML outcomes.

In 2019, Celent estimated that spending on technology and operations against money laundering have reached $8.3 billion and $23.4 billion. This investment is made to ensure compliance with AML and counter-terrorist financing (CTF). Chen et al. (2018) reviewed in their study various models applied for AML with the use of machine learning. They highlighted that most of the reviewed papers have used AML typologies, i.e., using algorithms to identify suspicious transactions. It is observed through their work that presently available work on AML and Machine learning does not have data quality assurance and there is a need for reinforcement learning. Singh and Best (2019) mentioned in their work that in the present economic scenarios, regulators and financial institutions are threatened by the latest scams and stop financial criminal activities. They explained that effective technological solutions are essential to assist investigators and they propose in their paper the use of visualization techniques that help in the identification of patterns of money laundering activities. The technique uses link analysis to detect fraudulent bank transactions. Tai and Kan (2019) proposed Mclays method based on machine learning and data analysis technique. The given method provides two-stage identification of fraud; laundering transactions and it work on recall and precision technology.

Han et al. (2020) in their study proposed a framework using advanced natural language processing and deep learning techniques for deploying the latest AML technologies. Their key contribution is to focus that external information (unstructured) must reduce the pressure on human investigators. Ullrich (2018) in his paper provided a three-tier compliance framework model using a risk-based approach for the AML system. Gikonyo (2018) conducted a study on Kenya's potential money laundering activities and analyzed the documents of crime and AML Acts and regulations. He further highlighted the loopholes and implementation challenges for detecting money laundering. Canhoto (2021) in her work examined the technical and contextual affordability of machine learning algorithms. The study concluded that nonavailability of good quality training datasets on money laundering methods hampers the use of controlled machine learning techniques.

Krishnapriya (2019) proposed in her paper a collaborative relational data screening model using big data and identified money laundering frauds by auto correlating the similar attributes in each transaction collaborative data analysis technique. Further, Umaru (2020) has studied the money laundering activity in sub-Saharan countries and concluded that financial institutions must use mobile money services to detect and adopt AML techniques. Alkahalili et al. (2021) developed a model that works on automating the watch list filtering system using machine learning and will perform three functions that include monitoring, advising, and taking action against money laundering activities.

8.3 AML Model

Traditional methods of curbing Money Laundering and Cyber laundering are not keeping pace with the new evolutions and advancements occurring in the banking and financial sectors all over the world. The change in **AML Models** is advanced by faster payments, digital-first approaches, and the ever-increasing cost of compliance.

Let's take a look at a few common and some not-so-common types of **AMLModels** and their pros and cons, and then consider some overall best practices for **AML Models** validation that will ensure that each model performs as intended.

8.3.1 The Walker Gravity Model

The Walker Gravity Model tries to estimate the flows of illegal funds and criminal money to and fro among many countries all over the world. This "Walker Model" was first developed in 1994 and recently improvised.

The formula developed by Walker and Unger (2009) is very close to the gravity model. International trade theories such as Heckscher Ohlin, Krugman, and Dixit-Stiglitz can relate theoretically with the Walker Model. The model does not receive global credit simply because flows of money laundering are hidden and are largely unrecognizable. The generalization and effective forecasting are difficult with the Walker model. Walker's "prototype" gravity formula assumes (Walker and Unger, 2009)

$$F_{ij}/M_i = (\text{GNP}/\text{capita})_j \times (3\text{BS}_j + \text{GA}_j + \text{SWIFT}_j - 3\text{CF}_j - \text{CR}_j + 15)/\text{Distance}_{ij}^2 \quad (8.1)$$

where GNP/capita is GNP per capita, BS is Banking Secrecy, GA is Government Attitude, SWIFT is SWIFT member, CF is Conflict, and CR is Corruption.

The model has challenges in terms of the availability of quality data, for which the only way out is to develop some sincere international effort and generate or collect better quality data or focus on the end result that fraud is more serious than possessing illegal drugs. The indicators in the Walker Model are good proxy variables but are rather ad hoc. The model can be enhanced by using behavioral analysis using big data or Machine Learning techniques.

8.3.2 The RBF Neural Network Model

An ultraprecision detection method in financial transactions is a contemporary requirement due to the presence of bulk data in financial institutions with a huge, frequent error detection rate. RBF neural network model can run timely calculations with its available data and can identify whether the transactions carried out are engaged in money laundering activity. The process does not involve complexity; hence, reduces the tracking time of ML activity.

The model gives promising results in enhancing ML detection rate and detects suspicious transactions to a larger extent. However, there are many problems in terms of the actual detection system for money laundering activities and the actual business account records.

8.3.3 Social Network Analysis Model

The social network model targets recognizing suspicious customers involved in group money laundering. The model identified and applied the social network functions such as degree centrality, clustering, and ego network under the.NET environment that utilized cryptoscape, an open-source software platform. The model uses customer's profile, financial data, and their transactions to classify the individuals and their nexus involved in money laundering (Shaikh et al., 2021). An iteration of experiments work to find the nexus of suspicious clients, such as shared ownership relationships, professional relationships, family relationships, sibling, spouse, and other close relations. The iteration results can benefit financial institutions to identify money laundering groups and events. Although to find a real-world financial data dependency of the AML analysis module on the list of suspicious customers are the drawback of the model.

There are various modules that have been created to identify money laundering activities but with the digitization and easy availability of technology, it has become all the more difficult to identify money laundering activities and trap the criminals effectively. However, the same technology can be effectively used to identify criminals with the help of artificial intelligence and data-driven models. Some of the emerging trends are presented in the forthcoming section.

8.4 Emerging Trends in the AML Space

8.4.1 Application of Analytics

Banks are relying on analytics for their money laundering detection and prevention. For fraud detection, banks are using sophisticated analytical tools and filtering technologies for real-time detection. Financial institutions generate warnings based on changes in behavior patterns. They also conduct high take linkage analysis to discover mistrustful activities and identify money trails. Anti-stripping technology is used to identify hidden transfers or any suspicious handling of wire transfer data (TCS BaNCS-Compliance-2020).

Banks are trusting social media as a supplementary source of information to establish authentication for customer identity, classify politically exposed persons (PEP). Banks and financial establishments are using analytics to identify entity-level linkages, uncover identities linked to the same consumer across streams of business, and identify multiple accounts under different names. They also use analytics to track transactions generated through common cyber infrastructure (see the report by Deloitte, 2020).

8.4.2 Application of Machine Learning and AML

Machine learning and data science have revolutionized the way financial ecosystem work, primarily in the area of uncovering hidden transactions, net systems, and mistrustful money laundering activities. It aims to identify money laundering typologies, peculiar and mistrustful transactions, behavioral alterations in customers, transactions of businesses from the same geography, age groups, and ethnic identities, leading to a reduction of fake positives. Financial institutions must make the detecting system smarter by using artificial intelligence. Exhibit 8.3 explains AML Solution Evolution, which will help to make detection system smarter for financial institutions.

For banks and financial institutions, now is the ideal opportunity to deploy AML models into their digital payment ecosystem where the total volume of transactions carried out each day direct toward thousands of daily financial transactions being flagged each month. These pseudo alerts are unproductive. Crores of rupees are spent each year to identify true alerts for investigation and the problem is only aggravating year by year. An emblematic challenge in transaction monitoring is the generation of innumerable alerts, which requires operation teams to identify and process the alarms. Adoption of AML models can identify and perceive unconvinced conduct and besides AML can help

EXHIBIT 8.3
Anti-Money Laundering (AML) Evolution.

to classify alerts as per the level of risk such as critical, high, medium, or low risk (Barthur, 2017).

Machine learning can play a key role in transforming the sector of AML, which is a complex and delimited field involving composite data and intricate workflows. It can be applied to discover the new risk segments and money laundering patterns that might point to money laundering or other types of illicit activity also revolutionizing the way the financial ecosystem work, especially in the area of detecting hidden patterns and suspicious activities. It helps to uncover money laundering typologies, bizarre and doubtful transactions, behavioral changes in customers, transactions of customers of the same geographical location, age groups, and other identities; and helps to reduce pseudo positives (International Finance Corporation, 2021).

Machine learning is not a completely changing approach to AML; however, it can improvise and augment the operational process for existing frameworks, such as transaction monitoring and risk assessments (Simonova, 2011).

8.4.3 Rule-Based AML Model

Rule-based AML models, also known as rules engines, are programmed with several if-then statements and intended to protect the bank or financial institutions from malicious activity, for example, waning cash transactions over a given amount like INR 20,000 over a certain time period such as more than SIX in two weeks. It works on a pattern and blocks transactions to other countries, use consumer data to identify accounts for added monitoring and categorize merchant accounts based on previous transactions. Such systems are pre-existing, but they require a substantial amount of bank resources to analyze the transactions that are categorized or blocked to clear out false positives. However, a rule-based approach to AML will not be applicable to changes in the criminal mode of operation aimed to avoid detection.

Rule-based methods have limitations such as it is a time-consuming process, it requires highly skilled analysts for manual investigation, it is subjective and inconsistent, and there can be a chance of a high false-positive rate. Based on the database and on the data mining techniques, a bank can obtain huge primary information with the use of cluster analysis, decision tree logistic regression analysis, correlation analysis, data mining Information to analyze a huge amount of data, and obtain the money laundering identification characteristics (Liu et al., 2011).

Here are examples of rule-based AML:

1. **Structuring over time:** This rule detects an excessive proportion of transactions which includes transaction limits. Take an example, the threshold for transactions is INR 10,000, and the system is looking for a pattern where transactions for the clients largely fall between INR 9,000 and INR 10,000 over a 60-day period or 90-day period. If transactions are above the limit they will be scrutinized.
2. **Suspicious users' expenditure pattern:** This rule identifies transactions that highly diverge from the client's usual expenditure pattern. This may specify an account takeover fraudulently or externally influenced transaction. Such transactions include a lower limit of INR 1000.
3. **Change in customer profile before large transaction:** This rule identifies a situation when a customer makes a change in profile to personally identifiable

information (PII) just before making a large transaction usually a transaction greater than INR 10000.

4. **Extraordinary increase in overall transaction volume:** The rule segregates out accounts that have been opened for a short time duration, accounts with a low balance, and little outgoing transaction value over the applicable time window. It identifies a significant increase in the value of an account's outgoing transactions when compared to their recent average. It searches for accounts with the latest activity where the transaction value of the account is substantially higher than the seven-day moving average.
5. **Self-payment using IP address:** This rule recognizes transfers between accounts with the same IP address and similar amounts or transactions.
6. **Small buyer diversity:** This rule is best applicable to a platform that generally observes many senders (buyers) transacting with a single recipient (seller). It recognizes merchants who receive payments from a less number of buyers, for example, fewer than 10. This rule is only applicable for accounts older than the prescribed threshold to validate low diversity over time and allow some time for merchants to ramp up their transactions.
7. **Seller to buyer messaging:** This method is applicable for platforms that track the frequency of communication between buyers and sellers on the transactions. It identifies merchants with high earnings but very few messages sent, which could direct toward agreement or money laundering rather than predictable commercial activity.

Forming rules can be a challenging task as every business situation has varied risk factors and appropriate thresholds. Rule-based methods have limitations such as it being a time-consuming process, requiring highly skilled analysis for manual investigation, it is subjective and inconsistent, and there can be a chance of a high false-positive rate.

8.4.4 Feature-Based Model

Financial institutions can adopt the feature-based model for AML in which help algorithms capture information from the data. Feature-based models use data from transactions or payments, account information, alerts from database like the average balance from the last 10 days, and captures suspicious transactions. Effective and efficiently designed feature-based models highlight transactional behavior of different customer segments, continuously track transactional behavior of an account, identify, and construct rule variables and can change the threshold limits of the transactions. The workflow of the feature-based model is explained in Exhibit 8.4.

The following variables can be constructed for developing feature-based AML models.

1. **Time-Since Variables:** This variable can be very useful to encapsulate the information of how fast the transactions are taking place for accounts. It calculates the time between when an account was last used for a transaction and the time of the current transaction. The faster the subsequent transactions for a single entity, the higher would be the probability of fraud. Hence, this would help in tracking the second stage namely the layering of money laundering.

2. **Velocity-Change Variables:** The workflow of a feature-based model is explained in Exhibit 8.5. The set of variables can track the sudden change in the normal behavior of an account by calculating how the number of transactions or the amount transferred in the past day (0 and 10 days) can be changed over the other set of periods (7, 14, and 30 days). The Velocity-change variables would help in calculating the average, maximum, median, and the total amount of the transaction from each account over the past 0, 1, 3, 7, and 10 days, which would help in tracking the third stage, namely, Integration where a large sum of money is withdrawn from a bank account without any adequate reason possibly for buying a property. It will assist in learning how frequently the account is used and in identifying a sudden change in the behavior of accounts.

8.4.4.1 Rule-Based and Feature-Based Model Workflow

Rule-based models are useful in identifying non-compliant activity and feature-based model helps to analyze the inputs about transaction data, account information and transaction history, average transaction volume from the last average of 30 days, card data and to identify unusual and fraudulent behavior in payment cards, loans, wires, and transfers (Barthur, 2017). Machine learning can be applied for advanced transaction monitoring to glean patterns or identify potentially suspicious transactions. Exhibit 8.5 explains the workflow of rule-based and feature-based models through machine learning.

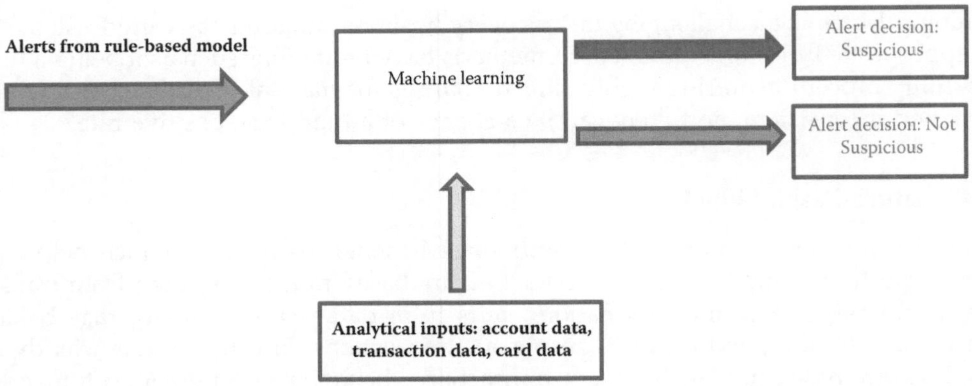

EXHIBIT 8.4
Feature-Based Model Workflow.

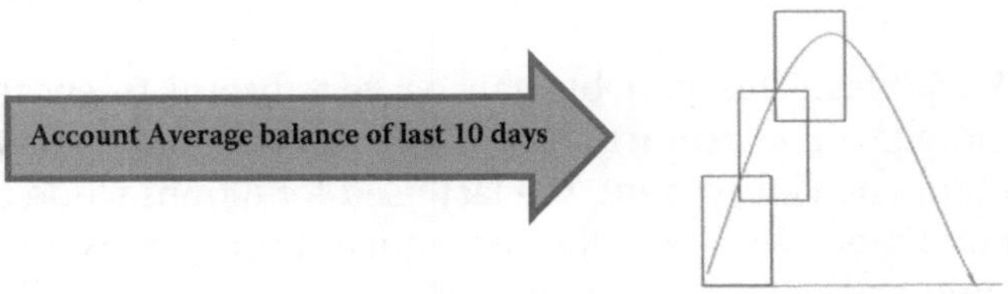

EXHIBIT 8.5
Example of Velocity-Change Variable Model for AML.

8.4.5 Data-Driven Model

Algorithms are smart to work without features and a data-driven model is based on algorithms that help in identifying any kind of anomalous behavior because algorithms understand malicious activities through data (Salehi et al., 2017). Data-driven model does not need alerts for training.

Exhibit 8.6 presents a slant of money laundering detection and run frequent pattern of data mining algorithms and data mining transactions to detect money laundering through transactions data, monitoring banking account transactions, card transactions, alert data, and KYC details (Barthur, 2017).

8.4.6 Website and Cyber Analytics-Based Model

Merchant view, control scam, and website watch (Ever Compliant US partner in 2016) are the solution software provided by the US-based Ever Compliant company to detect hidden transaction tunnels and merchant fraud from entering the e-commerce ecosystem by leveraging cyber intelligence. This platform is able to detect hidden mobile apps and fraudulent mobile payments being processed through illegal merchant accounts.

8.4.7 Behavioral Analytics-Based Model

This type of AML model is used by master card that monitors user behavior and traffic flow together when passed through highly developed algorithms alerts the acquirer and payment facilitator of possible transaction laundering or e-commerce laundering in real-time.

8.4.8 Risk-Based Model

Most of the AML model often contains risk factors that fail to differentiate between high- and low-risk customers, methods for assessing risk vary by nature of business and application of the model. Different risk factors must be used for different customers and different sections of transactions. In the context of money laundering, a risk-based approach is a process that includes the risk assessment of business transactions and customers using certain recommended elements such as products, services delivery

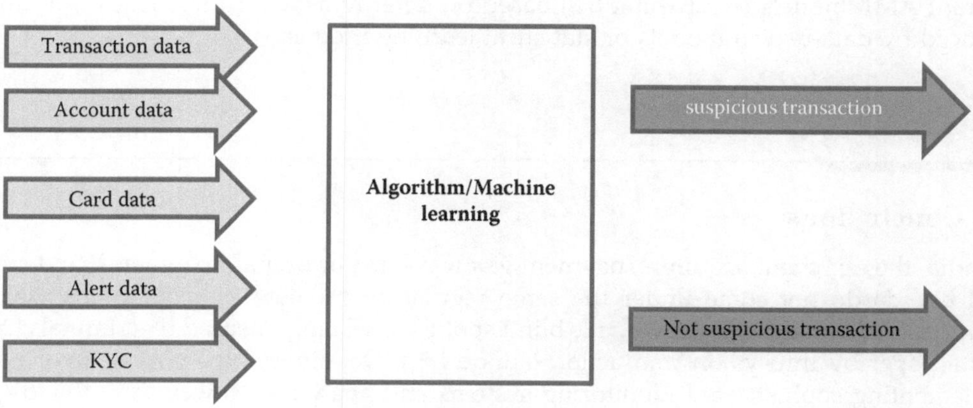

EXHIBIT 8.6
Data-Driven Model.

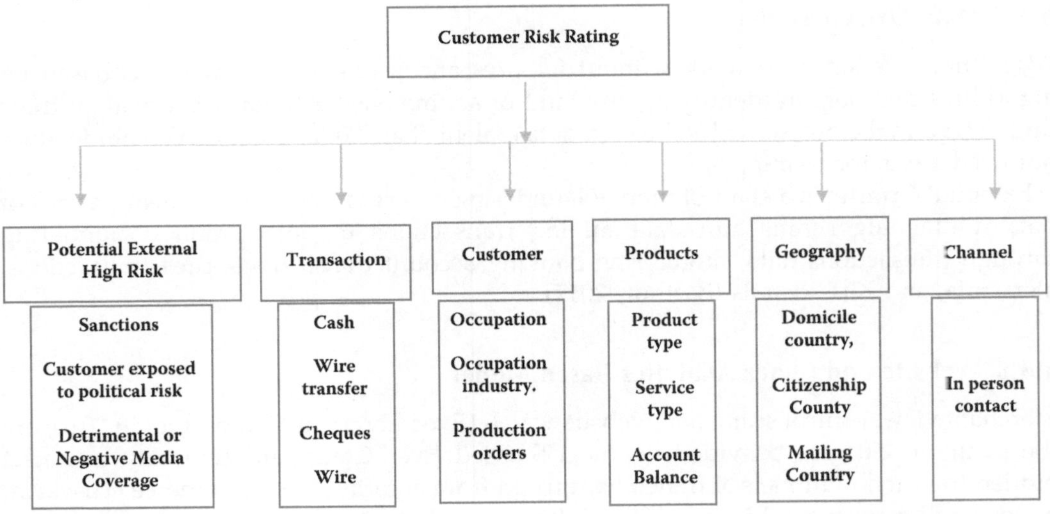

EXHIBIT 8.7
Risk Assessment Factors of Business Activities. (Source: Modified from Mckinsey, 2019.)

channels, geography, clients, and business relationship. Next is the alleviation of risk through the implementation of controls and measures suitable to determine the risks of identified customers. Evaluating and mitigating the risk of money laundering is not a one-time exercise. It is a continuous process to keep the information up to date in accordance with the assessed level of risk and constant monitoring of transactions and business relationships as per the level of risk. A risk-based approach should be reassessed and reorganized when the risk factors change with time. Effective and efficient risk rating models use a reliable set of risk factors through inputs and will differ by business line or customer segment (see Exhibit 8.7).

Most financial institutions already have an AML system, but they need to modify it to comply with current regulations. The updates to the institution´s AML system are assumed to be made by their personnel, according to their standards and procedures. Current AML models (see Exhibit 8.8) based on deterministic business rules need to be replaced by data-driven models or statistical learning models.

8.5 Conclusions

In India, the merchant acquirers, payment gateways, major prepaid payments, and credit card brands do not come under the same regulatory preview as regular financial institutions and banks do, however, this blind spot is now being misused by criminals (2017 White paper by Infosys on transaction laundering). Definitely, high cost is involved in implementing sophisticated monitoring systems and analytics. However, in this digital era payment industry must start reporting regularly suspicious and illegal activities

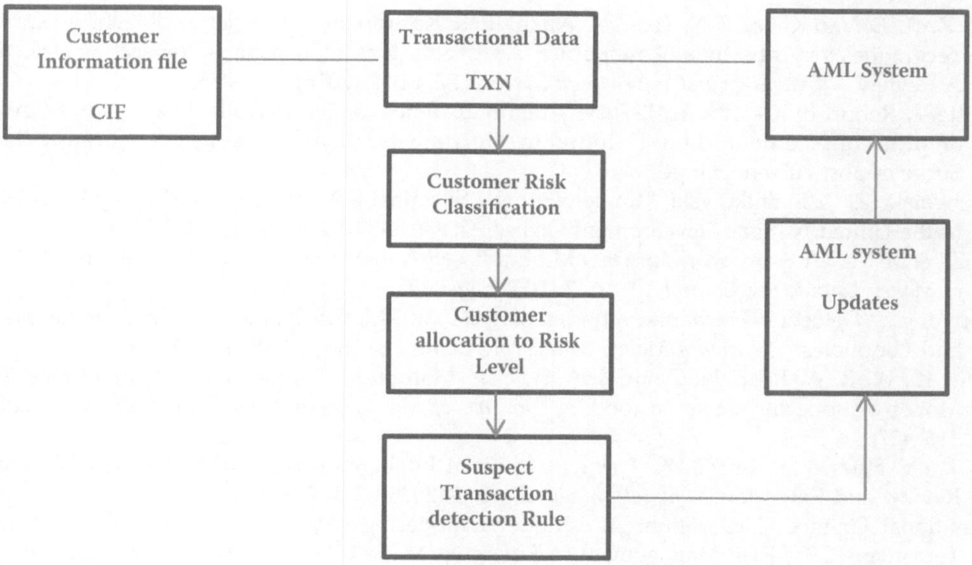

EXHIBIT 8.8
Current System for AML in Financial Institutions.

which will benefit the consumers, organizations, and at the same time, it will also improve financial institutions' reputation in a proactive manner.

Data mining, algorithms, and machine learning techniques are very convenient technologies to detect money laundering patterns or to take AML initiatives (Gao and Ye, 2007, Salehi et al., 2017). These technologies present to the financial institutions advanced filtering technologies and analytics for real-time fraud detection. Rule-based, feature-based, and data-based AML models will be more effective and crucial to enhance automated systems that can interact with the massive data. Although AML model implementations prompted a discussion about the practicability of these solutions and the degree to which AML should be trusted and potentially replace human analysis and decision-making, undoubtedly these technologies and models paved a way for the identification and reduction of fraudulent transactions safeguarding genuine consumers and financial losses from the economy.

References

Alford, D.E. "Anti-Money Laundering Regulations: A Burden on Financial Institutions." *North Carolina Journal of International Law* 19 (1993): 437.

Alkhalili, M., M. H. Qutqut, & F. Almasalha. "Investigation of Applying Machine Learning for Watch-List Filtering in Anti-Money Laundering." *IEEE Access*, 9 (2021), 18481–18496.

Barthur, A. Security Scientist, H2O, at MLconf Seattle. 2017. Available at: https://www.youtube.com/watch?v=1ujtVBimH8Y

Canhoto, A. I. "Leveraging Machine Learning in the Global Fight against Money Laundering and Terrorism Financing: An Affordances Perspective." *Journal of Business Research* 131 (2021): 441–452.

Chen, Z., L. D. Van Khoa, E. N. Teoh, A. Nazir, E. K. Karuppiah, & K. S. Lam. "Machine Learning Techniques for Anti-Money Laundering (AML) Solutions in Suspicious Transaction Detection: A Review." *Knowledge and Information Systems* 57, no. 2 (2018): 245–285.

Deloitte. A Report by DeloitteAML-Survey-report-2020-noexp. 2020. Available at: https://www2.deloitte.com/content/dam/Deloitte/in/Documents/finance/Forensic/in-forensic-AML-Surveyreport-2020-noexp.pdf

Dobrowolski, Z. & Ł. Sułkowski. "Implementing a Sustainable Model for Anti-Money Laundering in the United Nations Development Goals." *Sustainability*12, Issue 1 (2019): 244.

Gao, Z., & M. Ye. "A Framework for Data Mining-Based Anti-Money Laundering Research." *Journal of Money Laundering Control* 10, no. 2 (2007): 170–179.

Gikonyo, C. "Detection Mechanisms under Kenya's Anti-Money Laundering Regime: Omissions and Loopholes." *Journal of Money Laundering Control* 21, no. 2 (2018): 147–159.

Hamin, Z., W. R. W. Rosli, N. Omar, & A. A. P. A. Mahmud. "Configuring Criminal Proceeds in Money Laundering Cases in the UK." *Journal of Money Laundering Control* 17, no. 4 (2014): 416–427.

Han, J., Y. Huang, S. Liu, & K. Towey. "Artificial Intelligence for Anti-Money Laundering: A Review and Extension." *Digital Finance* 2, no. 3 (2020): 211–239.

International Finance Corporation. Anti-Money-Laundering (AML) & Countering Financing of Terrorism (CFT) Risk Management in Emerging Market Banks. 2021. Available at: https://www.ifc.org/wps/wcm/connect/e7e10e94-3cd8-4f4c-b6f81e14ea9eff80/45464_IFC_AML_Report.pdf?MOD=AJPERES&CVID=mKKNshy

Kaur, S. "Money Laundering a Fast Growing Menace: Emerging Trends and Measures to Curb." *International Journal of Research in Social Sciences* 9, no. 6 (2019): 247–262.

Krishnapriya, G. "Identifying Suspicious Money Laundering Transaction Based on Collaborative Relational Data Screening Model Using Decision Classifier in Transactional Database." *Journal of Critical Reviews* 7, no. 4 (2019): 2020.

Kumar, P. "Money Laundering in India: Concepts, Effects and Legislation." *International Journal of Research* 3, no. 7 (2015): 51–63.

Liu, R., X. L. Qian, S. Mao, & S. Z. Zhu. "Research on Anti-Money Laundering Based on Core Decision Tree Algorithm." In *2011 Chinese Control and Decision Conference (CCDC)*. IEEE (pp. 4322–4325), 2011.

Marques, J. F. O. *Risk Analysis in Money Laundering: A Case Study*. 2015, Instituto Superior Técnico Lisbon, Portugal.

Money Laundering Using New Payment Methods, FATF Report. October 2010. Available at: http://www.fatf-gafi.org/dataoecd/4/56/46705859.pdf

Palshikar, G. K., & M. Apte. Financial Security against Money laundering: A Survey. In *Emerging Trends in ICT Security* (pp. 577–590). Morgan Kaufmann, 2014.

Salehi, A., M. Ghazanfari, & M. Fathian. "Data Mining Techniques for Anti money Laundering." *International Journal of Applied Engineering Research* 12, no. 20 (2017): 10084–10094.

Shaikh, A. K., M. Al-Shamli, & A. Nazir. "Designing a Relational Model to Identify Relationships between Suspicious Customers in Anti-Money Laundering (AML) Using Social Network Analysis (SNA)." *Journal of Big Data* 8, no. 1 (2021): 1–22.

Singh, K., & P. Best. "Anti-Money Laundering: Using Data Visualization to Identify Suspicious Activity." *International Journal of Accounting Information Systems*, 34 (2019): 100418.

Simonova, A. The Risk-Based Approach to Anti-Money Laundering: Problems and Solutions. *Journal of Money Laundering Control* 14 (2011). 10.1108/13685201111173820

Tai, C. H., & T. J. Kan. Identifying Money Laundering Accounts. In *2019 International Conference on System Science and Engineering (ICSSE)*. July 2019. pp. 379–382.

Tata Consultancy Services. White paper on "Anti-Money Laundering: Challenges and Trends." 2020. Available at: https://www.tcs.com/content/dam/tcs/pdf/Industries/Banking%20and%20Financial%20Services/Anti-Money%20Laundering%20-%20Challenges%20and%20trends.pdf

Tata Consultancy Services. White paper on TCS BaNCS for Compliance – Anti-Money Laundering Solution. 2019. https://www.tcs.com › bancs › banking › compliance. Available at: https://www.tcs.com/content/dam/tcs-bancs/protected-pdf/Compliance.pdf

Ullrich, C. "A Risk-Based Approach towards Infringement Prevention on the Internet: Adopting the Anti-Money Laundering Framework to Online Platforms." *International Journal of Law and Information Technology* 26, no. 3 (2018): 226–251.

Umaru, K. K. "Corruption, Human Dignity, and an Ethic of Responsibility in Nigeria: A Theological-Ethical Inquiry." Unpublished *Ph.D. thesis*, Stellenbosch University, South Africa.

Walker, J., & B. Unger. "Measuring Global Money Laundering: 'The Walker Gravity Model.'" *Review of Law & Economics* 5, no. 2 (2009): 821–853.

9

Novel Cryptographic Hashing Technique for Preserving Integrity in Forensic Samples

S. Pooja[1], **Vikas Sagar**[2], **and Rohit Tanwar**[3]
[1]*GLA University, Mathura, Uttar Pradesh, India*
[2]*NIET, Greater Noida, Uttar Pradesh, India*
[3]*UPES, Dehradun, Uttarakhand, India*

CONTENTS

9.1 Introduction

Cryptography hash functions are the fundamental building blocks for information security and have plenty of security applications to protect the data integrity and authentication such as digital signature schemes, construction of Message authentication codes, and random number generators. Hash functions should follow the basic properties like one-way, second pre-image resistance, collision-resistant, and avalanche effect; and at least these are expected to be preserved. In Figure 9.1, a block diagram of a hash function is depicted.

A recent study shows that MD and SHA family cryptography hash functions are vulnerable to security flaws which leads to the designing of more secure hashing functions. This paper focuses on developing a novel and one-way lightweight and reliable cryptographic hash function that accepts input of arbitrary length and generates a fixed size output and satisfies all the basic properties of a cryptographic hash.

DOI: 10.1201/9781003204862-9

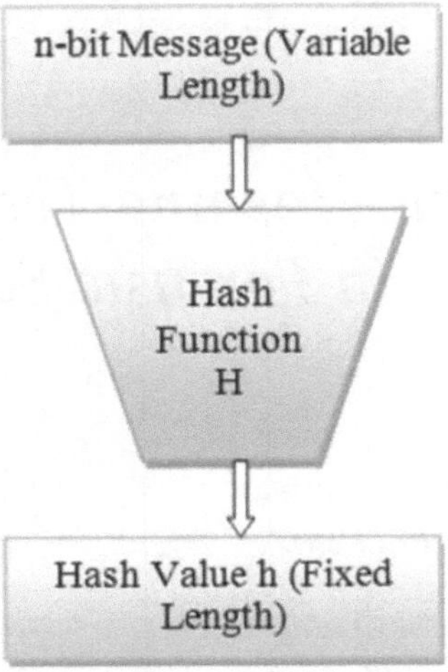

FIGURE 9.1
Block Diagram of Hash Function. (Source: http://pubs.sciepub.com/iteces/3/1/1/figure/7)

9.2 Attacks on Cryptography Hash Functions

Several attacks have been launched by an attacker on the hash functions to break the integrity of a message. The attacks are classified into two major categories and these are as follows:

1. **Brute Force Attack:** It works on all hash functions irrespective of their internal construction and any other functioning. The meaning of Brute force is trying all the possible combinations of keys to launch an attack. *Birthday attack* (Bellare & Kohno, 2004) is the most common example of this attack.
2. **Cryptanalytical Attacks:** It focuses on the structure of hashing function. It is further divided into two categories (Gauravram, 2003): Generic attacks and Specific attacks. Generic attacks work on the general hash function construction and major examples of this type of attack are Length extension attacks, Jouxmulti collision attacks, Herding Attacks, and Meet in the Middle Attacks (Gauravram, 2003). Specific attacks work on the compression function's algorithm and examples of these attacks are differential cryptanalysis, linear cryptanalysis, rotational cryptanalysis, and attacks on the underlying encryption algorithms (Gauravram, 2003).

The rest of the paper is organized as follows. In Section 9.3, a literature survey proposing a new cryptography hash technique is illustrated. In Section 9.4, the problem statement has been discussed. The proposed hashing technique is explained with the implementation and results of the algorithm in Sections 9.5 and 9.6. Finally, in Section 9.7, the conclusion and future directions are discussed.

9.3 Literature Survey

Kuznetsov et al. (2021) did a comparison of hashing techniques and analyzed their performance. They used parameters for comparisons such as number of cycles per byte, hashed message per second, and the hash rate (KHash/s). The purpose of the analysis was to choose the best hash function for designing a decentralized blockchain.

The authors of the paper (Chowdhury et al., 2014) developed a lightweight and one-way cryptography hash, which they named LOCHA. The algorithm was primarily designed in such a way that it is useful for energy-starved wireless networks by consuming low energy in transmission. Their algorithm produced a digest of 96 bits for any length of input string and satisfied all the main properties of hashing, that is, one-way, second pre-image resistance, and collision resistance.

Research in the paper by Arya et al. (2013) proposed a novel hashing scheme that incorporated the usage of the key so that intruders cannot break the hash code without the help of the key. Their algorithm produced a digest of 128 bits for an arbitrary message length. They have divided it into two phases: pre-processing and hash calculation.

After that Abutaha and Hamamreh (2013) designed a one-way hash algorithm that used two steps, that is, they have arranged the input data in a noninvertible matrix by using conversions and generated the initial hash initially. Second, they used the output of the previous step and added a salt value to it, which they have sent to the receiver. They have compared their proposed work with MD5, SHA-1, and SHA-512.

Raouf et al. (2013) gave a Pizer hash technique that was based on two methods, elliptic curve and expander graph. After computing the hash with the help of the Pizer function, they signed a message by ECDSA. They used MATLAB® to simulate their results and proved that their work was collision-resistant.

Mirvaziri et al. (2007) presented a hybrid cryptography hash function that was a combination of SHA-1 and MD5. The compression function used in the proposed hash function was made from the four rounds of encryption function; and each and every round consisted of 20 transformation steps.

Pooja and Chauhan (2020) proposed the Three-Phase Hybrid Cryptographic technique (TPHC) which was the combination of AES, DES, and modified-RSA. In this technique, the authors divided the plain text into three parts and applied these cryptographic algorithms simultaneously which results in less execution time. They also used another parameter to be compared with other existing techniques and that is nodes' energy. After simulation, they observed that nodes' energy after transmission of packets is more as compared to other techniques. They will enhance that algorithm by implementing security attacks on this.

Moe and Win (2017) developed a new honeyword generation technique that stored the users' passwords as honeywords to decrease the typo safety problem, storage overhead, and some other drawbacks which were existing in older honeyword generation methods. They have used a special hashing technique to store the passwords and honeywords in the database which reduced the time complexity of an algorithm.

Rubayya and Resmi (2014) designed a new technique that was based on HMAC/SHA-2. The results were analyzed and compared using various design goals and strategies like Balanced and Area Reduction. They proved that their proposed work utilized less area and consumed less power.

Tiwari and Asawa (2012) developed a dedicated cryptography hash technique called MNF-256 that was based on the concept of NewFork-256. Their design used a three-branch parallel structure and each branch consisted of eight operations. The results and rigorous analysis claimed that proposed work was robust against cryptanalytic attacks and faster than NewFORK-256.

Monadal and Mitra (2016) discussed the Timestamp-defined hash function called TDHA for the secure transmission among vehicles. In this technique, the sender vehicle transmitted deformed messages, an incomplete message digest and receiver vehicle produced a digest from the intermediate digest and distorted form of message. They have simulated their algorithm and compared it with MD5, SHA-1, and LOCHA using comparison metrics like overhead (communication and computation) and storage overhead. Their design outperforms the other techniques both qualitatively and quantitatively.

Chen and Wang (2008) developed an enhanced algorithm that followed the fundamentals of Store-Hash and Rehash for context-triggered piecewise hashing technique (CTPH) also known as FKsum. They have compared it with spamsum and the results proved that the performance and ability of the proposed method are better. The new design was valuable for forensics practice.

Rasjid et al. (2017) surveyed several types of attacks on hash algorithms. They reviewed existing and present methods which are used in digital forensic tools to create an attack. They have compared the common features of MD series and SHA series in terms of output size, number of rounds, collision found, and performance (MiB/s).

9.4 Problem Statement

After surveying the literature on the hash functions, it is observed that most of the algorithms are having more execution time due to their complex behavior and some algorithms have a large digest size. Therefore, in this paper, authors have designed a technique that can be implemented in less amount of time and will produce a small digest size.

9.5 Proposed Work

The hash function consists of two components: the first one is the compression function, a mapping function, used to transform a large input string into a small output; and the second component is construction, a method by which the compression function is being repeatedly called to process a variable-length message.

Flowchart of proposed algorithm is depicted in Figure 9.2.

9.5.1 Design of Proposed Hashing

Step 1. *Padding*: Perform padding in such a way that the length of message after padding is congruent to 448 modulo 512. In padding, the first bit is 1 and the rest of the bits are 0.

Step 2. *Appending*: After padding, append the length of the original message (represented in binary form) to the output of Step 1. After doing this step, the length of the message is now in multiples of 512.

Step 3. *Message into Blocks*: The message obtained from the previous step is divided into n Blocks of size 512 bits. That is

$B0, B1, B2, B3, B4, B5, B6, B7, \ldots\ldots\ldots\ldots Bn$

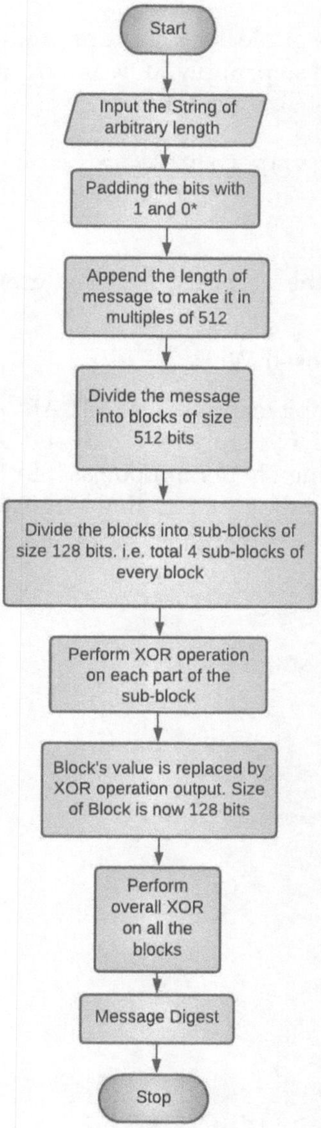

FIGURE 9.2
Flowchart of Proposed Algorithm.

Step 4. *Blocks into Sub-blocks*: Each block that is obtained in previous block is of bigger size. In this step, we have divided the blocks into sub-blocks of size 128 bits. That is

(B01, B02, B03, B04), (B11, B12, B13, B14), (B21, B22, B23, B24),................ (Bn1, Bn2, Bn3, Bn4)

Step 5. *Apply XOR operation*: Next step is to perform XOR among each part of the block and override the block's value with its output. As the size of the sub-block is 128 bits, after performing XOR the overridden block's size is 128 bits. That is

B0 = B01 XOR B02 XOR B03 XOR B04
B1 = B11 XOR B12 XOR B13 XOR B14
B2 = B21 XOR B22 XOR B23 XOR B24............ and so on.

Step 6. *Overall XOR*: The size of blocks which are produced from the previous step is 128 bits. In this final step, apply XOR among all the blocks. This will result in a message digest of size 128 bits.

output = B0 XOR B1 XOR B2 XOR B3

9.5.2 Algorithm

In Figure 9.3, the algorithm of the proposed hashing technique has been shown.

9.5.3 Implementation of Proposed Work

The proposed work has been implemented on MATLAB® and stepwise working of an algorithm has been demonstrated in Figures 9.4, 9.5, and 9.6. Initially, a file of 1 kb was considered which stores the string "helo I am poojas". In Figure 9.4, Steps 1 and 2 ASCII code of the string, padding, appending, and adding length to the string has been displayed.

```
Input: Message of arbitrary length.
Output: Digest of fixed size, i.e., 128 bits.
Begin
    1. Apply padding of 10* bits.
    2. Append length of message (binary form) to the previous step output,
    so that length of final message is in the multiples of 512.
    3. i=0, j=-1
    4. while (i<n) {
    5. j=j+1
    6. Bj=M(i,i+511)
    7. i=i+512}
    8. i=0
    9. while (i ≤ j) {
    10. Bi1=Bi (0,127)
    11. Bi2=Bi (128,255)
    12. Bi3=Bi (256, 383)
    13. Bi4=Bi (384,511)
    14. i= i+1}
    15. i=-1
    16. while (i <j) {
    17. i=i+1
    18. Bi=Bi1 XOR Bi2 XOR Bi3 XOR Bi4}
    19. digest=B0 XOR B1 XOR B2 XOR ........... Bj
End
```

FIGURE 9.3
Algorithm of Proposed Hash.

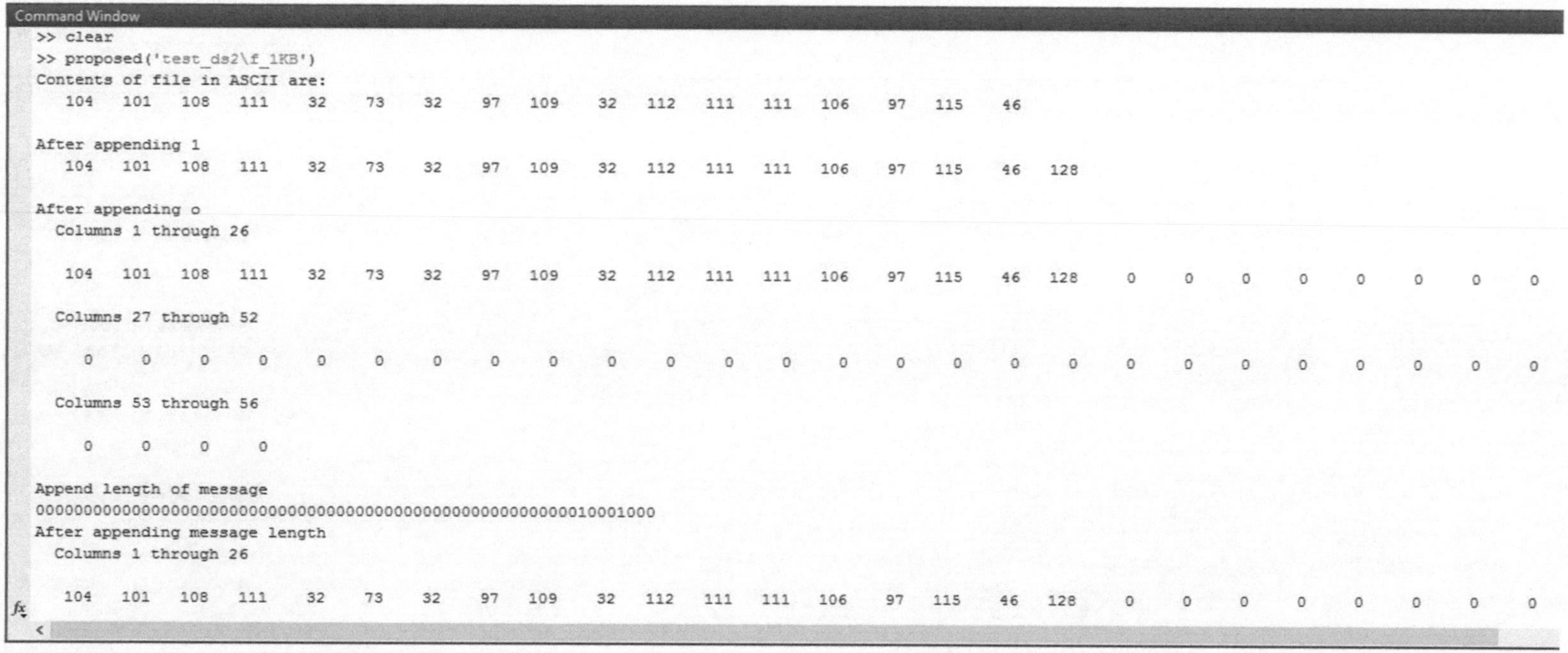

```
Command Window
>> clear
>> proposed('test_ds2\f_1KB')
Contents of file in ASCII are:
   104   101   108   111    32    73    32    97   109    32   112   111   111   106    97   115    46

After appending 1
   104   101   108   111    32    73    32    97   109    32   112   111   111   106    97   115    46   128

After appending o
  Columns 1 through 26

   104   101   108   111    32    73    32    97   109    32   112   111   111   106    97   115    46   128     0     0     0     0     0     0     0     0

  Columns 27 through 52

     0     0     0     0     0     0     0     0     0     0     0     0     0     0     0     0     0     0     0     0     0     0     0     0     0     0

  Columns 53 through 56

     0     0     0     0

Append length of message
0000000000000000000000000000000000000000000000000000000010001000
After appending message length
  Columns 1 through 26

   104   101   108   111    32    73    32    97   109    32   112   111   111   106    97   115    46   128     0     0     0     0     0     0     0     0
```

FIGURE 9.4
Steps 1 and 2 of Proposed Hashing.

```
Command Window
  Columns 1 through 26

   104   101   108   111    32    73    32    97   109    32   112   111   111   106    97   115    46   128     0     0     0     0     0     0     0     0

  Columns 27 through 52

     0     0     0     0     0     0     0     0     0     0     0     0     0     0     0     0     0     0     0     0     0     0     0     0     0     0

  Columns 53 through 64

     0     0     0     0     0     0     0     0     0     0     0   136

The number of Blocks formed are:
     1

After making Blocks of size 512 bits
  Columns 1 through 26

   104   101   108   111    32    73    32    97   109    32   112   111   111   106    97   115    46   128     0     0     0     0     0     0     0     0

  Columns 27 through 52

     0     0     0     0     0     0     0     0     0     0     0     0     0     0     0     0     0     0     0     0     0     0     0     0     0     0

  Columns 53 through 64

     0     0     0     0     0     0     0     0     0     0     0   136

fx
```

FIGURE 9.5
Step 3 of Proposed Hashing.

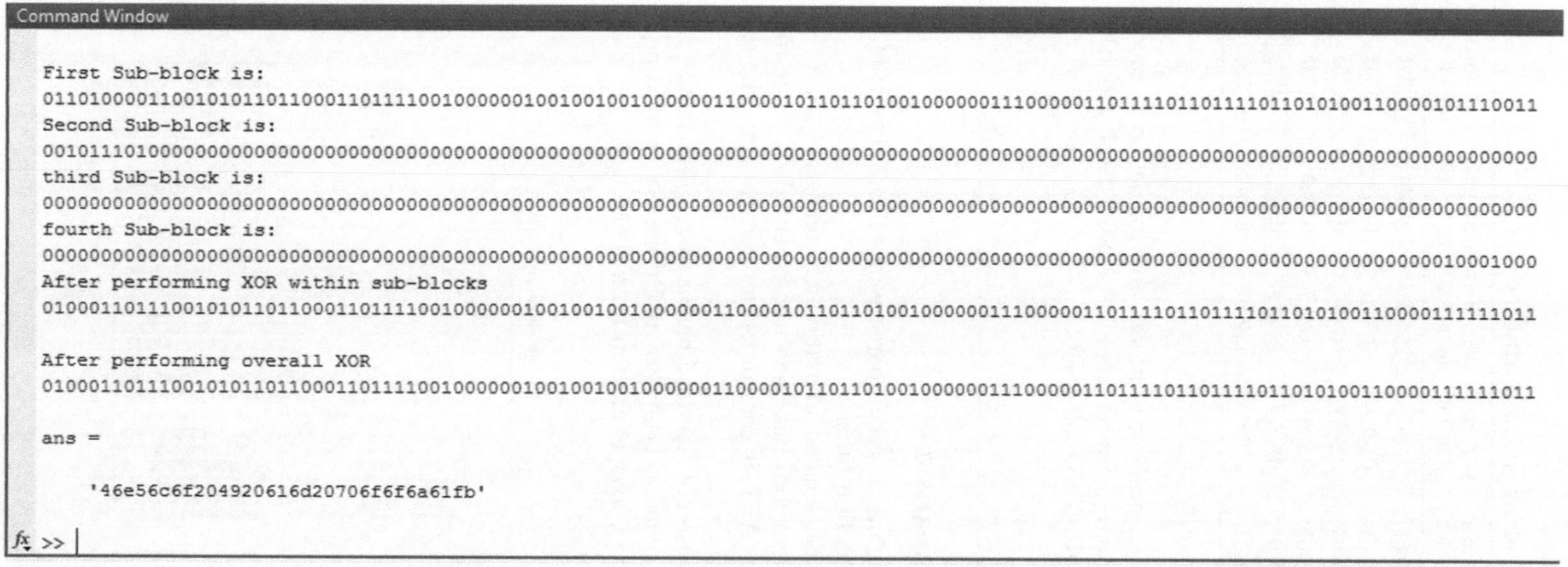

FIGURE 9.6
Final Step of Proposed Hashing.

TABLE 9.1

Comparison of Proposed Hashing with Standard Hashing

Parameters	AET (ms) of 10 KB	AET (ms) of 20 KB	AET (ms) of 30 KB	AET (ms) of 40 KB	AET (ms) of 50 KB	AET (ms) of 60 KB	AET (ms) of 70 KB	AET (ms) of 80 KB
MD5	0.1922	0.3901	0.5781	0.7655	0.9564	1.1561	1.3437	1.5343
SHA-1	0.1888	0.3906	0.5780	0.7656	0.9624	1.1562	1.3437	1.5311
SHA-256	0.1888	0.3906	0.5780	0.7656	0.9655	1.1500	1.3407	1.5326
SHA-384	0.1887	0.3905	0.5780	0.7655	0.9593	1.1562	1.3437	1.5311
SHA-512	0.1895	0.3905	0.5753	0.7651	0.9627	1.1528	1.3438	1.5312
Proposed	0.1211	0.2451	0.3715	0.4913	0.6042	0.7200	0.8249	0.9542

In Figure 9.5, Step 3, i.e., number of blocks and formation of blocks of the string has been shown. In Figure 9.6, remaining steps have been displayed. The hash value of the string is 46e56c6f204920616d20706f6f6a61fb.

9.6 Results and Comparisons

The proposed hashing technique is compared with MD5, SHA-1, SHA-256, SHA-384, and SHA-512 in terms of execution time.

Dataset of eight files has been considered which consists of 10, 20, 30, 40, 50, 60, 70, and 80 KB files. Proposed algorithm has been implemented on these files individually and Average Execution Time (AET) is considered for comparison. The results of comparison have been shown in Table 9.1.

In Figure 9.7, a comparison of standard hashing algorithms and proposed algorithm in terms of their execution time has been shown. On the x-axis, hashing techniques with file size are displayed and on y-axis, execution time is given.

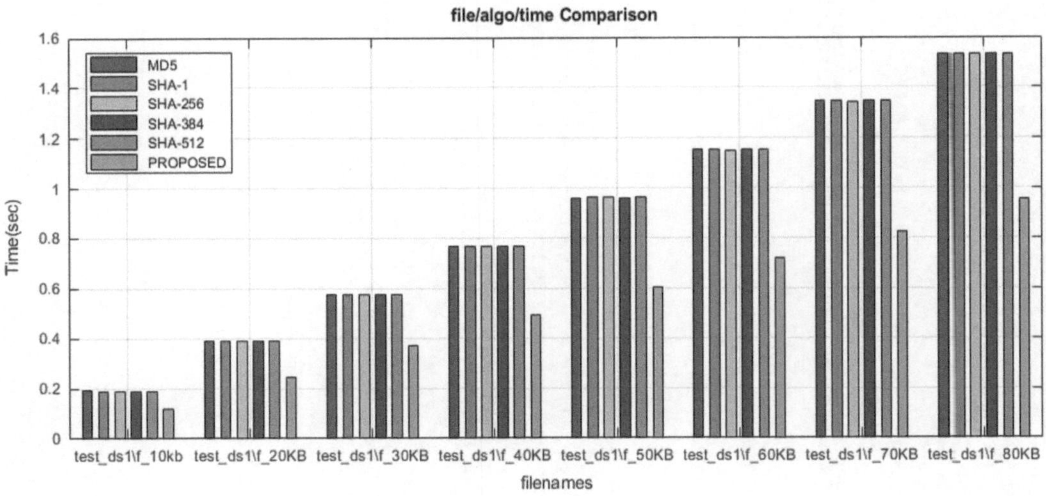

FIGURE 9.7
Comparison of Execution Time of Hashing Algorithms.

9.7 Conclusion and Future Scope

The present hashing algorithms for calculating message digests are time consuming. In this paper, a new hashing technique has been proposed which uses blocks subgrouping and XOR operation in a unique way to implement an algorithm very fast. It uses very simple mathematical operations that increase the speed of computation of message digest. Therefore, proposed hashing technique is simpler and lightweight than the existing ones.

Though the proposed algorithm satisfies the basic properties of hashing, we are trying to modify the proposed algorithm in the future so that it will be resistant to security attacks.

References

Abutaha, M., & Hamamreh, R. (2013). New One Way Hash Algorithm Using Non-invertible Matrix. In 2013 *International Conference on Computer Medical Applications (ICCMA)*, pp. 1–5.

Arya, R. P., Mishra, U., & Bansal, A. (2013). Design and Analysis of a New Hash Algorithm with Key Integration. *International Journal of Computer Applications*, 81, pp. 33–38.

Bellare, M., & Kohno, T. (2004). Hash Function Balance and Its Impact on Birthday Attacks. Advances in Cryptology -*EUROCRYPT*, 3027, pp. 401–418.

Chen, L., & Wang, G. (2008). An Efficient Piecewise Hashing Method for Computer Forensics. In *2008 Workshop on Knowledge Discovery and Data Mining*, pp. 635–638.

Chowdhury, A. R., Chatterjee, T., & DasBit, S. (2014). Locha: A Light-Weight One-Way Cryptographic Hash Algorithm for Wireless Sensor Network. *The 5th International Conference on Ambient Systems, Networks and Technologies, Procedia Computer Science*, 32, pp. 497–504.

Gauravram, P. (2003). Cryptographic Hash Functions: Cryptanalysis, Design and Applications. *Ph.D. thesis*, Faculty of Information Technology, Queensland University of Technology, Brisbane, Australia.

Kuznetsov, A., Oleshko, I., Tymchenko, V., Lisitsky, K., Rodinko, M., & Kolhatin, A. (2021). Performance Analysis of Cryptographic Hash Functions Suitable for Use in Blockchain. *International Journal of Computer Network and Information Security*, 2021, 2, pp. 1–15, doi: 10. 5815/ijcnis.2021.02.01.

Mirvaziri, H., Jumari, K., Ismail, M., & Hanapi, Z. M. (2007). A New Hash Function Based on Combination of Existing Digest Algorithms. In *2007 5th Student Conference on Research and Development*, pp. 1–6.

Moe, K. S. M., & Win, T. (2017). Improved Hashing and Honey-Based Stronger Password Prevention Against Brute Force Attack. In *2017International Symposium on Electronics and Smart Devices (ISESD)*, pp. 1–5.

Monadal, A., & Mitra, S. (2016). TDHA: A Timestamp Defined Hash Algorithm for Secure Data Dissemination in Vanet. *International Congress on Computational Modeling and Security, Procedia Computer Science*, 85, pp. 190–197.

Pooja & Chauhan, R. K. (2020). Triple Phase Hybrid Cryptography Technique in a Wireless Sensor Network. *International Journal of Computers and Applications*, doi: 10.1080/1206212X.2019. 1710342.

Raouf, D. M. O., Ramzi, H., & Mtibaa, A. (2013). Hash Function and Digital Signature Based on Elliptic Curve. In 14th *International Conference on Sciences and Techniques of Automatic Control Computer Engineering - STA'2013*, pp. 388–392.

Rasjid, Z. E., Soewito, B., Witjaksono, G., & Abdurachman, E. (2017). A Review of Collisions in Cryptographic Hash Function Used in Digital Forensic Tools. *2nd International Conference on Computer Science and Computational Intelligence*, 116, pp. 381–392.

Rubayya, R. S., & Resmi, R. (2014). Memory Optimization of hmac/sha-2 Encryption. In 2014 *First International Conference on Computational Systems and Communications (ICCSC)*, pp. 282–287.

Tiwari, H., & Asawa, K. (2012). A Secure and Efficient Cryptographic Hash Function Based on Newfork-256. *Egyptian Informatics Journal*, 13, 3, pp. 199–208.

10

Memory Acquisition and Analysis for Forensic Investigation

Tripti Misra, Vanshika Singh, and Tanisha Singla
University of Petroleum and Energy Studies,
Dehradun, Uttrakhand, India

CONTENTS

10.1 Introduction

The main aim of digital forensics is to investigate digital evidence present inside the storage devices. Conventional digital forensics methods are more focused on dead storage analysis, i.e., profoundly investigating the nonvolatile portion of the memory. These approaches work by first powering off the system at the scene of the crime and then performing a detailed investigation by imaging or cloning the hard drive of the seized system. Nevertheless, these methods have some shortcomings. The powering off the systems could lead to the loss of data present in the volatile memory. Moreover, in the contemporary scenario, digital attackers and criminals have turned out to be so inventive in committing crimes that they have begun discovering techniques to conceal information inside the RAM (Random Access Memory). With the increase of cybercrimes, live memory investigation has become a prerequisite for digital forensics because individuals especially the attackers have

DOI: 10.1201/9781003204862-10

started hiding the footprints inside the volatile memory in place of a storage device. Hence, to recover more important data the digital investigator needs to inspect the volatile memory. The collection of volatile data from the memory may help in determining any illegal activity that may vanish once the system is shut down. It might as well show a malware residing in the memory, which could remain undetected by an investigator. By performing live forensics (Hay et al., 2009), long months of wait can be avoided for a comprehensive exploration. Volatile memory, also known as RAM consists of a lot of useful information such as:

- Passwords used for encryption
- Indicators of anti-forensics usage
- Host-based indicators
- Network indicators
- Logged-on users

This art of investigating the live or volatile memory is called memory forensics. Memory forensics is a division of advanced legal sciences that for the most part underscores separating antiquities from the volatile memory of a compromised system. There are several tools available in the market for performing memory forensics. Some tools assist in memory acquisition and certain facilitate memory analysis. The FTK Imager helps to capture the live RAM, however, not supports the analysis of the captured memory dump. It stores the memory dump which later can be analyzed using some memory analysis tool. The Volatility Framework (2021) is one such command-line memory forensics tool that works on both, Windows and Linux frameworks. Volatility Workbench (2021) is a GUI form of one of a similar instrument Volatility for investigating the relics from a memory dump. It is accessibly liberated from cost, open-source, and runs on the Windows Operating System.

10.2 Memory Forensics

Memory Forensics is one of the promising areas in Digital Forensics Investigation, which comprises recovering, extracting, and analyzing evidence such as images, documents, chat histories, etc. from the structured volatile memory into nonvolatile devices such as hard drives or USB drives. The process is depicted in Figure 10.1.

Memory forensics has checked among the most extreme adaptable and mighty strategies to analyze systems (Case & Richard, 2017). It has come to be every day an incident reaction technique notwithstanding the riding tension toward the rear of proactive

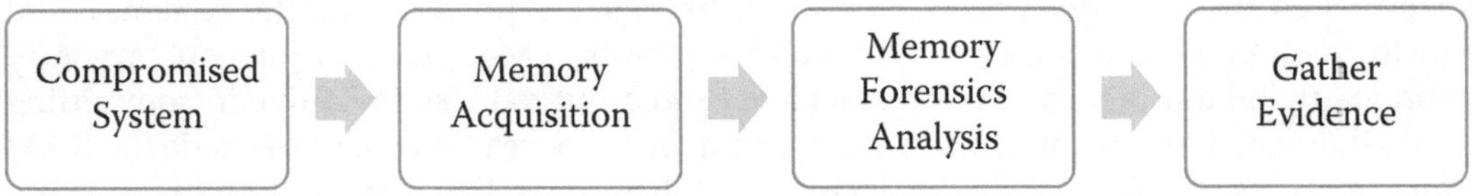

FIGURE 10.1
Memory Forensics Process.

assessment of conditions for noxious action. The cap potential to gather unstable memory in a solid means is the essence of memory forensics. Significantly, techniques of memory forensics can show a decent measured level of unpredictable proof that may be totally gone if customary "pull the plug" forensic strategies had been resulted. Memory forensics was ordinarily utilized in malware examination or in incident reaction while malware or predominant assailants had been available. This has rapidly adjusted over the past various years as examiners have discovered the expense of memory forensics sooner or later in a wide range of examinations. This comprises examinations zeroed in on maverick insiders, hostile to scientific applications, and eventually, common and hooligan claims concerning advanced gadgets. With a ton of those cases, memory crime scene investigation systems are equipped for improving the information that isn't constantly found in network or disk forensics.

Volatile memory stays for an exceptionally brief interval and this is the reason it is in every case difficult to break down such memory (Chaudhuri, 2019). It consists a lot of helpful data such as passwords, usernames, running cycles, and so on. Obtaining, breaking down, and analyzing are the three significant stages for memory forensics. Analyses are carried out using various instruments to comprehend the methodology of obtaining, examining, and recovering significant confirmations. A large portion of the devices function as uninvolved specialists that are passed on to the caution of the examiner to break down the confirmations gathered through various devices. The devices can be improved by consolidating them with AI methods. This paper additionally talks about the upgrades that should be possible in making the working of the instruments simpler and giving better outcomes.

Meera and Swamynathan (2013) incorporates challenges going up against current strategies amid gathering polymorphic computer worms in disseminated computing. A high-intelligent twofold honeypot has been proposed to address the recognized challenges. The proposed approach surveys VMs (Thangavel et al., 2021) from the exterior to recognize stowed absent cycles and to dodge recognizable proof by worms. In future scope, the paper proposed to look at how to reduce the hour of exploring VM memory and how to decrease the number of honeypots required to survey virtual organizations. Additionally, it'll propose to extend our approach to look at arrange activity adjoining to the memory and archive framework.

10.3 Memory Acquisition

Live memory acquisition is a strategy utilized to gather information when the system is discovered in a running state at the location of the crime. Live acquisition focuses on the data that might be lost from the memory, on shutting down a system, and centers on gathering such data while the system is yet running. The other target of live memory acquisition is to limit the effects on the trustworthiness of the information while gathering evidence from the suspect system. Live memory acquisition is a technique for extricating forensically strong proof from a "live" system. As per the conventional crime scene investigation procedure, a plug is forcefully pulled to turn off the system, when the system is in the running mode. However, in live crime scene investigation, prior to pulling the cord, data like subtleties in memory, running processes, network connections, and so forth is gathered from a running system that might be lost because of shut down.

10.3.1 Significance of Memory Acquisition

Live memory acquisition is a technique, which supports the removal of "live" system information prior to pulling the cable to save memory, cycle, and network data that would be lost with conventional forensic methodology. Data on a system have an order of volatility. Live Acquisition centers around the removal and assessment of the volatile legal information that would be lost on power off. Information from the swap space, memory, network cycles, and running frameworks is the most volatile in nature and is bound to get lost on a system reboot. The objective of live acquisition is to concentrate and safeguard the volatile information residing on a system while, to the degree conceivable, in any case sustaining the status of the system.

A huge amount of volatile data is lost, when shutting down a system. Along these lines, live memory acquisition is a significant piece of digital forensic investigations. These data will not be accessible for additional investigation, despite the fact that it might contain significant hints with respect to the occurrence, and there is now and then no alternate method to acquire it other than gathering it while the system is still in running state.

For memory forensics, first physical memory has to be acquired from the running/live system. For this, there are different memory dumping programs available such as FTK Imager, DumpIt, etc. Once the memory dump is collected, it can be analyzed to find crucial information available in the memory. The following information can be collected and then analyzed from RAM Dump:

- Running processes
- Network connections and details
- Login information of users
- Settings of firewall
- Different passwords and encryption keys, and much more

10.3.2 Case Scenario

An employee of an organization received a phishing mail from his bank. He unknowingly clicked on the link in the mail, which downloaded a ransomware. All his files and documents on WindowsXP ServicePack2 were encrypted. In addition, to decrypt those files he was being asked to pay a huge amount in bitcoin. Here, in this chapter, an investigation will take place to identify what exactly happened and how.

10.3.3 Tools for Memory Acquisition

A few tools out there are able to acquire an image/dump of the memory (RAM). Some of these tools are as follows:

1. AccessData FTK Imager
2. Belkasoft RAM Capturer

3. FireEye Memoryze
4. Zeltser DumpIt

10.3.4 Memory Acquisition Steps Using FTK Imager

FTK Imager (FTK Imager Tool, 2021) is a Windows acquisition tool and it can be downloaded directly from AccessData website free of cost. The version used here is FTK Imager 3.4.2.6.

Run FTK Imager.exe to start the tool. We will get the AccessDataFTK Imager window (Figure 10.2).

10.3.4.1 Steps to Collect RAM (Memory Dump) from a Live System

1. **Windows XP Service Pack 2:** Operating System is utilized here for memory acquisition. Capture RAM Dump, i.e., Volatile Memory: Click on File menu and then click on Capture Memory (Figure 10.3).
2. The memory Capture window will be displayed (Figure 10.4).
   The browse button needs to be clicked in order to choose a location, where RAM Dump will be stored.
   Note: Make sure an external storage media such as a pen drive, external hard drive, etc. is always chosen to store any evidence file.
3. Name the Memory Dump file. By default, file name will be memdump.mem. It can be changed as per the requirement. If the backup of Page file is required, check on Include Page file Box. Click on Capture Memory, to start capturing. Memory capture process will begin as illustrated in Figure 10.5.

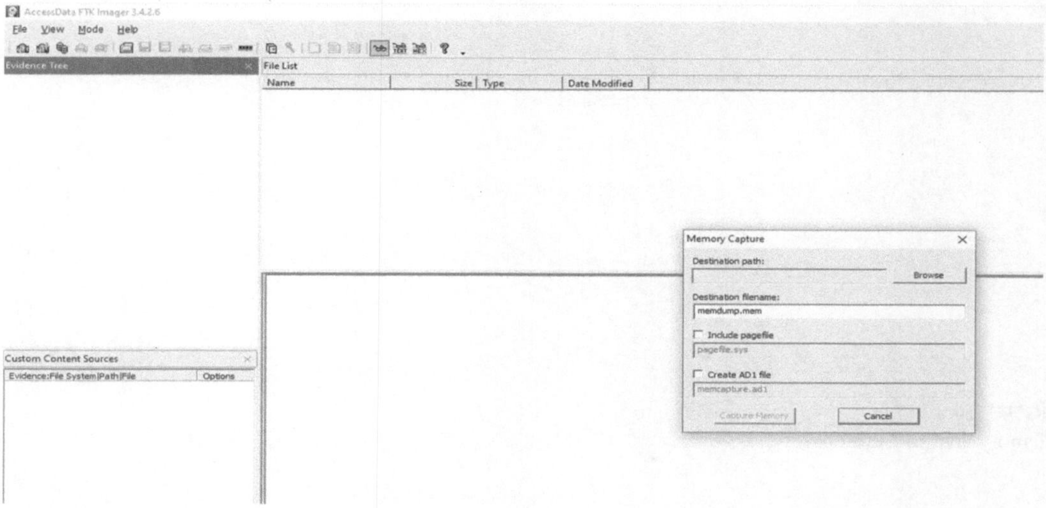

FIGURE 10.2
AccessData FTK Imager 3.4.2.6 Window.

FIGURE 10.3
Capture Memory Snapshot.

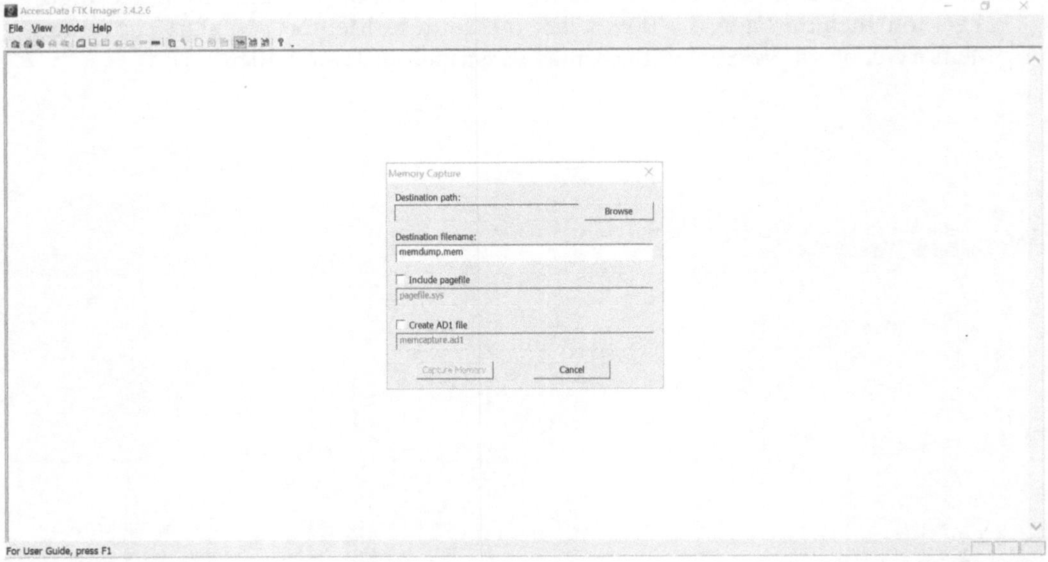

FIGURE 10.4
Memory Capture Window.

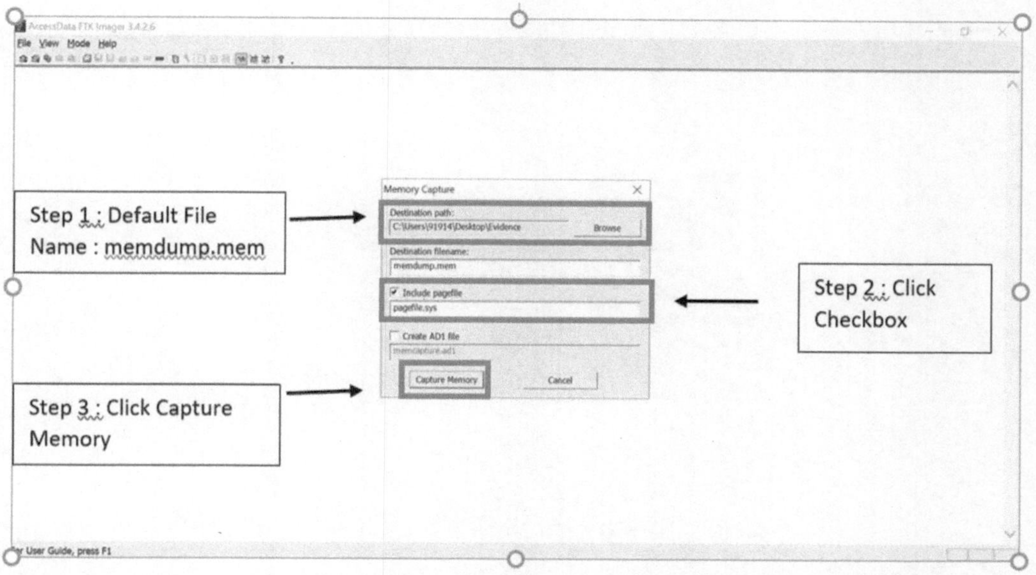

FIGURE 10.5
Naming and Capturing Memory Dump.

Total memory installed in the system can be found by looking at this window. Here, the total memory visible is 10 GB (Figure 10.6).

4. After waiting for some time, memory and page file capturing will be finished as visible in the images below (Figures 10.7–10.9).

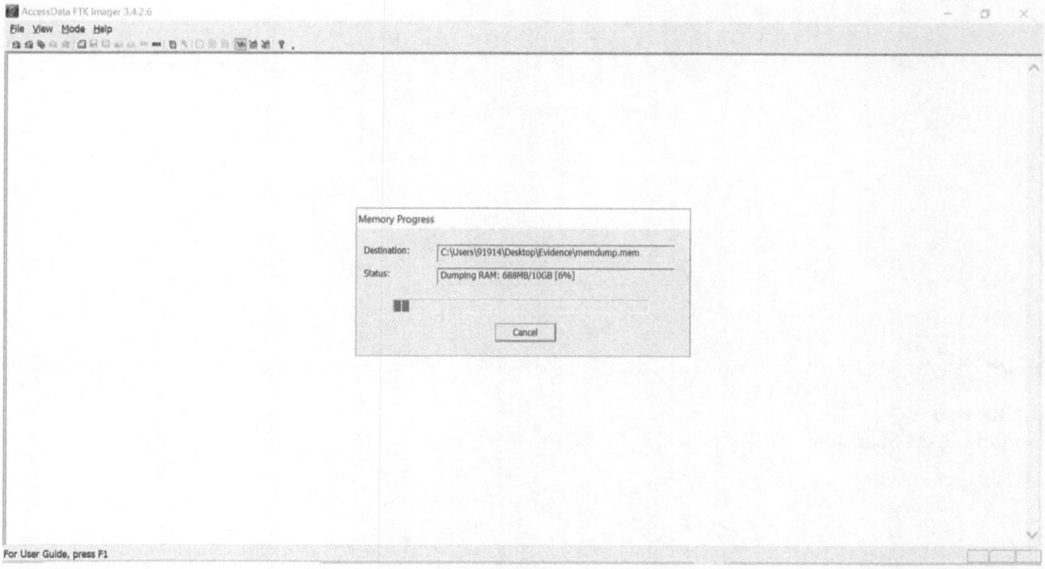

FIGURE 10.6
Memory Progress Snapshot.

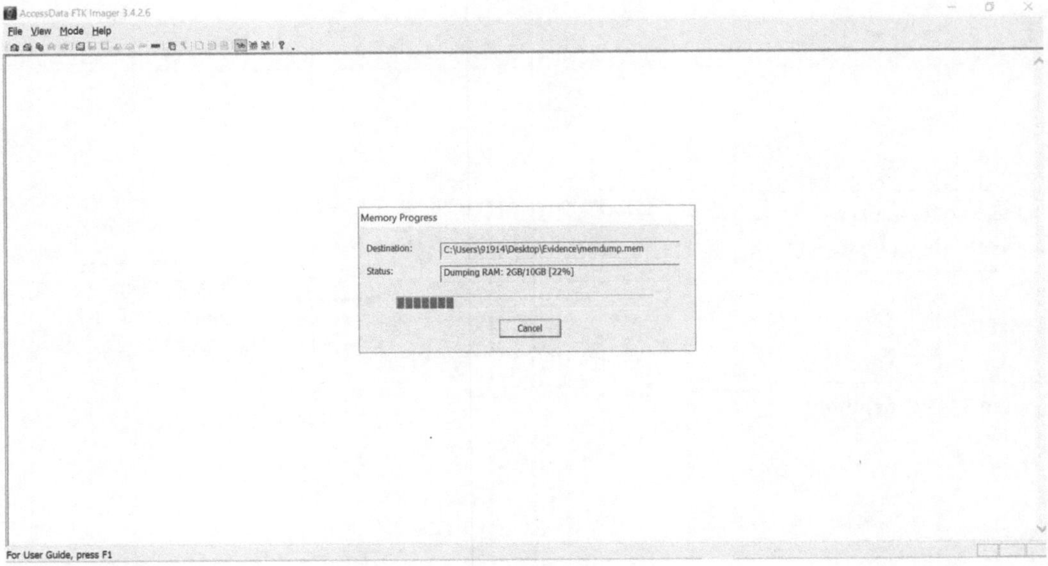

FIGURE 10.7
RAM Capture Progress Snapshot.

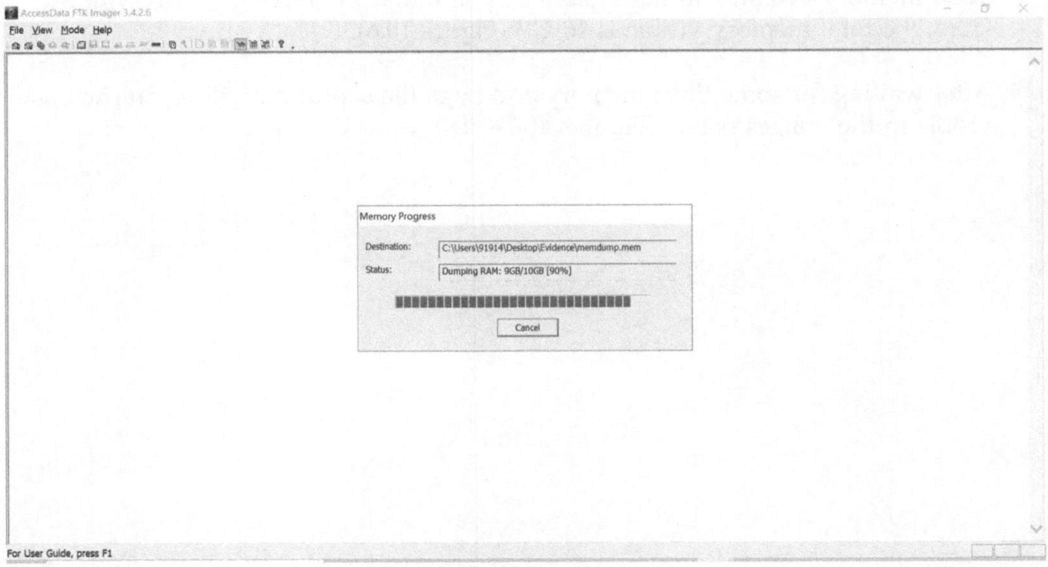

FIGURE 10.8
Dumping RAM Snapshot.

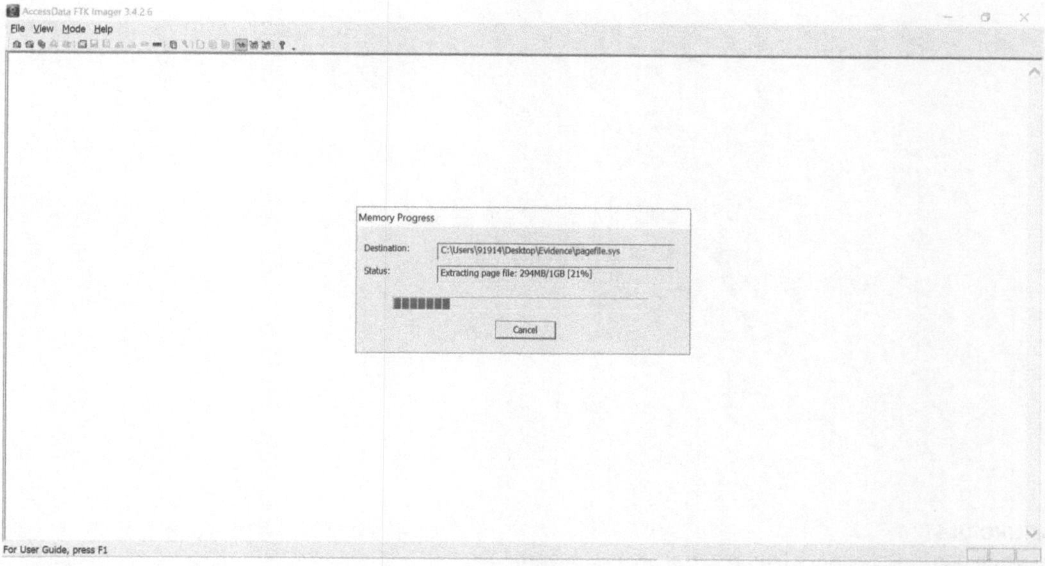

FIGURE 10.9
Extracting Page File Snapshot.

5. Click on close button after the memory capture is finished successfully (Figure 10.10).
6. Browse to the location where memdump.mem file is saved and memory analysis may start (Figure 10.11).

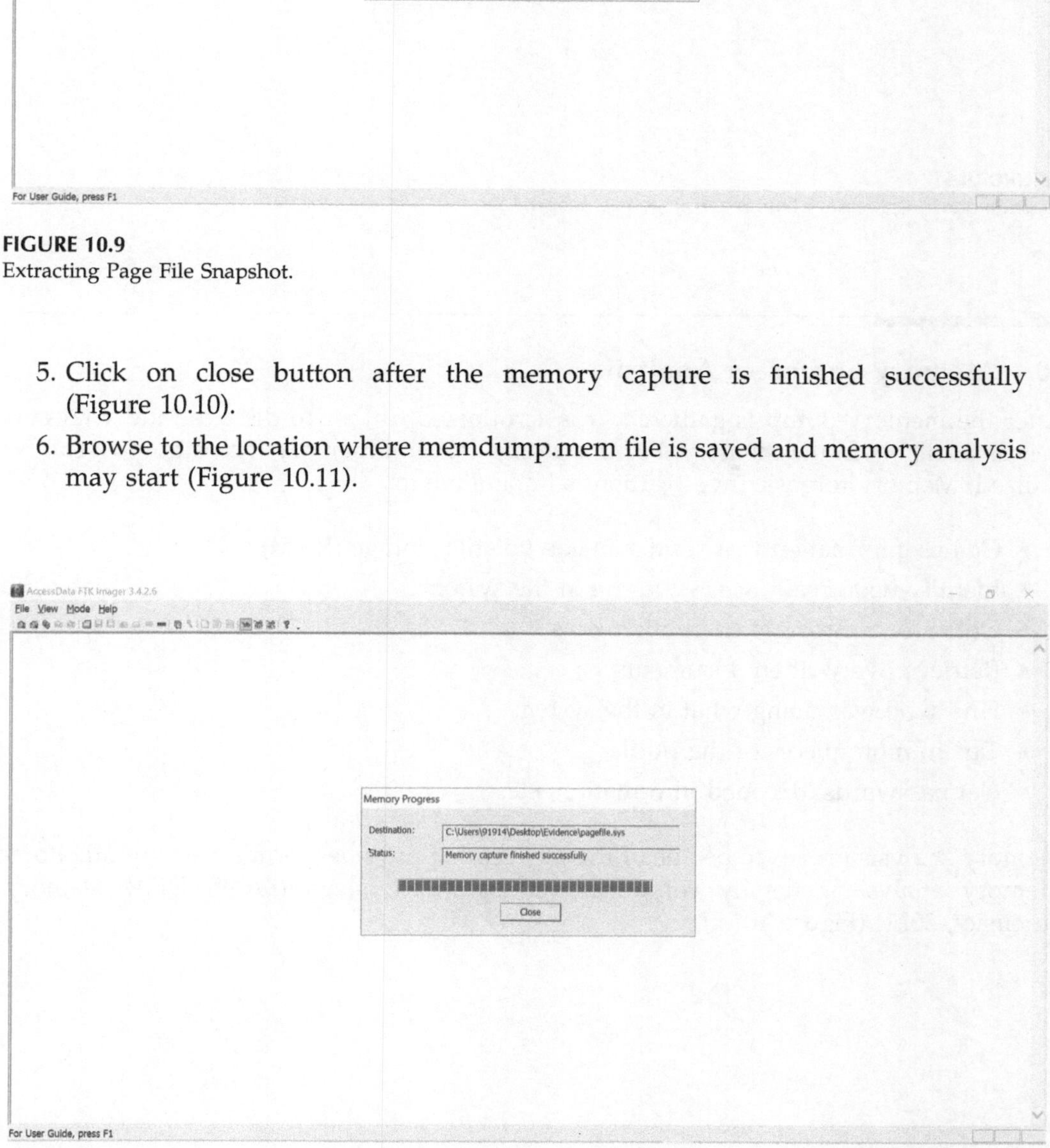

FIGURE 10.10
Memory Capture Finished.

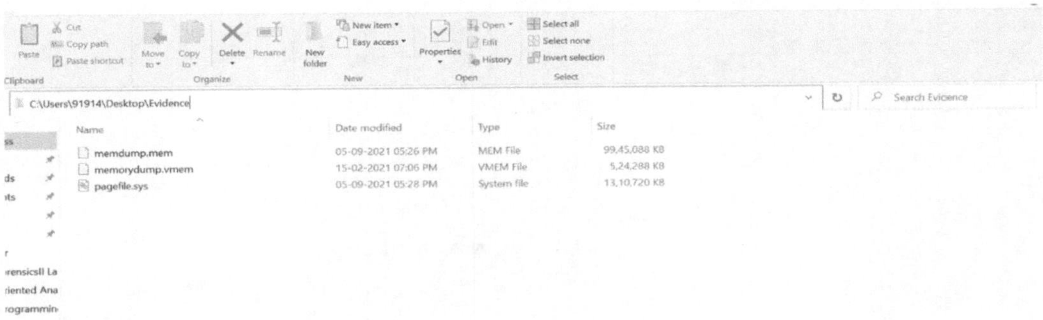

FIGURE 10.11
Location Showing Memory Dump and Page File Snapshot.

10.4 Memory Forensics Analysis

After the memory dump is gathered, it is scrutinized further to discover and vital evidences available in the memory. For this reason, several memory forensics tools can be utilized. Memory forensic investigation is imperative to

- Gather information that resides inside volatile storage (RAM)
- Identify what really was going on in the system
- Obtain or recuperate encryption keys
- Retrieve overwritten documents
- Find who was doing what in the system
- Obtain more pieces of the riddle
- Get passwords, decoded information, etc.

Memory analysis proves to be one of the powerful approaches for forensic investigators. Memory analysis generally comprises six significant steps (SANS DFIR Memory Forensics, 2021) (Figure 10.12).

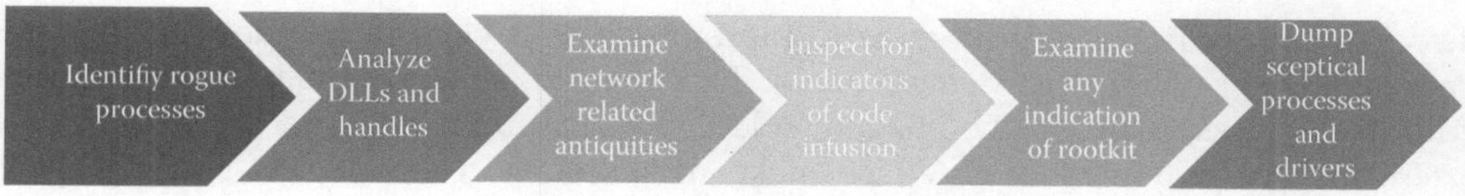

FIGURE 10.12
Six-Step Investigative Methodology by SANS.

Several memory analysis programs such as memorize, volatility framework, etc. are available that will help in extracting all the above necessary information available in the memory and thereafter prepare a final report with the gathered evidence. Here, *Volatility Framework* and *Volatility Workbench* tools have been demonstrated for memory forensic analysis. These tools help in uncovering answers to several questions like:

1. Identification of processes that were running on the suspect system at the time memory dump was taken.
2. Collection of artifacts associated with previous running processes.
3. Identification of any active or previous network connections.
4. Searching any suspicious files associated with a process.
5. Determining the purpose and intent of the suspicious files.
6. Extracting the suspicious files.
7. Examining the presence of any suspicious DLL modules.
8. Looking for any suspicious URLs or IP addresses, strings associated with a process.

10.4.1 Tools for Memory Analysis

Numerous tools are available that facilitate memory analysis after the memory dump has been captured. Some of them are as follows:

1. The Volatility Framework
2. The Volatility Workbench
3. Belkasoft Evidence Center
4. wxHexEditor
5. Autopsy

In this chapter, the memory analysis of the captured memory dump is performed using the Volatility Framework and the Volatility Workbench. Both these tools have been discussed in detail.

10.4.2 Volatility Framework

Volatility is an open-source tool written in python, which is a utility framework of artifact extraction of volatile memory. It is one of the most popular tools to analyze the data found in the volatile memory of the system. For an image of memory, volatility can remove running cycles, open organization attachments, memory maps for each interaction, or kernel modules. It processes memory dumps in various formats that are used to discover and extricate Indicators of Compromise (IoC). Here, a WindowsXP Service Pack2 memory dump is demonstrated for memory analysis named as memorydump.vmem as visible in the images. Volatility has a public API and accompanies an extendable module framework which makes it simple to compose new code, support more working frameworks, and add support for extricating extra ancient artifacts. Below mentioned steps are followed for memory analysis using the Volatility Framework (Memory Forensics using Volatility Framework, 2021):

Step 1: Identify System Profile

A profile incorporates information about explicit operating systems, their hardware configuration and versions. It includes metadata pertaining to operating systems.

1. **imageinfo:** At the point when a memory dump is taken, this plugin helps in knowing the information pertaining to the operating system being used. Volatility tries to examine the image and give recommendations for connected profiles having the particular memory dump. Date and Time of the given file that was acquired, the quantity of current CPUs, and so on, is displayed under this plugin (Figures 10.13 and 10.14).
2. **kdbgscan:** It is significant to get the right profile for memory examination. For this purpose, this command examines and discovers the profiles depending upon Kernel's Debugger Data Block. This plugin provides the right profile identified with the raw image (Figures 10.15 and 10.16).

FIGURE 10.13
Imageinfo Plugin.

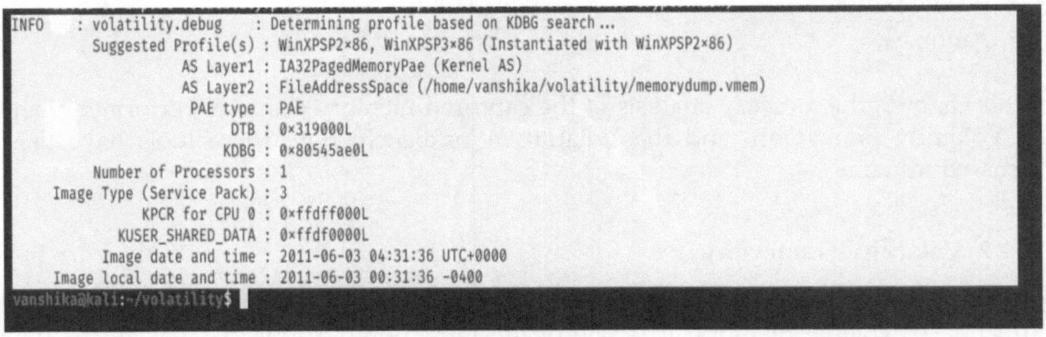

FIGURE 10.14
Imageinfo Plugin Result.

FIGURE 10.15
Kdbgscan Plugin.

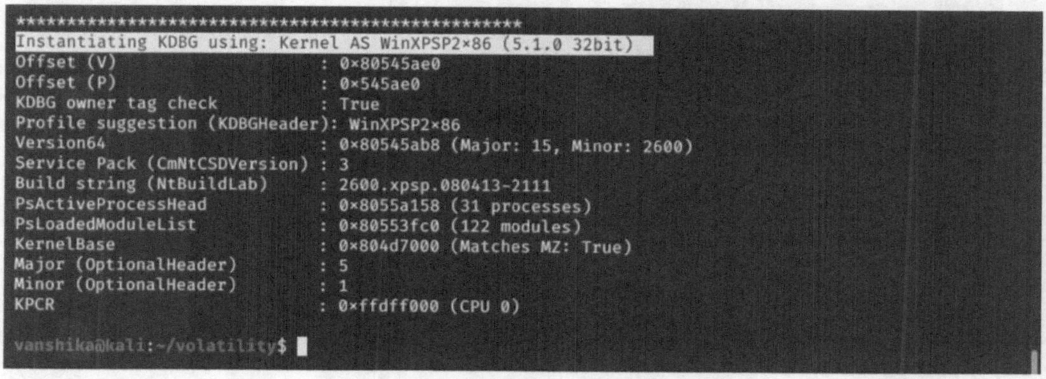

FIGURE 10.16
Kdbgscan Plugin Result.

Step 2: Identify Rogue Processes

3. **pslist:** This command lists down all the running processes in a system and recognizes the presence of any rogue processes. PIDs are allocated to them along with the parent's PID and the process name gets visible. The insights concerning the threads, handles, time period are additionally referenced. The beginning denoted by timestamp of the process is moreover shown. Recognition of this assists whether at current time or a while ago the process is running or not. No information about the concealed process or the processes that ended previously is revealed (Figures 10.17 and 10.18).
4. **psscan:** This command can be utilized to give a comprehensive list of processes found in the memory dump. On executing this plugin, running processes gets displayed along with its designated PID and parent's PID. The insights concerning the strings, sessions, handles are additionally referenced. Process creation and exit time are additionally shown. It serves to recognize either an obscure interaction is currently running or it was there running at an uncommon time (Figures 10.19 and 10.20).

FIGURE 10.17
Pslist Command.

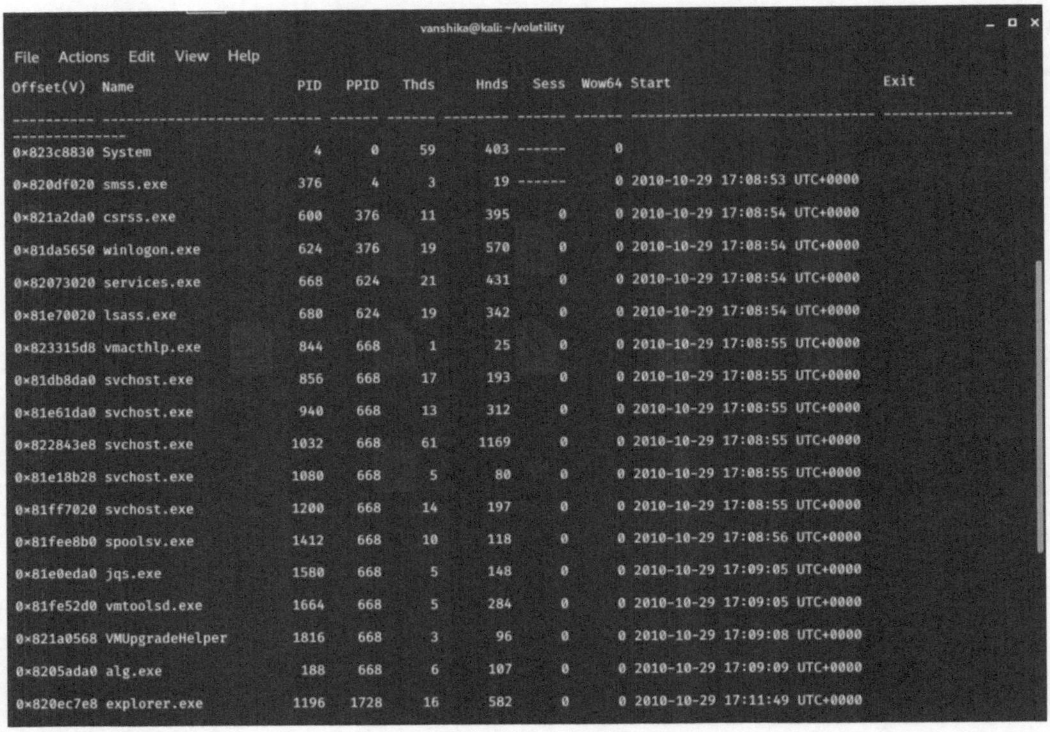

Offset(V)	Name	PID	PPID	Thds	Hnds	Sess	Wow64	Start	Exit
0×823c8830	System	4	0	59	403	------	0		
0×820df020	smss.exe	376	4	3	19	------	0	2010-10-29 17:08:53 UTC+0000	
0×821a2da0	csrss.exe	600	376	11	395	0	0	2010-10-29 17:08:54 UTC+0000	
0×81da5650	winlogon.exe	624	376	19	570	0	0	2010-10-29 17:08:54 UTC+0000	
0×82073020	services.exe	668	624	21	431	0	0	2010-10-29 17:08:54 UTC+0000	
0×81e70020	lsass.exe	680	624	19	342	0	0	2010-10-29 17:08:54 UTC+0000	
0×823315d8	vmacthlp.exe	844	668	1	25	0	0	2010-10-29 17:08:55 UTC+0000	
0×81db8da0	svchost.exe	856	668	17	193	0	0	2010-10-29 17:08:55 UTC+0000	
0×81e61da0	svchost.exe	940	668	13	312	0	0	2010-10-29 17:08:55 UTC+0000	
0×822843e8	svchost.exe	1032	668	61	1169	0	0	2010-10-29 17:08:55 UTC+0000	
0×81e18b28	svchost.exe	1080	668	5	80	0	0	2010-10-29 17:08:55 UTC+0000	
0×81ff7020	svchost.exe	1200	668	14	197	0	0	2010-10-29 17:08:55 UTC+0000	
0×81fee8b0	spoolsv.exe	1412	668	10	118	0	0	2010-10-29 17:08:56 UTC+0000	
0×81e0eda0	jqs.exe	1580	668	5	148	0	0	2010-10-29 17:09:05 UTC+0000	
0×81fe52d0	vmtoolsd.exe	1664	668	5	284	0	0	2010-10-29 17:09:05 UTC+0000	
0×821a0568	VMUpgradeHelper	1816	668	3	96	0	0	2010-10-29 17:09:08 UTC+0000	
0×8205ada0	alg.exe	188	668	6	107	0	0	2010-10-29 17:09:09 UTC+0000	
0×820ec7e8	explorer.exe	1196	1728	16	582	0	0	2010-10-29 17:11:49 UTC+0000	

FIGURE 10.18
Pslist Command Result.

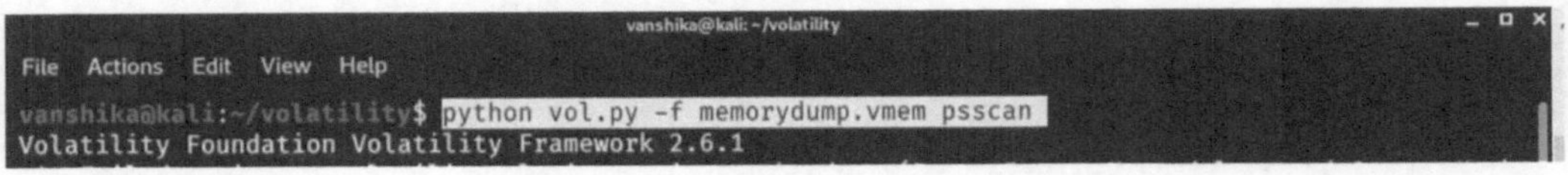

FIGURE 10.19
Psscan Command.

5. **pstree:** On execution of this command, the process names are listed with an inherited relationship, and obscure or abnormal processes are also displayed. The process of child is represented by indention and time intervals (duration) (Figures 10.21 and 10.22).

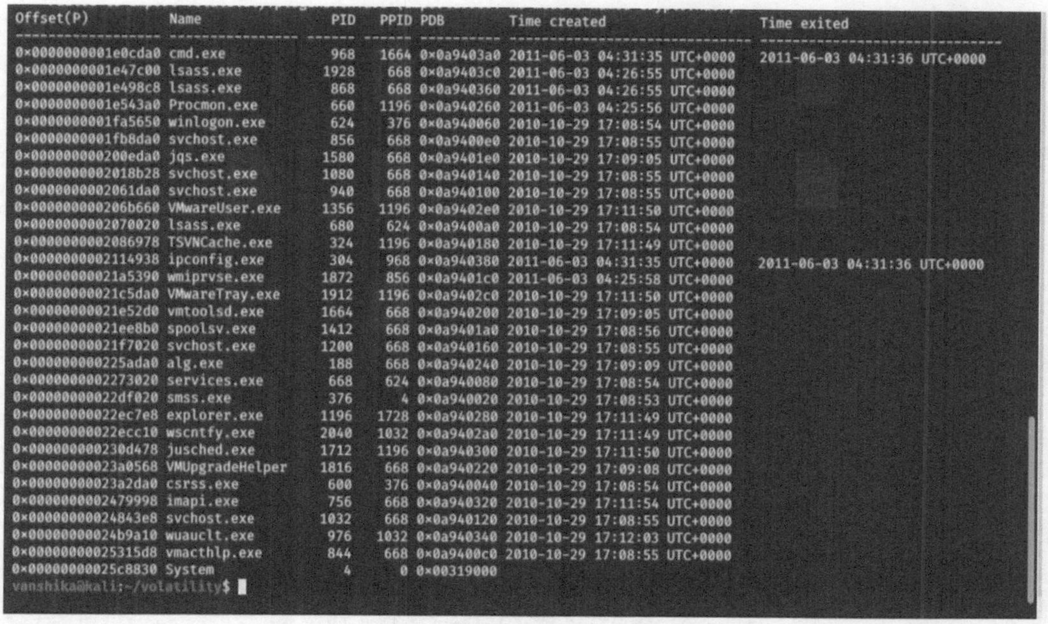

```
Offset(P)          Name             PID    PPID   PDB        Time created                   Time exited
------------------ ---------------- ------ ------ ---------- ------------------------------ ------------------------------
0x000000001e0cda0  cmd.exe          968    1664   0x0a9403a0 2011-06-03 04:31:35 UTC+0000   2011-06-03 04:31:36 UTC+0000
0x000000001e47c00  lsass.exe        1928   668    0x0a9403c0 2011-06-03 04:26:55 UTC+0000
0x000000001e498c8  lsass.exe        868    668    0x0a940360 2011-06-03 04:26:55 UTC+0000
0x000000001e543a0  Procmon.exe      660    1196   0x0a940260 2011-06-03 04:25:56 UTC+0000
0x000000001fa5650  winlogon.exe     624    376    0x0a940060 2010-10-29 17:08:54 UTC+0000
0x000000001fb8da0  svchost.exe      856    668    0x0a9400e0 2010-10-29 17:08:55 UTC+0000
0x0000000200eda0   jqs.exe          1580   668    0x0a9401e0 2010-10-29 17:09:05 UTC+0000
0x00000000002018b28 svchost.exe     1080   668    0x0a940140 2010-10-29 17:08:55 UTC+0000
0x00000000002061da0 svchost.exe     940    668    0x0a940100 2010-10-29 17:08:55 UTC+0000
0x0000000000206b660 VMwareUser.exe  1356   1196   0x0a9402e0 2010-10-29 17:11:50 UTC+0000
0x00000000002070020 lsass.exe       680    624    0x0a9400a0 2010-10-29 17:08:54 UTC+0000
0x00000000002086978 TSVNCache.exe   324    1196   0x0a940180 2010-10-29 17:11:49 UTC+0000
0x00000000002114938 ipconfig.exe    304    968    0x0a940380 2011-06-03 04:31:35 UTC+0000   2011-06-03 04:31:36 UTC+0000
0x000000000021a5390 wmiprvse.exe    1872   856    0x0a9401c0 2011-06-03 04:25:58 UTC+0000
0x000000000021c5da0 VMwareTray.exe  1912   1196   0x0a9402c0 2010-10-29 17:11:50 UTC+0000
0x000000000021e52d0 vmtoolsd.exe    1664   668    0x0a940200 2010-10-29 17:09:05 UTC+0000
0x000000000021ee8b0 spoolsv.exe     1412   668    0x0a9401a0 2010-10-29 17:08:56 UTC+0000
0x000000000021f7020 svchost.exe     1200   668    0x0a940160 2010-10-29 17:08:55 UTC+0000
0x0000000000225ada0 alg.exe         188    668    0x0a940240 2010-10-29 17:09:09 UTC+0000
0x00000000002273020 services.exe    668    624    0x0a940080 2010-10-29 17:08:54 UTC+0000
0x000000000022df020 smss.exe        376    4      0x0a940020 2010-10-29 17:08:53 UTC+0000
0x000000000022ec7e8 explorer.exe    1196   1728   0x0a940280 2010-10-29 17:11:49 UTC+0000
0x000000000022ecc10 wscntfy.exe     2040   1032   0x0a9402a0 2010-10-29 17:11:49 UTC+0000
0x0000000000230d478 jusched.exe     1712   1196   0x0a940300 2010-10-29 17:11:50 UTC+0000
0x000000000023a0568 VMUpgradeHelper 1816   668    0x0a940220 2010-10-29 17:09:08 UTC+0000
0x000000000023a2da0 csrss.exe       600    376    0x0a940040 2010-10-29 17:08:54 UTC+0000
0x00000000002479998 imapi.exe       756    668    0x0a940320 2010-10-29 17:11:54 UTC+0000
0x000000000024843e8 svchost.exe     1032   668    0x0a940120 2010-10-29 17:08:55 UTC+0000
0x000000000024b9a10 wuauclt.exe     976    1032   0x0a940340 2010-10-29 17:12:03 UTC+0000
0x000000000025315d8 vmacthlp.exe    844    668    0x0a9400c0 2010-10-29 17:08:55 UTC+0000
0x000000000025c8830 System          4      0      0x00319000
vanshika@kali:~/volatility$
```

FIGURE 10.20
Psscan Command Result.

```
vanshika@kali: ~/volatility
File  Actions  Edit  View  Help
vanshika@kali:~/volatility$ python vol.py -f memorydump.vmem pstree
Volatility Foundation Volatility Framework 2.6.1
```

FIGURE 10.21
Pstree Command.

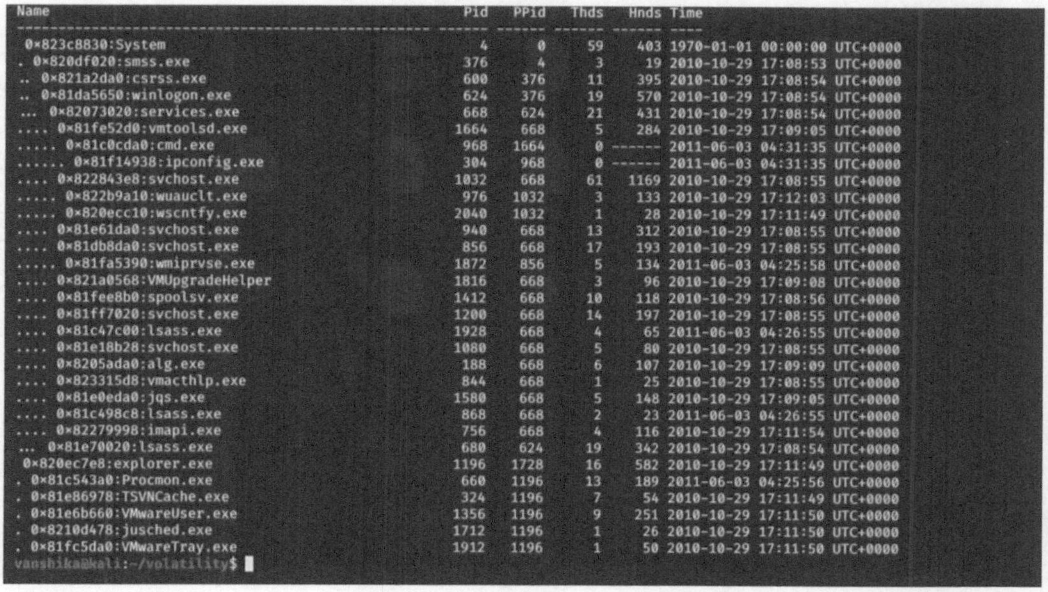

```
Name                                                  Pid    PPid   Thds   Hnds Time
-------------------------------------------------- ------ ------ ------ ------ ----
 0x823c8830:System                                      4      0     59    403 1970-01-01 00:00:00 UTC+0000
. 0x820df020:smss.exe                                 376      4      3     19 2010-10-29 17:08:53 UTC+0000
.. 0x821a2da0:csrss.exe                               600    376     11    395 2010-10-29 17:08:54 UTC+0000
.. 0x81da5650:winlogon.exe                            624    376     19    570 2010-10-29 17:08:54 UTC+0000
... 0x82073020:services.exe                           668    624     21    431 2010-10-29 17:08:54 UTC+0000
.... 0x81fe52d0:vmtoolsd.exe                         1664    668      5    284 2010-10-29 17:09:05 UTC+0000
..... 0x81c0cda0:cmd.exe                              968   1664      0 ------ 2011-06-03 04:31:35 UTC+0000
...... 0x81f14938:ipconfig.exe                        304    968      0 ------ 2011-06-03 04:31:35 UTC+0000
.... 0x822843e8:svchost.exe                          1032    668     61   1169 2010-10-29 17:08:55 UTC+0000
..... 0x822b9a10:wuauclt.exe                          976   1032      3    133 2010-10-29 17:12:03 UTC+0000
..... 0x820ecc10:wscntfy.exe                         2040   1032      1     28 2010-10-29 17:11:49 UTC+0000
.... 0x81e61da0:svchost.exe                           940    668     13    312 2010-10-29 17:08:55 UTC+0000
.... 0x81db8da0:svchost.exe                           856    668     17    193 2010-10-29 17:08:55 UTC+0000
..... 0x81fa5390:wmiprvse.exe                        1872    856      5    134 2011-06-03 04:25:58 UTC+0000
.... 0x821a0568:VMUpgradeHelper                      1816    668      3     96 2010-10-29 17:09:08 UTC+0000
.... 0x81fee8b0:spoolsv.exe                          1412    668     10    118 2010-10-29 17:08:56 UTC+0000
.... 0x81ff7020:svchost.exe                          1200    668     14    197 2010-10-29 17:08:55 UTC+0000
.... 0x81c47c00:lsass.exe                            1928    668      4     65 2011-06-03 04:26:55 UTC+0000
.... 0x81e18b28:svchost.exe                          1080    668      5     80 2010-10-29 17:08:55 UTC+0000
.... 0x8205ada0:alg.exe                               188    668      6    107 2010-10-29 17:09:09 UTC+0000
.... 0x823315d8:vmacthlp.exe                          844    668      1     25 2010-10-29 17:08:55 UTC+0000
.... 0x81e0eda0:jqs.exe                              1580    668      5    148 2010-10-29 17:09:05 UTC+0000
.... 0x81c498c8:lsass.exe                             868    668      2     23 2011-06-03 04:26:55 UTC+0000
.... 0x82279998:imapi.exe                             756    668      4    116 2010-10-29 17:11:54 UTC+0000
... 0x81e70020:lsass.exe                              680    624     19    342 2010-10-29 17:08:54 UTC+0000
 0x820ec7e8:explorer.exe                             1196   1728     16    582 2010-10-29 17:11:49 UTC+0000
. 0x81c543a0:Procmon.exe                              660   1196     13    189 2011-06-03 04:25:56 UTC+0000
. 0x81e86978:TSVNCache.exe                            324   1196      7     54 2010-10-29 17:11:49 UTC+0000
. 0x81e6b660:VMwareUser.exe                          1356   1196      9    251 2010-10-29 17:11:50 UTC+0000
. 0x8210d478:jusched.exe                             1712   1196      1     26 2010-10-29 17:11:50 UTC+0000
. 0x81fc5da0:VMwareTray.exe                          1912   1196      1     50 2010-10-29 17:11:50 UTC+0000
vanshika@kali:~/volatility$
```

FIGURE 10.22
Pstree Command Result.

FIGURE 10.23
Dlllist Plugin.

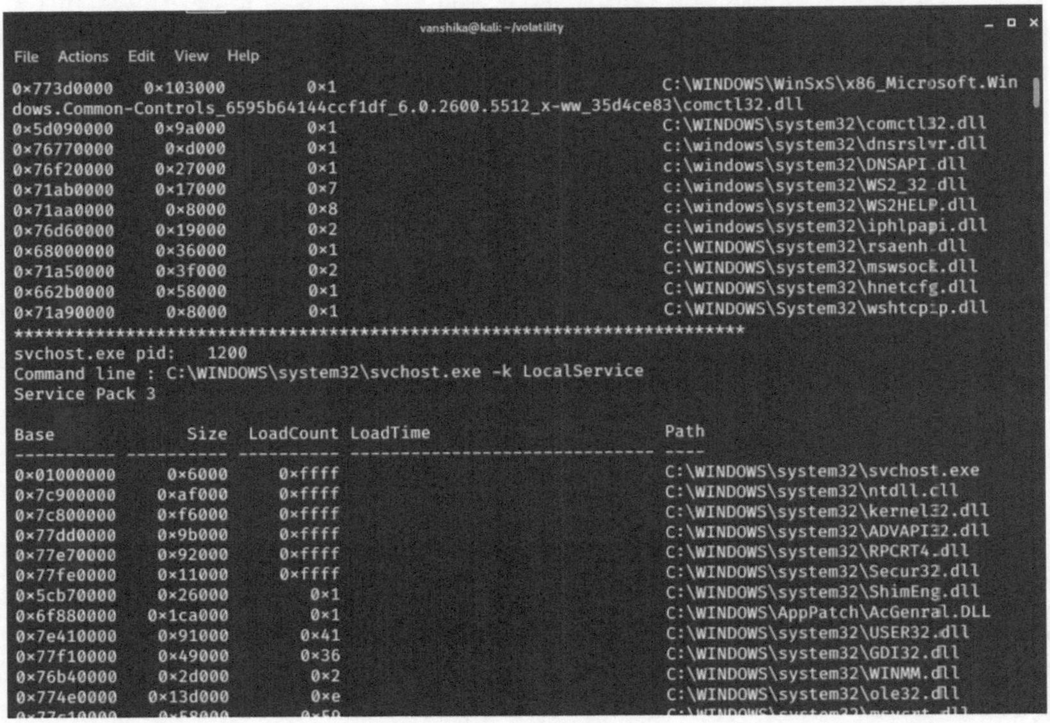

FIGURE 10.24
Dlllist Plugin Result1.

Step 3: Analyze Process DLLs and handles

6. **dlllist:** Several tools just can possibly recognize the DLLs which are utilized by an interaction by counseling the first of the three DLL records put away in the PEB, which tracks the request wherein each DLL is stacked. Accordingly, malware will now and then change that list to shroud the presence of a DLL (Figures 10.23–10.26).
   Dlllist plugin is performed on memorydump.vmem file in Kali terminal in order to analyze process DLLs.
7. **Handles:** Mentioned command is utilized for showing the handles of the process which are open and available. This module applies to keys of the registry, files, threads, events, strings, and related information (Figures 10.27–10.29).

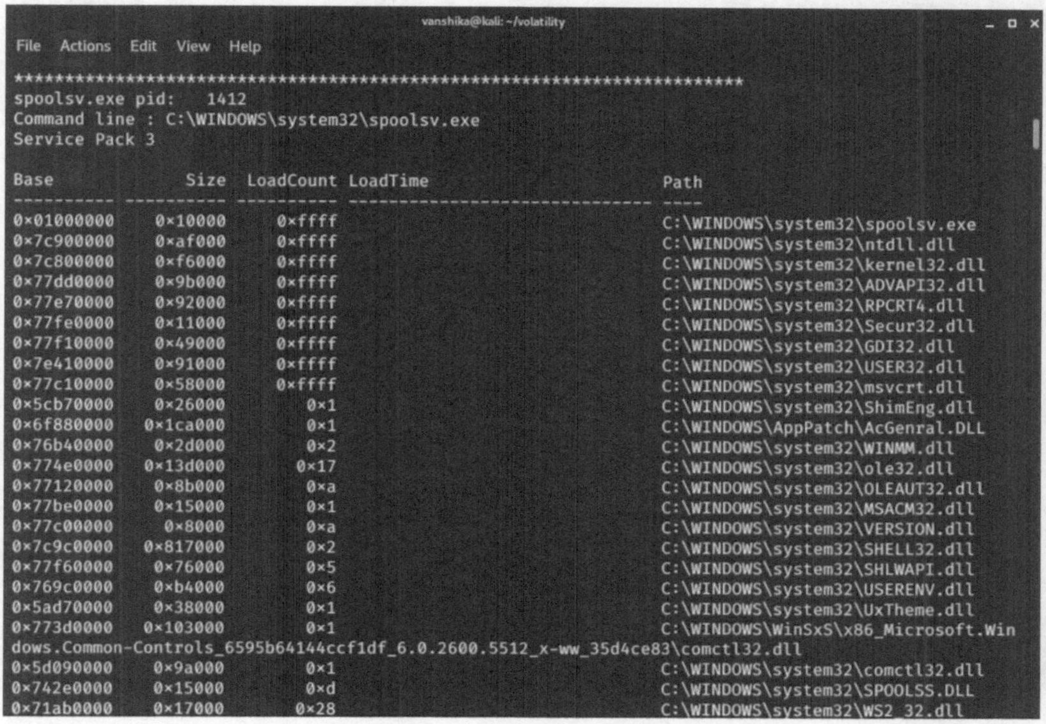

FIGURE 10.25
Dlllist Plugin Result2.

FIGURE 10.26
Dlllist Plugin Result3.

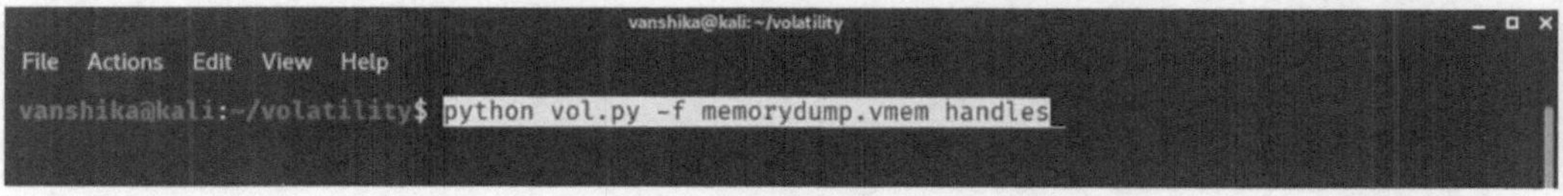

FIGURE 10.27
Handles Plugin.

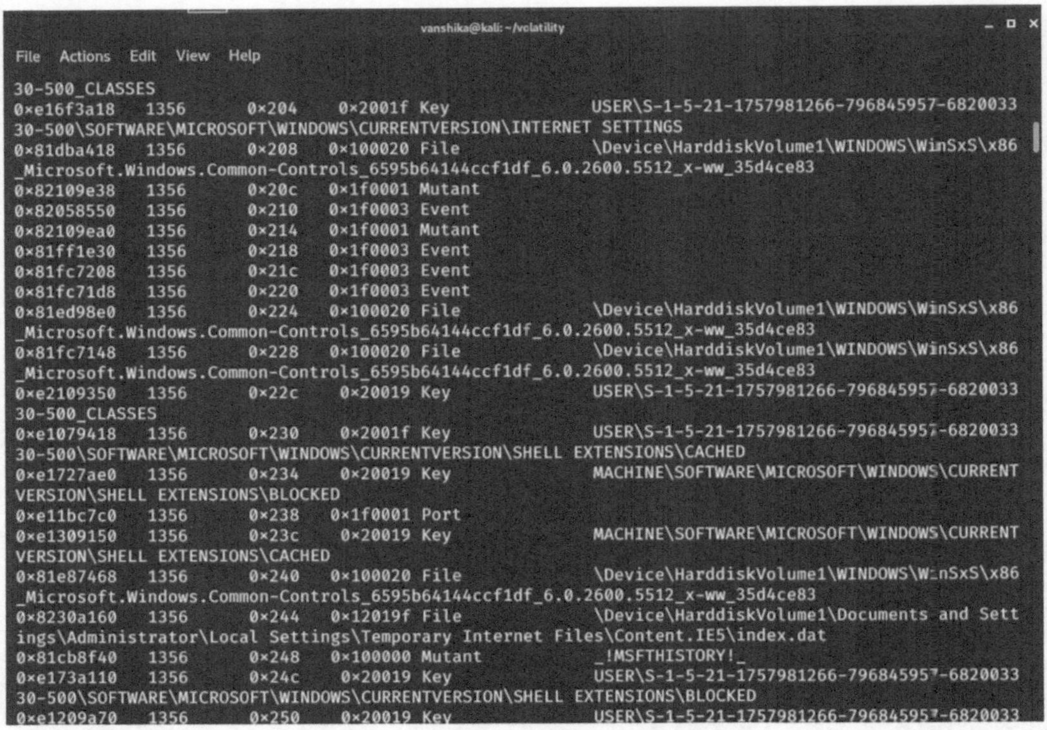

```
vanshika@kali: ~/volatility
File Actions Edit View Help
30-500_CLASSES
0xe16f3a18   1356      0x204    0x2001f Key             USER\S-1-5-21-1757981266-796845957-6820033
30-500\SOFTWARE\MICROSOFT\WINDOWS\CURRENTVERSION\INTERNET SETTINGS
0x81dba418   1356      0x208   0x100020 File            \Device\HarddiskVolume1\WINDOWS\WinSxS\x86
_Microsoft.Windows.Common-Controls_6595b64144ccf1df_6.0.2600.5512_x-ww_35d4ce83
0x82109e38   1356      0x20c   0x1f0001 Mutant
0x82058550   1356      0x210   0x1f0003 Event
0x82109ea0   1356      0x214   0x1f0001 Mutant
0x81ff1e30   1356      0x218   0x1f0003 Event
0x81fc7208   1356      0x21c   0x1f0003 Event
0x81fc71d8   1356      0x220   0x1f0003 Event
0x81ed98e0   1356      0x224   0x100020 File            \Device\HarddiskVolume1\WINDOWS\WinSxS\x86
_Microsoft.Windows.Common-Controls_6595b64144ccf1df_6.0.2600.5512_x-ww_35d4ce83
0x81fc7148   1356      0x228   0x100020 File            \Device\HarddiskVolume1\WINDOWS\WinSxS\x86
_Microsoft.Windows.Common-Controls_6595b64144ccf1df_6.0.2600.5512_x-ww_35d4ce83
0xe2109350   1356      0x22c    0x20019 Key             USER\S-1-5-21-1757981266-796845957-6820033
30-500_CLASSES
0xe1079418   1356      0x230    0x2001f Key             USER\S-1-5-21-1757981266-796845957-6820033
30-500\SOFTWARE\MICROSOFT\WINDOWS\CURRENTVERSION\SHELL EXTENSIONS\CACHED
0xe1727ae0   1356      0x234    0x20019 Key             MACHINE\SOFTWARE\MICROSOFT\WINDOWS\CURRENT
VERSION\SHELL EXTENSIONS\BLOCKED
0xe11bc7c0   1356      0x238   0x1f0001 Port
0xe1309150   1356      0x23c    0x20019 Key             MACHINE\SOFTWARE\MICROSOFT\WINDOWS\CURRENT
VERSION\SHELL EXTENSIONS\CACHED
0x81e87468   1356      0x240   0x100020 File            \Device\HarddiskVolume1\WINDOWS\WinSxS\x86
_Microsoft.Windows.Common-Controls_6595b64144ccf1df_6.0.2600.5512_x-ww_35d4ce83
0x8230a160   1356      0x244   0x12019f File            \Device\HarddiskVolume1\Documents and Sett
ings\Administrator\Local Settings\Temporary Internet Files\Content.IE5\index.dat
0x81cb8f40   1356      0x248   0x100000 Mutant          _!MSFTHISTORY!_
0xe173a110   1356      0x24c    0x20019 Key             USER\S-1-5-21-1757981266-796845957-6820033
30-500\SOFTWARE\MICROSOFT\WINDOWS\CURRENTVERSION\SHELL EXTENSIONS\BLOCKED
0xe1209a70   1356      0x250    0x20019 Key             USER\S-1-5-21-1757981266-796845957-6820033
```

FIGURE 10.28
Handles Plugin Result1.

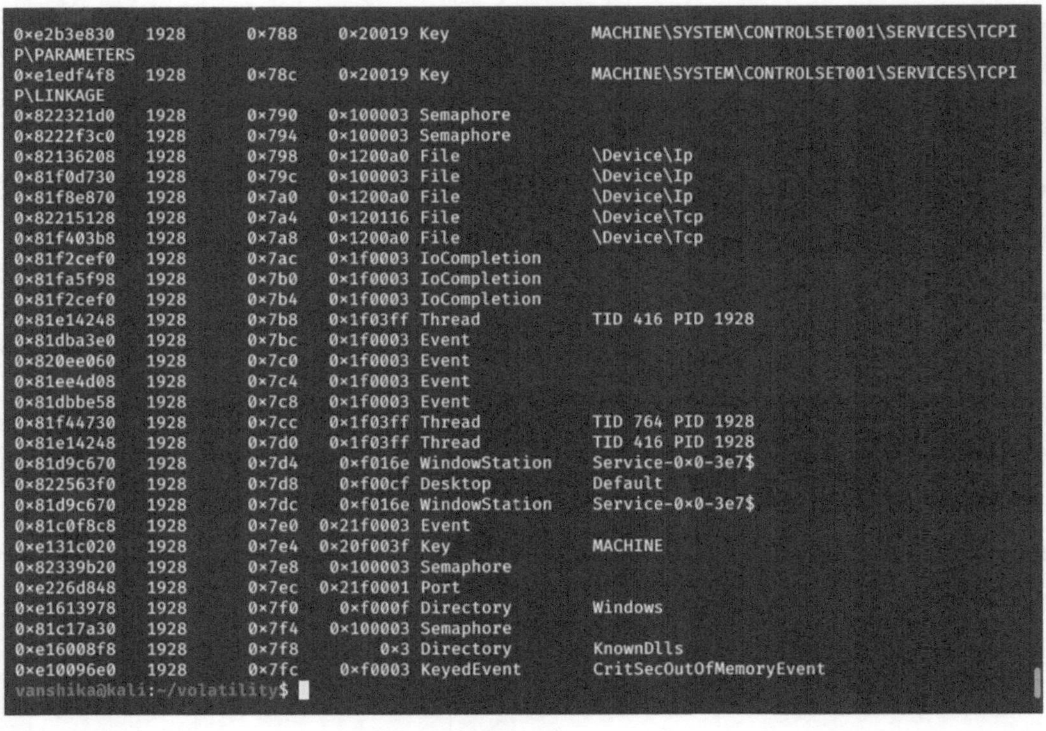

```
0xe2b3e830   1928      0x788    0x20019 Key             MACHINE\SYSTEM\CONTROLSET001\SERVICES\TCPI
P\PARAMETERS
0xe1edf4f8   1928      0x78c    0x20019 Key             MACHINE\SYSTEM\CONTROLSET001\SERVICES\TCPI
P\LINKAGE
0x822321d0   1928      0x790   0x100003 Semaphore
0x8222f3c0   1928      0x794   0x100003 Semaphore
0x82136208   1928      0x798   0x1200a0 File            \Device\Ip
0x81f0d730   1928      0x79c   0x100003 File            \Device\Ip
0x81f8e870   1928      0x7a0   0x1200a0 File            \Device\Ip
0x82215128   1928      0x7a4   0x120116 File            \Device\Tcp
0x81f403b8   1928      0x7a8   0x1200a0 File            \Device\Tcp
0x81f2cef0   1928      0x7ac   0x1f0003 IoCompletion
0x81fa5f98   1928      0x7b0   0x1f0003 IoCompletion
0x81f2cef0   1928      0x7b4   0x1f0003 IoCompletion
0x81e14248   1928      0x7b8   0x1f03ff Thread          TID 416 PID 1928
0x81dba3e0   1928      0x7bc   0x1f0003 Event
0x820ee060   1928      0x7c0   0x1f0003 Event
0x81ee4d08   1928      0x7c4   0x1f0003 Event
0x81dbbe58   1928      0x7c8   0x1f0003 Event
0x81f44730   1928      0x7cc   0x1f03ff Thread          TID 764 PID 1928
0x81e14248   1928      0x7d0   0x1f03ff Thread          TID 416 PID 1928
0x81d9c670   1928      0x7d4    0xf016e WindowStation   Service-0x0-3e7$
0x822563f0   1928      0x7d8    0xf00cf Desktop         Default
0x81d9c670   1928      0x7dc    0xf016e WindowStation   Service-0x0-3e7$
0x81c0f8c8   1928      0x7e0  0x21f0003 Event
0xe131c020   1928      0x7e4  0x20f003f Key             MACHINE
0x82339b20   1928      0x7e8   0x100003 Semaphore
0xe226d848   1928      0x7ec  0x21f0001 Port
0xe1613978   1928      0x7f0    0xf000f Directory       Windows
0x81c17a30   1928      0x7f4   0x100003 Semaphore
0xe16008f8   1928      0x7f8        0x3 Directory       KnownDlls
0xe10096e0   1928      0x7fc    0xf0003 KeyedEvent      CritSecOutOfMemoryEvent
vanshika@kali:~/volatility$
```

FIGURE 10.29
Handles Plugin Result2.

FIGURE 10.30
Connscan Command.

FIGURE 10.31
Connscan Command Result.

Step 4: Review Network Artifacts

8. **Connscan:** Following command is used to look for network connections that have expired as well as that are currently active (Figures 10.30 and 10.31).
9. **Sockscan:** This command filters the memory for _ADDRESS_OBJECT. By filtering the memory for this memory structure, one can get to know about the recently opened and currently opened endpoints of connection (Figures 10.32 and 10.33).

Step 5: Look for evidence of Code Injection

10. **malfind**: This command looks for any evidence of code infusion inside a memory process by searching any executable code's presence that has not been mapped to any file on the drive (Figures 10.34 and 10.35).

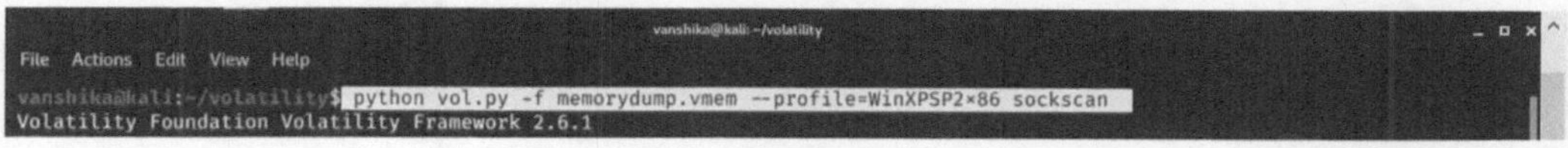

FIGURE 10.32
Sockscan Plugin.

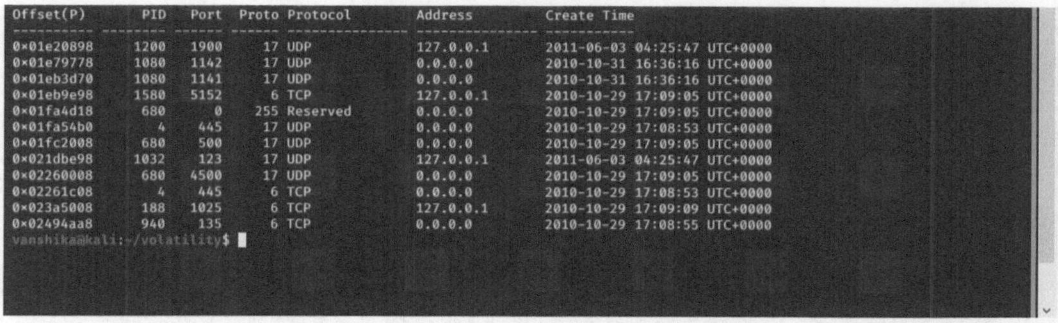

FIGURE 10.33
Sockscan Plugin Result.

FIGURE 10.34
Malfind Plugin.

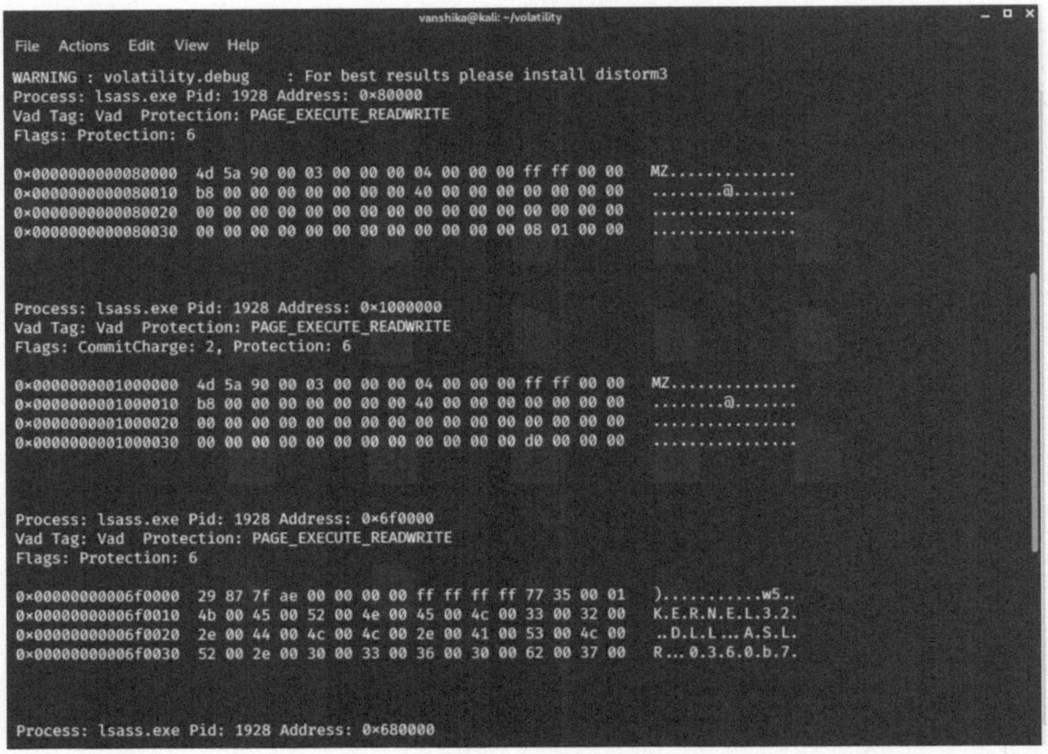

FIGURE 10.35
Malfind Plugin Result.

Step 6: Check for Signs of a Rootkit

11. **modscan:** Mentioned command is utilized for finding kernel memory and its connected attributes. This can get almost every already dumped drivers and furthermore concealed drivers or have been unlinked by rootkits in the system (Figures 10.36 and 10.37).

Step 7: Extract Processes, Drivers, and Objects

12. **moddump:** This command is used for extracting kernel driver to a file (Figures 10.38 and 10.39).

FIGURE 10.36
Modscan Plugin.

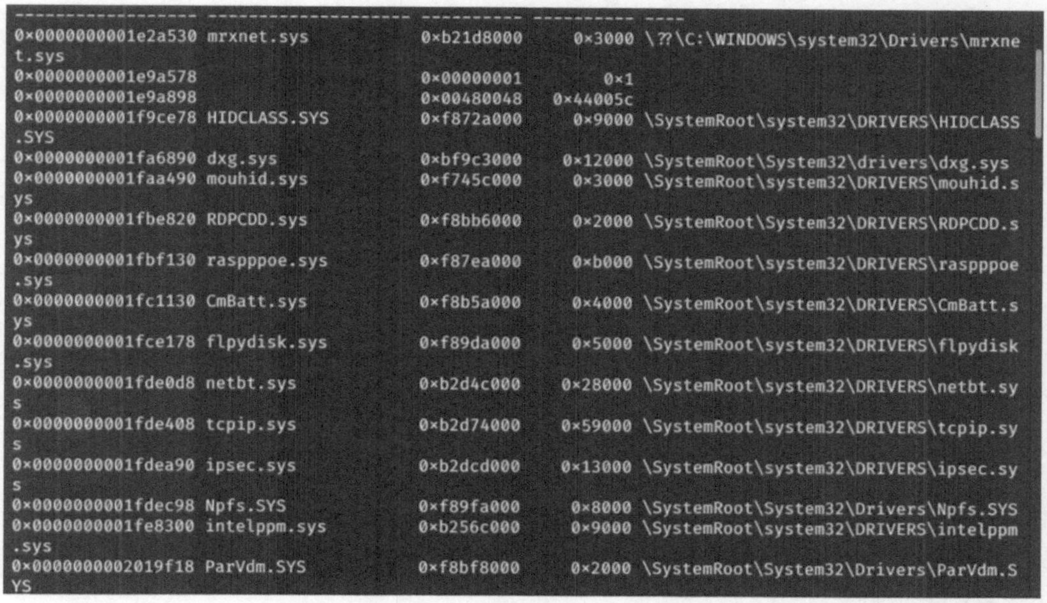

FIGURE 10.37
Modscan Plugin Result.

FIGURE 10.38
Moddump Command.

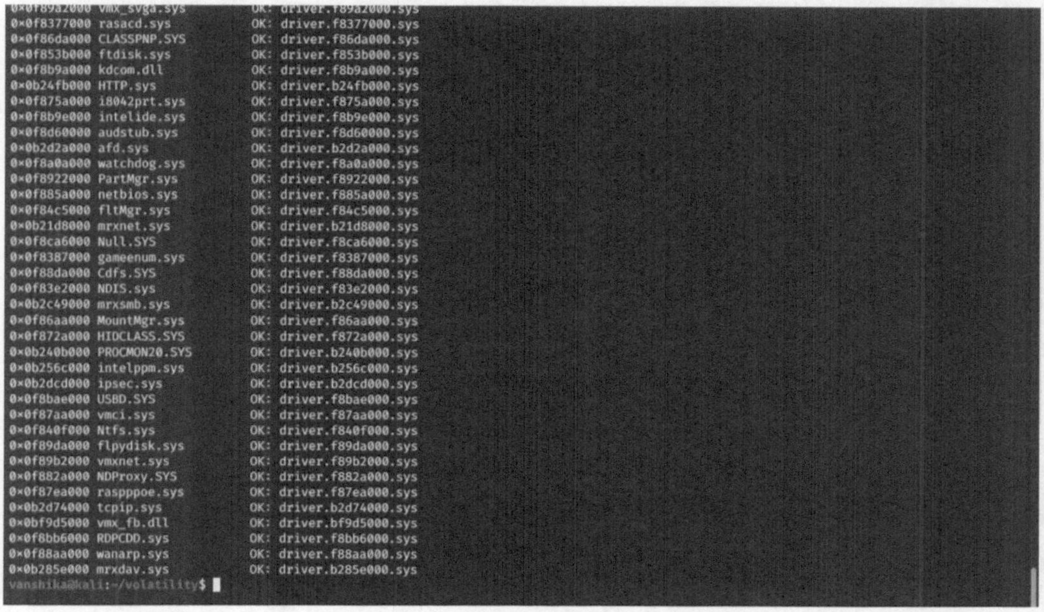

FIGURE 10.39
Moddump Command Result.

13. **procdump:** This command is used for dumping all executable files at one location. In case any malware is present, purposefully it molds PE header's size field for memory dumping tools to fall short (Figures 10.40 and 10.41).
14. **memdump:** Mentioned module gets utilized for dumping the pages of memory-resident of an interaction into a different document. You can likewise query a specific process by having - p and combine it with a directory path - D to create the result (Figures 10.42 and 10.43).
15. **filescan:** This module (Al-Sabaawi, 2020) is utilized to discover FILE_OBJECTs acquired in the actual part of memory by utilizing pool label examining. It also discovers records, which are open regardless of whether there is an obscure rootkit, present in the files (Figures 10.44–10.46).

```
vanshika@kali:~/volatility$ python vol.py -f memorydump.vmem --profile=WinXPSP2×86 procdump -D ./
Volatility Foundation Volatility Framework 2.6.1
```

FIGURE 10.40
Procdump Command.

```
Process(V) ImageBase  Name                 Result
---------- ---------- -------------------- ------
0×823c8830 ---------- System               Error: PEB at 0×0 is unavailable (possibly due to paging)
0×820df020 0×48580000 smss.exe             OK: executable.376.exe
0×821a2da0 0×4a680000 csrss.exe            OK: executable.600.exe
0×81da5650 0×01000000 winlogon.exe         OK: executable.624.exe
0×82073020 0×01000000 services.exe         OK: executable.668.exe
0×81e70020 0×01000000 lsass.exe            OK: executable.680.exe
0×823315d8 0×00400000 vmacthlp.exe         OK: executable.844.exe
0×81db8da0 0×01000000 svchost.exe          OK: executable.856.exe
0×81e61da0 0×01000000 svchost.exe          OK: executable.940.exe
0×822843e8 0×01000000 svchost.exe          OK: executable.1032.exe
0×81e18b28 0×01000000 svchost.exe          OK: executable.1080.exe
0×81ff7020 0×01000000 svchost.exe          OK: executable.1200.exe
0×81fee8b0 0×01000000 spoolsv.exe          OK: executable.1412.exe
0×81e0eda0 0×00400000 jqs.exe              OK: executable.1580.exe
0×81fe52d0 0×00400000 vmtoolsd.exe         OK: executable.1664.exe
0×821a0568 0×00400000 VMUpgradeHelper      OK: executable.1816.exe
0×8205ada0 0×01000000 alg.exe              OK: executable.188.exe
0×820ec7e8 0×01000000 explorer.exe         OK: executable.1196.exe
0×820ecc10 0×01000000 wscntfy.exe          OK: executable.2040.exe
0×81e86978 0×00400000 TSVNCache.exe        OK: executable.324.exe
0×81fc5da0 0×00400000 VMwareTray.exe       OK: executable.1912.exe
0×81e6b660 0×00400000 VMwareUser.exe       OK: executable.1356.exe
0×8210d478 0×00400000 jusched.exe          OK: executable.1712.exe
0×82279998 0×01000000 imapi.exe            OK: executable.756.exe
0×822b9a10 0×00400000 wuauclt.exe          OK: executable.976.exe
0×81c543a0 0×00400000 Procmon.exe          OK: executable.660.exe
0×81fa5390 0×01000000 wmiprvse.exe         OK: executable.1872.exe
0×81c498c8 0×01000000 lsass.exe            OK: executable.868.exe
0×81c47c00 0×01000000 lsass.exe            OK: executable.1928.exe
0×81c0cda0 ---------- cmd.exe              Error: PEB at 0×7ffd6000 is unavailable (possibly due to paging)
0×81f14938 ---------- ipconfig.exe         Error: PEB at 0×7ffde000 is unavailable (possibly due to paging)
vanshika@kali:~/volatility$
```

FIGURE 10.41
Procdump Command Result.

```
File  Actions  Edit  View  Help
vanshika@kali:~/volatility$ python vol.py -f memorydump.vmem --profile=WinXPSP2×86 memdump -D ./
Volatility Foundation Volatility Framework 2.6.1
```

FIGURE 10.42
Memdump Command.

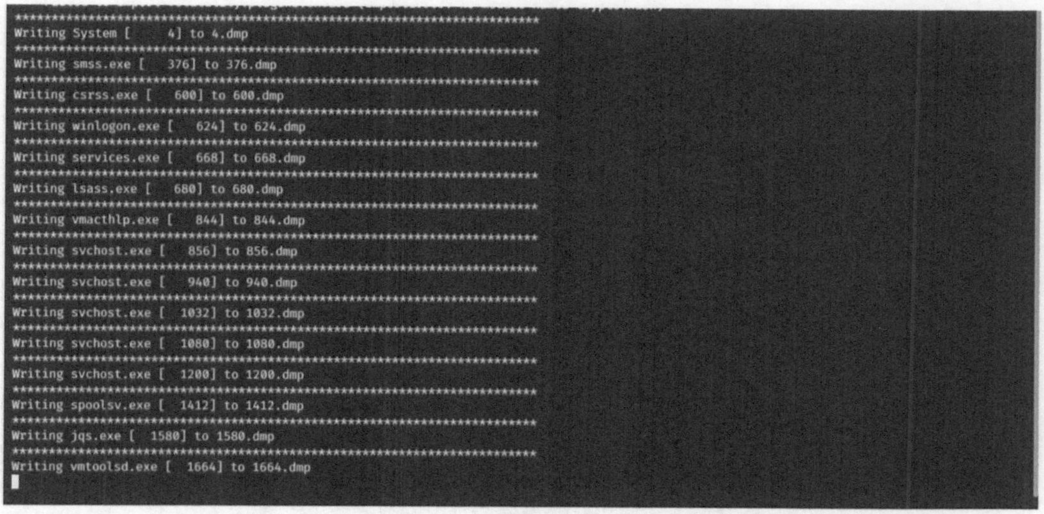

FIGURE 10.43
Memdump Command Result.

FIGURE 10.44
Filescan Plugin.

16. **hivelist:** Mentioned command is utilized to get the registry hive's virtual address in the memory, and drive's complete path to hive (Figures 10.47 and 10.48).
17. **iehistory:** The components of Internet Explorer history are retrieved using this plugin by searching index.dat cache file (Figures 10.49 and 10.50).
18. **notepad:** Files of the notepad are generally visible in the RAM Dump. For locating the existing content in the file of notepad, following command may be utilized (Figure 10.51).

FIGURE 10.45
Filescan Plugin Result1.

FIGURE 10.46
Filescan Plugin Result2.

FIGURE 10.47
Hivelist Plugin.

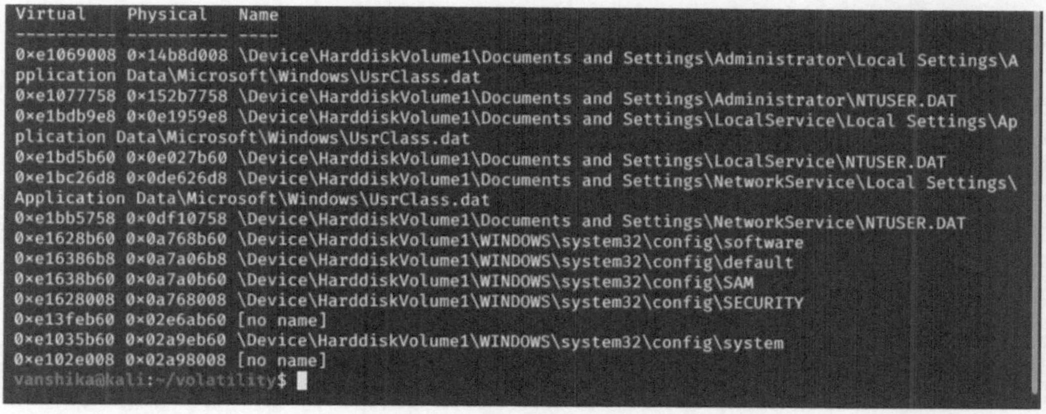

FIGURE 10.48
Hivelist Plugin Result.

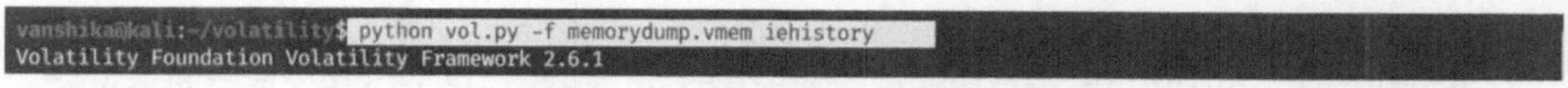

FIGURE 10.49
Iehistory Command.

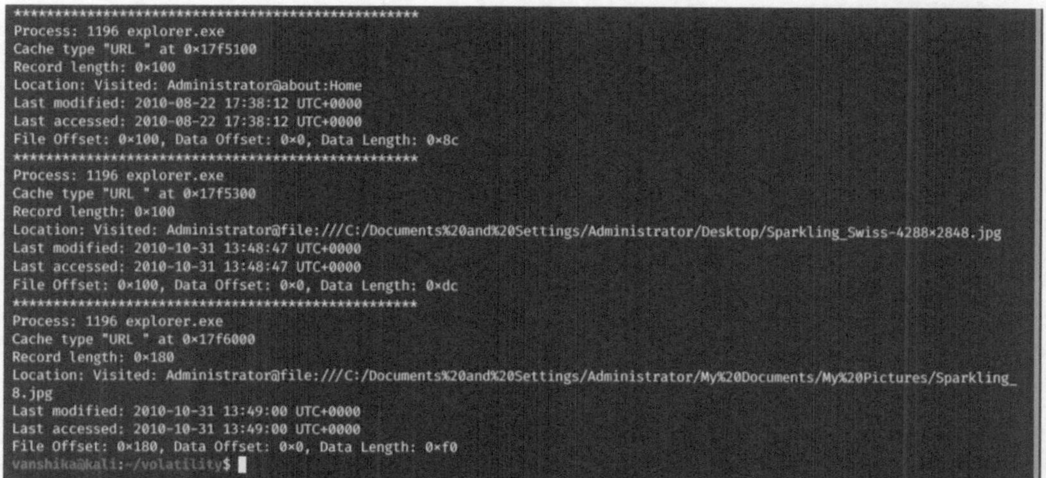

FIGURE 10.50
Iehistory Command Result.

FIGURE 10.51
Notepad Command.

10.4.3 Volatility Workbench

The Volatility framework has the most application-specific analysis plugins, but still implements a handful of them. Here, Volatility Workbench comes into picture that implements most of the application-specific analysis plugins. Volatility Workbench (Volatility Workbench, 2021) is a GUI rendition of one of the most prevalent tools, Volatility, for investigating the antiquities from a memory dump. It is supposed to be installed and executed on the Windows Operating System as it is available open-source and free of cost. It can be downloaded from the following link: https://www.osforensics.com/tools/volatility-workbench.html. The version used here is Volatility Workbench v2.1. Once it is downloaded, execute it. Now select the dump file you created earlier and choose the created image profile that can be used instead of imageinfo command. After doing all this, click on Refresh Process List and you will be able to run all the commands. Below mentioned commands are executed for more detailed analysis of memory dump (Memory Forensics Using Volatility Workbench, 2021):

1. **Malfind:** malfind command helps in searching hidden injected code and executable present inside each process. Once it encounters any suspicious activity it will print attributes like memory address and the PID where the suspicious activity has been found. You can also dump these code files if any present (Figures 10.52 and 10.53).

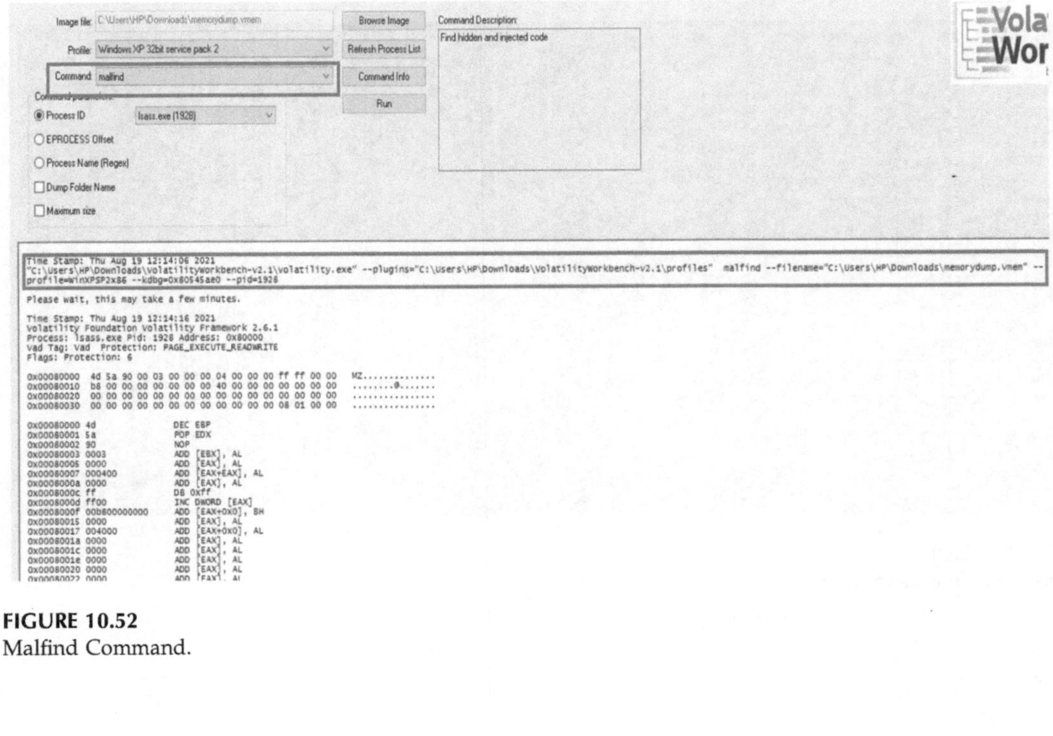

FIGURE 10.52
Malfind Command.

FIGURE 10.53
Files Dumped Using Malfind.

2. **Psxview:** Psxview is applied to list all the procedures which were running in the memory image and by what methods these processes have been discovered. This command also helps to detect hidden processes which were running in the memory but remained undetected by most of the commands (Figure 10.54).
3. **Timers:** All the kernel timers and their related module DPCs get listed on the output screen using this plugin (Figure 10.55).

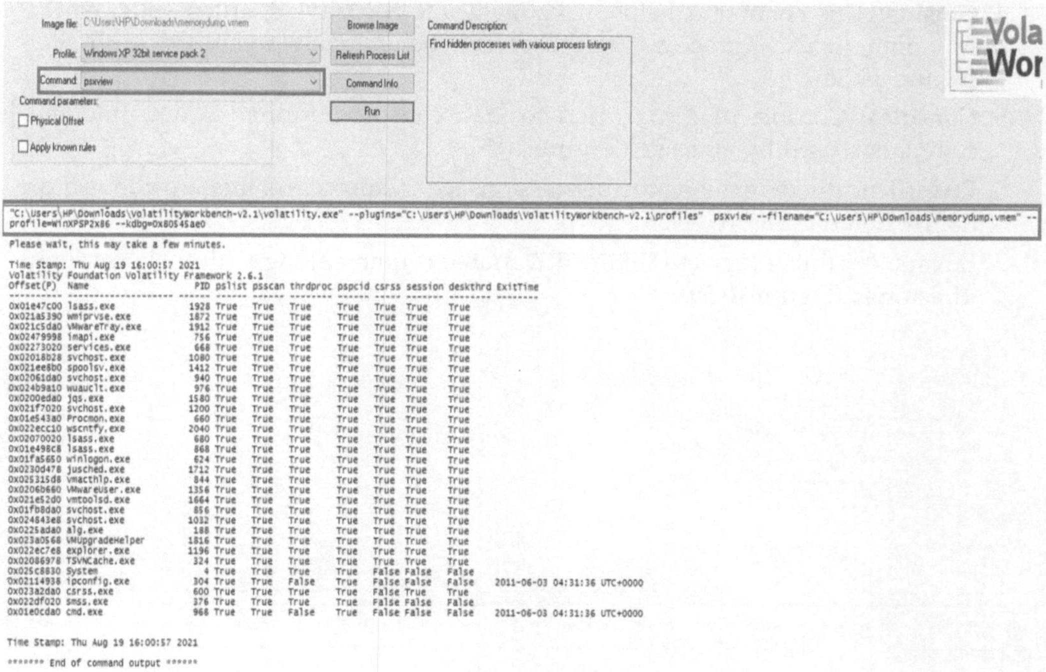

FIGURE 10.54
Psxview.

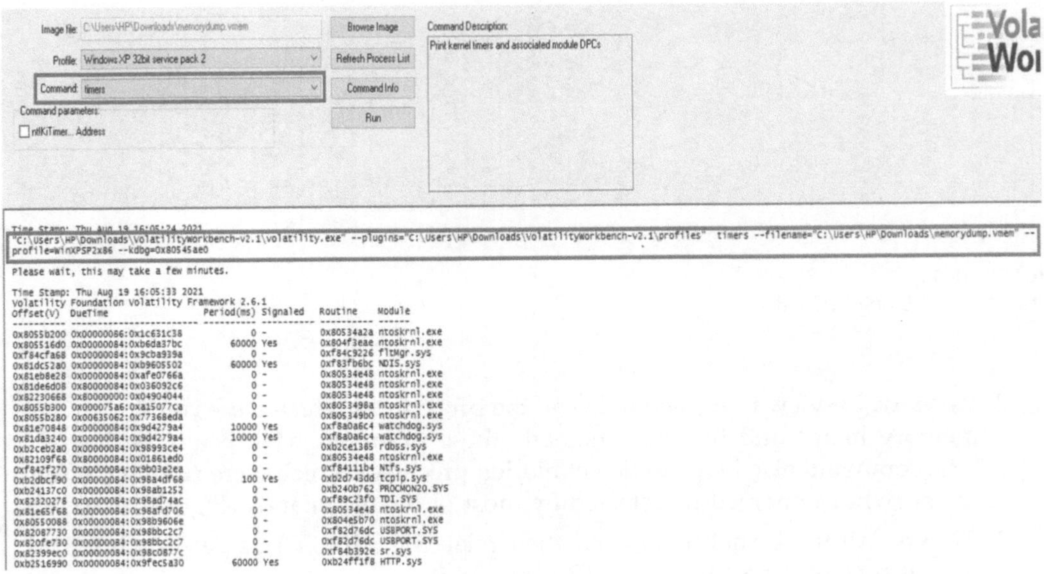

FIGURE 10.55
Timers.

4. **Getsids:** This command helps in knowing the Security Identifier (SID) corresponding to each process. Each user can be uniquely identified with SID (Figure 10.56).
5. **Consoles:** Console plugin is used to scan console information and find the commands used by attackers (Figure 10.57).
6. **Privs:** This plugin exhibits the permissions for the processes that are allowed or not by default (Figure 10.58).
7. **Envars:** It prints every environment variable running along with their working directories (Figure 10.59).

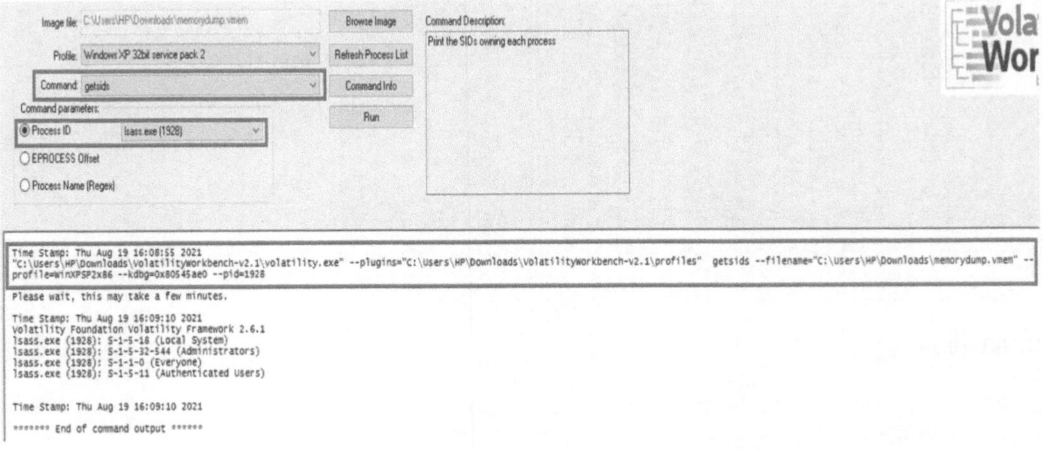

FIGURE 10.56
Getsids.

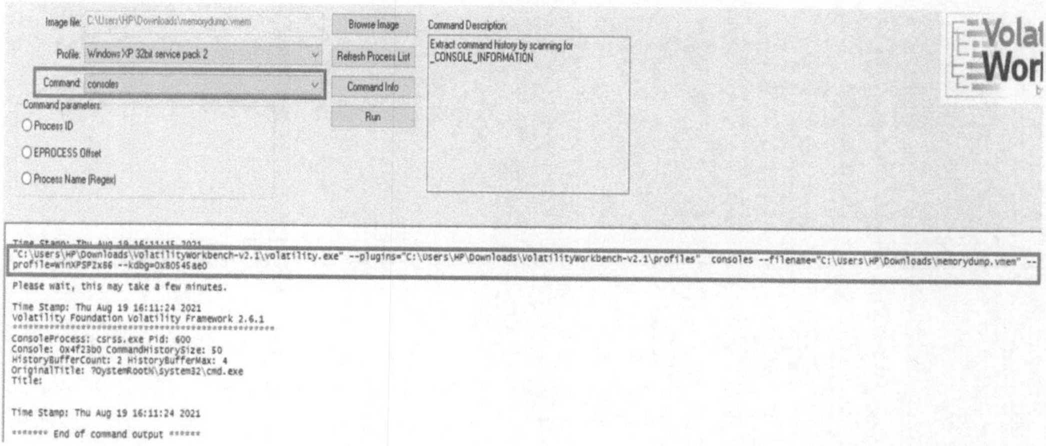

FIGURE 10.57
Consoles.

8. **Verinfo:** This will print out the version information that is available on the PE images. It distinguishes the binaries and in addition relates to different files (Figure 10.60).
9. **Memmap:** It prints the memory map, i.e., the exact pages of a particular process. It displays the virtual physical pages along with their sizes (Figure 10.61).

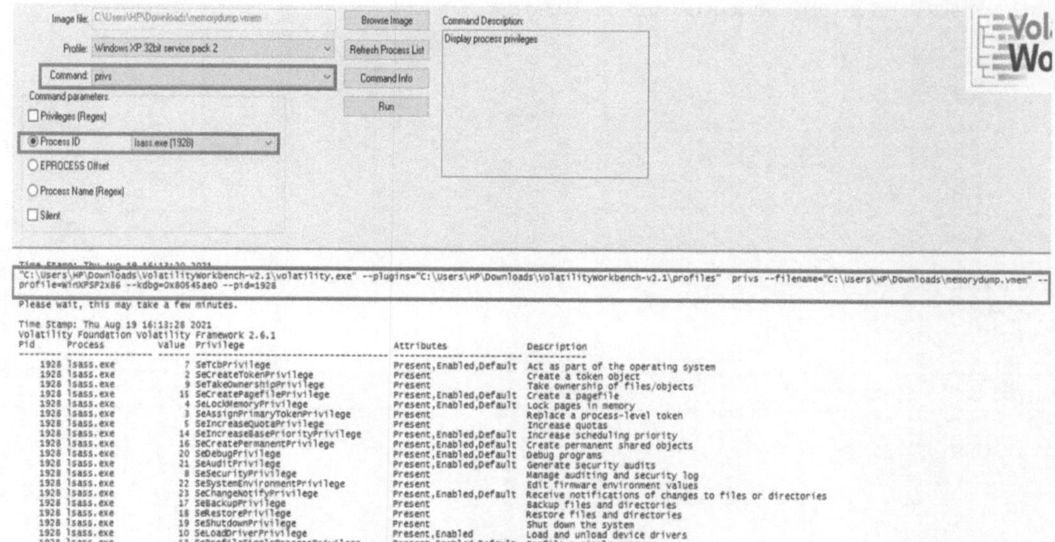

FIGURE 10.58
Privs.

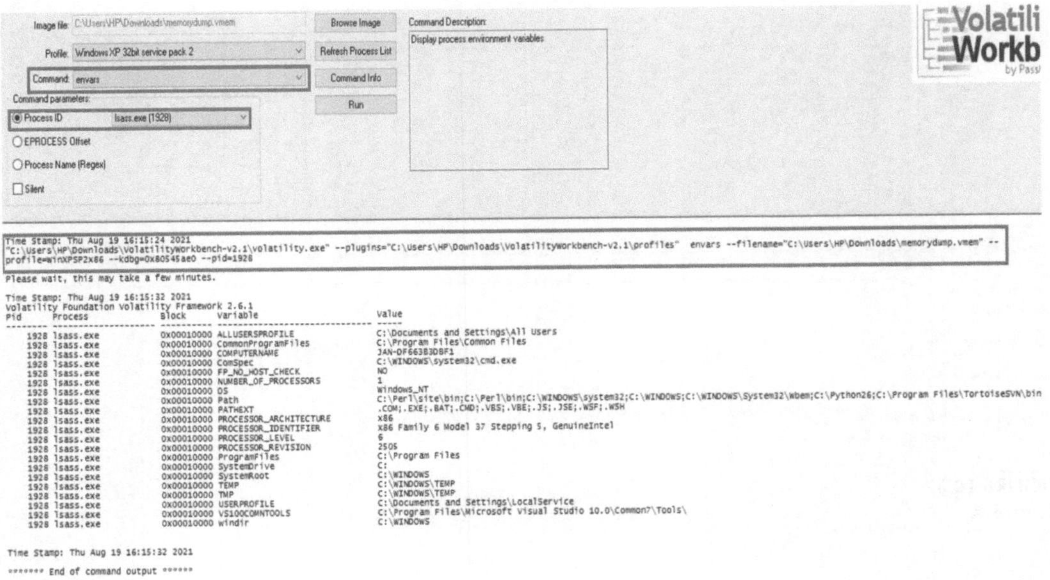

FIGURE 10.59
Envars.

10. **Vadinfo:** This command exhibits extensive details concerning the VAD nodes of a process. It displays VAD tags, VAD flags, control flags, etc. (Figure 10.62).
11. **Vadwalk:** Vadwalk plugin is used, in order to analyze the VAD nodes of a process in a tabular form (Figure 10.63).

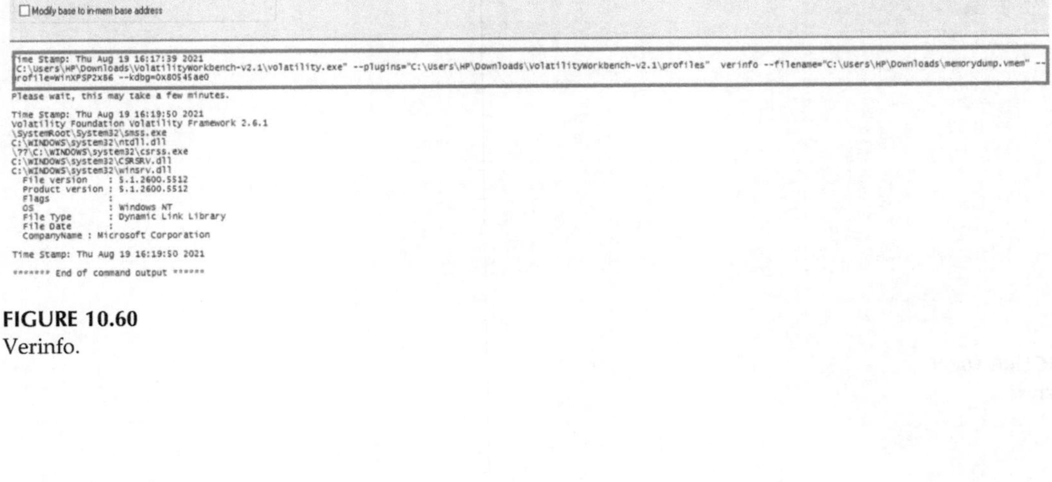

FIGURE 10.60
Verinfo.

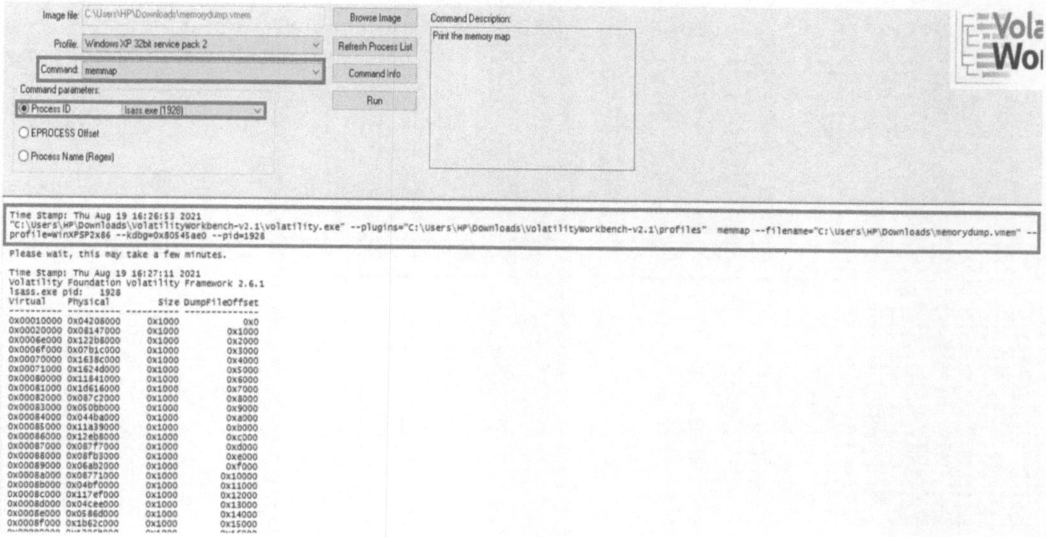

FIGURE 10.61
Memmap.

12. **Vadtree:** This command is used to show the VAD nodes of a process in a visual tree form (Figure 10.64).
13. **Iehistory:** This plugin is used to recover the Internet Explorer history components index.dat called cache files. It shows visited FTP and HTTP links, redirected links, or any remote entries (Figure 10.65).

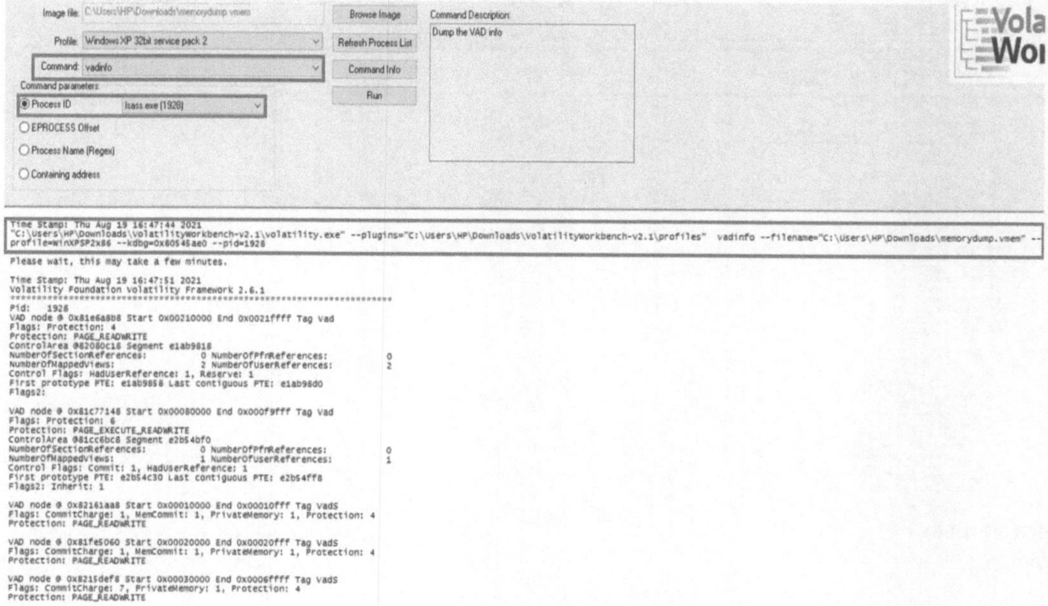

FIGURE 10.62
Vadinfo.

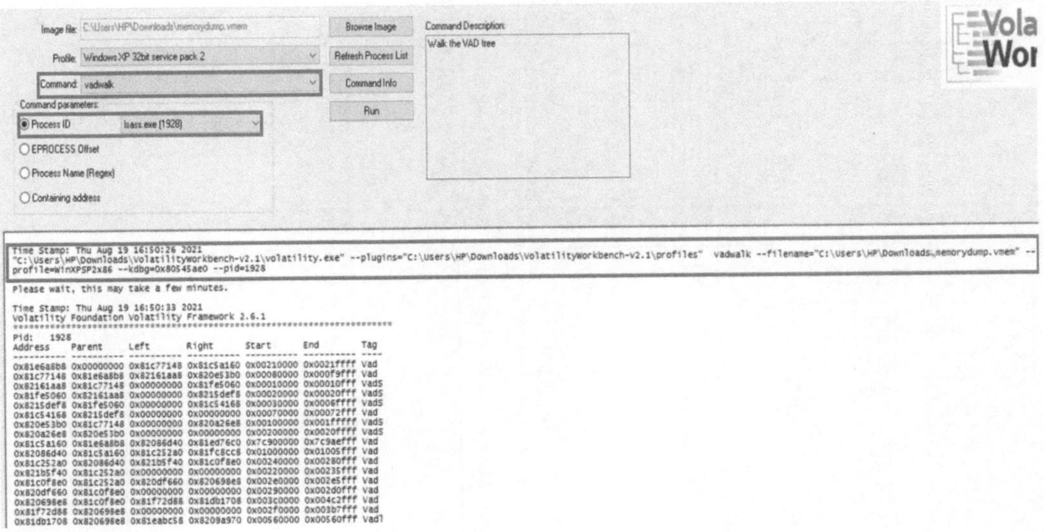

FIGURE 10.63
Vadwalk.

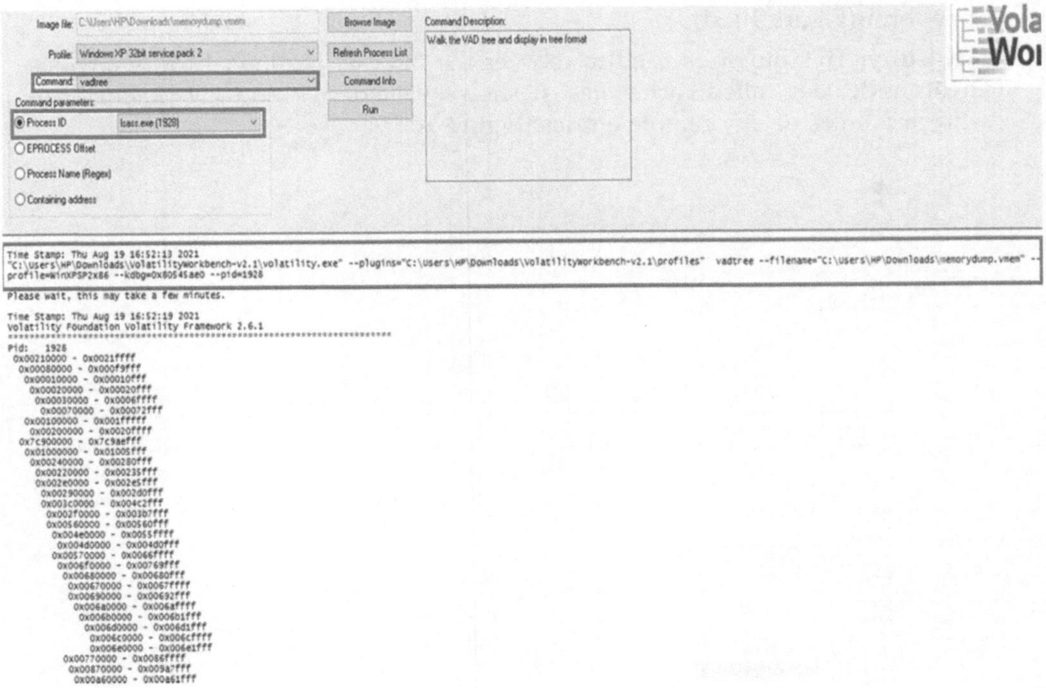

FIGURE 10.64
Vadtree.

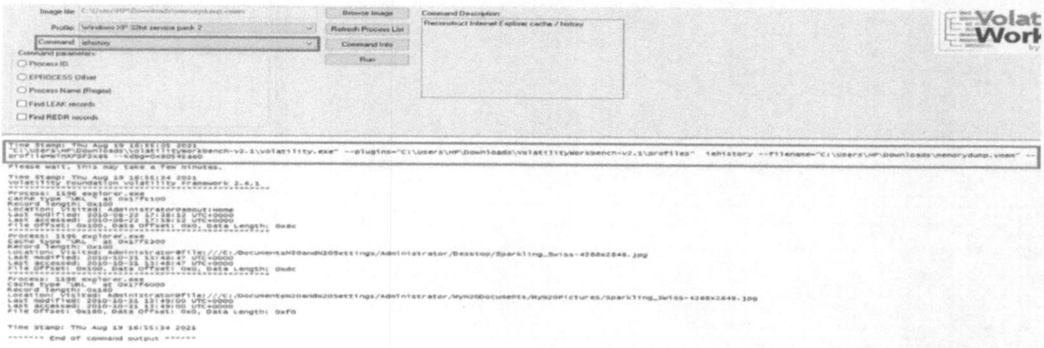

FIGURE 10.65
Iehistory.

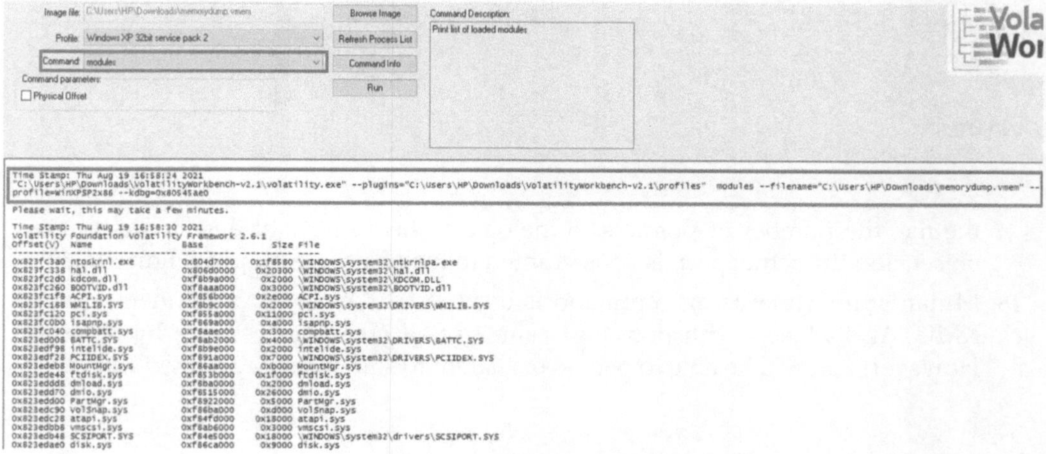

FIGURE 10.66
Modules.

14. **Modules:** In order to see the list of kernel drivers which are loaded on the system the modules command can be utilized (Figure 10.66).
15. **Ssdt:** This plugin can be utilized to display the functions within the Native and GUI SSDTs. This exhibits the index, function name, and owning driver for every entry in the SSDT (Figure 10.67).
16. **Driverscan:** In order to locate DRIVER_OBJECTs present in physical memory using pool tag scanning the driverscan command can be utilized. This is an alternative method to detect kernel modules, while not all kernel modules have a DRIVER_OBJECT linked with them. DRIVER_OBJECT consists of the 28 IRP (Main Function) tables, so the driverirp plugin is formulated on the ways utilized by driverscan (Figure 10.68).
17. **Filescan:** The filescan command is used to locate FILE_OBJECT present in physical memory using pool tag analysis. This will detect open files even if the rootkit hides files on disk and the rootkit hooks certain API functions to hide open handles on a live system. The physical offset of FILE_OBJECT, the name of

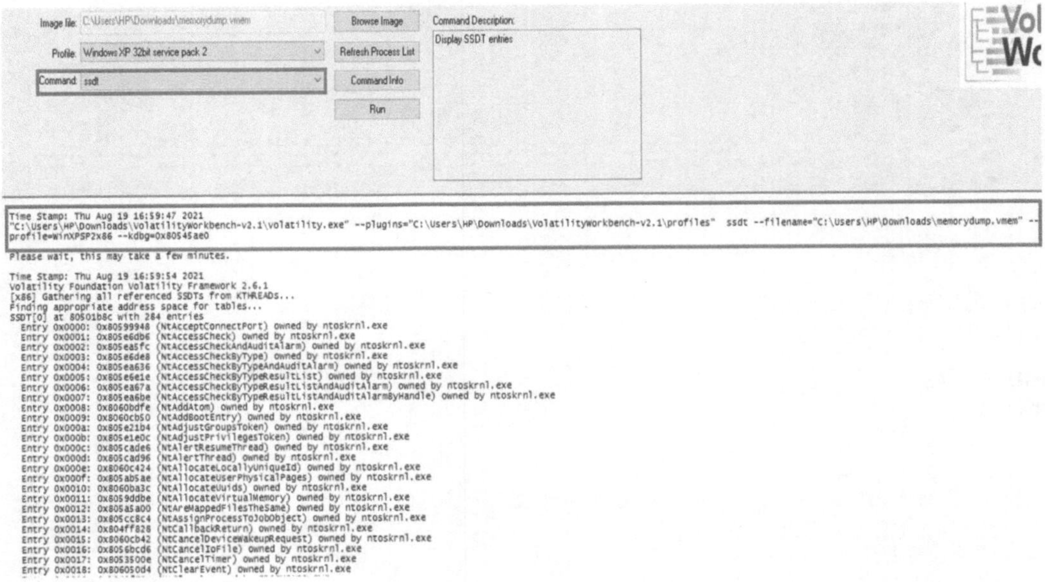

FIGURE 10.67
Ssdt.

the file, the number of pointers to the object, the number of descriptors to the object, and the actual permissions granted to the object are output (Figure 10.69).

18. **Mutantscan:** Mutantscan command is used to search the physical memory for KMUTANT objects with pool tag scanning. All objects are shown by default. However, you will be able to pass -s or --silent to solely display named mutexes.

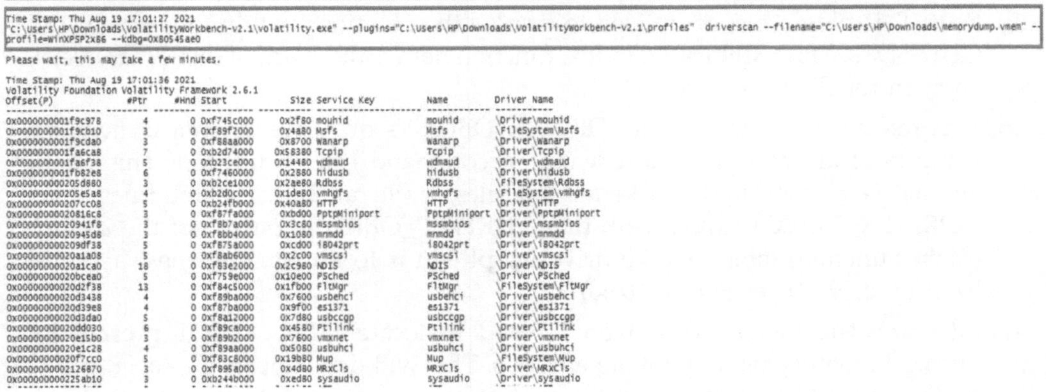

FIGURE 10.68
Driverscan.

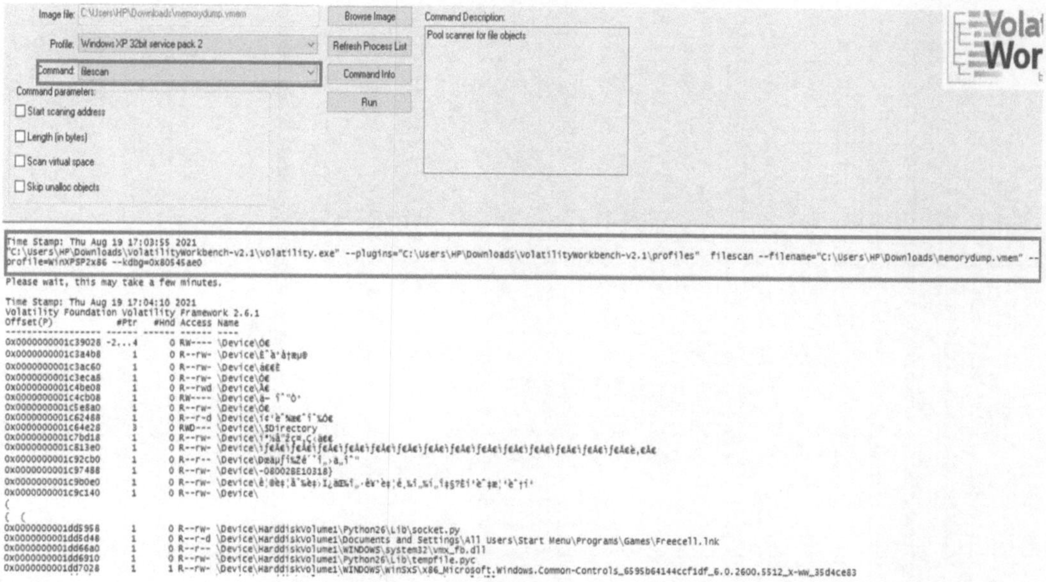

FIGURE 10.69
Filescan.

The process ID and thread ID of the mutex owner (if any) are contained in the CID column (Figure 10.70).

19. **Thrdscan:** It is used to inspect the thread objects contained in the physical memory using the pool scan. It also displays PIDs of different processes which is also useful in locating hidden processes if any (Figure 10.71).

FIGURE 10.70
Mutantscan.

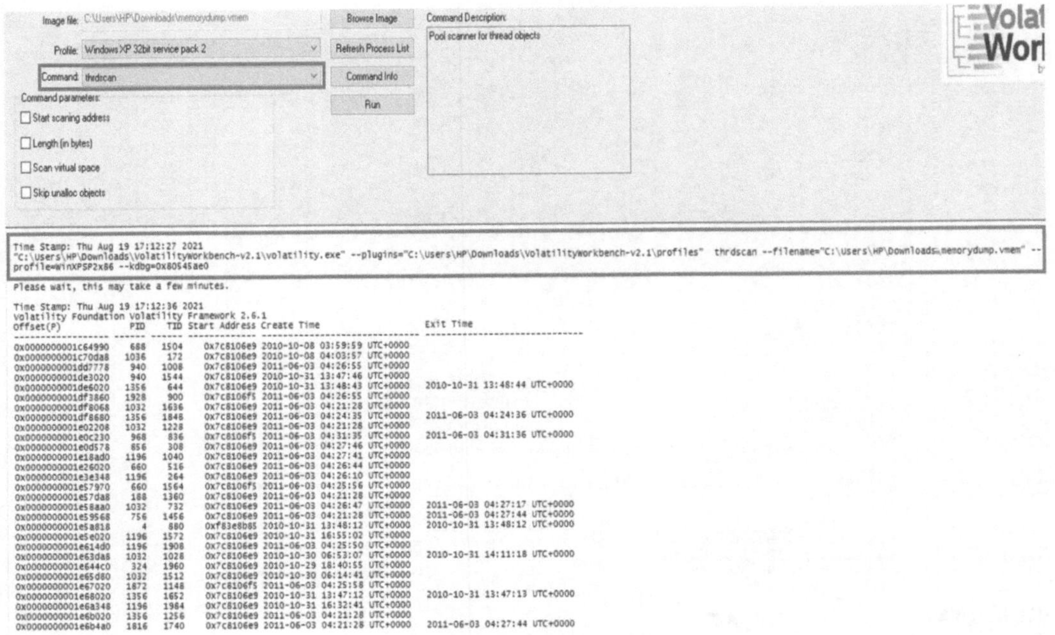

FIGURE 10.71
Thrdscan.

20. **Hivelist:** In general, this plugin is not useful on its own; it should be inherited from other plugins that rely on the information found in CMHIVE and interpret it (Figure 10.72).
21. **Hivescan:** Hivescan is used in order to locate the physical addresses of the registry hives (CMHIVEs) in memory (Figure 10.73).
22. **Printkey:** Utilize the printkey command to print the subkeys, values, information, and data types contained in an assigned register key. Printkey

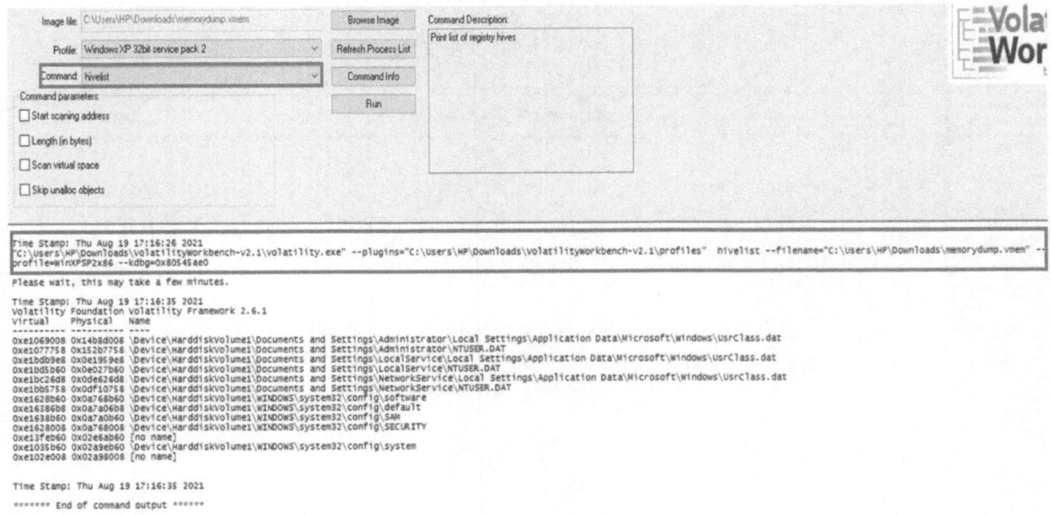

FIGURE 10.72
Hivelist.

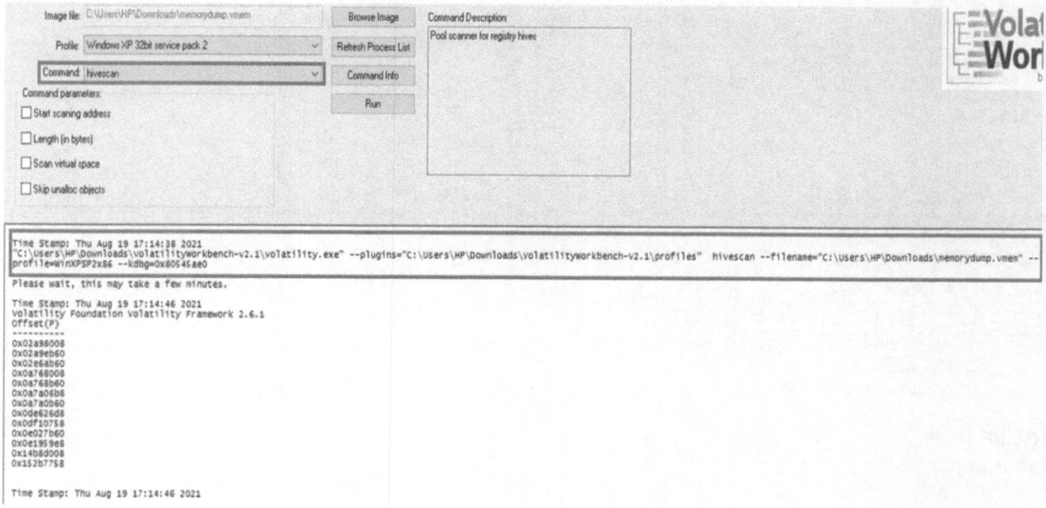

FIGURE 10.73
Hivescan.

consequently looks for all the hives and prints the key data (in case found) for the wished key. So, on the off chance that the key is found in more than one hive, the key subtle elements will be displayed for each hive that contains it (Figure 10.74).

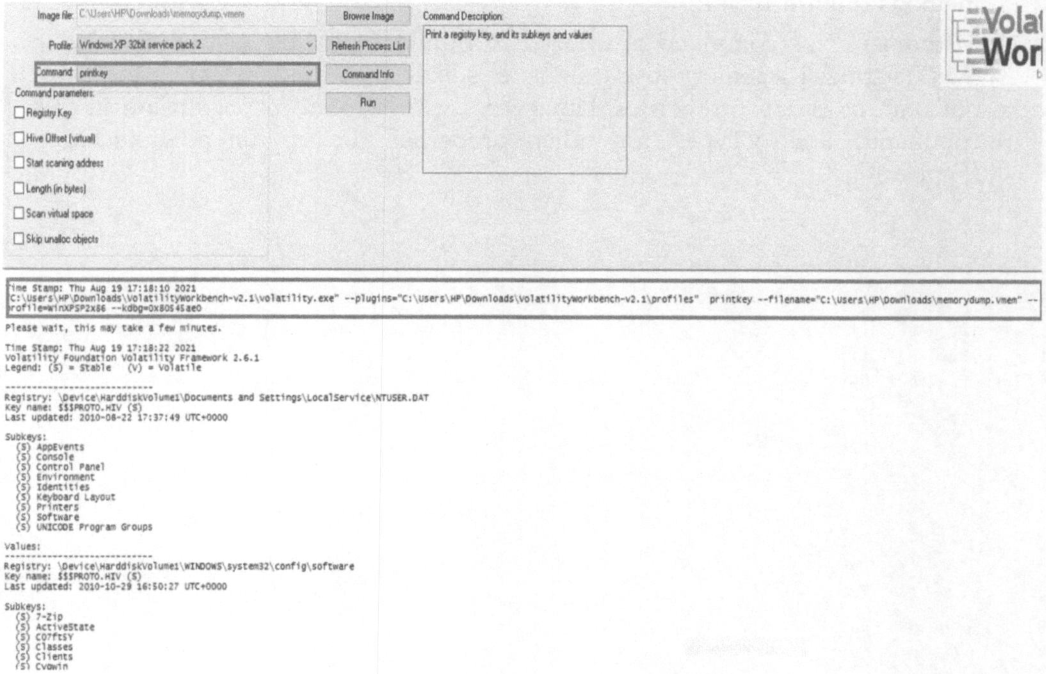

FIGURE 10.74
Printkey Command.

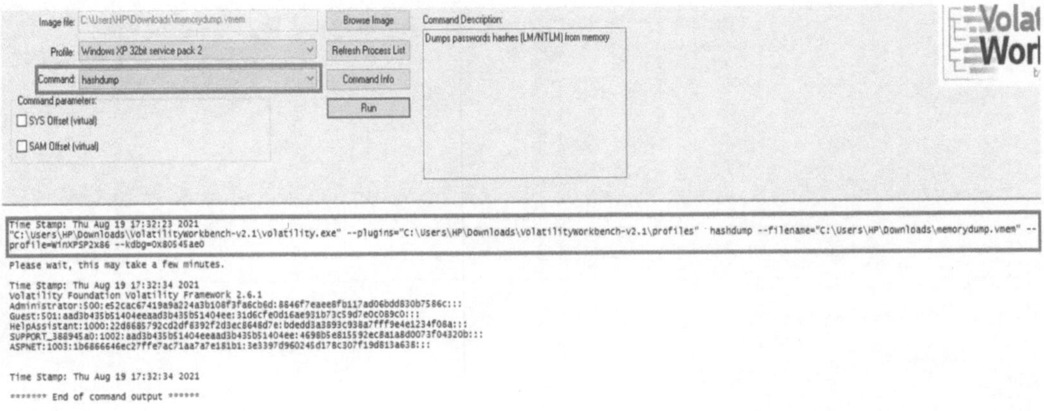

FIGURE 10.75
Hashdump.

23. **Hashdump:** The hashdump plugin is used to extract the hashes from the memory dump which might contain the domain credentials (Figure 10.75).
24. **Lsadump:** This command dumps the LS secrets from the registry. It is useful for obtaining information and credentials like passwords and hashes (Figure 10.76).
25. **Mbrparser:** This command looks for and parses possible MBRs (Master Boot Records). Locating MBRs and filtering results can be done using various methods (Figure 10.77).
26. **Mftparser:** This command is utilized to hunt for possible Master File Table (MFT) listings in memory (using signatures like "FILE" and "BAAD") and gives out data of certain properties. However, there is room for expansion in this command, and VTypes for other properties are as of now included (Figure 10.78).

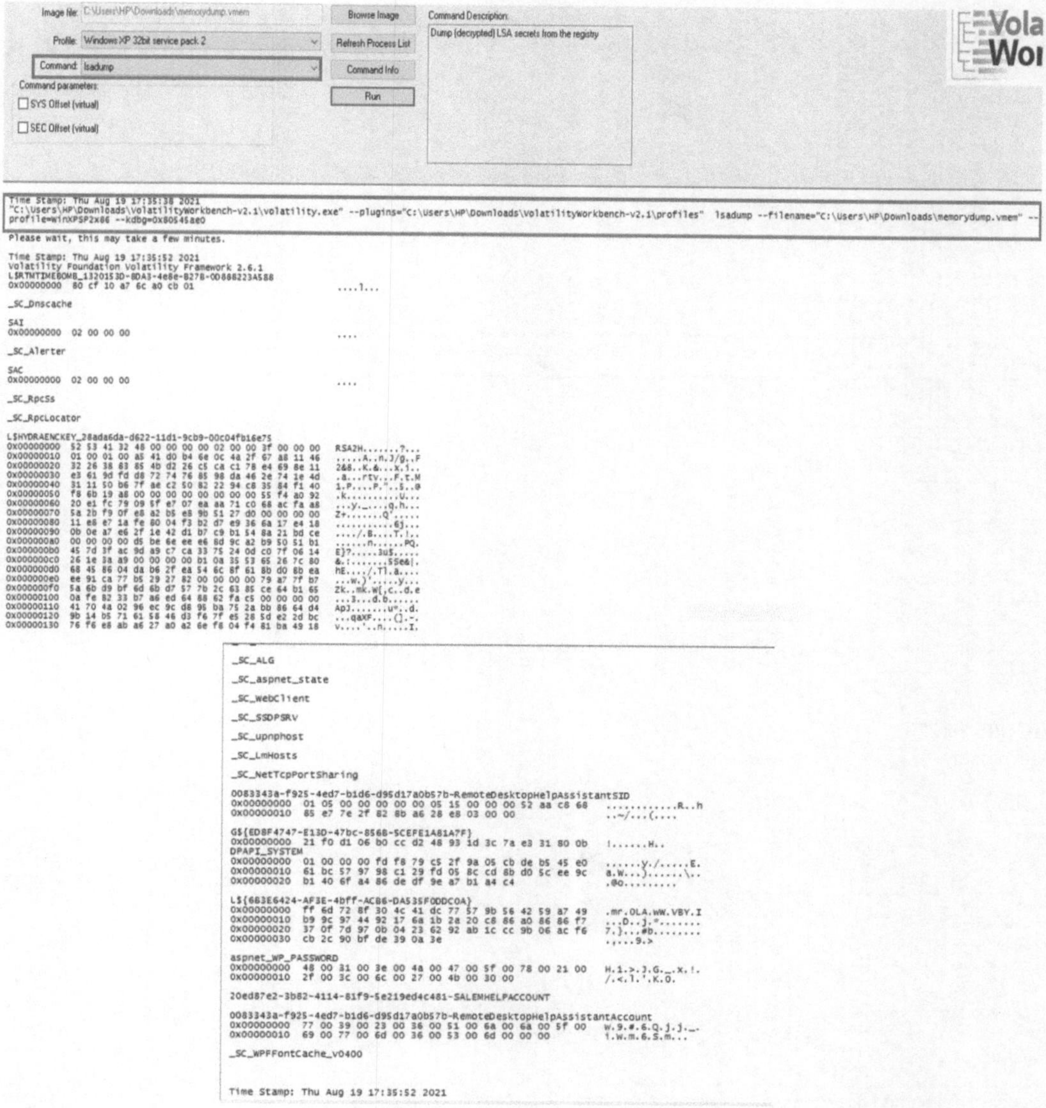

FIGURE 10.76
Lsadump.

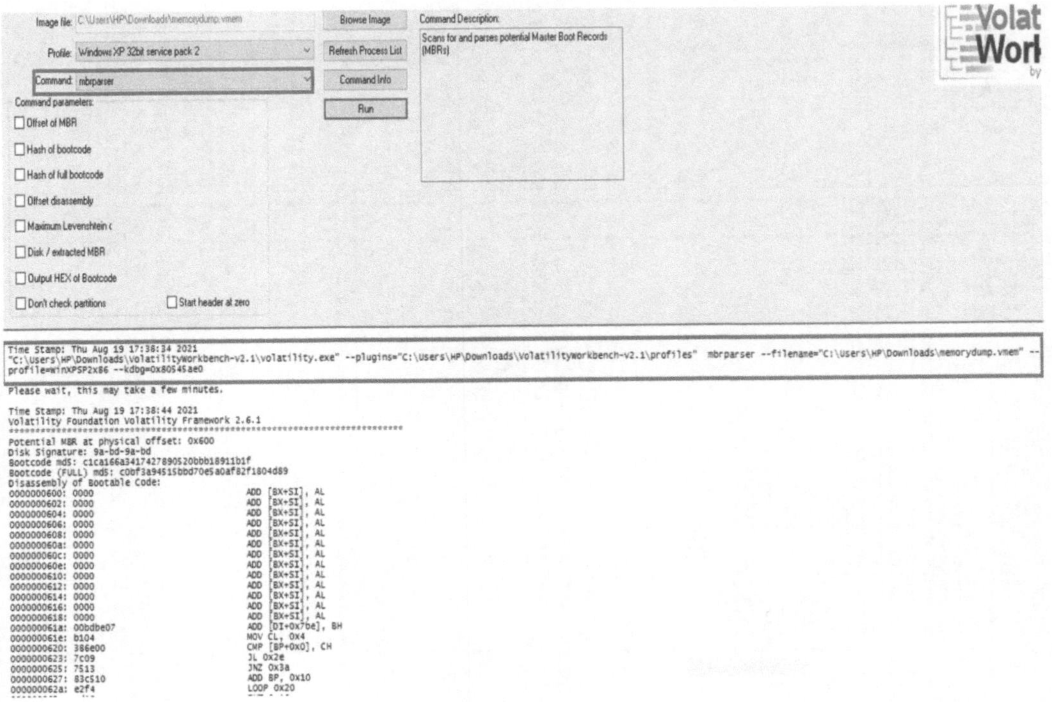

FIGURE 10.77
Mbrparser.

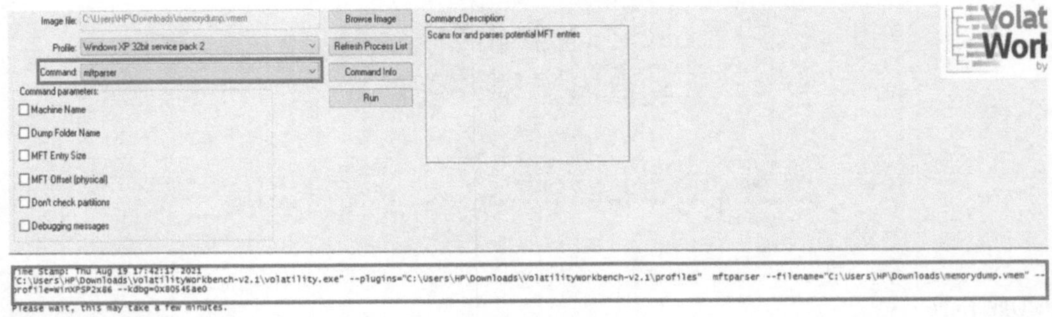

FIGURE 10.78
Mftparser.

10.5 Challenges in Live Memory Forensics

Though memory forensics is the need of the hour, it also has some challenges that need to be taken care of while performing an investigation:

1. Requires access to the system
2. Minimal impact on system
3. Some tools leave footprints and hence proper notes to be made
4. Timely evidence acquisition and analysis needs to be carried out

10.6 Conclusion

Memory forensics is a developing field and has huge scope in digital forensics. This field has an exceptionally splendid future regardless of the quick development in digital forensics in the last decade. The concentration on memory forensics is significant in order to control ever-increasing cybercrimes. There are many tools available in the market to handle and deal with cybercrime. This chapter has talked about FTK Imager by Access Data for memory Acquisition and the Volatility Framework and the Volatility Workbench for Memory Analysis. FTK Imager is an open-source tool that helps in capturing the live memory dump of the system of the employee in a forensically sound manner. One of its key advantages is that it is easy to use. The captured dump is further investigated with the Volatility Framework and Volatility Workbench to gather evidence in a comprehensive manner.

References

Al-Sabaawi, A. (2020, December). Digital forensics for infected computer disk and memory: Acquire, analyse, and report. In 2020 IEEE Asia-Pacific Conference on Computer Science and Data Engineering (CSDE) (pp. 1–7). IEEE.

Case, A., & Richard III, G. G. (2017). Memory forensics: The path forward. *Digital Investigation*, *20*, 23–33.

Chaudhuri, M., Gaur, J., Subramoney, S. (2019). Bandwidth-aware last-level caching: Efficiently coordinating off-chip read and write bandwidth. *2019 IEEE 37th International Conference on Computer Design (ICCD)*. pp. 109–118. doi:10.1109/ICCD46524.2019.00022

Dave, R., Mistry, N. R., & Dahiya, M. S. (2014). Volatile memory based forensic artifacts & analysis. *International Journal for Research in Applied Science and Engineering Technology*, *2*(1), 120–124.

FTK Imager Tool. (2021 October 16). Available from: https://accessdata.com/product-download/ftk-imager-version-3-4-2

Hay, B., Nance, K., & Bishop, M. (2009). Live analysis: Progress and challenges. *IEEE Security and Privacy*, *7*(2), 30–37.

Macht, H. (2013). Live memory forensics on android with volatility. Friedrich-Alexander University Erlangen-Nuremberg.

Memory Forensics Using Volatility Framework. (2021, October 16). Available from: https://www.hackingarticles.in/memory-forensics-using-volatility-framework/

Memory Forensics Using Volatility Workbench. (2021). https://cybersecurityconsultant.vn/blog/2021/12/01/memory-forensics-using-volatility-workbench/

Meera, A., & Swamynathan, S. (2013). Agent based resource monitoring system in IaaS cloud environment. *Procedia Technology*, 10, 200–207. https://doi.org/10.1016/J.PROTCY.2013.12.353

SANS DFIR Memory Forensics. (2021, October 16). Available from: https://www.sans.org/posters/dfir-memory-forensics/

Thangavel, M., Jeyapriya, B., & Suriya, K. S. (2021). Detection of worms over cloud environment: A literature survey. *Research Anthology on Architectures, Frameworks, and Integration Strategies for Distributed and Cloud Computing* (pp. 2472–2495).

The Volatility Framework. (2021 October 16). Available from: https://www.volatilityfoundation.org/releases

11

Forensics in Medical Imaging: Techniques and Tools

Bhavana Kaushik and Keshav Kaushik
School of Computer Science, University of Petroleum and Energy Studies, Dehradun Uttrakhand, India

CONTENTS

11.1 Introduction

Images are often considered a natural and efficient medium for a human being because image content is easy to grasp and understand. There has always been a question in the confidence of integrity of visual data, and images that are published in the newspaper are commonly considered authentic and accurate to be anticipated as primary substantial evidence in a court of law. Nowadays everybody has a probability of recording, storage, and communicating of huge quantity of digital imagery data because of the reasonably priced and comfortable to utilize gadgets. Plentiful obtainability of digital imagery and data can help scientific professionals to resolve the wrongdoings based on digital pictures. The manual processing of images is a cumbersome task and forensic pronouncements can be

DOI: 10.1201/9781003204862-11

exaggerated by numerous reasons such as cognitive framework and the brain, training and inspiration, managerial influences, base rate prospects, inappropriate case confirmation, reference substantial, and case evidence (W. D. Ferreira, Jul 2020). Healthcare industries and their allied domain have attained and accomplished boundless progression; instrumental expertise is very innovative today for calculating and monitoring human health factors. Ultrasounds, computed tomography (CT), X-ray, magnetic resonance (MR), and positron emission tomography (PET) are some general tools and mediums for clinical treatment of patients; detailed information is present in Table 11.1. The health practitioners and radiologists comprehensively depend upon the outcomes of such medical imagery data which is acquired from these medical sources along with their knowledge in building conclusions and deductions regarding treatment, medical illness, prescriptions, diagnosis, disease observation, planning of surgery, etc. Medical scans are exposed to be malevolently altered through transference over network, thus disturbing the findings of surgeons and clinicians. Furthermore, few imagery data in medical exploration work are purposefully influenced and transformed that decrease the reliability of the conclusions (Willemink MJ, 2020). Consequently, it is crucial to investigate an effective and strong process for medical image tamper uncovering and its position in the image. Such informative medical imagery data of patients has to be essentially systematized in a correct method in order to simplify consuming and retrieving such data and to avoid mismanagement and loss of data (Kelly, 2019) (Lou, Hu, & Liu, 2009). The presence of user-approachable and influential software and apps for modifying pictures like Photoshop makes altering of digital imagery data very simple. Lately, this matter has been confronted in medicinal imaging for the purpose of false insurance cover demands (Gadhiya, Mitra, & Mall, 2017). In the current scenario, the methods and procedure of image forensics have gained the consideration to authenticate the validity of the medical imagery data. These practices give confirmations about the reliability of the data and deliver indications about the manipulations' nature. Overall, methods of imagery data forensics are estimated under two main directions as

TABLE 11.1

Various Medical Imagery With **Its Method** and Usage (Goyal, Dogra, Agrawal, & Sohi, 2018)

Type of Medical Imaging	Imaging Method	Used to Diagnose
X-Ray	Ionizing Radiation	Bone rupture; knee issues; bone infections; other body diseases; abnormalities in breasts; issues in digestive tract
Computed tomography (CT) scan	Ionizing Radiation	Mental attack based injury; bone rupture; cyst and lumps; vascular ailment; heart-based issues; septicemia; for guiding biopsies
Magnetic resonance imaging (MRI)	Magnetic Waves	Stenosis; aortic; ganglion; neurological disorder; Multiple Sclerosis (MS); stroke; issues in spinal bones; lumps and tumors; issues in vein; damages in bone joints
Ultrasound	Sound Waves	Gall-bladder injury; lumps and cysts in breasts; prostate injury; swelling in body; blood flowing injury; gestation period diagnosis; guiding biopsies
PET (positron emission tomography) Scan	Radiotracer	Cancerous tissue; heart based concerns; coronary artery and blood vessel diagnosis; Alzheimer's disease; paroxysm and strokes; attack and contortion; Parkinson's ailment

active forensic procedures and inactive "blind" forensic practices (Vaishnavi & Subashini, 2019). The methods of medical image forensics are discussed thoroughly in the subsequent section. Under the banner of active forgery detection methods, digital watermarking is applied to cover a reliable and genuine watermark in the image data, and the digital signature is employed to augment signatures or message digests for prevention of tampering of visual data or information. Even though watermarking is an effective and efficient practice to authenticate the originality and reliability of imagery data, its execution desires that a watermark is concealed over the progression of imageries creation, thus, its consumption is narrowed down with the scope of its application that is proficient of creating digital objects with built-in watermarking. Today, most of the captured images are not watermarked. So, there is a severe obligation and need for passive forensic detection techniques. These practices are exploited to recognize signal and indication that remains after altering the imagery data (Mahmood, Mehmood, Khan, Shah, & Ashraf, 2016).

The intent of users varies with their different motives; a person can do tampering with the image intentionally or unintentionally. The innocent altering comprises various activities performed such as corrections, zooming, contrast brightness, and so on, which do not considerably modify the image. The wicked or malicious user's purpose is to modify and manipulate the matter of the imagery data, this is likely to change the inference of the visual data (Rajalakshmi, Alex, & Balasubramanian, 2017). In situation of medical imagery method, dim light environments and inadequate exposure forms result in degradation of samples by increasing the clatter effect. Considering medical images, exact and correct facts mining is of utmost significance for treatment and understanding disease. Because of accessibility of multi-sensor imaging machineries and tools, multi-type scans are freely bonded together to collect additional evidence. A boisterous scan still confines the fidelity of the merged image as well its truthful conception and therefore results in hindering the victim's carefulness and cure (Dance, Christofides, Maidment, McLean, & Ng, 2014). To protect digital medical scans and data, numerous types of picture safety devices have been engaged so far. Among these schemes, the image validation schemes are the superlative known and the most broadly used process by the current systems. The present image validation schemes may be categorized into two classes: hard authentication and soft authentication. (Lin & Chang, 2001). However, the approaches stated above not only change but also mislead the original image in an irreparable means. The distortion, no matter how trivial, may cause the changed medical images to be not used for further diagnosis because of the likelihood of misdiagnosis and wrong treatment. Considering the previous schemes and methods, the way to deal with imagery forensics is centrally grounded on descriptive study and pattern matching. Further, lately, developments in calculating competences ignited a transformed attentiveness in procedures constructed on machine learning. In specific, deep learning-based structures haave been efficaciously useful in the domain of foundation image forensics, and have substantiated their usefulness and efficiency in a number of applications area (Guan et al., 2019) (Figure 11.1).

After appraising Section 11.1 which consists of an overview of digital medical image falsification, the remaining of the study is structured as follows: Section 11.2 deals with the general schematic architecture of image tamper detection techniques. Section 11.3 is all about giving a brief overview of the tampering detection techniques, Section 11.4 presents a conversation on free forensics tools and approaches employed for identification of fake images. Section 11.5 is presenting the comparative study of different types of proposed algorithms for medical image forensics.

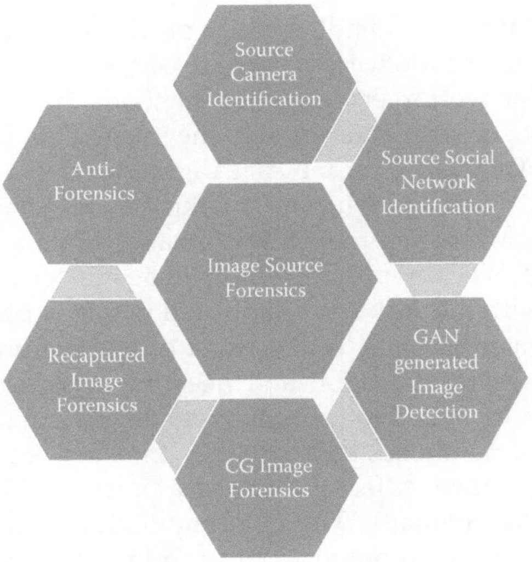

FIGURE 11.1
Various Image Source Forensics.

11.2 Comprehensive Phases for Image Forgery Identification

The fundamental objective of fake image identification procedure stays to categorize a specified digital photograph as genuine or reformed. The schematic architecture of imagery forgery identification system is shown in Figure 11.2.

Step 1. Image Preprocessing: It is the opening phase of the framework. The initial level processing is executed on the imagery data underneath discussion like image cleaning, image enhancement, pruning, modification in DCT factors, RGB to grayscale alteration beforehand usage of the picture to the procedure of fetching of the features (Makandar & Halalli, 2015).

Step 2. Feature Extraction: Choosing features set for each category split up the collection of images from other categories, nevertheless, intervening time stays persistent planned for a particular set elected. The striking section of the picked set of features is to have a little size so that processing overhead can be lessened and have a widespread peculiarity with added categories (Phkan & Borah, 2014).

Step 3. Choice of Classifier: Subject to the set of features that is mined in feature fetching phase, preferable classifier is either nominated or self-possessed. The outsized training sets will return the value-added presentation of classifier (Munirah, Nawi, Wahid, & Shukra, 2016).

Step 4. Classification: The mere aim behindhand arrangement is to decide if the imagery data is genuine or not. Neural network-based classifications (Lu, Sun, & Huang, 2018), LDA (Luo, Huang, & Qiu, 2016), and SVM are classifiers cast-off for this objective.

Step 5. Postprocessing: Some falsifications will probably demand post treating of an image that contains influences like localization of replica spots (Christlein, Riess, Jordan, & Angelopoulou, 2012)

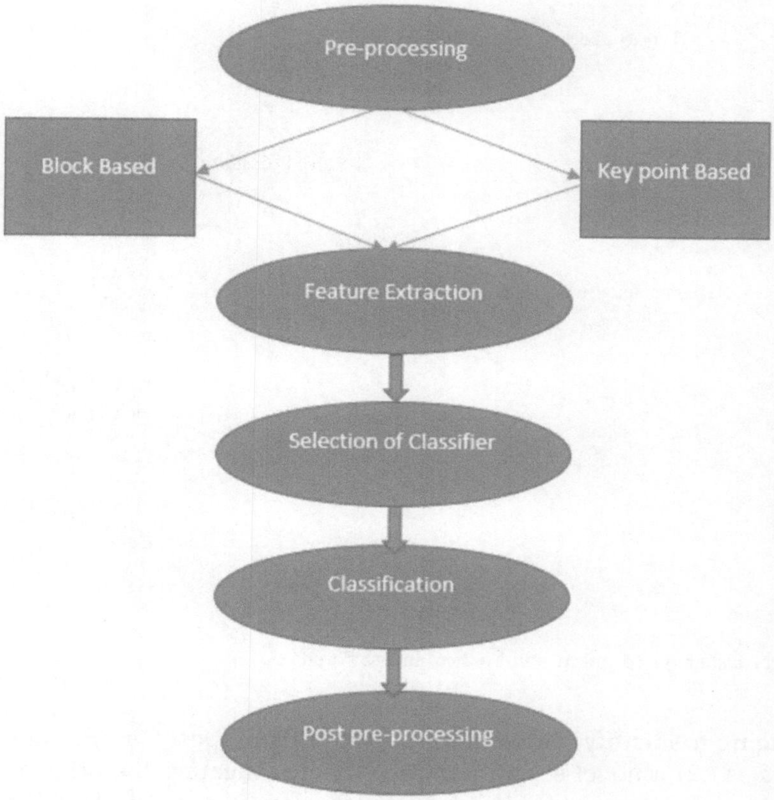

FIGURE 11.2
General Scheme of Forgery Identification in Medical Imaging.

11.3 Forgery Detection in Medical Imaging

Tampering or forgery of medical imagery data is fundamentally the act of mutating or adding characteristics structures to imageries, such as varying or removing some essential features and deprived perceptible clues (Kashyap, 2017). Many practices are applied for falsifying digital images. Considering the account of means used for medical image forgery, the most prominent methods and practices are enumerated below (Figure 11.3).

11.3.1 Active Forgery Detection Technique

A detection technique in an active forgery scheme wants pre-mined or pre-rooted information. Digital signature and Digital watermarking are normally acknowledged approaches under the active method of identification (Zhang, Ren, Ping, & Zhang, 2008).

11.3.1.1 Digital Watermarking

In this style of method, an alphanumeric watermark is embedded on the image, which is extremely unnoticeable to visualize. Then, the attached material is see-through, so it is

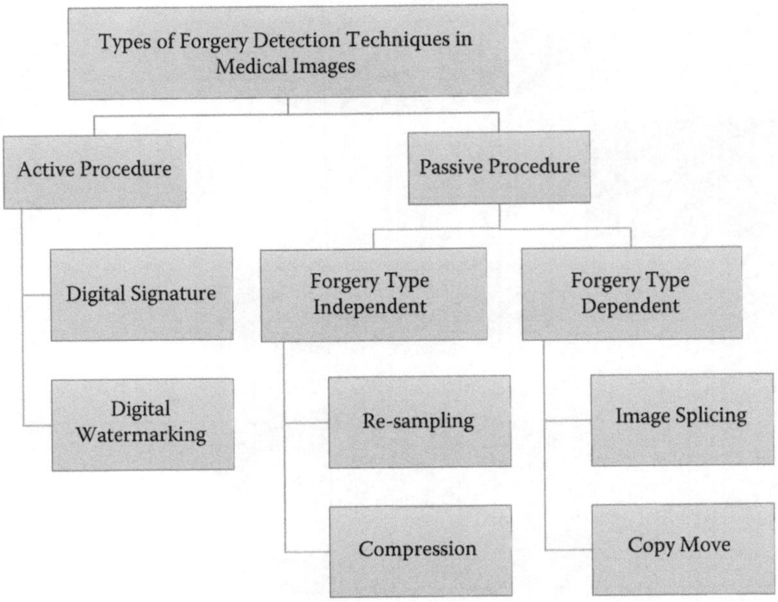

FIGURE 11.3
Different Forgery Detection Techniques in Medical Image Forensics.

very challenging to identify the mark or imprint. It is proposed in (Ferrara, Bianchi, De Rosa, & Piva, 2012) a novel scientific device for investigating the original picture and tampered area of an image grounded on the interpolation scheme, where it consumes the third ordinarily statistical characteristics throughout the falsification discovery; these marking algorithms are classified as reversible and irreversible. The irreversible distortions in the images are evaded constructed on the actual characteristics of the imagery by means of the reversible watermarking modus operandi. Watermarking can be principally utilized to direct the foundation or accredited user of the imagery. It is an arrangement of bytes that is implanted into a digital multimedia for pinpointing the initiator (Mushtaq & Mir, 2014). Hussain, Muhammad, Saleh, Mirza, and Bebis (2013) proposed a multi-resolution Weber Local Descriptors (WLD) for discovering and identifying the medical imagery counterfeits and tampering centered on the features gained from the chrominance modules. Also in this, the WLD histogram representation is considered and the Support Vector Machine (SVM)-based classifier is consumed to distinguish the tampering. In the current study, two diverse categories of counterfeits, for example, splice and copy-move are distinguished through means of the multiple resolution WLD methodology. The main modules of watermarking schemes are watermark generation, watermark embedding, and watermark extraction; all the above modules are shown in detail in Figures 11.4, 11.5, and 11.6, respectively.

11.3.1.2 Digital Signature

Habitually, the legitimacy of the alphanumeric communications is authenticated established on the digital signature. The addressee can have faith in the message that is designed by the known and authorized sender with the help of a legal signature. Thus, the digital signature is broadly exploited in the domain of financial trades, contract administration

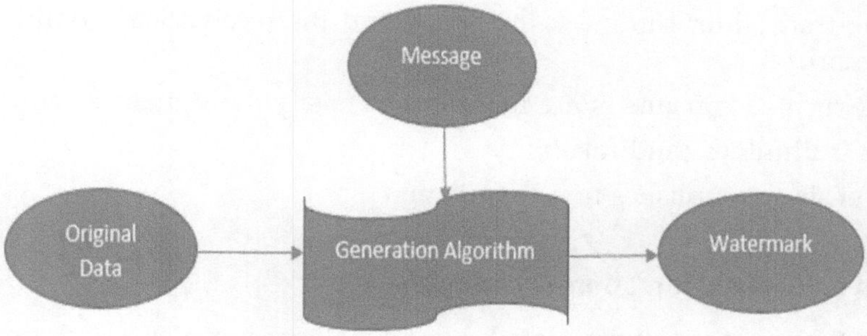

FIGURE 11.4
Watermark Generation. (Courtesy: Qasim, Meziane, & Aspin, 2018.)

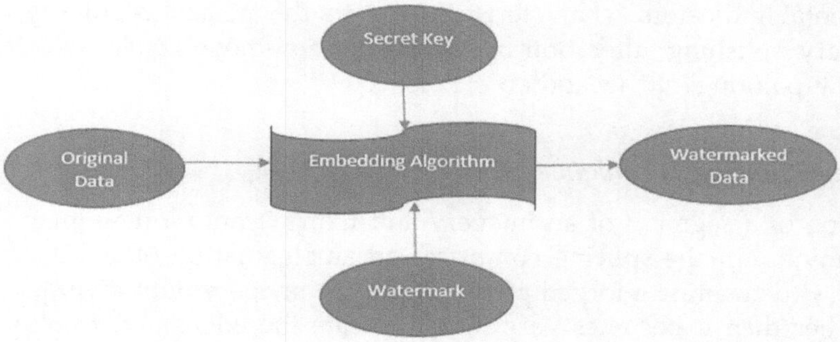

FIGURE 11.5
Watermark Embedding. (Courtesy: Qasim, Meziane, & Aspin, 2018.)

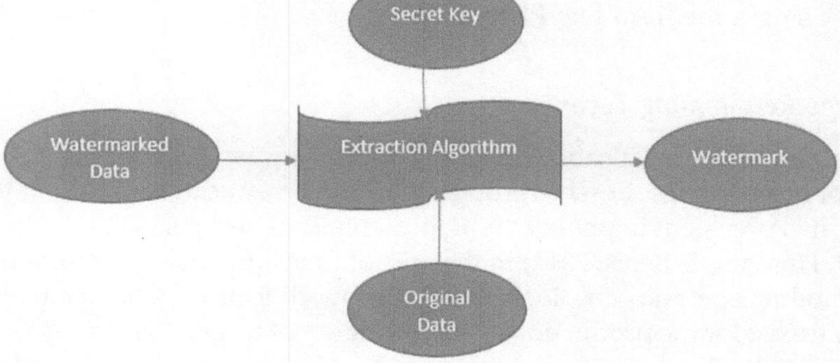

FIGURE 11.6
Watermark Extraction. (Courtesy: Qasim, Meziane, & Aspin, 2018.)

devices, and its dissemination (Mushtaq & Mir, 2014). Routinely, the digital signature implants some tributary facts, which are acquired from the imagery. In another scheme, the discrete characteristics are mined from the imagery throughout the preliminary period, grounded on these, the image legitimacy is authenticated (Mahmood et al., 2015). Classically, the digital signature has subsequent benefits:

- Only the transmitter can mark the image and the receiver can confirm the signature mark
- Unauthenticated consumers are incapable to falsify the signature
- It offers truthfulness and reliability
- Moreover, it accomplishes non-repudiation

11.3.2 Passive Forgery Detection Technique

When the legitimacy of the digital data by investigating its contents and arrangement is confirmed then this type of approach is called Passive Forensics. Passive systems, prevalently acknowledged as blind methods, simply use the image itself for its confirmation and reliability (Luo, Qu, Pan, & Huang, 2007). This scheme adopts that even though there might be no graphical signs of altering within the data, interfering possibly will intrude the fundamental indicators' characteristics due to the noise irregularity, blurring of image, imagery polishing, alteration by means of copy-move (Zhao, Liao, Shih, & Shi, 2013), image inpainting, etc. (Mahdian & Saic, 2009).

11.3.2.1 Image Splicing Technique

The replication of a segment of an imagery and fixing it onto a new image is called as splicing technique. Image splicing comprises an amalgamation of at least two or more visual imagery to generate a forged picture. If all the imagery with divergent footing are pooled together then it becomes very firm to create the edges and frontiers disjointed (Ibrahim, Moghaddasi, Jalab, & Noor, 2015). The procedure in which images are cut and pasted in areas from similar or dissimilar images is also known as splicing. It is also labeled as photomontage, which is cast-off for denoting an art form or deed of generating fused image that can be drawn back to the phase of camera origination (Sharma & Abrol, 2013). Image splicing is also used in the photomontage technique so that two images can be combined using a medium like Photoshop.

11.3.2.2 Image Re-sampling Technique

Among the other image falsifications, image re-sampling is identified as a slightly lesser destructive forgery practice, in which roughly improvement can be done on the imagery. Furthermore, it is prevalent in photo editing presentations and periodicals. The researchers (Muhammad, Hussain, & Bebis, 2012) in the area of image forensics put forward a wavelet conversion modus operandi for identifying the modification. Characteristically, other classy software exist for the production of such category of forgery by simply putting up the lenient changes at the boundaries. So, it is very problematic to discriminate the color and texture of the moved fragment with the unoriginal part. Image re-sampling includes crafting an extraordinary value counterfeit imagery by performing a few conversions like turning, resizing, enlarging, twisting, overturning, etc., in order to yield a substantial amalgamation of two items of dissimilar dimensions. This method has need to resample the real image onto a fresh one by familiarizing definite periodic correspondences among adjoining pixels. At this time, it is also specified that the conversion procedures which can identify and discover the falsification in an extremely packed down image. Some of the scholars also mentioned a Discrete Cosine Transform Quantization Coefficients

Decomposition (DCT-QCD) for distinguishing and removing this particular approach of forgery (Ghorbani, Firouzmand, & Faraahi, 2011).

11.3.2.3 Copy-Move Forgery Technique

Amid the other forgery approaches, the copy-move process is a widely preferred style of tampering of image, where the definite segment is fetched and inserted on another portion of the image (Mohamadian & Pouyan, 2013). The central intention of this scheme is to conceal a noteworthy component or signifies a detailed and particular entity. The researchers (Bayram, Sencar, & Memon, 2009) instigated a super-efficient scheme for discovering the alteration by copy-move process. The researchers indicated that the block matching technique is employed to identify this category of tampering by unraveling the imagery into overlying portions. Likewise, it classifies the reproduced associated data chunks by discovering the position between the neighbor blocks. To finally take conclusion regarding fake images, merely the replicated blocks recognition is not adequate, for the reason that the ordinary imageries have several alike blocks. Additionally, the Fourier Mellin Transform (FMT) is utilized to accomplish the processes like scaling, transformation, and rotation for medical scan forgery recognition (Zheng, Hao, & Zhu, 2012).

11.3.2.4 Compression Technique

Because of the accessibility to a number of powerful image handling tools or software, it is convenient to transform and alter the digital information without the addition of any indications or hints. Tampering indicators based on JPEG compression techniques are most profoundly employed in digital imagery forensics. A competent anti-forensic modus operandi is obligatory to measure the competency of JPEG forensic indicators. Shifted block DCT methodology on the specific JPEG compacted image to cover the voids in the comb-like scattering of DCT factors (Kaushik, Kumar, Jalal, & Bhatnagar, 2018). This shifted block DCT style headed to the insertion of indecisive noise itself deprived of any essential adaptive dithering framework (Kumar, Kansal, & Singh, 2019).

11.4 Forensic Approaches and Tools

Some of the proposed works that are proficient for digital imagery forgery detection are explored in this section. Oommen, Jayamohan, and Sruthy (2016) developed an algorithm based on fractal dimension and Support Vector Decomposition (SVD) to discover and insulate the replicated sections in the imagery data. In this structure, the image is categorized into different classes grounded on the value of its fractal dimension, which is used to recognize the discrepancies and deviations in the data. Then and there, the unoriginal and attached areas are recognized by means of a proficient texture-based grouping procedure. Chierchia, Poggi, Sansone, and Verdoliva (2014) instigated a Bayesian Markov Random Field (MRF) practice to categorize the photograph counterfeits centered on the sensor arrangement clatter. At this juncture, the detected facts and previous facts were stabilized by the usage of a Bayesian methodology. Murali, Chittapur, and Anami (2013) scrutinized and explored several image forgery discovery algorithms for classifying the forged areas in the tampered image. Pan and Lyu (2010) proposed a feature corresponding practice for detecting the reproduced segment in the digital imagery. Piva (Bianchi & Piva, 2012) established an innovative forensic system for distinguishing the difference between the real and forged sections in the image. Here, the special effects of cumulation among innumerable DCT factors are mined with the streamlined map by means of the unified statistical framework.

The software/tools that can be used for medical image forensics are as follows:

a. **Forensically**: It is an open source and free tool in digital imagery forensics that provides services and facilities such as cloning identification and reliable mining of metadata of the image easily (Wagner, 2020). The magnifier and the zooming capability attached in the tool support expert forensic specialists to catch concealed characteristics in an image by amplifying the pixels' dimensions, magnitude, and chromatic property. Magnification of image for recognition generally makes use of the subsequent 3 things grounded on data of the original image. This tool relates various parameters of image documents such as chrominance fidelity, fault ratio, image enlargement capabilities, and denseness of image. Study of noise is an additional facility of Forensically, which is employed as a median filter to detect disturbances in an imagery document that can be utilized for tampering recognition like airbrushing and enfolding. Level sweep functionality in it supports the forensic community to find out copy-pasting by making an allowance for sweep through a histogram of the digital picture. Additionally, the altered zones are likely to be noticeable and observable owing to the use of zooming capabilities of the tool. With the JPEG exploration mechanism, data miners can mine information from JPEG imagery, like quantization details of imagery data.
b. **Assembler**: In early 2020, Google circulated Assembler, which is a software implemented for media and reports community to perceive forgery in the images (Google, 2020). Assembler practices and makes usage of numerous prevailing procedures to distinguish general image manipulation findings like improvement of an image, copy-move, and splicing. Assembler software also contains an indicator to detect deep fakes, which is produced through StyleGAN methodology. Assembler can support forensic community to faithfully find which area of the imagery is altered, defining copy-paste and splicing in the existence of image illumination and intensity parameter. Despite the fact that Assembler can give assistance to journalists for spotting manipulated images, it does not take account of other prevailing tampering schemes for noticing the alteration in multimedia documents. Additionally, the Assembler tool is required to be employed on real-time medical scans for a better purpose.
c. **JPEGsnoop**: This, as described by (Hass, 2020), is a free tool that can calculate and fetch veiled and out-of-sight particulars of compacted imagery, video, and image created by various editing software. JPEGsnoop is also proficient in investigating the image's foundation to attain data from reduced imagery, such as fidelity parameter, and reportage on facts such as color-based quantization array, assessment of image quality features, Huffman counters, and histogram for color statistics data.

TABLE 11.2

Comparative Analysis of Various Forensics Tools

Tools	Pros	Cons
Forensically	Helps to identify clone finding, metadata abstraction, magnifier, study of error and noise in the image.	Localization discovery is not up to the mark.
Assembler	Enhancement and splicing in the image are identified easily.	Only a few processing capabilities are provided.
JPEGsnoop	Support in the mining of the veiled particulars of the compacted image and movable JPEG.	Identifies only a single compression technique e.g., JPEG not TIFF.

The above discussed free forensics tools that are available for the forensics communities are presented in Table 11.2 with their pros and cons.

11.5 Comparative Analysis

This section analyzes the prevailing forgery recognition procedures with respect to their own positive and negative aspects of the techniques. This investigation is primarily concentrated on the finding of image forgery by means of a number of forensic methodologies. The approaches which are inspected in the current inquiry are based on numerous forensics techniques that have been proposed by several researchers of image forensics community. The detailed comparative analysis of all the approaches is presented in Table 11.3. The merits and demerits along with the associated methods are also detailed in Table 11.3, which will give the proper insight to the researcher for better understanding and comprehension of all trending procedures in the field of medical image forgery detection.

11.6 Conclusion

With the development of innovative communication knowledge and machineries, new structures and services are delivered in a recent healthcare framework dealing with the different kinds of medical imagery and scans. The main objective of features and services is to give effortless, simple-to-use, precise, and real-time healthcare and medical support to the consumer and patients. As fitness and healthism are delicate concerns, it is better to be taken care of with extremely promising safety, carefulness, and alertness. This investigative study gauged numerous image forensics methodologies for detecting and preventing the malicious and harmful tampering executed on the computerized imagery. The methods considered in the current study are based on various methods like digital signature, digital watermarking, copy-move, image splicing, and image re-sampling with the general structure of its algorithm. Most of the researchers quantified that image forgery recognition is an exceedingly difficult and intricate practice due to the introduction of numerous manipulation and editing software. The properties and

TABLE 11.3

Comparative Analysis of Various Image Forensic Approaches

S. No.	Methods Used	Detection Techniques	Merits	Demerits
1	Deep convolution neural network CNN, a 2 branch CNN utilized with automatically learning hierarchy (Yuan Rao, Ni, & Zhao, 2020)	Image splice identification and localization process	Resiliency against JPEG compression Extreme recognition precision	High computational overheads while using 3 linear high pass filter Future hybrid transformation is complex
2	Novel procedure used, "AttentionDM" for CISDL (Liu & Zhao, 2020)	Splice-based forgery recognition, and finds whether one picture has forged segment attached from another image.	High throughput Better computational efficiency	Equal error results and identification rates are diminished Less efficient than DMAC
3	Mathematical morphological filter forgery identifier by means of Gaussian low pass and Median filtering (Boato, Dang-Nguyen, & Denatale, 2020)	Functioned on grayscale digital imagery data and stated a fresh and novel extension of a deterministic scheme specifically detecting erosion and dilation of binary imagery data	Highly robust to image compression Extremely good accuracy	Mathematical and time overheads and its management is high
4	Enhanced deep learning-based model which is low in computation and complexity (Le-Tien, Phan-Xuan, Nguyen-Chinh, & DoTieu, 2019)	Daubechies wavelet transform is employed, presenting YCrCb segments inside the image, neural network used to categorize forged segments of the tampered image.	Reduce computational cost Increase accuracy	Not highly robust Time complexity is high
5	Three classifiers Multiclass Model using SVM Learner, K-NN and Naïve Bayes are utilized to train the classifier model (Jaiswal & Srivastava, 2019)	Spliced image forgery detection using image as input for CNN and processed through numerous levels of training	Increase the accuracy Localization of spliced forged image efficiently	Not preferable for copy-move fake image identification High performance system to execute the technique is required
6	Pixel-based image forgery detection (Kashyap, Parmar, Agrawal, & Gupta, 2017)	Image splicing, copy-move, and image resampling forgeries are identified.	Improved precision Enhanced reliability	Does not perform well in the clattered image. Time overheads are high

(*Continued*)

TABLE 11.3 ***(Continued)***

Comparative Analysis of Various Image Forensic Approaches

S. No.	Methods Used	Detection Techniques	Merits	Demerits
7	Brute-force, block based and key point based technique (Gill, Garg, & Doegar, 2017)	A common architecture is prepared for detecting a copy move image tampering.	Reduced complexity Highly efficient and robust	Not preferable for complexed background details and texture Less accurate
8	Lateral Chromatic Aberration (LCA) and block matching scheme (Mayer & Stamm, 2018)	Image falsification is identified by exploiting the hypothesis testing problem.	Increased efficacy Reduced overheads	Increased calculation error Not preferable for clattered imagery
9	Passive digital imagery forensic methods (Lin, Li, Wang, Cheng, & Huang, 2018)	It identifies the image tampering grounded on the artefacts.	Better generalization capabilities Reduced time overheads	Most forgery cases are not properly treated Performance degradation

parameters also play a critical role in forgery identification for the reason that the structures are utterly subtle to some forgery processing. Furthermore, diverse image processing methods, such as prior processing of the image, extraction of feature, feature selection, and categorization, are greatly beneficial and advantageous for recognizing tampering in a precise mode. The passive methods in forensics techniques are highly appropriate for forgery detection in the domain of medical imaging as compared to the active approaches. A passive method of medical image forensics analyzes the pixel dissimilarities and evaluates the geometrical illuminations and chrominance in a full effectual style. Among the other passive forgery identification techniques in the field of medical image forensics, copy-move and image splicing are extensively executed by several investigators because of their advantage of condensed and lower computational overheads and improved accurateness. Also people and community present in image forensics also have many free tools for forgery detection in images and it can easily be applied to medical scans and pictures for better reliability and precision.

References

Bayram, S., Sencar, H., & Memon, N. (2009). An efficient and robust method for detecting copy-move forgery. *International Conference on Acoustics, Speech and Signal Processing*, 1053–1056.

Bianchi, T., & Piva, A. (2012). Image forgery localization via block-grained analysis of JPEG artefacts. *IEEE Transactions on Information Forensics and Security*, 1003–1017.

Boato, G., Dang-Nguyen, D.-T., & Denatale, F. G. (2020). Morphological filter detector for image forensics application. *IEEE Access*.

Chaitra, B., & Reddy, P. V. (2019). A study on digital image forgery techniques and its detection. *International Conference on Contemporary Computing and Informatics (IC3I)*, 127–130.

Chierchia, G., Poggi, G., Sansone, C., & Verdoliva, L. (2014). A Bayesian-MRF approach for PRNU based image forgery detection. *IEEE transactions on Information Forensics and Security*, 554–567.

Christlein, V., Riess, C., Jordan, J., & Angelopoulou, E. (2012). An evaluation of popular copymove forgery detection approaches. *IEEE Transactions on Information Forensics and Security*, 1841–1854.

Dance, R., Christofides, S., Maidment, A. D., McLean, I. D., & Ng, K. H. (2014). Diagnostic radiology physics. *International Atomic Energy Agency*.

Ferrara, P., Bianchi, T., De Rosa, A., & Piva, A. (2012). Image forgery localisation via fine-grained analysis of CFA artefacts. *IEEE transactions on Information Forensics and Security*, 1566–1577.

Gadhiya, T. R., Mitra, S., & Mall, V. (2017). Use of discrete wavelet transform method for detection and localization of tampering in a digital medical Image. *IEEE Region 10 Symposium*, 1–5.

Ghorbani, M., Firouzmand, M., & Faraahi, A. (2011). DWT-DCT (QCD) based copy-move image forgery detection. *International Conference on Systems, Signal and Image Processing*, 1–4.

Gill, N. K., Garg, R., & Doegar, E. A. (2017). A review paper on digital image forgery detection techniques. *International Conference on Computing, Communication, and Networking*, 1–7.

Google. (2020). Assembler.

Goyal, B., Dogra, A., Agrawal, S., & Sohi, B. (2018). Noise issues prevailing in various types of medical images. *Biomedical and Pharmacology Journal*, 11(3).

Guan, H., Kozak, M., Robertson, E., Lee, Y., Yates, A., Delgado, A., … & Kheyrkhah, T. (2019). MFC Datasets: Large scale benchmark dataset for media forensics challenge evaluation. *IEEE Winter Application of Computer Vision Workshops*, 63–72.

Hass, C. (2020). JPEGsnoop.

Hussain, M., Muhammad, G., Saleh, S. Q., Mirza, A. M., & Bebis, G. (2013). Image forgery detection using multi-resolution weber local descriptors. *IEEE EUROCON*, 1550–1577.

Ibrahim, R. W., Moghaddasi, Z., Jalab, H. A., & Noor, R. M. (2015). Fractional differential texture descriptor based on the mach ado entropy for image splicing detection. *Internal Journal of Computer Science*, 4775–4786.

Jaiswal, A. K., & Srivastava, R. (2019). Image splicing detection using deep residual network. *International Conference on advanced computing and software engineering*.

Kashyap, A. (2017). An evaluation of digital image forgery detection approaches.

Kashyap, A., Parmar, R. S., Agrawal, M., & Gupta, H. (2017). An evaluation of digital image forgery detection.

Kaushik, B., Kumar, M., Jalal, A. S., & Bhatnagar, C. (2018). A context based tracking for similar and deformable objects. *International Journal of Computer Vision and Image Processing*, *8*(4), 1–15.

Kelly, C. K. (2019). Key challenges for delivering clinical impact with artificial intelligence. *BMC Med*, *17*.

Kumar, A., Kansal, A., & Singh, K. (2019). An improved anti-forensic technique for JPEG compression. *Multimed Tools Appl*, *78*, 25427–25453.

Le-Tien, T., Phan-Xuan, H., Nguyen-Chinh, T., & DoTieu, T. (2019). Image forgery detection: A low computational-cost and effective data driven model. *International Journal of Machine Learning and Computing*.

Lin, C. Y., & Chang, S. F. (2001). A robust image authentication method distinguishing JPEG compression from malicious manipulation. *IEEE Transactions* on *Circuits* and *Systems* for *Video Technology*, 153–168.

Lin, X., Li, J. H., Wang, S. L., Cheng, F., & Huang, X. S. (2018). Recent advances in passive digital image security forensics: A brief review. *Engineering*.

Liu, Y., & Zhao, X. (2020). Constrained image splicing detection and localization with attention aware encoder decoder and atrous convolution. *IEEE Access*.

Lou, D.-C., Hu, M.-C., & Liu, C.-L. (2009). Multiple layer data hiding scheme for medical images. *Computer Standards & Interfaces*, 329–335.

Lu, W., Sun, W., & Huang, J. W. (2018). Digital image forensics using statistical features and neural network classifiers. *International Conference on Machine Learning and Cybernetics*, 12–16.

Luo, W., Huang, J., & Qiu, G. (2016). Robust detection of region-duplication forgery in digital images. *Internation Conference on Pattern Recognition*, 746–749.

Luo, W., Qu, Z., Pan, F., & Huang, J. (2007). A survey of passive technology for digital image forensics. *Front Computer Science China*, 166–179.

Mahdian, B., & Saic, S. (2009). Using noise inconsistencies for blind image forensics. *Image and vision computing*, 1497–1503.

Mahmood, T. N., Mehmood, Z., Khan, Z., Shah, M., & Ashraf, R. (2016). Forensic analysis of copy-move forgery in digital images using the stationary wavelets. *Sixth International Conference on Innovative Computing Technology*, 578–583.

Mahmood, T., Nawaz, T., Ashraf, R., Shah, M., Khan, Z., & A, I. (2015). A survey on block based copy move image forgery detection techniques. *Emerging Technologies*, 1–6.

Makandar, A., & Halalli, B. (2015). A review on preprocessing techniques for digital mammography images. *International Journal of Computer Applications*.

Mayer, O., & Stamm, M. C. (2018). Accurate and efficient image forgery detection using lateral chromatic aberration. *IEEE Transactions on Information Security and Forensics*.

Mohamadian, Z., & Pouyan, A. A. (2013). Detection of duplication forgery in digital images in uniform and non-uniform regions. *International Conference on Computer Modelling and Simulation*, 455–460.

Muhammad, G., Hussain, M., & Bebis, G. (2012). Passive copy move image forgery detection using undecimated dyadic wavelet transform. *Digital Investigation*, 49–57.

Munirah, M. Y., Nawi, N. M., Wahid, N., & and Shukra, M. (2016). A comparative analysis of feature selection techniques for classification problems. *ARPN Journal of engineering and applied sciences*, 13176–13187.

Murali, S., Chittapur, G. B., & Anami, B. S. (2013). Comparison and analysis of photo image forgery detection techniques.

Mushtaq, S., & Mir, A. H. (2014). Digital image forgeries and passive image authentication techniques: A survey. *International Journal of Advanced Science and Technology*, 15–32.

Oommen, R. S., Jayamohan, M., & Sruthy, S. (2016). Using fractal dimension and singular value for image forgery detection and localisation. *Procedia Technology*, 1452–1459.

Pan, X., & Lyu, S. (2010). Region duplication detection using image feature matching. *IEEE Transactions on Information Forensics and Security*, 857–867.

Phkan, A., & Borah, M. (2014). A survey paper on the feature extraction module of offline handwriting character recognition. *International Journal of Computer Engineering and Application*, 875–887.

Qasim, A. F., Meziane, F., & Aspin, R. (2018). Digital watermarking: Applicability for developing trust in medical imaging workflows state of the art review. *Computer Science Review*, 45–60.

Rajalakshmi, C., Alex, M. G., & Balasubramanian, R. (2017). Study of image tampering and review of tampering detection techniques. *IJARCS*, *8*(7), 963–967.

Sharma, D., & Abrol, P. (2013). Digital image tampering – a threat to security. *IJARCCE*, 4120–4123.

Vaishnavi, D., & Subashini, T. (2019). Application of local invariant symmetry features to detect and localize image copy move forgeries. *Journal of Information Security*, 44, 23–21.

W. D. Ferreira, C. B. (Jul 2020). A review of digital image forensics. *Computers & Electrical Engineering*, *85*, 106685. doi: 10.1016/j.compeleceng.2020.106685.

Wagner, J. (2020). Forensically tool.

Willemink MJ, K. W. (2020). Preparing medical imaging data for machine learning. *Radiology*, *295*(1), 4–15.

Yang, P., Baracchi, D., Ni, R., Zhao, Y., Argenti, F., & Piva, A. (2020). A survey of deep learning-based source image forensics. *Journal of Imaging*.

Yuan Rao, Y., Ni, J., & Zhao, H. (2020). Deep learning local descriptor for image splicing detection and localization. *IEEE Access*.

Zhang, Z., Ren, X., Ping, Z., & Zhang, S. (2008). A survey on passive blind image forgery by doctor method detection. *International Conference on Machine Learning and Cybernetics*, 3463–3467.

Zhao, Y. Q., Liao, M., Shih, F. Y., & Shi, Y. Q. (2013). Tampered region detection of impainting JPEG images. *International Journal on Light Electron Optics*, 2487–2492.

Zheng, J., Hao, W., & Zhu, W. (2012). Detection of copy-move forgery based on keypoints positional relationship. *Journal of Information and Computational Science*, 4729–4735.

12

Exploring Face Detection and Recognition in Steganography

Urmila Pilania[1], **Rohit Tanwar**[2], **and Neha Nandal**[3]
[1]*Manav Rachna University, Faridabad, Haryana, India*
[2]*University of Petroleum & Energy Studies, Dehradun, Uttarakhand, India*
[3]*Gokaraju Rangaraju Institute of Engineering and Technology, Hyderabad, India*

CONTENTS

12.1 Introduction

With the advancement of technology, almost everyone prefers the internet for information transmission all over the world. Possible ways for transmitting information through the internet are e-mails, chats, social sites, etc. Information transmission is made very fast

DOI: 10.1201/9781003204862-12

using a high-speed internet connection. One major problem with transmitting information online is the security of unauthorized users. Transmitted information can be hacked by an unauthorized person in many different ways. For providing safety to online information, certain methods already exist like cryptography, digital signature, watermarking, steganography, and many more.

Steganography is the way of hiding secret data inside a carrier file. Steganography is categorized as text, image, audio, and video based on the type of carrier file. Among all these types, video steganography is found to be the most efficient for concealing secret information. Because it has the option of hiding secret data inside inaudible frequencies and images as well. Again, videos are large in size, therefore, secret data can be hidden randomly in the number of frames. Also, concealing secret information in the selected area improves imperceptibility. The selected area is the human face is known as ROI—Region of Interest. For finding ROI, first, by applying a face detection algorithm, skin portion in an image is identified. Then, features like eyes, nose, and lips are identified for finding the human face.

The human faces have almost all information in low-frequency components, so high-frequency components can be used for concealing secret information. That's why steganography is combined with face detection. With the help of steganography methods, a secret key can be concealed in human faces. Then, that face can be recognized by the face recognition method. Face recognition can be used to recognize the input and output face at both ends. By doing so, secret information can be sent to a third party without being known, anyone. However, the challenges associated with steganography methods are low capacity, poor visual quality of output files, and exposure to various image-processing attacks. It's very difficult to establish a balanced relationship between the parameters of the magic triangle, as shown in Figure 12.1 [1]. For avoiding or reducing the impact of all these challenges, steganography is combined with face detection and recognition methods [2].

12.1.1 Face Detection Using Viola-Jones Algorithm

Face detection is an electronic process of identifying a face in an image/video with the help of computer technology. It finds the position and dimension of a human face in the image. In this process, facial features such as eyes, nose, lips, etc., are identified first and other items such as hills, trees, walls, etc., if any, are discarded from the image. It could be defined as a particular case of entity class identification, where the main task is the identification of the position and dimensions of all entities in the input file that lies

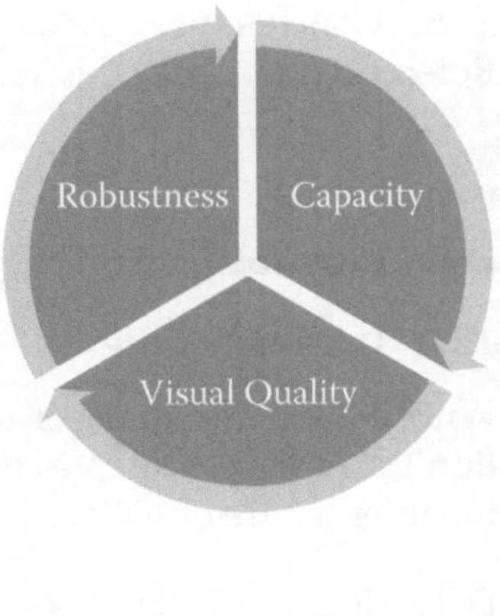

FIGURE 12.1
Magic Triangle for Steganography.

in the given class. Finally, if face is found in an image, then return position of face, dimensions of face, and put boundary box around the face [3]. The process of face detection by using the Viola-Jones algorithm is shown in Figure 12.2 [4].

- **Haar Feature:** The face of every human has some common features such as eyes, nose, chin, lips, etc., all of these features could be used for detecting edges in the image [5].
- **Integral Image:** It is a transitional illustration of an image in terms of pixels. Location (x, y) on the integral image is equivalent to the summation of pixels above and left of (x, y) on the original image.
- **Adaboost:** By using this feature, irrelevant portions of the image are calculated to decrease the complexity of relevant features. Adaboost is a machine learning technique trained on the dataset.
- **Cascade:** If features like eyes, lips, chin, and mouth are found, then the face is detected. Face and non-face regions are identified using this algorithm.

Some basic face detection methods available are shown in Figure 12.3 [6]. Mainly for detecting a face in an image, two types of methods exist that are based on characteristics and image [7]. The characteristics-based method attempts to retrieve characteristics of the image and match it with the understanding of facial features. In contrast, the image-based method attempts to find the finest match among training and testing images. The method of face detection is commonly applied to still images or videos. In an image, face detection is very challenging as the user is not aware of facial expressions, varying poses, scares, angles, etc. All these factors make detection of the face very difficult because the overall appearance of the face varies with the changing parameters [8].

In 2001, Viola and Jones introduced the concept of object detection. It is targeted to identify images in real-time. After this, the concept of face detection predominantly inspired researchers to provide the required solution. These days several face detection software exists. Open-Source Face detection software are listed in Table 12.1 with its pros and cons.

The face detection software has various features. Some of these software are also able to handle the challenges associated with face detection methods. Face detection can be done by installing software on the computer.

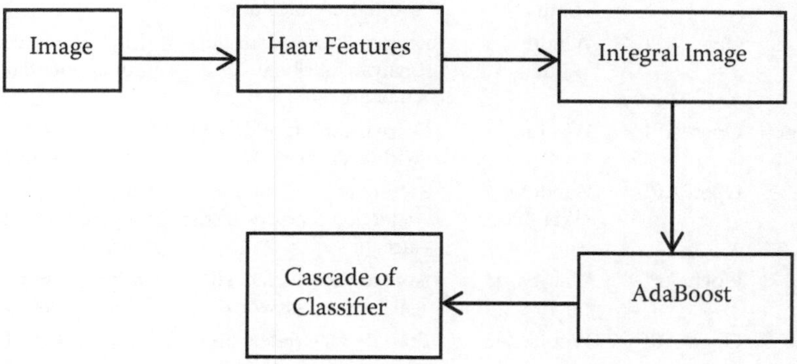

FIGURE 12.2
Viola-Jones Face Detection Process.

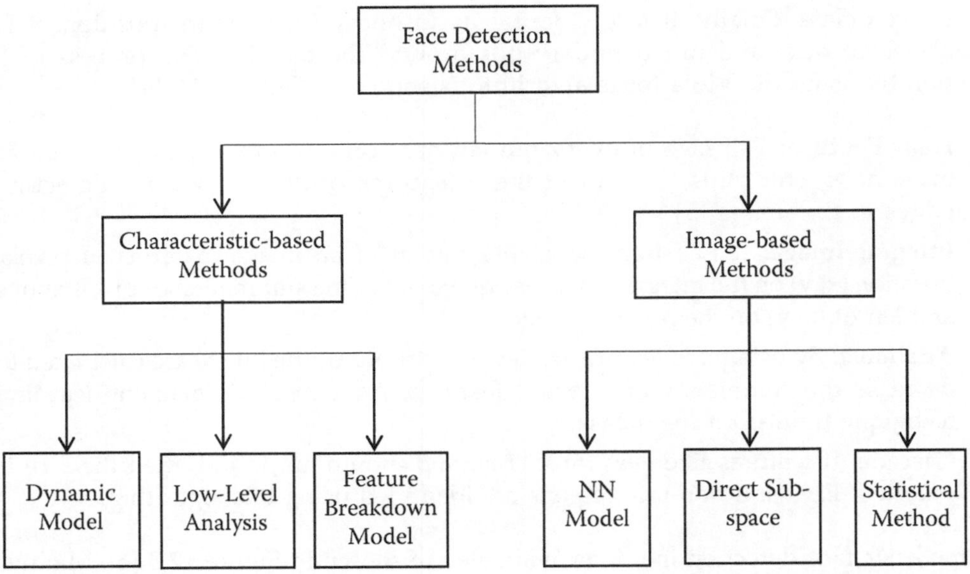

FIGURE 12.3
Face Detection Methods.

12.1.2 Face Recognition

For face recognition, the first face is perceived in the image using some face detection methods. A face recognition system is used to identify a given face in a data set. Components of the face recognition process are explained in Figure 12.4 [9,10].

TABLE 12.1
Open-Source Face Detection Software

Face Detection Software	Deployment	Operating System	Feature	Web Link
OpenBR	Open API	Window, Mac, Linux	Age estimation, gender estimation, face detection	http://openbiometrics.org/
Flandmark	Open API	Window, Linux	Do face tracking, attribute analysis, attribute comparison	http://cmp.cvut.cz/uricamic/flandmark/
OpenFaceTracker	Open API	Window	Do real-time face detection with accuracy	http://www.openfacetracker.net/
OpenEBTS	Open API	Window, Web-based	Secure and accurate in detection features of the face	http://www.openbiometricsinitiative.org/
Bioenable Tech-iFace	Open API	Web-Based	Able to detect a face, finger, card, and password	http://www.bioenableface.com
Bioenble Tech-vFace	Open API	Web-Based	Provide face detection and recognition with accuracy	http://www.bioenableface.com/bioenable-vface
DeepFace	Cloud-hosted	Web-Based, Window, Mac	Handle issues: age, gender, pose, eye position, and skin color	http://www.deepface.ir

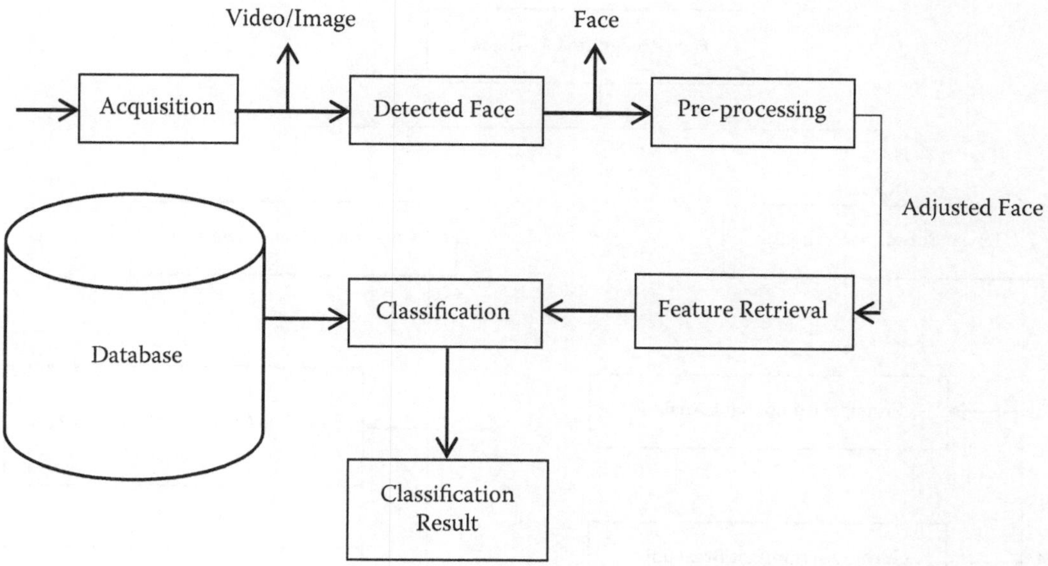

FIGURE 12.4
Face Recognition Process.

- **Acquisition:** It is the first step for the recognition of the face in an image. An existing image can be used for the purpose or a live image can also be taken [11].
- **Detection of Face:** For a given image, the detector algorithm is said to be efficient if it recognizes faces irrespective of their size, position, rotation, scale, orientation, age, intensity, illumination, contrast, angle, and expression [12].
- **Pre-Processing:** This method enhances the excellence of the source image in terms of color, contrast, illumination, and intensity. By doing pre-processing, the complexity of the recognition procedure could be reduced [13].
- **Feature Retrieval:** This method focusses on collecting useful detail of images for differentiating faces of a set of persons [14].
- **Classification:** Images stored in the database are identified based on the comparison in the feature retrieval phase [15]. Face recognition is a complex procedure and has many components. Time is also a major constraint for these algorithms, especially in the case of sequential execution of the recognition algorithms.

Some of the face recognition methods are shown in Figure 12.5. These methods are classified as "linear" and "nonlinear." All these methods have some challenges owing to the pros and cons associated with them. Many experiments have been performed by different authors on different databases. Experimental results are verified against various conditions such as varying face expression, glasses, scares, age, illumination, cosmetics, different hairstyle, and many more. It has been established that among these face recognition methods, the principal component analysis (PCA) revealed good performance as compared to other methods [16,17].

Facial features can be recognized by software tools that also first create various representations by examining the face of an image, comparing it against many human faces, and then recognizing a person's identity. Some of the best open-source face recognition software available are listed in Table 12.2.

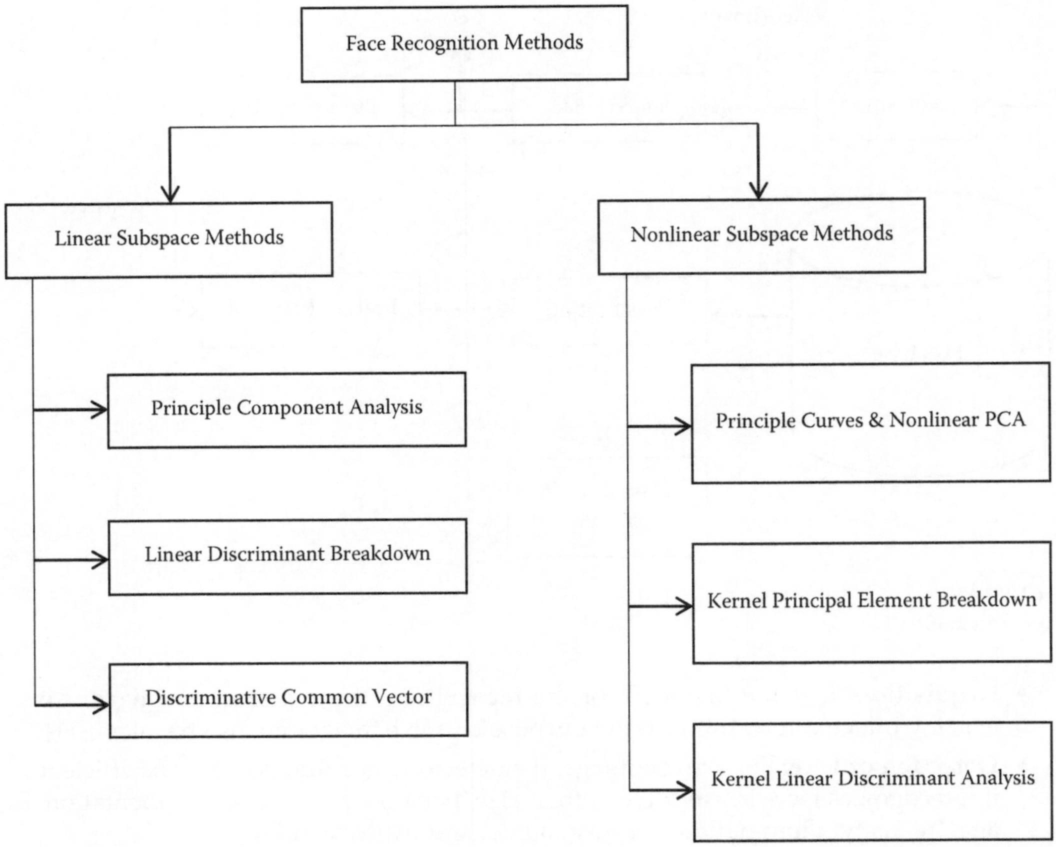

FIGURE 12.5
Face Recognition Methods.

Face recognition has applications in various fields one of the most widely used applications is the biometric system. Face recognition allows a secure, user-friendly, and convenient way to perform applications. But still, it has many shortcomings in which work needs to be done. The first shortcoming is many attacks exist with face recognition methods and these attacks can affect the performance of the system or can be misused by an unauthorized person. Attacks may be categorized based on parameters of authentication proof to recognize faces such as stolen images, the face of the image, recorded video, 3D face copies with different movements, varying poses, and various expressions [18,19].

Face detection and recognition methods are combined to attain better results as shown in Figure 12.6. Face detection is the initial step in the whole process. Face detection can act as an application of face recognition methods. The basic difference between face detection and recognition methods is shown in Table 12.3.

Face detection and recognition have various applications in common like in the military, nuclear power plants, multimedia banking, medical, personal computers, etc. Some of the applications are listed as follows [8]:

TABLE 12.2

Open-Source Face Recognition Software

Face Recognition Software	Deployment	Operating System	Features	Web Link
Deep Vision AI	DeepVision	Windows, Linux, Android	Provide real-time processing, work with both images & video, fast responsive	https://deepvision.se/download/
Kairos	Open API	Android, Windows, IOS, Linux, Mac	Provide data security, avoid attacks like scares, age, color difference	https://rapidapi.com/KairosAPI/api/kairos-face-recognition
TrueKey	McAfee	Android, Windows, Mac	Powerful face localization, face tracking, accuracy, check for age, gender, pose variation, glasses, work with 3D data also	https://www.techspot.com/downloads/7064-true-key.html#download_scroll
Face	Megvii	Windows, Mac	It can identify faces with high accuracy with a variety of databases	https://face.en.softonic.com/download
OpenFace	SourceForge	Windows, Web-based, Linux	Able to detect faces, facial action recognition, head pose estimation, eye-gaze estimation	https://sourceforge.net/projects/openface.mirror/
3D Face Recognition System 3.14	Biometric Recognition Code	Android, Windows, IOS, Linux, Mac	3D face recognition, lightening condition does not affect its working, able to recognize a face from different angles	https://3d-face-recognition-system.soft112.com/download.html

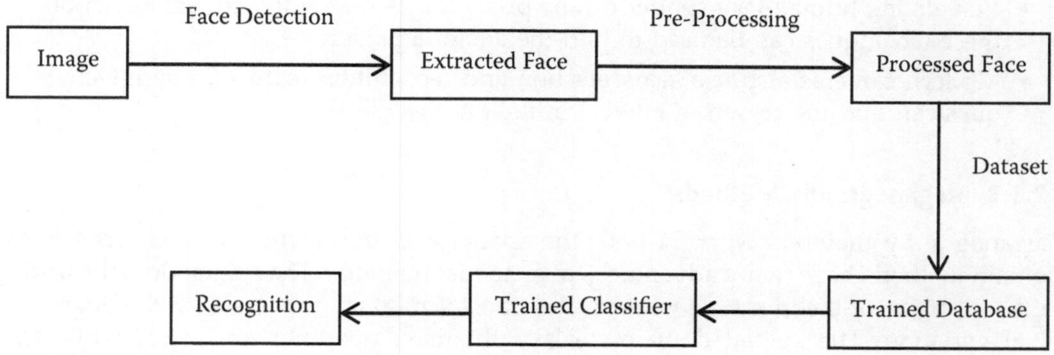

FIGURE 12.6
Combined Face Detection and Recognition System.

- In the computerized investigation, where the main objective is to identify and track a person whether he is on a watch list or not.
- CCTV can identify the face of a criminal.
- It is also used in the identification of the Image database of licensed drivers, assistance receivers, colonizers, and police bookings.

TABLE 12.3

Face Detection and Recognition difference

Face Detection Method	Face Recognition Method
Face detection is the initial step of face recognition.	After face detection, it does face recognition.
It detects features of the human face using the pattern detection algorithms for concluding the location, presence, or absence of a face, coordination, and measure of the face which exists in either image or the video.	It predicts whether the face matches the face in the dataset.
It locates the size and dimensions of the human face in images or videos.	Capable to tell whose face is it bypassing the received information into several classifiers.
It can find the number of people in a group.	It can also find the number of people who repeatedly visit a particular location.
It does not have a memory element.	It has memory. After detection of the face, it can recognize the face of a person after matching it to the dataset.

- At airports for investigation purposes, face identification plays a significant role.
- It plays a significant role in face spoofing and antispoofing.
- It is very useful in smart cards for the recognition of authorized persons.
- It also provides personal security through face recognition such as logging in to your personal computer or phone.
- It is also useful in entertainment programs like video games or virtual reality.
- It also has useful applications in law enforcement like in suspicious alerts, detecting cheats, and stopping corruption.
- Visualizing human face gender can be predicted. Along with gender prediction, these techniques can be used to find the age of a person.
- Modern cameras also use face detection and recognition features. These techniques can find the region of interest in the photo slide show.

12.1.3 Steganography Methods

Steganography methods work in both the spatial and transform domains. Transform domain methods have many advantages over spatial methods. The spatial domain works in the bit plane of the input file whereas the transform domain works with the degree of pixel variation. The spatial domain deals with direct operation on pixels while the transform domain deals with adapting Fourier transform. Concealing secret information in the spatial domain is easy and fast as compared to the transform domain [20]. The difference between spatial and transform domains is revealed in Table 12.4.

Spatial and transform domain methods are further can be divided into different categories. Many more types of these methods exist. Some most important types of these methods are shown in Figure 12.7 [22].

A few generally used steganography tools are depicted in Table 12.5. For briefing the tools some features have been integrated. Some tools are capable of concealing secret data in a variety of multimedia files and dissimilar formats of the same multimedia files. Mainly almost all tools offer compression, cryptography, hashing, and password security.

TABLE 12.4

Difference between Spatial and Transform Domain [21]

Spatial Domain	Transform Domain
It works with the image plane.	Transform domain works a change in the rate of pixels.
It deals with the direct operation of pixels.	It deals with altering Fourier transform.
It is simple.	It is complex.
Computation is easy in the spatial domain.	Computation is time-consuming and difficult.
It is less secure.	It is more secure.
It has exposure to attacks.	It is robust.

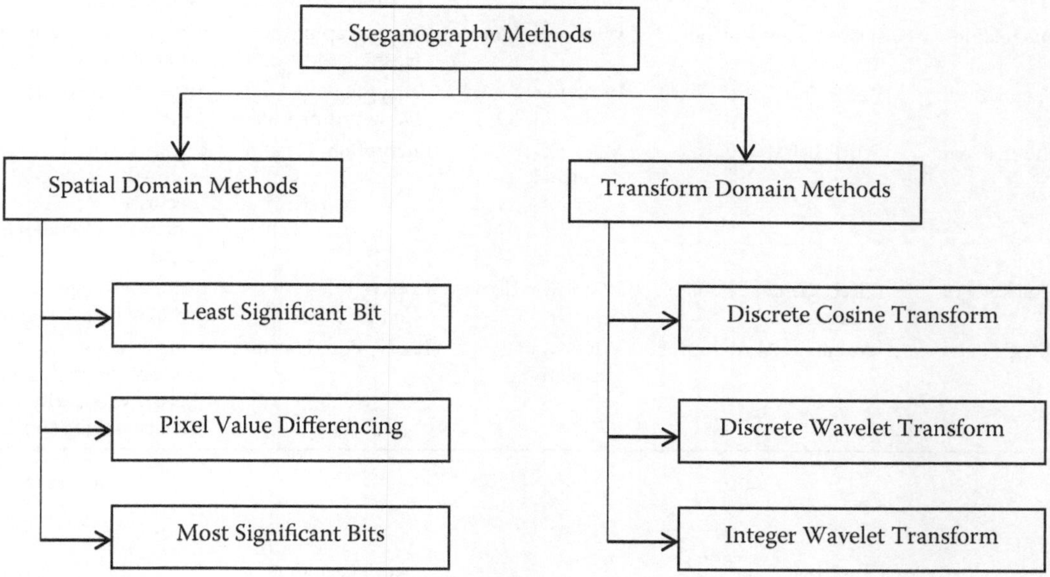

FIGURE 12.7
Steganography Methods.

All these tools are freely available on the web so can be installed on a personal computer free of cost. These tools are also capable of providing encryption, hashing, compression, and password protection. Because of these features, double security can be achieved by the system. All these tools can work with windows.

12.1.4 Face Detection and Recognition in Steganography

By combining face detection, face recognition, and steganography method a robust integrated system can be created. Face detection finds a suitable region for concealing secret information. Steganography conceals secret information in the obtained suitable region. Then finally face recognition is applied to find the quality of input and output faces. Face detection and recognition in steganography are shown in Figure 12.8. In Table 12.6, some

TABLE 12.5
Open-Source Steganography Tools

Steganography Tool	Deployment	Operating System	Features	Web Link
SteganPEG	Kango Abhiram	Windows, Linux	Encryption, Password protection	https://www.softpedia.com/get/Security/Encrypting/SteganPEG.shtml
OurSecret	SecureKit.net	Windows all versions, Web-based	Encryption	https://oursecret.soft112.com/
S-tool	stools.sf.net	Windows, Linux, Android,	Encryption, Hashing, Compression	https://stools.soft112.com/
ImageHide	Dancemammal.Com	Windows, Linux	Cryptography, Hashing	https://imagehide.apponic.com/
DeepSound	Jpinsoft	Windows, Android, iOS	Encryption, Password protection	https://deepsound.soft112.com/
Hide'N'Send	MRP Lab	Mac, iOS, Android	Encryption, Hashing	https://www.softpedia.com/get/Security/Encrypting/Hide-N-Send.shtml
QuickStego	GNU General Public License	Windows, Linux	Copyright, Compression	http://wbstego.wbailer.com/
rSteg	Abhinav, Alok, Saurabh	Windows all versions	Encryption, Hashing	https://www.softpedia.com/get/Security/Security-Related/rSteg.shtml

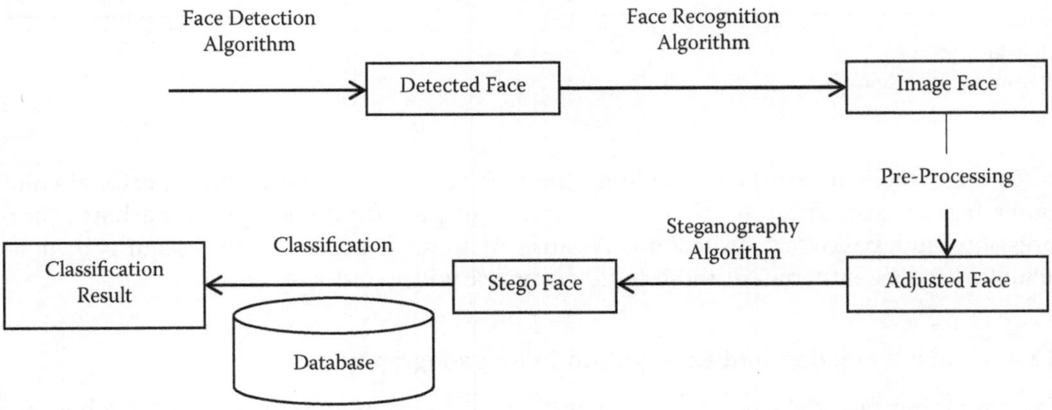

FIGURE 12.8
Integrated Method.

TABLE 12.6

Face Detection and Recognition in Steganography

Author	Year of Publication	Face Detection/ Recognition Method	Steganography Method
Najme Zehra, Mansi Sharma, Somya Ahuja, Shubha Bansal [5]	2010	Fast Fourier Transform (FFT) and Sobel Filters	List-Based Steganography
Anjali A. Shejul, Umesh L. Kulkarni [23]	2011	HSV & Cropping	Discrete Wavelet Transform (DWT)
Kavitha Raju and S K Srivatsa [24]	2012	PCA	Principal component analysis with sign cryption Algorithm (PCASA)
ShamiJhodge, GirijaChiddarwar, and Gitanjali Shinde[25]	2013	Local Binary Pattern (LBP) &Gabor features	DWT
Rasber Rashid, HarinSellahewa, Sabah Jassim [26]	2013	Local Ternary Pattern (LTP)	Least Significant Bit (LSB)
Qiangfu Zhao, YutaroMinakawa, Yong Liu, and Neil Y. Yen [27]	2013	Iterative Evolutionary Algorithm (IEA) based on Neural Network	Morphing-Based steganography
Ekta Chauhan [28]	2016	Image-Based method	DWT
Jean-Christophe Burie, Jean-Marc Ogier, Cu Vinh Loc[29]	2017	LTP (Local Ternary Pattern)	LSB
Parth Agarwal, Dhruve Moudgil, S. Priya [30]	2020	PCA	LSB

of the face detection and recognition methods are shown in combination with steganography methods [31].

By combining these three methods, securities of the communication system increased to a satisfactory level. Every method has some pros and cons associated with it. For combining more than one method, we have to analyze many conditions [32]. If all methods are comfortable with a set of conditions, then only an integrated system can be prepared to provide better results. Assessment of face detection, recognition, and steganography methods concludes that the present state of research in this field is not so far satisfactory for many applications.

12.2 Literature Review

In this section review of various faces detection, face recognition and steganography methods has been detailed from 1997 to 2021. Face detection and recognition are useful for making steganography methods more robust, improved concealing capacity, and carrying a good visual quality. These methods use a large dataset of different types of faces to compare with the given image for the detection/recognition of faces in the image/video. Many datasets are available for these methods and some online datasets are shown in Table 12.7. In almost all papers, Indian faces are used to check the performance of these methods [33].

TABLE 12.7

Online available Datasets for Face Detection and Recognition

Face Detection & Recognition dataset	Publication Year	Web URL	Number of Images/Size
Flickr-Faces-HQ Dataset	2019	https://github.com/NVlabs/ffhq-dataset	70000 Images
Tufts-Face-Database	2019	https://www.kaggle.com/kpvisionlab/tufts-face-database	10000 Images
Real and Fake Face Detection	2019	https://www.kaggle.com/ciplab/real-and-fake-face-detection	215 MB
Google Facial Expression Comparison Dataset	2018	https://research.google/tools/datasets/google-facial-expression/	220 MB
Face Images with Marked Landmark Points	2018	https://www.kaggle.com/drgilermo/face-images-with-marked-landmark-points	497 MB
Labeled Faces in the Wild Home (LFW) Dataset	2018	http://vis-www.cs.umass.edu/lfw/	173 MB
UTKFace Large Scale Face Dataset	2017	https://susanqq.github.io/UTKFace/	20000 Images
YouTube Faces Dataset with Facial Keypoints	2017	https://www.kaggle.com/selfishgene/youtube-faces-with-facial-keypoints	10 GB
Large-scale CelebFaces Attributes (CelebA) Dataset	2015	http://mmlab.ie.cuhk.edu.hk/projects/CelebA.html	200000 Images
Yale Face Database	2001	http://vision.ucsd.edu/content/yale-face-database	6.4 MB

Already a lot of work is done on face detection and recognition in combination with steganography methods but still, there are some issues associated with these methods. Literature is categorized as face detection methods, face recognition methods and steganography in combination with face detection and recognition methods. A literature survey of a few papers is given as follows:

12.2.1 Papers on Face Detection Methods

Face detection is the process of identifying a face in an input file. There are many methods through which face can be identified. Some of these methods are listed in the literature survey with their merits and demerits as follows:

Extended face detection research work was recommended by Viola-Jones in 2001. The author also worked on various views from different angles initiated by Rowley and Schneider man. He created many different detectors for various views of faces in an image. A decision tree was also used for determining different viewpoint classes at an angle of 60 degrees. The proposed technique works efficiently to overcome the issue of different viewpoints [34]. Research work [35], was done to enhance the actual face detection Viola-Jones method for making it more accurate and faster. Three parameters of an image were selected one for feature detection, Adaboost to select features and attentional cascade for effective computational resource distribution. The algorithmic description was proposed, a learning code and a learned face indicator were applied to all color images.

A novel technique of face detection using a skin color model and AdaBoost was proposed by the authors in [36]. The non-skin color model applied on the source image was quickly detected and created on skin color replicas in RGB and YCbCr color spaces. Face detection is done with AdaBoost by providing percentages of skin color pixels to non-skin color pixels outside convinced thresholds. Simulation results proved that the proposed technique decreases false alarms significantly. It is well known that face expression delivers valuable information during communication so all vision-based human-computer communication system needs fast and consistent face or facial feature identification. Issues associated with face detection methods [37], were carried out in this work. One of the furthermost face detection methods is the Viola-Jones method which is very efficient and reliable. Open CV is also the most commonly used public domain classifier for face identification purposes. These classifiers are trained on various situations like varying face poses, different lighting conditions, skin color, and also on different datasets.

As in the world of the internet and computers, multimedia information is increasing day by day. Based on various features such as eyes, lips, and nose, various face detection algorithms were analyzed [38]. So, for proper organization and understanding of this information, an artificial intelligence system was required. Coming to a particular domain, one of the greatest specific objects which can be traced in images are the faces of humans. Face detection is gaining the attention of many researchers in various applications. Face detection from a large distance was facing a lot of issues [39]. The distance was calculated between face features through configurable theories. An error of about 8 to 13% was found during the extraction of these features. These errors were occurring due to resizing of faces to the original. Extending the concept of distance between camera and object. In the paper [40], the author has established a model of dynamic vision face detection from a large distance system. The first related literature was examined by the author to find the shortcomings of existing work in this field. The experimental result showed that objects at a large distance like from 25–30 meters could be identified easily with accuracy and good quality with the proposed method.

12.2.2 Papers on Face Recognition Methods

For the face recognition process, first face detection algorithm was applied to identify the face, and then the detected face is identified in a given database. Coming from face detection to face recognition method some more papers are reviewed to find their pros and cons as follows:

Some of the demerits of 2D face recognition techniques over 3D techniques were listed in the work [41]. 2D techniques have problems in handling varying poses, brightness, looks, aging, and obstructions. 3D techniques could handle problems like feature recognition, and classifiers that report appearance and obstruction variation issues. 3D techniques were also able to work with face databases and their types used for performance assessment. Face recognition techniques differentiate between various facial features.

Three features distorted faces, pose, and resize faces were studied in [42]. Plastic surgery on faces has issues: not able to properly recognition of surgery faces, low accuracy, and no ability to deal with the face shape. Understanding the range and scope of the alteration created through many kinds of actions were carried out. Many techniques available for plastic surgery were also reviewed with their merits and demerits. In the last four decades, many face recognition techniques have been already explored and designed by researchers. Still, a lot of improvement is needed in this area. Face recognition techniques have diverse applications in our daily life. Issues with the existing face recognition techniques are varying faces, different poses, angles, scaling and lighting conditions, etc.

in both images and videos both. The conception of face fusion for enhancing precision and identification rate on many face records such as ORL, AR, and LFW was explained in [43].

In work [44], nine existing face recognition techniques for finding issues, merits and demerits were reviewed. The author has used the IJB-A database which is a very large database having many images and videos in it. The purpose of the research work was to find the challenges related to these techniques. Even many tops most algorithms are also not able to work with varying facial expressions, different angles, poses, and low illumination conditions. Approximate 20% of total faces fails during the process of face recognition by all algorithm used in this paper. One of the conclusions of the paper was faster identification algorithms were less accurate as compared to the slower ones.

Face recognition has many applications in computer vision for the identification of the right person. In work [45] have reviewed these techniques and found issues like lighting, color, contrast, poses, angle, obstruction, plastic surgery, etc. Datasets were used for finding the performance of existing techniques in terms of accuracy. Again, some more issues related to face recognition techniques were reviewed in the paper [46]. Mainly plastic surgery faces were studied in this paper. The author concluded that plastic surgery faces need a lot of work to be done to enhance their capacity. A large database of about 500 images and videos was taken to analyze existing plastic surgery techniques. The proposed technique gives fewer effective results when pre-and post-surgery images were matched. Many researchers are working on face detection and recognition techniques. These techniques have had many applications in recent years. In the paper [47], issues like frontal view, different facial expressions like anger, delight, gloom, and static images were discussed. Author generated enhanced face detection and recognition technique with improved results in relation to accuracy. The execution period and complexity of the proposed technique were also optimized.

Removal of distortion in the facial expression was carried out. Also reviewed different face recognition techniques based on different age groups persons. The performance and accuracy of the proposed technique were greatly affected by age group. With the increase in age challenges also increased for the proposed technique [5]. Another attempt to carry out issues associated with the face recognition methods was performed in [43]. One key issue was complications in controlling changing poses or in-depth rotations as face image transformations produced by rotations were greater than inter-person alterations applied for differentiating identities. The proposed paper delivered a deep review of image identification through different poses.

12.2.3 Papers on Face Detection and Recognition in Combination with Steganography Methods

Now reviewed papers are based on the combination of face detection and recognition technique in steganography. To improve the shortcomings of steganography methods like low capacity, poor quality of stego file, and less robustness against different image processing and geometric attacks. A literature survey based on these methods is as follows:

In real life, biometric technology is very useful for providing identity to people. But storing biometric patterns in the central database makes it susceptible to various attacks. These attacks can take place during information communication. Thus, a substitute is required for the safety of information during communication. In the paper [48], a review of various biometric steganography techniques was done. Various challenges and motivations associated with steganography were listed by the author. LBP and Gabor features were combined to improve the performance of face recognition and detection techniques in the paper [25]. Face recognition has its application in identification proofs like biometrics, net banking, security, etc. For authentication purposes username, password, and face image could be used. While transferring this sensitive information steganography is used to make the system more robust. An image recognition technology has many issues with it like varying poses, facial expressions, lighting effects, illumination, etc. For making the proposed technique [49], a more robust spatial steganography technique was used to conceal secret information on lips. Concealing information in the skin part of an image ensures good visual quality and high capacity. The author's reviewed many existing steganography techniques on the skin part of images and concluded it doesn't obstruct the recognition speed of the biometric system. They also confirmed the future framework on NITRLipV1 and NITRLipV2 to compare individuality concealing and recognition along with steganography performance.

LSB is concealing secret information inside the least significant bit of the cover file. LSB technique [50], has been applied to conceal secret information in any feature of the face like the nose, mouth, eyes, chin, etc. An image was selected from the database having 8-bit color. Randomly any feature from the face was selected to conceal secret data in the LSB of that feature. The proposed method was very strong against image processing attacks and has a high capacity. Paper [51], used Eigenvalue to identify the face in an image. After matching the face with the existing database, these faces were used to authenticate and verify tools beyond the recent requirement for a password. Face detection and recognition techniques have been integrated with steganography for providing more security to applications.

Face detection and recognition techniques have many applications in real life. Voting is one example of these techniques. Paper [52], proposed web-based voting which permits the voter to vote from anywhere. According to the author image of the voter could be captured by the camera and then it was sent to face recognition technology to detect it. After detection, it was saved for further processing. Then voter card number is used to extract the saved image of the face from the database to compare the image captured by the camera and check if the voter is a legitimate voter. Steganography was also used to offer security to voters' accounts by embedding personal information inside voter images.

Face recognition was combined with steganography to deliver more safety to the secret data. Work proposed face recognition using PCA with steganography [24]. The proposed technique was suitable in numerous applications like surveillance, biometrics, banking, industry, and the safety of secret data. The author employed a secure verification through face detection based on Eigenvalue and correlation of source image in the frequency domain. Video steganography has been implemented on skin tone [53]. A skin tone detection algorithm was used to find skin parts in a frame. Then secret information was concealed inside skin portions of the detected frame. Many spatial and transforms domain steganography tools were reviewed for concealing secret information. YCbCr color model was used to conceal information with steganography tools. The experimental result proved that concealing information in the transform domain in skin portions was more robust as compared to the spatial domain.

Various face detection and recognition techniques along with steganography were reviewed [54] and challenges associated with these techniques were detailed. Viola-Jones algorithm was used to identify the face in an image. This algorithm has four parts to detect faces that is: Haar Feature, Integral Image, Adaboost, and Cascade. Many existing steganography methods conceal secret information randomly without choosing ROI.

Concealing secret information on the human face enhances the visual excellence of the cover file. Considering the region of interest author proposed the LSB technique to conceal secret information [55]. The first face was detected using face detection algorithms and then steganography was applied. For face detection, two databases were used MIT and PIE. Along with face detection and steganography, cryptography has been also used to add more robustness.

A novel steganography system for concealing and transmitting biometric information in mobile multimedia entities such as images, audio, and video over open networks was proposed [34]. As compared to the existing techniques of image steganography, the planned technique has high accuracy. For concealing secret information LSB was used in the spatial domain. Simulation results proved that the research work was robust against attacks in comparison with other variants of LSB. It has a high concealing capacity with face biometric characteristics while preserving the precision of face recognition. Extending work cryptography along with the steganography technique was used to encode secret information so that hacker was not able to detect it [56]. Biometric patterns kept in the dataset were generally in the form of images, cryptography could be well implemented for encrypting these patterns from attacks. Cryptography and steganography together could provide a double level of security to biometric information. LSB steganography was used for keeping usernames and passwords hidden from the detectors.

In the last three decades, data safety has become an important measure of information communication. To report data safely in information communication steganography, face detection, and recognition technique needs to be combined. Steganography is an act of concealing secret information carrier files. LSB steganography on the face of an image to make the system more robust was proposed [30]. The objective of steganography is robustness, security, capacity, and imperceptibility. The skin tone-based secure image steganography technique was proposed in [57]. The first skin portion inside the image was detected and then conceals secret information about that part of the image. Experimental observations showed good results in terms of security, capacity, and robustness. Nowadays biometrics is very common in real-life activities like accessing mobile phones, laptops, automobiles, etc.

The author proposed a Self-Organizing Map (SOM) based on face recognition with steganography and DWT compression algorithm [33]. A large dataset was used to recognize the face in the image. These extracted faces were compressed using the DWT algorithm. Then secret information was inserted inside the face to send to the other party. The proposed technique was robust geometric attacks. Again, the invisible face biometric transmission method was proposed in [58]. The face image was divided into multiple sub-bands of different frequencies with wavelet transform. Then these sub-bands were decomposed into non-overlapping regions. After that LBPHs were retrieved from sub-bands with 4 neighbors. By using all LBPH an image was constructed with the help of a histogram. These retrieved faces were concealed inside a carrier file using some robust steganography technique. Simulation results proved the good visual quality of the watermark and security both.

Researchers in the field of face biometrics are facing a common problem of selecting a suitable color space, making a skin model, and then processing this model. Almost every existing system has the problem of de-correlation of illumination from the color channel. For separating skin and non-skin portion illumination plays an important role? Detected skin portions were used to conceal secret information. The proposed technique has good quality of output file and good capacity as compared to existing work in the field [59].

Again, in this work skin portion of the image was targeted for concealing secret information [60]. Concealing information in the skin portion is less sensitive to the Human Visual System (HSV) related to concealing it in any other part of the image. The image was taken as input in Hue, Saturation, and Value (HSV) and then it was converted to the frequency domain by using the Haar wavelet transform. The image was converted into four sub-bands and the LL sub-band was used to conceal information. The proposed technique was robust against image processing attacks and the watermark carried good visual quality.

Object-oriented steganography has its application in biometrics to improve the safety of the system. One biometric feature is skin used to conceal secret information with steganography. By applying the skin tone detection algorithm first skin was detected in the HSV color model [61]. For steganography DWT and DCT techniques were used by the author to conceal secret information. The result of the proposed work has good visual quality of the stego file. Combining steganography and the biometric system could decrease the risk of information loss from hackers. Steganography was used to conceal secret information in any cover file like text, image, audio, video, etc. Image steganography using DWT along with a biometric system was proposed in [2]. The proposed system was more robust as compared to existing techniques and provided high concealing capacity.

In the field of face recognition with steganography, another novel video steganography method for defending biometric data from detectors was proposed in [62]. In the HVS model, both inter and intraframe motion data were considered for making the concealing technique more imperceptible and robust. Instead of concealing secret information excessively for repelling attacks, a biometric image set was concealed inside video frames randomly using DWT. Particularly, the sequence number of every frame was concealed inside corresponding frames as a stego for maintaining the veracity of the stego frame and assuring correct retrieval of the biometric image set. Finally, the retrieved image set was recognized by the biometrics system. Extending the concept of face recognition with steganography, face detection was introduced in [63]. A biometric steganography technique in the skin part of an image was proposed. Concealing secret information in the skin part of an image makes the proposed system more robust. Concealing information in skin tone is less sensitive to HVS instead of concealing it in other parts of the image. The first skin region was detected and then using DWT secret information was concealed in the detected part of the image. By DCT technique compression was done after concealing secret information. The proposed biometric steganography technique improved the robustness of the system.

Detecting the skin portion in an image is not an easy task. Challenges associated with face biometrics include selecting a color model, the angle on which the face is mounted, illumination, and the color of the image. After detection of skin tone, secret information was concealed in the region of interest i.e., face. For information concealing DWT technique was used in [64]. The proposed technique was more robust as compared to existing techniques. Experimental results proved that it has a high concealing capacity and good visual excellence of the stego file. Whereas in research work an image steganography method for verifying printed images of the face was proposed [65]. The verification of the image face was done by a biometric process. For steganography to be effective, stego quality must not be compromised due to the print scan process. The process of concealing secret information through the print scan process was affected after concealing secret information. The experimental result proved the good quality of stego and high concealing capacity.

Medical records are very sensitive information; alteration by anyone may result in incorrect analysis for diagnosis. So, the transfer of this secret information requires a robust steganography technique. The author of this paper proposed two solutions for providing security to secret information [66]. The first one was to provide a secure link between patients and communicating devices, and the second was to provide a secure link between devices and networks. First biometric authentication was used and then steganography has been applied for enhancing security. The author has used the CASIA Iris image dataset for implementing the proposed work. Concealing secret information in the usual part of an image could be detected during filtering content of the image, compression, and color balancing. The author proposed a steganography technique for embedding secret data in the skin part of the image along with cryptography to deliver improved safety [23]. Biometric features were used for selecting skin tone in the image. By concealing secret information in the skin portion secret information was not affected by even cropping, scaling, translation, etc.

Steganalysis is the process of detecting secret data hidden in the carrier file. The author in [67] proposed steganography technique recognition as a sub-section of steganalysis. Exploration proved when a steganalysis sensor was trained on one carrier file then it works for that image only. Whenever you apply to a new image set it will not work or its capacity decreases. To handle, this problem author proposed steganography technique recognition. CNN's classical model was trained on a training dataset for retrieving deep features of testing and matching images. The final decision was based on the matching features of both images. Simulation of work proved that the technique could improve the precision of testing when the image from an unknown dataset was picked. Automated Teller Machine (ATM) permits users to do activities like deposits, transfers of money from one account to another, balance checking and withdrawal of money, etc. Authorized persons at ATMs could access the secret information of a person.

In paper [68] novel steganography with a recognition technique was proposed. Biometric identity was required first to handle problems of existing techniques. In recent face recognition techniques gained a lot of attention among researchers. For face recognition, PCA was applied and then LSB was used for concealing secret information on that face. Pattern recognition allowed users to conceal secret information of good size. Paper [38], proposed an adaptive information concealing technique with pattern recognition. By using the Speed up Robust Features (SURF) detector suitable region for concealing secret information was constructed. Then LBP was applied for checking the pattern of the concealing region. Finally, LTP was used for finding suitable concealing locations. For making the proposed technique more robust Hough transform was used for rotating the document to its original position. The proposed steganography technique conceals information in the spatial domain and could detect the suitable region of interest for concealing secret information. It was robust against attacks and has a high hiding capacity as equated to existing techniques.

Extending the concept of steganography with the recognition system IRIS information was concealed in the image [69]. A logistic map was used for producing two pseudorandom sequences. The first sequence was used for scrambling biometric information before concealing it and the second for encoding of hiding location. Finally, Joint Photographic Expert Group (JPEG) compression was also used for reducing the risk of image processing attacks. Experimental observation proved that the proposed technique enhances the security of the IRIS feature and also produces good quality of the stego file. Storing and communicating secret information through the web is very challenging for users. If this secret information is lost or hacked by anyone then it is very difficult to handle.

Paper [70] proposed concealing secret information of biometric data in combination with cryptography and steganography. The proposed technique could handle the problem of information storing, recovering, and transferring. First Eigenvalues were retrieved for the face of the image then-secret information was concealed. Then cryptography and steganography were performed for improved the security of biometric data. Currently with the advancement of technology face images are generally stored in 3D format. The author of this paper proposed the steganography technique on 3D face images [71]. So, for concealing secret information first face was detected by face detection methods. Detecting a face was also a challenging task as it becomes difficult to detect a face with varying face poses, different facial expressions, lighting effects, etc. The proposed technique has a large concealing capacity and good visual quality of the stego file.

Challenges associated with reviewed papers are shown in Table 12.8. Challenges with steganography are low capacity, less robustness and poor quality of stego files [72]. These challenges can be improved to some extent by using face detection and recognition methods along with steganography. The human face has high frequency and concealing secret information in high-frequency components of an image is more robust as compared to any other part of an image. So, concealing secret information in face of an image has less chance of detection.

A total of 103 papers are studied related to various methods of face detection, face recognition, and steganography as shown in Figure 12.9. From the literature survey, it has also been concluded that by combining two or more methods better results can be obtained. From the survey, it also has been concluded that on improving one parameter

TABLE 12.8

Challenges associated with Face Detection and Recognition Method

Method of Face Detection and Recognition	Working Domain	Face Dataset	Challenge
IRIS and steganography-based method for concealing secret key	Transform domain	CASIA-IrisV3-Interval, MMU-VI	Eye color, location and size of the eye, distance
ROI for robust steganography	Spatial domain	USC-SIPI,	Varying poses, age, illumination, lightening, Expression
Face recognition using DWT steganography	Transform domain	ORL, JAFFE, NRI, YALE	Occlusion, face marks, angle of the face, hairs on face, haircut
Technique and issues of face recognition	Integrated	ORL, AR, LFW	Color of face, face makeup, contrast, similar looks, poses
PCA and LDA based face recognition techniques	Transform domain	JAFFE, PIE	Environment, image quality, background, face expression
FRVT based face recognition system	Integrated	MIT	Similar faces, low resolution, pose, face expression
Face recognition using Laplacian of Gaussian and DCT	Spatial domain	Yale, PIE	Illumination, thermal image, motion, angle, similar faces
SVM face recognition technique	Integrated	AT & T, AR, FERET, ORL,	Partial Occlusion, aging, the effect of illumination, pose
Face recognition using Eigen's faces	Integrated	FRAV3D	A different view of the face, pose
Curvelet transform and LSSVM face recognition system	Integrated	ORL	Viewpoint, illumination, facial expression
Angular LDA and SVM based face recognition technique	Integrated	XM2VTS	Varying illumination conditions, varying poses, angle of face, resolution

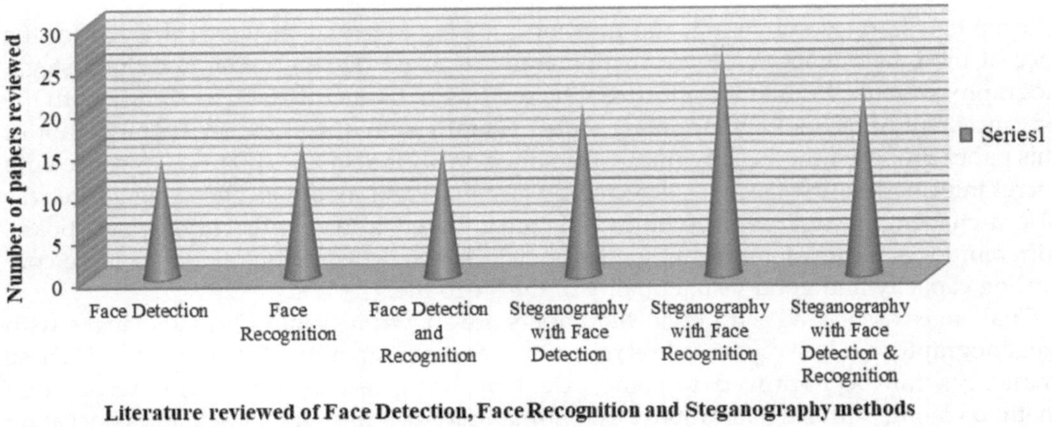

FIGURE 12.9
Total Papers Reviewed.

others got affected and resulting in some challenges. Combining two or more methods results in consuming more time. Also, the complexity of the scheme rises in terms of cost and effort. But the overall performance of the system is improved in terms of quality, safety, and robustness.

12.3 Challenges

From the literature survey, it has been found that these methods have many challenges. Almost all face detection and recognition methods are facing challenges like varying lighting conditions, variation in poses, facial expressions, aging, face makeup, facial marks, haircut, angle, rotation, illumination, color, contrast, and partial occlusions in images. Steganography methods also have many challenges like low concealing capacity, less robustness, and poor excellence of stego files. In this section challenges associated with all these three methods are shown as follows:

12.3.1 Challenges with Face Detection and Recognition Methods

In the case of videos, visual surveillance is another challenge that is motion effects identification and recognition of faces. Some of these challenges are listed below along with their explanation. These challenges are also shown in Figure 12.10.

- **Acquisition Time:** Usually smaller acquisition periods are good than extended acquisition periods for minimizing objects because of subject motion. But in smaller acquisition time some systems could have a problem in getting the opaque selection of face surface. Systems that depend on controlled light generally have a problem in areas like eyebrows, which may create a smooth picture, and sometimes create spike objects during multiple reflections [73].
- **2D Sensor:** There are many datasets available for 2D face detector sensors but when researcher work with these datasets the following challenges occurs: 2D represents face only by their intensity value, 2D sensors work by measuring the

FIGURE 12.10
Challenges with Face Detection & Recognition Methods.

distance between facial features, Face orientation in 2D sensors can be done up to 20 degrees, 2D face detection is slow as compared to 3D and many more [74].

- **Illumination disparities:** When an image is generated by a camera then some characteristics affect the quality of the image like spectra, source scattering, rotation degree, and intensity. Illumination disparities could do this due to skin reflectance properties and the camera's internal setting. For building a good face detection and recognition system illumination challenges play an important role [75].
- **Pose:** The image of the face may vary due to camera position, angle of the camera, and facial expression. Usually varied poses greatly affect the detection and recognition process due to projective distortions and self-occlusion. Pose variation becoming a major issue for face identification and recognition systems that depend on only a single [76].
- **Wrinkles due to aging:** Wrinkles due to aging greatly affect the performance of face identification and detection algorithm. Wrinkles can also be created with the help of makeup tools that also affect the performance of the identification algorithm. Less work is done on this issue because of the unavailability of the data set. It is very challenging to gather a dataset of images having the face of individuals taken at different ages [77].
- **Expression:** Face appearance gets affected when the expression of a person changes. Hairs on the face, stubble, and mustache could change facial appearance. A hairstyle carried by a person also affects face appearance [78].
- **Occlusion:** Sometimes images of faces might be partly or completely obstructed by other objects. This might occur in group photographs some faces in an image may be partially or fully blocked by other objects. Because of this identification and detection of the face become difficult [74].

- **Facial Marks:** Marks on the face is also a challenge for detection and recognition algorithms. Face marks like scars, moles, and spots show an important part in the recognition of faces in criminal applications. As sensors used to detect and recognize faces in the image are very advanced. These sensors can easily detect even a minor change in image face [12].
- **Lighting Condition:** As face detection and recognition techniques have lots of applications in various fields but despite their success, many challenges are there for these techniques. One of the measurement challenges is lighting conditions. Lighting conditions include direction of light, the intensity of light, angle of light occurring on the face, etc. Capturing various features of the face under these conditions affects the quality of the image face [79].
- **Thermal Image:** Thermal imaging is a process of enhancing the visibility of the image face in a dark background. In this process, an image is created based on infrared radiation on the face. For detection of the thermal image, the face requires proper illumination. For the detection and recognition of thermal images, the special dataset is required to have some specific characteristics. Recognition and detection accuracy rates are also not good for thermal images [74].
- **IRIS:** Some of the challenges associated with IRIS are: dilation, lenses, twins, time variability, contact surgery, etc. In biometrics analysis, IRIS plays a significant role in the detection and recognition of a particular face. In the filtering and synthesis phase of face recognition IRIS corner information defeat on bin base structure. These IRIS-based recognition techniques have their applications in Bio-Hashing [80].
- **Similar Looks:** Designing a face recognition system for persons having the same looks or for twins is very challenging. As twins have very similar locks, expressions, features, textures, etc. Even sometimes humans also fail to recognize the faces of twins [81].
- **Image conditions:** When an image is captured from a camera then factors like spectra, source spreading, sensor, lenses, and power intensity affect the look of the face in the image. Capturing images under different conditions results in discrepancies in the quality of the image. Face detection in an image depends on the excellence of the face in the image [80].
- **Size of Face:** Person to person size and appearance of the face vary a lot. Distance of face from the camera effect size of an image. Closer faces look larger as compared to faces that are at distance from the camera [6].
- **Resolution:** Low resolution is also a challenge for many of the existing face detection and recognition techniques. Images in low-resolution conditions have very poor quality. Because of degradation in quality, some information may be lost from the face of the image. This challenge affects face detection and recognition systems specifically for safety applications [82].
- **Facial Features:** Features like mouth, hairs, face cut, eyes, nose, and chin are very significant for recognizing and detecting faces. The literature survey, also found that both external and internal features of an image play important role in the detection and recognition of faces. It is also reported that the upper face plays a significant role than the lower face in the detection and recognition of faces [16].
- **Motion in Face Recognition:** Movement in images results in a challenge for the detection and recognition of faces. Because of motion, it becomes very difficult to identify individual features. Detection and recognition system capacity also degrades due to motion [83].

- **Size Variation:** Variation in size of actual face and template face create difficulty in detection. In this case, the pattern matching algorithm fails to perceive the face due to a low similarity score [84].
- **Composite background:** Composite background means many entities exist in the image due to which precision and percentage of face identification decreases [85].
- **Many Faces in the image:** One of the major challenges is the existence of many faces in the image. Among many faces detecting a particular face is very challenging [86].
- **Skin Color:** The color of skin changes with geographic localities. The color of the skin of Indians is different from that of the USA and so on. Change in color of the individual is also interesting for face identification [7].
- **Long Distance:** Long distance between camera and face decreases the percentage of detection of faces in the image [45].

12.3.2 Challenges with Steganography Methods

Steganography methods have the challenge of robustness, poor visual quality of stego files, and less capacity. On rectifying one challenge another challenge got affected. All the challenges are related to each other. Some of the challenges associated with steganography methods are listed as follows along with Figure 12.11.

- **Relationship between Security and Capacity:** Maintaining high security along with large concealing capacity is a significant challenge for the existing steganography techniques. From the literature survey, it has been found that concealing a large amount of secret data leads to losing security to some degree. This fact is also proven mathematically. Concealing a large amount of secret data leads to the detection of secret information [87].
- **Robustness:** Steganography techniques also have the challenge of detecting secret information when attacks are applied to these techniques. On increasing concealing capacity robustness of steganography techniques decreases. Degradation in the

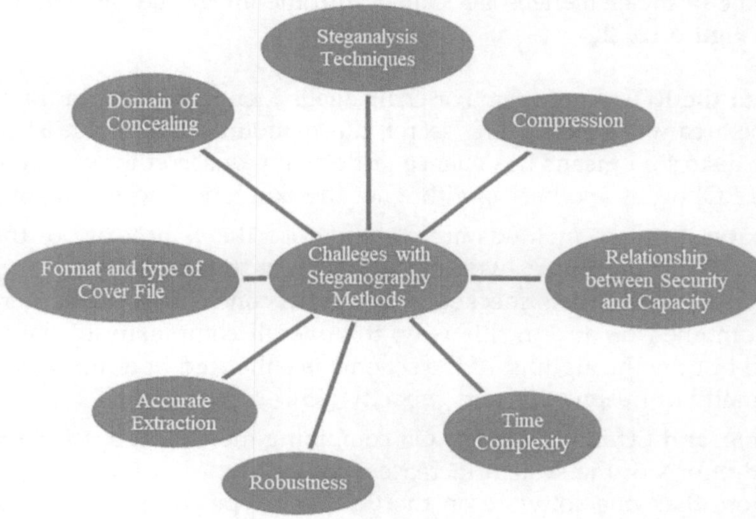

FIGURE 12.11
Challenges with Steganography Methods.

visual excellence of the stego file also results in the detection of secret information [88].

- **Accurate Extraction:** One more challenge with steganography techniques is the extraction of secret information at the recipient side. On receiving information at the recipient side, it needs to compare with the original secret information. If there is any modification or loss of information then report it at the source [89].
- **Format and type of Cover File:** Steganography techniques are specific to the format and type of cover file. Change in format and type of cover file using same technique leads to degradation of stego file. Low quality of setgo file means more chance of detection of secret information [90].
- **Time Complexity:** More complexity means more robust is the steganography technique. The time complexity of a particular technique varies with the domain used. The applicability of the technique also depends on time complexity [91].
- **The domain of Concealing:** The domain of concealing secret information plays a significant role in calculating the overall performance of the steganography technique. Spatial domain techniques are not much robust but have high concealing capacity. But transform domains are more robust against attacks and carry good visual quality [92].
- **Compression:** Compression techniques are of two types lossy and lossless. Lossy compression sometimes results in the loss of useful information. Loss of information also results in the detection of the steganography technique [93].
- **Steganalysis Techniques:** Steganalysis techniques create a challenge for the steganography techniques. These techniques can find the existence of secret information concealed inside the cover file [94].

12.3.3 Challenges in Steganography with Face Detection and Recognition Method

When steganography is combined with face detection and face recognition system then the number of challenges increases. Integration of these methods requires checking many conditions. Some of the challenges associated with the integrated method are explained and shown in Figure 12.12:

- **Identity of the ROI:** Another major challenge is identifying ROI in the cover file. ROI is the area where concealing secret information leads to the least distortion. The least distortion means less chance of detection of secret information. But detection of ROI needs another algorithm i.e., the skin tone detection algorithm [95].
- **Complexity:** As three methods are combined so the complexity of the system increases. First individually working of all these three systems is understood. Then their compatibility is checked with a set of conditions on whether they are can be combined or not. In this way, the overall complexity of the system is increased but the throughput of the scheme is enhanced in terms of robustness, visual quality of output file, and capacity [65].
- **Cost, Time, and Efforts increases:** On combining more than one technique cost, time, and efforts of the system increase. For such types of systems, we need to install more than one software on the PC. Such types of activities increase the overall cost, time, and efforts of the system.
- **Multiple Faces:** When a video has multiple faces then identifying a suitable face for concealing secret information increases the complexity of the system. The

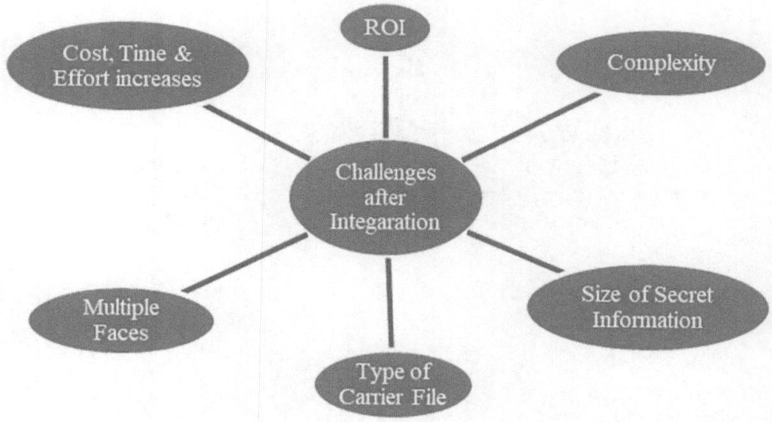

FIGURE 12.12
Challenges with Integrated Method.

identification of the face also has the challenge of the age, angle, varying expression, similar looks, eyeglasses, illumination, resolution, and many more [67].

- **Size of secret information:** In case the size of secret information is large then the chances of detection of secret information increase. For the safety of the secret information face detection and then recognition can be used. It will increase the robustness of the system avoiding different image processing attacks [68].
- **Type of Carrier File:** Detecting faces in the video is difficult; every face detection algorithm is not capable to work with video files. In face detection many challenges like motion, quality of the video, varying poses and background takes place. After this, a strong steganography technique needs to select for concealing secret information. In the end, the face recognition algorithm is used to compare the quality of input and output files [55].

These challenges are faced by society for a long time but researchers are still not able to fix them. A lot of research in this area is still required to fix these challenges. Among the existing face detection, face recognition, and steganography methods no one can handle *100%* of all of these challenges. Almost every method works well when a large set of similar images is available to the system. But in actual face detection and recognition applications like law enforcement and ID card verification, only a single image is provided to the system. For such cases removing robust and discriminant structures which create intra-person faces close and expand the boundary between unlike persons is very problematic in face detection and recognition [96]. When steganography is combined with these two methods the challenges are increased. But combining these methods improves the robustness, capacity, and visual excellence of the output file.

12.4 Expected Resolutions

After the literature survey, some solutions are suggested to resolve the challenges associated with face detection, face recognition, and steganography techniques. The suggested list of resolutions is shown in Figure 12.13.

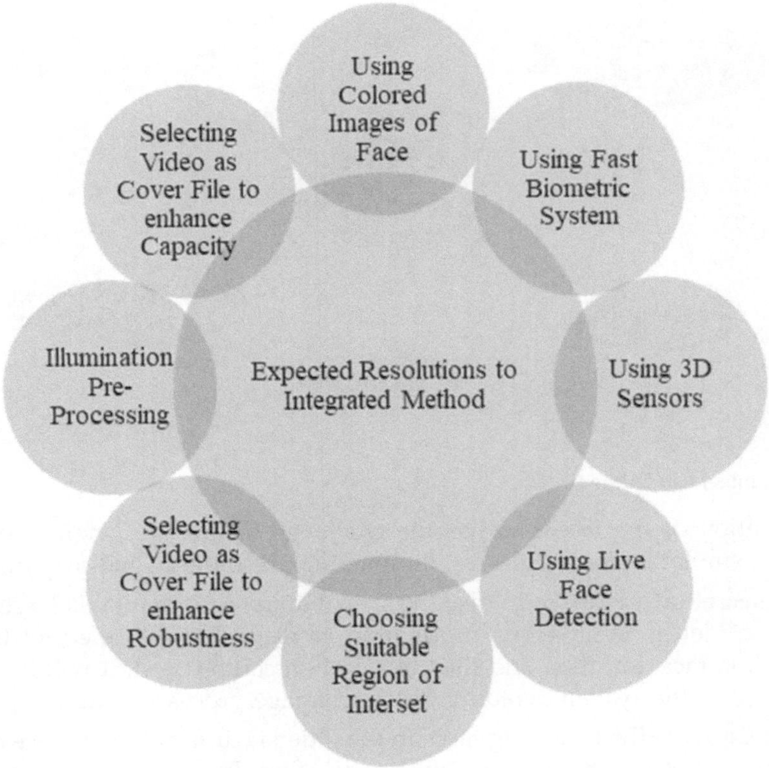

FIGURE 12.13
Expected Resolution to Integrated Method.

- **The solution to Illumination Disparities:** Illumination can be explained as light energy striking the surface of the object. Illumination is various with the area of an object on which it strikes in a period. Illumination pre-processing helps in resolving some issues associated with face detection and recognition. Features of image face change with change in illumination conditions [72].
- **Colored Images of Face:** As we already know that many challenges are associated with face detection and recognition techniques. Some of these are varying poses, different angles, aging, skin color, lighting conditions, resolution, and many more. Working with colored images these challenges can be overcome to some extent instead of working with grey images [23].
- **Fast Biometric System:** To enhance the speed of the face recognition system soft biometric traits may be used. It enhances the quality of faces in image detection and recognition systems. Good quality images can easily be detected and recognized by the system [8].
- **3D Sensors:** Challenges associated with 2D sensors can be handled by 3D sensors. In recent years 3D sensors are gaining attention with many qualities but still require improvements. 3D sensors give decent results in terms of correctness when videos are taken as input. 3D sensors are efficient to work with distant objects also. It also deals efficiently with different poses, eyeglasses, different angles, age wrinkles, etc. [97].

- **Protection from Attacks using Live Face Detection:** To resist various face detection and recognition attacks live face detection system work well. The live face detection system has anti-imposture capabilities to expose these attacks. The vein chart of faces by ultra-violet cameras is the utmost secure system for detecting a live person. But this whole process needs the most expensive devices and increases the cost of the system increases [98].
- **Improved Robustness using Video as Cover File:** By utilizing more pixels around the secret information security of the system can be improved [99]. Concealing secret information in the complex area of the image provides more robustness against image processing attacks.
- **Enhancing Capacity using Video as Cover File:** Utilizing video steganography concealing capacity and robustness can be improved. As video has many frames and concealing secret information randomly into these frames enhances the capacity as well robustness of the system [100].
- **Suitable Region:** ROI can be calculated with the help of face detection techniques and then secret information is concealed by using steganography. ROI provides a suitable region, and concealing secret information in the selected region provides robustness to the steganography technique [101].

12.5 Performance Measure of Steganography Techniques with Face Detection and Recognition

The quality of any steganography technique can be measured with the help of Performance Metrics. Performance metrics include Peak Signal to Noise Ratio (PSNR), Mean Square Error (MSE), Structure Similarity Index Matrix (SSIM), Histogram Analysis, Concealing Capacity, and Entropy [102], etc. In this research work, PSNR, MSE, and the Concealing capacity of existing steganography techniques are compared to find the quality. PSNR, MSE, and Concealing capacity are the quantitative values.

Concealing capacity is the quantity of secret data which can be concealed in a carrier file without the knowledge of a third party. The concealing capacity for some of the techniques is shown in Figure 12.14. Here in the given figure concealing capacity is calculated in the number of bits hiding in the carrier file.

PSNR checks the imperceptibility of the output file. High is the imperceptibility good is the quality of the output file. Good quality output file avoids the chance of detection of hidden secret information resulting in high robustness against different types of attacks.

Figure 12.15 compares the PSNR value of some of the existing steganography techniques along with face detection and recognition techniques. PSNR value is found to be very high on combining steganography with face detection and recognition techniques resulting in more robust techniques.

MSE measures the amount of error present between the original and output file. A smaller is difference means good is the quality of the output file resulting in more robustness against different signal processing attacks. Figure 12.16 shows the MSE value of some of the existing steganography techniques.

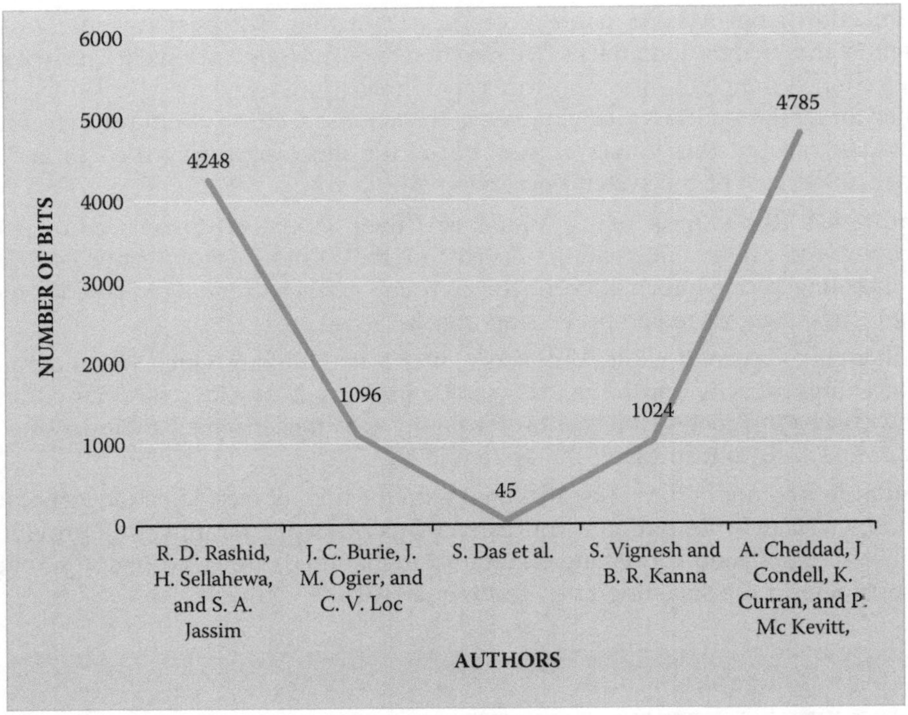

FIGURE 12.14
Concealing Capacity Comparison.

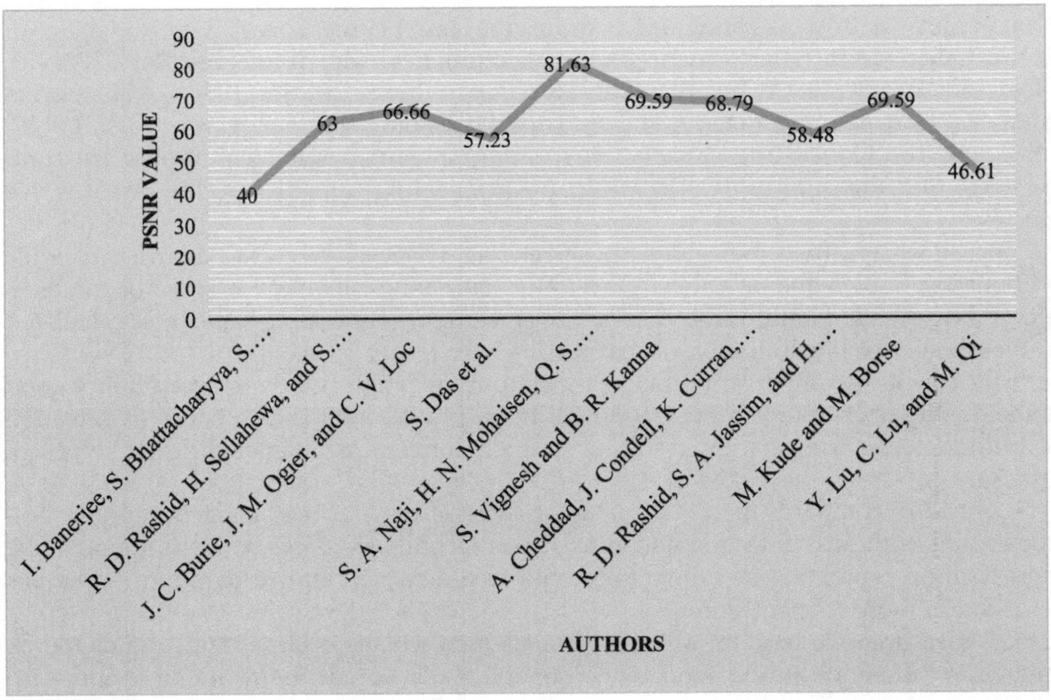

FIGURE 12.15
PSNR Comparison.

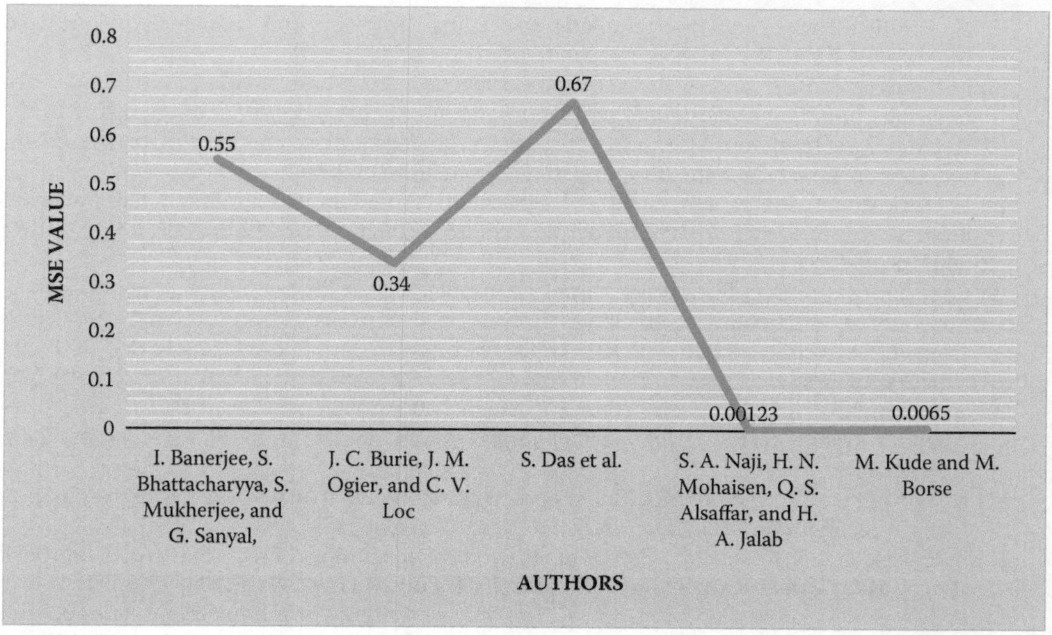

FIGURE 12.16
MSE Comparison

12.6 Conclusion

In this chapter, a review of steganography, face detection, and recognition techniques is done. From the literature review, it has been found that these techniques are gradually used in real-world applications and attain improved results. By combining more than one technique results are improved but challenges increase gradually. Challenges associated with these techniques are listed individually as well as in combination. Finally, some solutions are suggested to overcome these challenges. The researcher can take these solutions as the topic for future research.

References

[1] M. Dalal and M. Juneja, "Video steganography techniques in spatial domain—a survey," *Lect. Notes Networks Syst.*, vol. 24, pp. 705–711, 2018, doi: 10.1007/978-981-10-6890-4_67

[2] I. Banerjee, S. Bhattacharyya, S. Mukherjee, and G. Sanyal, "Biometric steganography using face geometry," *IEEE Reg. 10 Annu. Int. Conf. Proceedings/TENCON*, vol. 2015-Janua, 2015, doi: 10.1109/TENCON.2014.7022450

[3] N. Hazim, S. Sameer, W. Esam, and M. Abdul, "Face detection and recognition using Viola-Jones with PCA-LDA and square Euclidean distance," *Int. J. Adv. Comput. Sci. Appl.*, vol. 7, no. 5, 2016, doi: 10.14569/ijacsa.2016.070550

[4] T. M. Effendi, H. B. Seta, and T. Wati, "The combination of viola-jones and eigen faces algorithm for account identification for diploma," *J. Phys. Conf. Ser.*, vol. 1196, no. 1, 2019, doi: 10.1088/1742-6596/1196/1/012070

[5] A. Lanitis, "Facial biometric templates and aging: Problems and challenges for artificial intelligence," *CEUR Workshop Proc.*, vol. 475, pp. 142–149, 2009.
[6] H. Hatem, Z. Beiji, and R. Majeed, "A survey of feature base methods for human face detection," *Int. J. Control Autom.*, vol. 8, no. 5, pp. 61–78, 2015, doi: 10.14257/ijca.2015.8.5.07
[7] A. Kumar, A. Kaur, and M. Kumar, "Face detection techniques: a review," *Artif. Intell. Rev.*, vol. 52, no. 2, pp. 927–948, 2019, doi: 10.1007/s10462-018-9650-2
[8] L. Hock Koh, S. Ranganath, and Y. V. Venkatesh, "An integrated automatic face detection and recognition system," *Pattern Recognit.*, vol. 35, no. 6, pp. 1259–1273, 2002, doi: 10.1016/S0031-3203(01)00117-0
[9] G. R. Bradski and V. Pisarevsky, "Intel's computer vision library: applications in calibration, stereo, segmentation, tracking, gesture, face and object recognition," *Proc. IEEE Comput. Soc. Conf. Comput. Vis. Pattern Recognit.*, vol. 2, pp. 796–797, 2000, doi: 10.1109/cvpr.2000.854964
[10] Z. QasemJaber and M. Issam Younis, "Design and implementation of real time face recognition system (RTFRS)," *Int. J. Comput. Appl.*, vol. 94, no. 12, pp. 15–22, 2014, doi: 10.5120/16395-6014
[11] M. Bartlett and T. J. Sejnowski, "Independent components of face images: A representation for face recognition," *4th Annu. Jt. Symp. Neural Comput.*, 1997.
[12] B. Heisele and T. Koshizen, "Components for face recognition," *Proc. - Sixth IEEE Int. Conf. Autom. Face Gesture Recognit.*, pp. 153–158, 2004, doi: 10.1109/AFGR.2004.1301523
[13] L. Torres, J. Y. Reutter, and L. Lorente, "Importance of the color information in face recognition," *IEEE Int. Conf. Image Process.*, vol. 3, pp. 627–631, 1999, doi: 10.1109/icip.1999.817191
[14] R. K, K. B. Raja, V. K. R, and L. M. Patnaik, "Feature extraction based face recognition, gender and age classification," *Int. J. Comput. Sci. Eng.*, vol. 02, no. 01S, pp. 14–23, 2010.
[15] W. Huang, X. Wang, Z. Jin, and J. Li, "Penalized collaborative representation based classification for face recognition," *Appl. Intell.*, vol. 43, no. 4, pp. 722–731, 2015, doi: 10.1007/s10489-015-0672-z
[16] M. P. Beham and S. M. M. Roomi, "A review of face recognition methods," *Int. J. Pattern Recognit. Artif. Intell.*, vol. 27, no. 4, 2013, doi: 10.1142/S0218001413560053
[17] J. Shah, M. Sharif, M. Raza, and A. Azeem, "A survey: Linear and nonlinear PCA based face recognition techniques," *Int. Arab J. Inf. Technol.*, vol. 10, no. 6, 2013.
[18] E. Kheirkhah and Z. S. Tabatabaie, "A hybrid face detection approach in color images with complex background," *Indian J. Sci. Technol.*, vol. 8, no. 1, pp. 49–60, 2015, doi: 10.17485/ijst/2015/v8i1/51337
[19] F. Ahmad, A. Najam, and Z. Ahmed, "Image-based face detection and recognition: 'State of the art,'" pp. 3–6, 2013, [Online]. Available: http://arxiv.org/abs/1302.6379.
[20] A. O. Vyas and S. V. Dudul, "Comparative analysis of different wavelet families, applied for steganography on two cover images," *2019 IEEE 5th Int. Conf. Converg. Technol. I2CT 2019*, pp. 1–6, 2019, doi: 10.1109/I2CT45611.2019.9033752
[21] G. Prabakaran and R. Bhavani, "A high capacity video steganography based on integer wavelet transform," *J. Comput. Appl.*, 5, no. 4, December 2015.
[22] U. Pilaniaand P. Gupta, "A proposed optimized steganography technique using ROI, IWT and SVD," *Int. J. Informat. Syst. Manag. Sci.*, 2019 (Forthcoming).
[23] R. Roy, S. Changder, A. Sarkar, and N. C. Debnath, "Evaluating image steganography techniques: Future research challenges," *2013 Int. Conf. Comput. Manag. Telecommun. ComManTel 2013*, pp. 309–314, 2013, doi: 10.1109/ComManTel.2013.6482411
[24] K. Raju and S. K. Srivatsa, "Video Steganography for Face Recognition with Signcryption for Trusted and Secured Authentication by using PCASA," *Int. J. Comput. Appl.*, vol. 56, no. 11, pp. 1–5, 2012, doi: 10.5120/8932-3055
[25] S. Jhodge, G. Chiddarwar, and G. Shinde, "A new SAFR tool for face recognition using EGVLBP-CMI-LDA wrapped with secured DWT based steganography," *Proc. 2013 3rd IEEE Int. Adv. Comput. Conf. IACC 2013*, pp. 1040–1050, 2013, doi: 10.1109/IAdCC.2013.6514370

[26] R. D. Rashid, H. Sellahewa, and S. A. Jassim, "Biometric feature embedding using robust steganography technique," *Mob. Multimedia/Image Process. Secur. Appl. 2013*, vol. 8755, no. May, p. 875503, 2013, doi: 10.1117/12.2018910
[27] Q. Zhao, Y. Minakawa, Y. Liu, and N. Y. Yen, "Feature point detection in image morphing based steganography," *Proc. - 2013 IEEE Int. Conf. Syst. Man, Cybern. SMC 2013*, pp. 2837–2842, 2013, doi: 10.1109/SMC.2013.484
[28] A. Lanitis, "Facial biometric templates and aging: Problems and challenges for artificial intelligence," *CEUR Workshop Proc.*, vol. 475, no. March, pp. 142–149, 2009.
[29] J. C. Burie, J. M. Ogier, and C. V. Loc, "A Spatial Domain Steganography for Grayscale Documents Using Pattern Recognition Techniques," *Proc. Int. Conf. Doc. Anal. Recognition, ICDAR*, vol. 9, pp. 21–26, 2018, doi: 10.1109/ICDAR.2017.391
[30] S. Vignesh and B. R. Kanna, *Encrypted Transfer of Confidential Information Using Steganography and Identity Verification Using Face Data*, vol. 1056. 2020.
[31] M. Kawulok and J. Szymanek, "Precise multi-level face detector for advanced analysis of facial images," *IET Image Process.*, vol. 6, no. 2, pp. 95–103, 2012, doi: 10.1049/iet-ipr.2010.0495
[32] V. M. Praseetha, A. Dattagupta, R. Suma, and S. Vadivel, "Novel Web Service Based Fingerprint Identification Using Steganography and Xml Mining," *IOP Conf. Ser. Mater. Sci. Eng.*, vol. 396, no. 1, 2018, doi: 10.1088/1757-899X/396/1/012026
[33] B. M. Sujatha, N. Ramapur, S. Lagali, K. S. Babu, K. B. Raja, and K. R. Venugopal, "SOM based Face Recognition using Steganography and DWT Compression Techniques," *Int. J. Comput. Sci. Informat. Secur.*, vol. 14, no. 9, pp. 806–826, 2016.
[34] M. J. Jones and P. Viola, "Fast Multi-View Face Detection," *Mitsubishi Electric Research Lab TR-20003*-96, vol. 3, no. 14, p. 2, December 2003.
[35] Y.-Q. Wang, "An Analysis of the Viola-Jones Face Detection Algorithm," *Image Process. Line*, vol. 4, pp. 128–148, 2014, doi: 10.5201/ipol.2014.104
[36] N. Zehra, M. Sharma, S. Ahuja, and S. Bansal, "Bio-Authentication based Secure Transmission System using Steganography," vol. 8, no. 1, pp. 318–324, 2010, [Online]. Available: http://arxiv.org/abs/1005.4264.
[37] M. Castrillón, O. Déniz, D. Hernández, and J. Lorenzo, "A comparison of face and facial feature detectors based on the Viola-Jones general object detection framework," *Mach. Vis. Appl.*, vol. 22, no. 3, pp. 481–494, 2011, doi: 10.1007/s00138-010-0250-7
[38] S. K. Mondal, I. Mukhopadhyay, and S. Dutta, "Review and Comparison of Face Detection Techniques," *Adv. Intell. Syst. Comput.*, vol. 1065, pp. 3–14, 2020, doi: 10.1007/978-981-15-0361-0_1
[39] A. Sandford and A. M. Burton, "Tolerance for distorted faces: Challenges to a configural processing account of familiar face recognition," *Cognition*, vol. 132, no. 3, pp. 262–268, 2014, doi: 10.1016/j.cognition.2014.04.005
[40] F. W. Wheeler, R. L. Weiss, and P. H. Tu, "Face recognition at a distance system for surveillance applications," *IEEE 4th Int. Conf. Biometrics Theory, Appl. Syst. BTAS 2010*, 2010, doi: 10.1109/BTAS.2010.5634523
[41] E. Nandhini, M. Nivetha, S. Nirmala, and R. Poornima, "MLSB Technique Based 3D Image Steganography Using AES Algorithm," *J. Recent Res. Eng. Technol.*, vol. 3, no. 1, p. 2936, 2016.
[42] M. Nappi, S. Ricciardi, and M. Tistarelli, "Deceiving faces: When plastic surgery challenges face recognition," *Image Vis. Comput.*, vol. 54, pp. 71–82, 2016, doi: 10.1016/j.imavis.2016.08.012
[43] X. Zhang and Y. Gao, "Face recognition across pose: A review," *Pattern Recognit.*, vol. 42, no. 11, pp. 2876–2896, 2009, doi: 10.1016/j.patcog.2009.04.017
[44] J. Cheney, B. Klein, A. K. Jain, and B. F. Klare, "Unconstrained face detection: State of the art baseline and challenges," *Proc. 2015 Int. Conf. Biometrics, ICB 2015*, no. iii, pp. 229–236, 2015, doi: 10.1109/ICB.2015.7139089
[45] M. O. Oloyede, G. P. Hancke, and H. C. Myburgh, "A review on face recognition systems: recent approaches and challenges," *Multimed. Tools Appl.*, vol. 79, no. 37–38, pp. 27891–27922, 2020, doi: 10.1007/s11042-020-09261-2

[46] R. Singh, M. Vatsa, and A. Noore, "Effect of plastic surgery on face recognition: a preliminary study," *2009 IEEE Conf. Comput. Vis. Pattern Recognition, CVPR 2009*, pp. 72–77, 2009, doi: 10.1109/CVPR.2009.5204287

[47] T. S and M. N, "Detection, Segmentation and Recognition of Face and its Features Using Neural Network," *J. Biosens. Bioelectron.*, vol. 7, no. 2, 2016, doi: 10.4172/2155-6210.1000210

[48] A. H. Mohsin *et al.*, "Real-Time Medical Systems Based on Human Biometric Steganography: a Systematic Review," *J. Med. Syst.*, vol. 42, no. 12, 2018, doi: 10.1007/s10916-018-1103-6

[49] S. Das *et al.*, "Lip biometric template security framework using spatial steganography," *Pattern Recognit. Lett.*, vol. 126, pp. 102–110, 2019, doi: 10.1016/j.patrec.2018.06.026

[50] P. Marella, J. Straub, and B. Bernard, "Development of a facial feature based image steganography technology," *Proc. - 6th Annu. Conf. Comput. Sci. Comput. Intell. CSCI 2019*, pp. 675–678, 2019, doi: 10.1109/CSCI49370.2019.00126

[51] I. McAteer, A. Ibrahim, G. Zheng, W. Yang, and C. Valli, "Integration of Biometrics and Steganography: A Comprehensive Review," *Technologies*, vol. 7, no. 2, p. 34, 2019, doi: 10.3390/technologies7020034

[52] M. Vijay, S. Suvarna, K. Dipalee, and P. S. K. Patil, "Face Base Online Voting System Using Steganography," *Int. J. Emerg. Technol. Adv. Eng.*, vol. 3, no. 10, pp. 462–466, 2013.

[53] A. Cheddad, J. Condell, K. Curran, and P. Mc Kevitt, "Skin tone based steganography in video files exploiting the YCbCr colour space," *2008 IEEE Int. Conf. Multimed. Expo, ICME 2008 - Proc.*, no. December 2013, pp. 905–908, 2008, doi: 10.1109/ICME.2008.4607582

[54] A. Bukis, T. Proscevičius, V. Raudonis, and R. Simutis, "Survey of Face Detection and Recognition Methods," In *Proceedings of the International Conference on Electrical and Control Technologies, Kaunas*, pp. 51–56, 2011.

[55] S. A. Naji, H. N. Mohaisen, Q. S. Alsaffar, and H. A. Jalab, "Automatic region selection method to enhance image-based steganography," *Period. Eng. Nat. Sci.*, vol. 8, no. 1, pp. 67–78, 2020, doi: 10.21533/pen.v8i1.1092.g489

[56] D. Aeloor and A. A. Manjrekar, "Securing Biometric Data with Visual Cryptography and Steganography," *Commun. Comput. Inf. Sci.*, vol. 377 CCIS, pp. 330–340, 2013, doi: 10.1007/978-3-642-40576-1_33

[57] A. Cheddad, J. Condell, K. Curran, and P. Mc Kevitt, "Biometric inspired digital image Steganography," *Proc. - Fifteenth IEEE Int. Conf. Work. Eng. Comput. Syst. ECBS 2008*, no. January 2017, pp. 159–168, 2008, doi: 10.1109/ECBS.2008.11

[58] R. D. Rashid, S. A. Jassim, and H. Sellahewa, "Covert exchange of face biometric data using steganography," *2013 5th Comput. Sci. Electron. Eng. Conf. CEEC 2013 - Conf. Proc.*, no. September, pp. 134–139, 2013, doi: 10.1109/CEEC.2013.6659460

[59] A. Cheddad, J. Condell, K. Curran, and P. Mc Kevitt, "A skin tone detection algorithm for an adaptive approach to steganography," *Signal Processing*, vol. 89, no. 12, pp. 2465–2478, 2009, doi: 10.1016/j.sigpro.2009.04.022

[60] M. Kude and M. Borse, "Skintone detection based steganography using wavelet transform," *Int. Conf. Autom. Control Dyn. Optim. Tech. ICACDOT 2016*, pp. 440–443, 2017, doi: 10.1109/ICACDOT.2016.7877624

[61] K. M. Goud, K. Radhika, and D. Jamuna, "Survey on Steganography Using Wavelet Transform and Biometrics," *Int. J. Eng. Res. Technol.*, vol. 1, no. 6, pp. 2278–0181, 2012.

[62] Y. Lu, C. Lu, and M. Qi, "An effective video steganography method for biometric identification," *Lect. Notes Comput. Sci. (including Subser. Lect. Notes Artif. Intell. Lect. Notes Bioinformatics)*, vol. 6059 LNCS, pp. 469–479, 2010, doi: 10.1007/978-3-642-13577-4_42

[63] S. Barve, U. Nagaraj, and R. Gulabani, "Efficient and secure biometric image stegnography using discrete wavelet transform," *Int. J. Comput. Sci. Commun. Networks*, vol. 1, no. 1, pp. 96–99, 2011.

[64] A. Cheddad, J. Condell, K. Curran, and P. Mc Kevitt, "A skin tone detection algorithm for an adaptive DWT based approach to steganography using biometrics," *Signal Processing*, vol. 89, no. 12, pp. 2465–2478, 2009, doi: 10.1016/j.sigpro.2009.04.022

[65] W. Kasprzak, M. Stefanczyk, and A. Wilkowski, "Printed steganography applied for the authentication of identity photos in face verification," *Proc. - 2015 IEEE 2nd Int. Conf. Cybern. CYBCONF 2015*, pp. 512–517, 2015, doi: 10.1109/CYBConf.2015.7175987

[66] S. Barkathunisha and R. Meenakumari, "Secure transmission of medical information using IRIS recognition and steganography," In *2013 Int. Conf. Comput. Power, Energy, Inform. Commun. (ICCPEIC)* pp. 89–92, 2013.

[67] X. Xu, Y. Sun, J. Wu, and Y. Sun, "Steganography algorithms recognition based on match image and deep features verification," *Multimed. Tools Appl.*, vol. 77, no. 21, pp. 27955–27979, 2018, doi: 10.1007/s11042-018-6010-9

[68] K. Lavanya and C. N. Raju, "An approach to enhance level of security to the ATM customers by hiding face biometric data using steganography," *I-manager's J. Inf. Technol.*, vol. 1, no. 3, pp. 25–30, 2012, doi: 10.26634/jit.1.3.1911

[69] W. Na, Z. Chiya, L. Xia, and W. Yunjin, "Enhancing iris-feature security with steganography," *Proc. 2010 5th IEEE Conf. Ind. Electron. Appl. ICIEA 2010*, pp. 2233–2237, 2010, doi: 10.1109/ICIEA.2010.5515145

[70] C. Whitelam, N. Osia, and T. Bourlai, "Securing multimodal biometric data through watermarking and steganography," *2013 IEEE Int. Conf. Technol. Homel. Secur. HST 2013*, vol. 5, no. 1, pp. 61–66, 2013, doi: 10.1109/THS.2013.6698977

[71] M. Moradi and M.-R. Sadeghi, "Combining and steganography of 3D face textures," no. 3, pp. 3–8, 2017, doi: 10.22061/JECEI.2017.690

[72] S. Bhattacharyya, I. Banerjee, A. Chakraborty, and G. Sanyal, "Biometric steganography using variable length embedding," *Int. J. Comput. Inform. Eng.*, vol. 8, no. 4, pp. 668–679, 2014.

[73] K. W. Bowyer, K. Chang, and P. Flynn, "A survey of approaches and challenges in 3D and multi-modal 3D + 2D face recognition," *Comput. Vis. Image Underst.*, vol. 101, no. 1, pp. 1–15, 2006, doi: 10.1016/j.cviu.2005.05.005

[74] D. Smeets, P. Claes, D. Vandermeulen, and J. G. Clement, "Objective 3D face recognition: Evolution, approaches and challenges," *Forensic Sci. Int.*, vol. 201, no. 1–3, pp. 125–132, 2010, doi: 10.1016/j.forsciint.2010.03.023

[75] J. Xie, "Face recognition based on curvelet transform and LS-SVM," *Proc. Int. Symp. Inf. Process.*, no. January 2009, pp. 140–143, 2009.

[76] G. M. Zafaruddin and H. S. Fadewar, "Face recognition using eigenfaces," *Adv. Intell. Syst. Comput.*, vol. 810, pp. 855–864, 2018, doi: 10.1007/978-981-13-1513-8_87

[77] N. Gandhi, "Study on security of online voting system using biometrics and steganography," *IJCSC*, vol. 5, no. 1, pp. 29–32, 2014.

[78] A. Singh and A. Mehta, "Hiding of text in a 3D image using steganography," vol. 4, no. 10, 2017.

[79] P. N. Belhumeur, "Ongoing challenges in face recognition," *Front. Eng. reports leading-edge*, 2005, [Online]. Available: http://scholar.google.com/scholar?hl=en&btnG=Search&q=intitle:Ongoing+Challenges+in+Face+Recognition#0.

[80] I. Pavlidis and P. Symosek, "The imaging issue in an automatic face disguise detection system," In *Proc. IEEE Workshop Comput. Vision Visible Spectrum: Methods and Appl. (Cat. No. PR00640)*, pp. 15–24, 2000.

[81] Z. Akhtar and A. Rattani, "A face in any form: New challenges and opportunities for face recognition technology," *Computer (Long. Beach. Calif).*, vol. 50, no. 4, pp. 80–90, 2017, doi: 10.1109/MC.2017.119

[82] R. S. Smith, J. Kittler, M. Hamouz, and J. Illingworth, "Face recognition using angular LDA and SVM ensembles," *Proc. - Int. Conf. Pattern Recognit.*, vol. 3, pp. 1008–1012, 2006, doi: 10.1109/ICPR.2006.529

[83] X. Wang, H. Xu, X. Chen, and H. Li, "Fast and robust face detection with skin color mixture models and asymmetric AdaBoost," *MIPPR 2009 Pattern Recognit. Comput. Vis.*, vol. 7496, p. 749618, 2009, doi: 10.1117/12.832569

[84] K. Hidai, H. Mizoguchi, K. Hiraoka, M. Tanaka, T. Shigehara, and T. Mishima, "Robust face detection against brightness fluctuation and size variation," *IEEE Int. Conf. Intell. Robot. Syst.*, vol. 2, pp. 1379–1384, 2000, doi: 10.1109/iros.2000.893213

[85] M. Sharif, F. Naz, M. Yasmin, M. A. Shahid, and A. Rehman, "Face recognition A survey," *J. Eng. Sci. Technol. Rev.*, vol. 10, no. 2, pp. 166–177, 2017.
[86] F. Navabifar, M. Emadi, R. Yuso, and M. Khalid, "A short review paper on face detection using machine learning," *Proc. 2011 Int. Conf. Image Process. Comput. Vision, Pattern Recognition, IPCV 2011*, vol. 1, no. 1, pp. 391–398, 2011.
[87] J. Fridrich, T. Pevný, and J. Kodovský, "Statistically undetectable jpeg steganography," p. 3, 2007, doi: 10.1145/1288869.1288872
[88] Shivani Gupta, Gargi Kalia, and Preeti Sondhi, "Video Steganography using discrete wavelet transform and artificial intelligence," *Int. J. Trend Sci. Res. Dev.*, vol. 3, no. 4, pp. 1210–1215, 2019, doi: 10.31142/ijtsrd25067
[89] J. Blue, J. Condell, and T. Lunney, "Identity document authentication using steganographic techniques: The challenges of noise," *2017 28th Irish Signals Syst. Conf. ISSC 2017*, 2017, doi: 10.1109/ISSC.2017.7983646
[90] A. S. Ansari, M. S. Mohammadi, and M. T. Parvez, "A multiple-format steganography algorithm for color images," *IEEE Access*, vol. 8, pp. 83926–83939, 2020, doi: 10.1109/access.2020.2991130
[91] L. Zhai, L. Wang, and Y. Ren, "Universal detection of video steganography in multiple domains based on the consistency of motion vectors," *IEEE Trans. Inf. Forensics Secur.*, vol. 15, no. c, pp. 1762–1777, 2020, doi: 10.1109/TIFS.2019.2949428
[92] A. Rashid and M. K. Rahim, "Critical analysis of stegauography 'An art of hidden writing,'" *Int. J. Secur. its Appl.*, vol. 10, no. 3, pp. 259–282, 2016, doi: 10.14257/ijsia.2016.10.3.24
[93] A. K. Sahu and M. Sahu, "Digital image steganography and steganalysis: A journey of the past three decades," *Open Comput. Sci.*, vol. 10, no. 1, pp. 296–342, 2020, doi: 10.1515/comp-2020-0136
[94] Y. Xue, J. Zhou, H. Zeng, P. Zhong, and J. Wen, "An adaptive steganographic scheme for H.264/AVC video with distortion optimization," *Signal Process. Image Commun.*, vol. 76, no. March, pp. 22–30, 2019, doi: 10.1016/j.image.2019.04.012
[95] A. A. Attaby, M. F. M. Mursi Ahmed, and A. K. Alsammak, "Data hiding inside JPEG images with high resistance to steganalysis using a novel technique: DCT-M3," *Ain Shams Eng. J.*, vol. 9, no. 4, pp. 1965–1974, 2018, doi: 10.1016/j.asej.2017.02.003
[96] Y. Hirano, C. Garcia, R. Sukthankar, and A. Hoogs, "Industry and object recognition: Applications, applied research and challenges," pp. 49–64, 2006, doi: 10.1007/11957959_3
[97] B. Lahasan, S. L. Lutfi, and R. San-Segundo, "A survey on techniques to handle face recognition challenges: occlusion, single sample per subject and expression," *Artif. Intell. Rev.*, vol. 52, no. 2, pp. 949–979, 2019, doi: 10.1007/s10462-017-9578-y
[98] m. m. hashim, a. k. mohsin, and m. s. m. rahim, "all-encompassing review of biometric information protection in fingerprints based steganography," *ACM Int. Conf. Proceeding Ser.*, no. June 2020, 2019, doi: 10.1145/3386164.3389079
[99] S. Kamil, M. Ayob, S. N. H. Sheikh Abdullah, and Z. Ahmad, "Challenges in multi-layer data security for video steganography revisited," *Asia-Pacific J. Inf. Technol. Multimed.*, vol. 07, no. 02(02), pp. 53–62, 2018, doi: 10.17576/apjitm-2018-0702(02)-05
[100] R. Amirtharajan, and J. B. B. Rayappan, "Steganography-time to time: A review," *Res. J. Inf. Technol.*, vol. 5, no. 2, pp. 53–66, 2013, doi: 10.3923/rjit.2013.53.66
[101] S. Venkatraman, A. Abraham, and M. Paprzycki, "Significance of steganography on data security," *Int. Conf. Inf. Technol. Coding Comput. ITCC*, vol. 2, pp. 347–351, 2004, doi: 10.1109/ITCC.2004.1286660
[102] M. M. Hashim, M. S. M. Rahim, F. A. Johi, M. S. Taha, and H. S. Hamad, "Performance evaluation measurement of image steganography techniques with analysis of LSB based on variation image formats," *Int. J. Eng. Technol.*, vol. 7, no. 4, pp. 3505–3514, 2018, doi: 10.14419/ijet.v7i4.17294

13

Authentication and Admissibility of Forensic Evidence under Indian Criminal Justice Delivery System: An Analysis

Bharti Nair Khan and Sujata Bali
School of Law, University of Petroleum and Energy Studies (UPES), Dehradun, Uttarakhand, India

CONTENTS

13.1 Introduction to Forensic Evidence and Criminal Investigation

13.1.1 Forensic Evidence

Forensic Science can be defined as the use and application of scientific methods and procedures to the recognition, collection, identification, and comparison of physical evidence gathered during legal proceedings. It involves a systematic coherence of various scientific specialties and disciplines. Analysis of evidence is done with the use of various disciplines like physics, chemistry, biology, and computer science. The study of chemistry helps in learning the composition and chemical content present in the drugs, similarly study of

DOI: 10.1201/9781003204862-13

biology helps in associating a suspect with the crime likewise DNA profiling helps in ascertaining the identity of a person.

Forensic evidence functions within the ambit of legal framework. Forensic science assists experts entrusted with carrying on criminal investigations and helps in recognition of authentic information, which can be relied on by the court to adjudicate criminal cases (Kaul Shali, 2018).

13.1.2 Criminal Investigation

With the commission of any unlawful act, the law comes into force immediately. Even when no such report is made, *suo moto* cognizance can be taken against such unlawful acts. The police start with the criminal investigation, which includes search and seizure, interrogation, discovery of various facts relevant to the case. A criminal investigation is a continuous process and continues until trial and even beyond. During an investigation, forensic scientists are involved in collection, identification, and examination of evidence gathered from the crime scene. Their aid and involvement are necessitated because they are well equipped and trained in analyzing and preserving evidence. The assistance of forensic scientists is generally (The Indian Evidence Act, 1872, Sec 3 as amended by Act 21 of 2000) sought in high-profile cases or cases of notorious nature, which are widely condemned (Houck and Siegel, 2015).

13.2 Significance of Forensic Science in Criminal Investigation

Society is growing complex day by day and advanced technology and science have been one of the reasons for the same. The criminals have turned much smarter and frequently make use of such advanced technology and science for the commission of an offense. This has led to the emergence of new crimes that necessitates the use of forensic science in criminal investigation.

Forensic science is extremely pertinent in criminal justice system. It is helpful in detecting, recognizing, and collecting physical clues from a crime scene. It discloses and establishes the identity of the suspect committing the crime. The analysis of evidence by applying forensic science indicates the nature of the offense. Forensic evidence also helps in locating the place where the offense was committed.

Investigation including forensic science helps in determining the methods opted by the offender for committing the crime. Forensic science is equally important in proving the innocence of a person, and this is established when the evidence and clues collected do not match or link the accused with the crime (Kaul Shali, 2018).

13.3 Overview of Historical Development of Forensic Science as Recorded by Hebrard and Daoust

Hebrard and Daoust (2013) give a detailed record of development of forensic science. Below mentioned is a brief summary of their recordings:

> Before the application of legal and scientific principles for resolving the cases, evidence was obtained and verified in an unscientific and superficial manner and these

techniques were quite different in various countries. There has been a long influence of religion and spiritual belief on evidence. A suspect was subjected to various tests like judicial duel and cross ordeal to draw evidence in line with God's judgment. Despite these methods of extracting data believed to have a Godly origin, it still turned out to be limited and societies looked forward toward other methods like confessions and statements and testimony of witnesses. Simultaneously help from various experts like physicians were taken for the disclosure of facts and their opinion would help the jury to know the cause of demise of the deceased. At the beginning of the 16th century, in France, assistance of handwriting experts were taken by the courts to adjudicate forgery cases. Technical and scientific expertise was frequently required during the investigations and trials even when relying on confession and statements of witnesses was the modus operandi in criminal proceedings. Sir William Herschel was the pioneer to advocate the use of fingerprinting for the purpose of identification of criminals. In 1876, there was a new research movement started in Italy. This movement discarded the old and obsolete-born criminal theory and held different observations such as a man with a tattoo being a potential criminal or a man with a sharp nose and eyes having a criminal tendency to be absurd and unscientific. Fingerprints as evidence were for the first time accepted in the court of Argentina in the year 1890 and in the English Court in 1902. In early 1893, Austria imposed mandatory training in forensic science for judicial officers and lawyers. The training helped the judges to understand the importance of science in legal proceedings.

Therefore, there was an advancement of scientific and technical progression in the field of law, which was necessary to corroborate the evidence drawn through testimony, admission, and confession but was not used to replace it. In the mid of 19th century because of the growing role of forensic scientists and experts, altogether new perceptions and ideas with respect to science and law were introduced. The societies were not satisfied with the criminal proceeding being completely dependent on confession. Therefore, science had to intrude into criminal proceedings in order to restore the faith of the public in the criminal justice system.

The adversarial Judicial System in the United States led to the rapid acceptance and frequent use of forensic science in criminal proceedings. Hence, the first US Police crime laboratory was established in the year 1920. Forensic science is evolving and expanding in different new fields by devising new techniques and procedures, therefore, proving to be more significant and relevant. After the US Daubert case (Daubert v. Merrell Dow Pharmaceuticals, Inc., 509 U.S. 579, 1993), the judges are required to establish that the evidence and testimony furnished by the expert are authenticating and reliable. The courts have to verify that the expert possessed the required scientific knowledge, experience and had diligently made use of the process and methods while applying it to the facts at hand.

(Hebrard & Daoust 2013)

13.4 Status of Forensic Investigative Facilities in India

The success and reliability of forensic evidence depend on availability of investigative facilities.

In India, it was the state of Kolkata where the first Central Fingerprint Bureau was established in 1897, which got operationalized in 1904. This was the starting point for the growth and development of forensic science and since then many efforts were made to ensure its steady growth.

Forensic laboratories were now being set at both State and Center levels. Various toxicological and crime laboratories were made operational in various parts of the country under the supervision of police and health department. The continuous efforts have enabled the establishment of 7 central and 37 state forensic science laboratories. In addition to this, there are 29 fingerprints bureaus and several Regional Forensic Science Laboratories along with Districts Mobile Forensic Units. In Hyderabad, DNA Fingerprinting and Diagnostic, Advanced Center has been established.

DNA profiling in criminal cases in India is carried out in pioneering institutions such as the Cellular and Molecular Biology in Hyderabad and the Central Forensic Science Laboratory in Kolkata (Kathane, 2021).

13.5 Defining Evidence

Evidence helps in proving or disapproving an important fact in a given case. It includes oral evidence, the statements that are permitted by the court to be made by the witness concerning a fact under inquiry. It also includes documentary evidence comprising of electronic records submitted before the courts for examination (The Indian Evidence Act, 1872, Sec 3 as amended by Act 21 of 2000).

13.6 Authentication of Evidence: The Chain of Custody

Generally, all the evidence drawn from the events is subjected to authentication. The Universal practice is to check the tampering of the evidence and ensure that it remains unaffected right from its seizure from the crime scene until it is produced before the court. The process of authentication is initiated right at the scene of a crime or any place from where the evidence is collected. The chain of custody preserves the sanctity of the evidence.

The chain of custody is a documented process, which is usually followed by the forensic experts of different countries like the United States and the UK for keeping detailed account of the transfer of evidence from one custody to another. Each evidence has to be mandatorily sealed distinctly and marked with a unique identifier by an official, whose signature along with the time is to be affixed on the package. The examination of the evidence is done with the utmost care by the forensic expert to not tamper with the original seal. Whenever the evidence is unpacked for examination it should again be resealed and marked with a unique identifier along with the initials and signature of the expert so as to keep a track of all those who unpacked the seal. The evidence is circulated along with a document, i.e., chain of custody which consists of the details of the evidence and signatures of all the experts who have examined the evidence along with the dates and times.

This chain of record helps the court to know as to who all had the custody of the evidence so the experts can be called to the courts to testify about the description, usage, storage, and condition of evidence (Houck and Siegel, 2015).

13.7 Admissibility of Evidence

One of the important questions faced by the experts and lawyers is to decide as to what kind of evidence should be furnished before the court and how the judges can utilize the evidence during the proceedings of the case. Certain sections under various statutes are stipulated to determine the admissibility of evidence under certain circumstances, which has been discussed in detail below. However, very few rules are laid which state that how evidence is to be used by the judges that are admissible. A proper legal framework governing the admissibility and use of evidence by the court will help to preserve the integrity and sanctity of evidence.

While deciding on the admissibility of the evidence submitted by the forensic experts, the court refer to section 293 (The Code of Criminal Procedure, 197, Sec. 293 (1)) of the criminal procedure code, whereby a report submitted by a senior scientific expert is admissible in evidence and can be used in inquiry and in a trial in the court. Laying emphasis on the evidentiary value and admissibility of the reports furnished by forensic experts, the court reiterated that report of a chemical examiner in case of murder by poisoning could be used as evidence during the proceedings in a court (Bhupinder Singh v. State of Punjab, (1988) 3 SCC 513: 1988 SCC (Cri) 694).

In another case, Supreme Court held that the opinion of the doctor based on the report of the chemical analyzer can be used as evidence in the court (State of A.P. v. Gangula Satya Murthy, (1997) 1 SCC 272: 1997 SCC (Cri) 325).

13.8 Procedural and Substantive Provisions Encouraging Application of Forensic Science in Criminal Investigation

The Code of Criminal Procedure, 1973, encourages the use of forensic evidence in criminal investigations in India. Under Section 53 of the above stated Act, A medical practitioner can conduct the medical examination if ordered by a police officer of the rank of sub-inspector, if the accused has been alleged to commit an offense under such circumstances that it is reasonably believed that an examination of such a person will offer evidence necessary to ascertain facts (The Code of Criminal Procedure, 1973, Sec. 53). The extent of this section was widened by an amendment in 2005. Such medical examination now includes examination of blood, bloodstains, semen, swabs in case of sexual offenses, sputum and sweat, hair samples, and fingernail clippings by the application of new and scientific measures involving DNA profiling (The Code of Criminal Procedure, 1973, Sec. 53. Exp.1).

In cases of sexual offenses, victims against whom rape is committed or attempted are proposed to undergo a medical examination by a registered medical expert. Such examination can be carried out only with the prior permission of the victim or parents or guardians. The medical practitioner is therefore required to examine the victim immediately and submit a report of the examination to the investigating officer, which is further to be submitted by him to the Magistrate (The Code of Criminal Procedure, 1973, Sec. 164-A, cl. (2) cl. (6)).

Any report submitted by the government scientific expert upon any case or issue deposited to him for examination may be utilized as evidence in an inquiry, trial, or proceeding of the case (The Code of Criminal Procedure, 1973, Sec. 293, cl. (1)). The court may summon such expert and examine him as to the subject matter and authentication of his report (The Code of Criminal Procedure, 1973, Sec. 293, cl. 2). A girl of 16 years was raped and throttled to death in 1991. The Supreme Court of India held that the reports submitted by the forensic examiner are to be used as evidence for the conviction of the accused (A.P. v. Gangula Satya Murthy, (1997) 1 SCC 272: 1997 SCC (Cri) 325).

The testimony given by a medical witness or civil surgeon and same being attested by the Magistrate in the presence of the accused may be used by the court as evidence in an inquiry or trial (The Code of Criminal Procedure, 1973, Sec. 291, cl.1). The court may call and question the medical witness regarding the veracity and subject matter of his report (The Code of Criminal Procedure, 1973, Sec. 291, cl. 2).

Section 45 of the Indian Evidence Act, 1872 defines the term "Expert." Whenever the court has to formulate a decision upon a matter, which is not much known, to them or a question pertaining to science or art, or to verify the handwriting and finger expressions of the suspect, generally the opinion of the experts especially skilled in all such areas are considered relevant. Such especially skilled persons are called experts (The Indian Evidence Act, 1872, Sec. 45).

The court expressed that it is expected from the experts to aid and assist the court by providing authentic reports based on the expertise and his reasons. Assessing such reports and the grounds laid by the experts for inferring such conclusions, the court tries to form its independent opinion and adjudicates accordingly (Pattu Rajan v. State of T.N., (2019) 4 SCC 771).

13.9 Legal Constraints While Applying Forensic Science in Criminal Investigation

The application of forensic science in the administration of the criminal justice system is required to stand the test of law and specifically clause 3 of Article 20 of the Constitution of India (The Constitution of India, Art. 20 cl. 3). It includes statements given by a suspect admitting his crime, which is later made use against him to prove him guilty Article 20 (3) is applicable only when the accused is compelled to give testimony against him. If such a statement is given voluntarily out of free will, the same cannot be said to be violating the constitutional provision.

The criminal justice delivery system is founded on the principle that a person is innocent until proven guilty beyond reasonable doubts, this has been provided under Article 11 of United Declaration of Human Rights (United Nation Declaration of Human Rights (UNDHR), 1948). The aim and purpose of Article 20(3) is to protect the accused from unwanted torture and violence during the investigation. The right against self-incrimination is not absolute. The courts in India have been authorized to seek a specimen of the handwriting of any person in order to match and compare it with the handwriting of such person (Indian Evidence Act, 1872, Sec. 11).

The Supreme Court of India has clarified that an accused can be asked to give his footprints as well as fingerprints for corroboration of evidence and that would not tantamount to the violation of the rights and safeguards guaranteed under Article 20(3) of the Constitution of India (State of U.P v. Sunil, 2017 SCC OnLine SC 520). The Supreme

Court of India further stated that directing an accused to give his specimen of handwriting and signature, or thumb impressions, fingers, palm, or footprints to the investigating officer as per the orders of a court would not result in infraction of Art. 20(3) of the Constitution (State of Bombay v. KathiKalu Oghad & Others, AIR 1961 SC 1808, 1962 SCR (3) 10).

If the accused does not cooperate and misguides the investigating team by not revealing the truth, in such cases the investigating agency may resort to the scientific tests and the same would not amount to any sort of compulsion for obtaining testimony from the accused. When there is a clamor from the general masses and staunch supporters of human rights demanding for a speedy trial, it is surely high time that recourse to scientific methods of investigation should be taken by the investigating agency.

The constitutional validity of certain scientific techniques, namely Narco-analysis Test, Polygraph Examination, and the Brain Electrical Activation Profile (BEAP) Test administered forcefully, for improving investigation efforts in criminal cases, were raised before the Supreme Court. Accordingly, the Court held that no individual should be forcibly or involuntarily subjected to any of the techniques in question. The court further stated that this would amount to an unwanted transgression into personal liberty of a person. Further, it was clarified that voluntary administration of the impugned techniques would not tantamount to violation of constitutional safeguards (Selvi v. State of Karnataka, (2010) 7 SCC 263).

13.10 Conclusion and Suggestions

In India, the study of forensic science suffers from various pitfalls and drawbacks, which require immediate attention from the administration. The Supreme Court while emphasizing the importance of application of forensic science, held that forensic techniques and tools should not simply be used in high-profile cases but same be encouraged in most cases related to sexual violence and homicides (Dharam Deo Yadav v. State of Uttar Pradesh, 2014 SCC OnLine SC 321). Lack of research, scarcity of resources, absence of professional code of ethics and unequipped and untrained experts are various factors that affect the reliability of forensic evidence in India.

There is a need to have an immediate reform in forensic science discipline. Based on the above conclusion, the following suggestions are proposed for increasing the role of forensic evidence in criminal investigation:

1. In order to check the error rates, it is important that the experts are well trained and equipped with updated scientific skills in collection, examination, and preservation of evidence.
2. The strength of forensic scientists and experts working in various state and central forensics is extremely low as compared to the population of India. Whereas the crime rate is disproportionately increasing and the workload on forensic scientists are increasing excessively.
3. India being heavily populated and with highly reported crimes, it is important that there is an increase in the number of forensic laboratories.

4. There is also a need to have a revised education system promoting forensic studies in the universities.
5. Along with forensic experts, it is important that criminal justice professionals like lawyers and judges are also trained and specialized in forensic science.
6. There is a need to have a strong legal framework for the regulation of application of forensic science in India. The DNA Technology (Use and Application) Regulation Bill, 2019, which is pending in the Rajya Sabha, needs to be passed immediately.
7. Lastly, capacity building of forensic science is the need of the hour in order to provide speedy and effective justice to the people of the country.

References

A.P. v. Gangula Satya Murthy, (1997) 1 SCC 272: 1997 SCC (Cri) 325. Available at https://main.sci.gov.in/jonew/judis/14766.pdf

Bhupinder Singh v. State of Punjab, (1988) 3 SCC 513: 1988 SCC (Cri) 694. Available at https://main.sci.gov.in/judgment/judis/8375.pdf

The Code of Criminal Procedure, 197, Sec. 293 (1). Available at https://www.indiacode.nic.in/show-data?actid=AC_CEN_5_23_000010_197402_1517807320555&sectionId=22701&sectionno=293&orderno=335

The Code of Criminal Procedure, (1973), Exp. 1, Sec. 53. Available at https://www.indiacode.nic.in/show-data?actid=AC_CEN_5_23_000010_197402_1517807320555&sectionId=22425&sectionno=53&orderno=59

The Code of Criminal Procedure, (1973), Sec. 53. Available at https://www.indiacode.nic.in/show-data?actid=AC_CEN_5_23_000010_197402_1517807320555&sectionId=22425&sectionno=53&orderno=59

The Code of Criminal Procedure, (1973), Sec. 164-A, cl. (2) cl. (6). Available at https://www.indiacode.nic.in/show-data?actid=AC_CEN_5_23_000010_197402_1517807320555&sectionId=22554&sectionno=164A&orderno=188

The Constitution of India, Art. 20 cl. (3). Available at https://legislative.gov.in/sites/default/files/COI_1.pdf

The Code of Criminal Procedure, (1973), Sec.164-A, cl. (1). Available at https://www.indiacode.nic.in/show-data?actid=AC_CEN_5_23_000010_197402_1517807320555&sectionId=22554&sectionno=164A&orderno=188

The Code of Criminal Procedure, (1973), Sec. 291, cl. (1). Available at https://www.indiacode.nic.in/show-data?actid=AC_CEN_5_23_000010_197402_1517807320555&sectionId=22698&sectionno=291&orderno=332

The Code of Criminal Procedure, (1973), Sec. 291, cl. (2). Available at https://www.indiacode.nic.in/show-data?actid=AC_CEN_5_23_000010_197402_1517807320555&sectionId=22698&sectionno=291&orderno=332

The Code of Criminal Procedure, (1973), Sec. 293, cl. (1). Available at https://www.indiacode.nic.in/show-data?actid=AC_CEN_5_23_000010_197402_1517807320555&sectionId=22701&sectionno=293&orderno=335

The Code of Criminal Procedure, (1973), Sec. 293, cl. (2). Available at https://www.indiacode.nic.in/show-data?actid=AC_CEN_5_23_000010_197402_1517807320555&sectionId=22701&sectionno=293&orderno=335

Daubert v. Merrell Dow Pharmaceuticals, Inc., 509 U.S. 579 (1993). Available at https://supreme.justia.com/cases/federal/us/509/579/case.pdf

Dharam Deo Yadav v. State of Uttar Pradesh, (2014) SCC OnLine SC 321. Available at https://main.sci.gov.in/jonew/judis/41403.pdf

Hebrard & F. Daoust. *History of Forensic Sciences,* (Cambridge: Academic Press, 2013), 273–277.

Indian Evidence Act, (1872), Sec. 11. Available at https://www.indiacode.nic.in/show-data?actid=AC_CEN_3_20_00034_187201_1523268871700&sectionId=38806&sectionno=11&orderno=11

The Indian Evidence Act, (1872), Sec. 45. Available at https://www.indiacode.nic.in/show-data?actid=AC_CEN_3_20_00034_187201_1523268871700&sectionId=38840&sectionno=45&orderno=46

The Indian Evidence Act, (1872), Sec92. Available at https://www.indiacode.nic.in/handle/123456789/2188?sam_handle=123456789/1362

Kathane, Prachi. The development, status and future of forensics in India. Forensic Science International: Reports, 4 (2021): 1–5.

Kaul Shali, Sonia. *Applicability of Forensic Science in Criminal Justice System in India with Special Emphasis on Crime Scene Investigation.* Medico-Legal Desire Media and Publications, Medico-Legal Reporter, (2018). 1–16.

Max M. Houck & Jay A. Siegel. *Fundamentals of Forensic Science,* (Cambridge: Academic Press, 2015), 623.

Pattu Rajan v. State of T.N., (2019) 4 SCC 771. Available at https://main.sci.gov.in/supremecourt/2009/10392/10392_2009_Judgement_29-Mar-2019.pdf

Selvi v. State of Karnataka, (2010) 7 SCC 263. Available at https://main.sci.gov.in/jonew/judis/36303.pdf

State of A.P. v. Gangula Satya Murthy, (1997) 1 SCC 272: 1997 SCC (Cri) 325. Available at https://main.sci.gov.in/jonew/judis/14766.pdf

State of U.P vs Sunil, (2017) SCC OnLine SC 520. Available at https://main.sci.gov.in/jonew/judis/44862.pdf

The State of Bombay v. KathiKalu Oghad & Others, AIR 1961 SC 1808, 1962 SCR (3) 10. Available at https://main.sci.gov.in/judgment/judis/4157.pdf

United Nation Declaration of Human Rights (UNDHR) (1948). Available at https://www.un.org/en/about-us/universal-declaration-of-human-rights

Index